Tools and Techniques for Economic Decision Analysis

Jelena Stanković
University of Niš, Serbia

Pavlos Delias
Eastern Macedonia and Thrace Institute of Technology, Greece

Srđan Marinković
University of Niš, Serbia

Sylvie Rochhia
Université Côte d'Azur, CNRS, GREDEG, France

A volume in the Advances in Finance, Accounting, and Economics (AFAE) Book Series

IGI GLOBAL
DISSEMINATOR OF KNOWLEDGE

www.igi-global.com

Published in the United States of America by
IGI Global
Business Science Reference (an imprint of IGI Global)
701 E. Chocolate Avenue
Hershey PA, USA 17033
Tel: 717-533-8845
Fax: 717-533-8661
E-mail: cust@igi-global.com
Web site: http://www.igi-global.com

Library of Congress Cataloging-in-Publication Data

Names: Stankovic, Jelena, 1976- author.
Title: Tools and techniques for economic decision analysis / Jelena Stankovic, Pavlos Delias, Srdjan Marinkovic, and Sylvie Rochhia, editors.
Description: Hershey, PA : Business Science Reference, [2017] | Includes bibliographical references and index.
Identifiers: LCCN 2016032833| ISBN 9781522509592 (hardcover) | ISBN 9781522509608 (ebook)
Subjects: LCSH: Decision making. | Managerial economics.
Classification: LCC HD30.23 .T66 2017 | DDC 658.4/03--dc23 LC record available at https://lccn.loc.gov/2016032833

This book is published in the IGI Global book series Advances in Finance, Accounting, and Economics (AFAE) (ISSN: 2327-5677; eISSN: 2327-5685)

British Cataloguing in Publication Data
A Cataloguing in Publication record for this book is available from the British Library.

Advances in Finance, Accounting, and Economics (AFAE) Book Series

Ahmed Driouchi
Al Akhawayn University, Morocco

ISSN: 2327-5677
EISSN: 2327-5685

Mission

In our changing economic and business environment, it is important to consider the financial changes occurring internationally as well as within individual organizations and business environments. Understanding these changes as well as the factors that influence them is crucial in preparing for our financial future and ensuring economic sustainability and growth.

The **Advances in Finance, Accounting, and Economics (AFAE)** book series aims to publish comprehensive and informative titles in all areas of economics and economic theory, finance, and accounting to assist in advancing the available knowledge and providing for further research development in these dynamic fields.

Coverage

- Wages and Employment
- Risk Analysis and Management
- Development Economics
- Economics of Intellectual Property Rights
- Economic Indices and Quantitative Economic Methods
- Investments and Derivatives
- Accounting information systems
- Entrepreneurship in Accounting and Finance
- Microfinance
- Evidence-Based Studies

IGI Global is currently accepting manuscripts for publication within this series. To submit a proposal for a volume in this series, please contact our Acquisition Editors at Acquisitions@igi-global.com or visit: http://www.igi-global.com/publish/.

The Advances in Finance, Accounting, and Economics (AFAE) Book Series (ISSN 2327-5677) is published by IGI Global, 701 E. Chocolate Avenue, Hershey, PA 17033-1240, USA, www.igi-global.com. This series is composed of titles available for purchase individually; each title is edited to be contextually exclusive from any other title within the series. For pricing and ordering information please visit http://www.igi-global.com/book-series/advances-finance-accounting-economics/73685. Postmaster: Send all address changes to above address.

Titles in this Series

For a list of additional titles in this series, please visit: www.igi-global.com

Handbook of Research on Global Indicators of Economic and Political Convergence
Ramesh Chandra Das (Katwa College, India)
Business Science Reference • copyright 2016 • 616pp • H/C (ISBN: 9781522502159) • US $345.00 (our price)

Global Perspectives on Trade Integration and Economies in Transition
Vasily Erokhin (Moscow University of Finance and Law, Russia)
Business Science Reference • copyright 2016 • 407pp • H/C (ISBN: 9781522504511) • US $210.00 (our price)

Handbook of Research on Social Entrepreneurship and Solidarity Economics
José Manuel Saiz-Álvarez (Tecnológico de Monterrey, Mexico)
Business Science Reference • copyright 2016 • 606pp • H/C (ISBN: 9781522500971) • US $230.00 (our price)

Economic Modeling, Analysis, and Policy for Sustainability
Anandajit Goswami (The Energy and Resources Institute (TERI), India) and Arabinda Mishra (ICIMOD, Nepal)
Business Science Reference • copyright 2016 • 388pp • H/C (ISBN: 9781522500940) • US $210.00 (our price)

Financial Market Regulations and Legal Challenges in South Asia
Amit K. Kashyap (Nirma University, India) and Anjani Singh Tomar (Gujarat National Law University, India)
Business Science Reference • copyright 2016 • 346pp • H/C (ISBN: 9781522500049) • US $200.00 (our price)

Economics and Political Implications of International Financial Reporting Standards
Efobi Uchenna (Covenant University, Nigeria) Matthias Nnadi (Rivers State University of Science and Technology, Nigeria) Sailesh Tanna (Coventry University, UK) and Francis Iyoha (Covenant University, Nigeria)
Business Science Reference • copyright 2016 • 417pp • H/C (ISBN: 9781466698765) • US $220.00 (our price)

Handbook of Research on Impacts of International Business and Political Affairs on the Global Economy
Norhayati Zakaria (Universiti Utara Malaysia, Malaysia) Asmat-Nizam Abdul-Talib (Universiti Utara Malaysia, Malaysia) and Nazariah Osman (Universiti Utara Malaysia, Malaysia)
Business Science Reference • copyright 2016 • 450pp • H/C (ISBN: 9781466698062) • US $235.00 (our price)

Relational Methodologies and Epistemology in Economics and Management Sciences
Lucio Biggiero (Università dell' Aquila, Italy) Pier Paolo Angelini (Interuniversity Research Centre for Sustainable Development (CIRPS), Italy) Mario Basevi (Italian National Institute of Statistics, Italy) Nunzia Carbonara (Politecnico di Bari, Italy) Antonio Mastrogiorgio (Interuniversity Research Centre for Sustainable Development (CIRPS), Italy) Eliano Pessa (University of Pavia, Italy) Enrico Sevi (Università dell' Aquila, Italy) and Marco Valente (Università dell' Aquila, Italy)
Information Science Reference • copyright 2016 • 485pp • H/C (ISBN: 9781466697706) • US $200.00 (our price)

IGI GLOBAL
DISSEMINATOR OF KNOWLEDGE
www.igi-global.com

701 E. Chocolate Ave., Hershey, PA 17033
Order online at www.igi-global.com or call 717-533-8845 x100
To place a standing order for titles released in this series, contact: cust@igi-global.com
Mon-Fri 8:00 am - 5:00 pm (est) or fax 24 hours a day 717-533-8661

Table of Contents

Detailed Table of Contents

This chapter is a review of different approaches academics take to find right answers on the question how investors' community makes decisions on optimal portfolio of securities and how this process converges toward capital market equilibrium. Authors will try to reconcile the approaches that come from different intellectual traditions. The authors start with the Capital Assets Pricing Model (hereafter CAPM). For decades long the model has been a cornerstone of modern finance literature and a guide for investment decision making. The model assumes that the choice of investment portfolio is directed toward optimization between statistically defined risk and observable return of a universe of available investments, in the setting of rational and homogeneous agents where information is common knowledge. The rigidity of CAPM assumptions led to a plethora of studies where some of those assumptions are relaxed. An important breakthrough to the extant body of knowledge has been made by the introduction of the asymmetric information in the decision-making process.

This chapter is focused on building investment portfolios by using the Markowitz Portfolio Theory (MPT). Derivation based on the Capital Asset Pricing Model (CAPM) is used to calculate the weights of individual securities in portfolios. The calculated portfolios include a portfolio copying the benchmark made using the CAPM model, portfolio with low and high beta coefficients, and a random portfolio. Only stocks were selected for the examined sample from all the asset classes. Stocks in each portfolio are put together according to predefined criteria. All stocks were selected from Dow Jones Industrial Average (DJIA) index which serves as a benchmark, too. Portfolios were compared based on their risk and return profiles. The results of this work will provide general recommendations on the optimal approach to choose securities for an investor's portfolio.

Since decision on making an investment in exchange rate is one of the main problems faced by financial players acting in markets around the world, it is extensively discussed in the literature. In this study, it is investigated whether judgmental factors affect the decision in behavioral environment or not, and, if such an effect exists, its impact is whether positive or negative. In order to achieve that purpose, multi-criteria decision making approach is integrated with time series analysis approach which leads to clearly question the existence and direction of such an impact if it exists. The proposed model is applied to the Turkish market, indicating that judgmental factors prevent the financial player from misleading which is caused by considering solely profitability criterion. Thus, it is demonstrated that judgmental factors have a positive impact on the decision regarding exchange rate selection problem. Ultimately, it is demonstrated that the proposed integrated model provides accurate and reliable results.

This chapter utilizes multi-agent modeling to study the effects of prudential supervision on bank resiliency and profitability within a simulated environment of persistent crisis conditions. It focuses on the stabilizing effect of prudential supervision introduced alongside three "traditional" regulatory instruments: a norm, a market-based CDS insurance mechanism and a tax in the form of a bail-in instrument. The results show that: (1) supervision enhances the regulatory instruments' efficiency, (2) the regulatory norm can postpone the bank's default, but not avoid it, (3) the CDS mechanism only produces positive results on resiliency and profitability if the regulator supervises, and (4) the tax bail-in instrument is the most powerful tool in the regulator's arsenal as it potentiates profitable bank operation under long-lasting crisis conditions.

The governance concept has become very popular in recent decades and in this regard has increased interest in measuring its quality. The most widely used measures of governance are World Governance Indicators, which represent composite perceptions-based indicators, published by World Bank Institute. There are six composite indicators and the data for constructing those indicators are obtained from 32 individual data sources. The objective of this chapter is to highlight the applicability of Grey Relational Analysis in the ranking of EU countries according to the governance quality. The Grey Relational Analysis entails calculation of Grey relational grade for governance quality. The final stage of the Grey Relational Analysis procedure involves ranking of EU countries according to Grey relational grade and their comparison with ranks obtained from World Bank Institute. The full contribution of Grey Relational Analysis arises on this stage, where ranks of countries have been changed.

survey of 66 mussel producers in the area, a typology is elaborated, by means of which three types of mussel farmers are discerned. "Professionals" are the ones continuing their family tradition, "Newcomers" are those who chose mussel farming as their main occupation and recently invested in the sector and "Aged amateurs" are the oldest and least educated group, members of which plan to pass their farm to younger family members. There is strong evidence that the sampled "Newcomers" achieve considerably higher financial results, however the sample size is not adequate to generalize for all results except for the farm income. When it comes to their environmental attitudes, mussel farmers comply to bans in cases where high toxin concentrates are detected, but they are not convinced about the effectiveness of controls. They discern very clearly between the environmental and regulatory measures necessary to boost the productivity of the sector, but they seem to proclaim by far the latter type of adjustments, including the resolution of location issues. Based on the profile of each cluster and the general results of the sample proposals are made concerning the implementation of the new Common Fisheries Policy.

The energy system studies include a wide range of issues from short term to long term horizons. The decision making chain is fed by input parameters which are usually subject to uncertainties. The art of dealing with uncertainties has been developed in various directions and has recently become a focal point of interest. Decision making is certainly the most important task of Oil and Gas managers and it is often a very difficult one. The purpose of this chapter is to review and investigate the decision making processes under risk and uncertainty of Oil and Gas companies. Questionnaires were distributed to eight Oil and Gas companies in Ghana to solicit their view on decision making under risk and uncertainty. Results indicate that most managers use Maximax, Minimax Regret and Expected Value when making decisions under risk and uncertainty.

Corporate managers are faced with one important role in managing company's overall communications, especially when one crisis event occurred. Since the whole business world was preoccupied with the crisis that has gripped the year 2008, it is interesting to explore the content and the level of development of crisis management teams and crisis communications guidelines in the biggest Croatian companies. The results of research showed that Croatian companies do not stay behind their peers in the rest of the business world in the terms of establishment and development crisis management and crisis communications. Deep business crisis did not stop Croatian companies to invest in their workforces and their communication skills in order to achieve competitiveness in the market. Even though the business environment was very turbulent during the observed period, and suffered from many cutoffs the research results showed even some improvements in 2014 compared to the research from 2011.

Preface

Decision analysis in business economics is a set of quantitative tools that in a systematic manner carries out the evaluation of strategies and choices necessary for successful business. Decision analysis is based on hundreds of years of philosophical and practical thought about uncertainty and decision-making. The state-of-art of the field is very impressive, algorithms and problem-solving techniques are delicate and tailor made, yet the decision analysis has not become commonplace even in very important decisions. While there is no doubt that human nature is an ultimate limitation, maintaining clarity of concept and exploiting progress in the realms of scope, skill, and efficiency should lead to more widespread use.

The subject area of Handbook of Research on Tools and Techniques for Economic Decision Analysis is decision analysis in business economics and it is dedicated to promoting the advances in decision methodology and theory, but also in application possibilities of decision models in various aspects of business, and techniques for facilitating decision-making such as computer modelling software and expert systems for decision support.

Handbook of Research on Tools and Techniques for Economic Decision Analysis represents a comprehensive approach of decision analysis to business economics including all the relevant aspects from methods for decision-making under conditions of uncertainty or existence of multiple criteria, techniques of risk assessment and portfolio analysis to economic analysis of competitive and strategic decisions and research on decision-making in the field of operations management and business process management.

This book also aims at developing a systemic approach of economic decision while pointing out the importance of an analysis of both actors and their interactions so as to allow a better understanding of economic decision in a complex and changing world. In such an environment, the coordination of activities is characterized by a set of attributes that evolve over time while specifying the components and modes of interaction of the system. These attributes are the knowledge bases and technologies, the institutions (markets and economic policies), the organizations (firms and networks), which all together help to explain the constraints linked to the specificity of economic decision processes.

Because it involves some microscopic and macroscopic features, a systemic approach aims at providing a bridge between the two levels in studying emergent macro or collective regularities from the interaction of microeconomic diverse entities. Some chapters shall here try to import, on an appreciative mode, some of such concepts in the analysis of decision processes.

Thematically speaking, this book covers three sections: *Finance* (in particular financial markets, and finance and institutions), *Economic Policy* (discussing topics like governance, export promotion policy, labour markets, and sectoral policy), and *Firms & Networks* (including works about business decisions under risk and uncertainty, communication and management, multiple criteria decision aid, and social networks). The three sections are balanced in size and illustrate how economic decision analysis can be applied in business economics problems.

The idea to start the book with contributions related to the finance literature came from the fact that finance has for a long been a fruitful ground for studying how individuals and organizations reach decisions that grant individual well-being and how such self-interest motivated actions bring optimal solutions to the society as a whole. The papers selected for this section of the book vary from those of general (conceptual) content to those that are mainly applicative, covering a specific segment of the financial market, or institution, or dealing with some specific decision making issue.

Chapter 1 – *Investment decision making: where do we stand*? gives a comprehensive overview of more than half a century long academia attempts to explore main drivers of securities return.

Elaborations start with the traditional perfect market model (CAPM), which assumes that the choice of investment portfolio is directed toward optimization between statistically defined risk and observable return of a universe of available investments, while the equilibrium assets pricing is determined simply by copying the superior investment strategy, in the setting of rational and homogeneous agents where information is common knowledge. The rigidity of assumptions on which traditional models are built has led to a plethora of variations where some of those assumptions are relaxed. An important breakthrough to the extant body of knowledge has been made by the introduction of the asymmetric information (and other forms of incomplete knowledge and judgmental bias) in the decision-making process. The chapter points out the main research dilemmas, i.e. academia response to the fact that real life may depart from "blackboard" theory. In their contributions here, authors rely on the legacy of renowned scholars of the relevant fields of expertise, but also on those coming from different intellectual traditions.

Chapter 2 – *Application of Markowitz portfolio theory by building optimal portfolio on the US stock market* is a test of traditional Sharpe-Lintner-Mossin CAPM. In a well-established tradition, the authors divided the genuine basket of US stocks (represented by Dow Jones Industrial Average) into several subsamples: low-beta portfolio, high-beta portfolio, and randomly (computer-driven) selected portfolio of stocks. Consequently, the optimal weights schemes were calculated.

Opposite to the suggestions of the mainstream theory, the authors showed that large beta portfolios could underperform low-beta portfolios. The authors advocate for the extension of the mainstream model assuming that size (market capitalization), book-to-market value and price/earnings ratios might have some explanatory power along with betas. Hence, it is another proof that more than a single variable is required to characterize the multidimensional nature of risk.

Chapter 3 – *Do judgmental factors lead to a good decision on investing in a currency or mislead the financial player? An application in Turkey* is an empirical study of different methods and techniques available to investors (traders) on financial markets. The author compares different time series models that are frequently used in forecasting the return on foreign exchange markets. The models were fed by the official transaction data for the most frequently used currency pairs in the foreign exchange market of Turkey. The selected methods (Moving Average, Single Exponential Smoothing Method, Holt's Method, Winter's Method, and Autoregressive Integrated Moving Average) are tested for accuracy with a battery of performance criteria, and within different forecasting horizons. The forecasting/decision making model delivered in this chapter allows using both objective forecast values and judgmental criteria, and it can be easily adapted in order to be used in a family of other time series models.

The *Finance* section closes with the Chapter 4 titled *The effects of prudential supervision on bank resiliency and profits in a multi-agent setting*. Once again, the asymmetric information was taken to be the feature of the ambience in which contributors were studying complex decision making interplay between actors. In this chapter the arena is financial regulation (prudential supervision), the game that is played between regulator and regulated entities in order to achieve a resilient financial intermediation. The authors investigated the choice that a regulator made between three regulatory solutions (tools): a monitoring norm, a market-based credit default swap (CDS) insurance mechanism and a tax (imposed on borrowers' profit) in the form of a bail-in instrument. Asymmetric information is explicitly introduced by assuming that a bank does blind credit screening (unable to defer between good and bad borrowers at initial credit allocation phase) and a costly monitoring process. The authors employed numerical simulations in the multi-agent (prudential supervisor, a bank, their borrowers and in specific cases a CDS fund) virtual environment which allows agents to advance their decision making abilities by being able to learn from the past experience and respond in innovative ways. The chapter contributes to the general knowledge because it ranks different regulatory approaches in the novel way, and delivers clear-cut guidelines for regulatory policy. The findings indicate that prudential supervision is indisputably beneficial; the monitoring norm has at its best limited effects, market-based (CDS) solution is dependent on supervision efficiency, while tax bail-in mechanism provides a superior tool able to get a bank back to profitability and liquidity, and sustain long-lasting crisis conditions.

The second part of the book includes contributions that deal with application of contemporary quantitative economic analysis in economic policy decision-making. The papers selected for this section of the book vary from subjects of governance quality and its measurement to labor market flows and analysis of export significance in terms of growth dynamic and sustainability.

Chapter 5 - *Measuring Governance: The Application of Grey Relational Analysis on World Governance Indicators* provides an in-depth analysis of fundamental political economy issues - the quality of governance and the performance of government institutions in managing country's economic and social resources. Based on rich theoretical and empirical literature, the chapter deals with the key problems related to state-level decision making. It offers a thorough elaboration of the issue of conceptual clarity of the term "governance", the channels that link good governance to economic growth and the increasing interest in measuring the quality of governance. The research presented in this chapter accentuate that managing resources of national economies requires competent and informed decision-making, based on systematic measuring of government performance and propose an alternative tool for measuring the progress of the countries in providing an environment conducive to economic growth and social development.

Chapter 6 - *Export-led Recovery in Portugal. Can it Also Sustain Growth?* broadly analyzes connection between the significance of exports and the growth dynamic and its sustainability. This chapter focuses mainly on the nature of exporting activity - which industries, what share of domestic produced value added and which regional destination - as well as on the importance of domestic market for sustaining a well-established competitiveness for the exporters. This chapter investigates the dynamics among exports and output over the period 1970-2012 for Portugal. The methods of choice for the purpose of estimation are a bivariate VAR model with output and exports and apply co-integration and Granger causality and impulse response analysis.

In terms of sectoral policy, a fundamental problem is to discover which sectors are more correlated with creation of jobs and understand the aggregated fluctuations of the labor force. Authors of Chapter 7 make an interesting claim that shifts in labor demand among sectors, rather than changes in the level of aggregate demand, are the cause of cyclical variation in unemployment-to-employment transition. They apply an econometric model at European level to empirically discover three kinds of outflow rates (the speed with which an unemployed person can find an employed position). The panel analysis is the method applied and the data are provided using the KILM comprehensive database of country-level data

(Key Indicators of the Labor Market) including 33 European countries over 5 year period (from 2008 to 2012). This kind of results are valuable tools for policy makers in their efforts to develop specific policy measures, i.e. targeting sectors with greater impact on outflow rates in order to mitigate the negative effects of economic crisis on labor force.

Last, numerical and quantitative approaches for economic policies design, can take the shape of unsupervised techniques. Popular applications under this setting are segmentation through clustering, rules generation (often by association analysis), social network analysis to infer connections among subjects, latent variables assessment through factor analysis, etc.

Chapter 8 illustrates how such an unsupervised methodology (cluster analysis) can be used to guide management decisions. Essentially, such a methodology is recommended to safeguard that the findings (e.g. survey findings) reflect substantial behaviors of the sample, and to allow legitimate, evidence-based decisions. Policy design implications for the specific domain of mussels farming are presented, revealing the potentials of typologies for economic decision analysis.

Manager and administrators in business and public sector organizations are perhaps the largest group of potential users of economic decision analysis. Therefore, the topic of the third section *Firms & Networks* comes without any surprise. Considering the implementation of decision analysis to this area, there are of course associated behavioral issues, however chapters of this section illustrate how quantitative methods are designed to support (groups of) decision makers to confront decision problems.

Perhaps the most evident obstacle for making economic decisions is the inherent large scale uncertainty of basic input data. Chapter 9, provides a comprehensive presentation of the basic concepts and the mainstream models, exemplified in an industry where large uncertainties are a regularity. Through running examples of hydrocarbon exploration and oil field development, readers can be introduced to the principles of making decisions under risk and uncertainty. As the relevant survey of managers demonstrated, these principles, as well as the basic models are of great practical importance for the industry.

As most economic issues, the theory of organizations has been erected in the light of the allocation of scarce resources inquiry. Such a theory takes it that (i) the purpose is to investigate the behaviour of firms as it affects allocation and distribution, (ii) the decision process of the firm is reduced to the fiction of one sole rational maximizing agent, (iii) the role of the firm is not qualitatively different from the role of market.

While considering the firm as a by-product of the exchange paradigm seems interesting when one investigates a static market coordination of isolated agents, it becomes quite inappropriate when one tries to deal with economic agents embedded in changing and interactive environments. It is through interactions and retroactions that the agents experiment their 'model of the world'; it is through action that the agents put their own representation under control so that communications operate as a feedback mechanism on the construction of knowledge. Chapter 10 - *Crisis communication and crisis management during the crisis, case study of Croatia* – is particularly interested in the role of communication during crisis. The empirical study tends to confirm the growing importance given by firms to interactions and retroactions both for organizational learning or change management.

In every decision, using a single criterion approach is equivalent to deliberately discarding certain aspects of reality. Therefore, to reach an effective decision, it is necessary to develop a family of criteria that preserves, for each of them, the original concrete meaning of the decision's objective. Considering multiple criteria appears therefore, a natural process, and probably every researcher of economic decision analysis will encounter at some point problems that need to be supported by solid multiple criteria decision aid methodologies. Chapter 11 mixes two MCDA techniques (AHP and TOPSIS) in an integrated methodology that eventually suggests a ranking of to-be improved business processes. A modified Delphi method was implemented to create the family of criteria, AHP was used to assign significance weights to criteria, and then TOPSIS was applied to deliver the final ranking. An interesting point of this chapter is that it discusses the comparison of the proposed MCDA methodology with an established Six Sigma approach, that is commonly followed for the same goal (prioritize business processes for improvement).

Finally, beyond a certain level of complexity, the firm should take in account the benefits that can be derived from participating in organizational networks and increasing social capital. For this purpose, Chapter 12 - *Rethinking social capital measurement* – should allow economic actors to get a strategic positioning within their social sphere. By using graph theory, the chapter develops a direct measurement of social capital by means of two operational indicators, which are the "relational strength" and the "relational potential". These indicators might be useful for designing network strategies especially in the global digital economy.

The Information and Communication Technologies (ICTs) have made networks pervasive and a widespread access to data possible. But data have no value if organizations, institutions and firms, are unable to combine and process them through complex decision processes. The rise of related technologies, like Internet, social networks or cloud computing, have increased the availability of data in such a way that the challenges of decision are no longer on information but on knowledge. And because they help to decipher data on changes in markets and organizations, Tools and Techniques for Economic Decision Analysis still matter.

Chapter 1
Investment Decision Making: Where Do We Stand?

Aleksandar Šević
Trinity College Dublin, Ireland

Srđan Marinković
University of Nis, Serbia

ABSTRACT

This chapter is a review of different approaches academics take to find right answers on the question how investors' community makes decisions on optimal portfolio of securities and how this process converges toward capital market equilibrium. Authors will try to reconcile the approaches that come from different intellectual traditions. The authors start with the Capital Assets Pricing Model (hereafter CAPM). For decades long the model has been a cornerstone of modern finance literature and a guide for investment decision making. The model assumes that the choice of investment portfolio is directed toward optimization between statistically defined risk and observable return of a universe of available investments, in the setting of rational and homogeneous agents where information is common knowledge. The rigidity of CAPM assumptions led to a plethora of studies where some of those assumptions are relaxed. An important breakthrough to the extant body of knowledge has been made by the introduction of the asymmetric information in the decision-making process.

INTRODUCTION

In the process or investment decision-making agents are imbued with beliefs about potential returns, but until mid-1960s it was rather difficult to find a comprehensive story that would link returns to the evaluation of risk. Markowitz (1952) examines the so-called second stage of portfolio construction in an attempt to link the beliefs to the final asset selection and refers to the relevance of both anticipated return and variance in the process, with a specific focus being paid to diversification. Depending on the level of risk averseness investors would choose to invest in cash, or a combination of cash and risky assets (Tobin, 1958). Following these studies an additional step seemed inevitable in an attempt to provide a more stylized theory on the selection of assets in a two-dimensional risk-return space.

DOI: 10.4018/978-1-5225-0959-2.ch001

Sharpe (1964) uses the utility theory to create a market equilibrium theory for asset prices and risks involved in asset allocation, and creates the early version of the Capital Asset Pricing Model. Investors select the universe of potential investment choices and then choose the most efficient portfolios, i.e. those that secure the highest return for the given level of risk or the lowest risk for the assumed expected return. By paying special attention to varying levels of risk aversion and probability assessments, including the cases of limited short sales and unavailability of riskless assets, Lintner (1965) further improves the model. Black (1972) examines the assumption that an investor can take a long or short position in any asset, which may not be readily confirmed in the investment process. Therefore, a more restrictive environment without riskless assets, borrowing or lending has been analyzed, just to conclude that the CAPM model is still valid with statistically significant beta coefficients in explaining individual returns.[1] In the CAPM modelling efficient portfolios could comprise short sales, since the expected value of the individual asset return could be smaller than the risk-free interest rate or the asset could be shorted so as to achieve diversification goals even though its expected value could be higher than the risk-free rate of return. In certain cases, shorted assets could account for as much as 50 percent or more of the entire efficient portfolio (Levy, 1983; Sharpe, 1991; Levy, 2010).

Merton (1973) extends the model to multiple periods, while Breeden (1979) applies this approach to a multi-good Consumption CAPM. Following attempts to find a comprehensive model in the international settings Stulz (1981) manages to evaluate the expected return without reference to the exchange rate risk. In addition, int order to assuage differences between *ex-ante* assumptions and *ex-post* testability a Conditional CAPM has been suggested. Fama and French (1992, 1993, 1996, 2013) suggest the introduction of a range of variables to examine the validity of beta coefficient estimates.

In this chapter we first examine the studies leading to the creation of the basic CAPM model. Then we'll discuss issues faced by empiricists in testing CAPM caused by the rigidity of *ex-ante* assumptions that cannot be easily confirmed *ex-post* due to the lack of stable betas and market proxies that do not represent all tradeable risky assets in respective markets. Then we shall discuss variations in CAPM, which have evolved over more than half a century of persistent research to find the best fit for markets and investors. Afterwards, our attention will turn to challenges faced by advocates of CAPM.

CAPM

The CAPM is a market equilibrium theory with very strict requirements such as:

- Investors maximize the expected utility of their wealth at the end of the period
- Investors are risk averse and act as price takers. Normality of distribution has been assumed in addition to homogenous expectations across the investment universe
- Frictionless markets without imperfections are associated with costless information available to all investors.
- A risk-free rate is available and investors may borrow and lend without restrictions
- Assets are marketable, divisible and available in fixed quantities.

Following these requirements, it is possible to create an efficient set of investments in the two-dimensional risk-return space. Less risk-averse investors will opt for higher return and a commensurate increase in risk, while cautious agents will be more inclined to achieve lower returns with a proportion-

Figure 1.

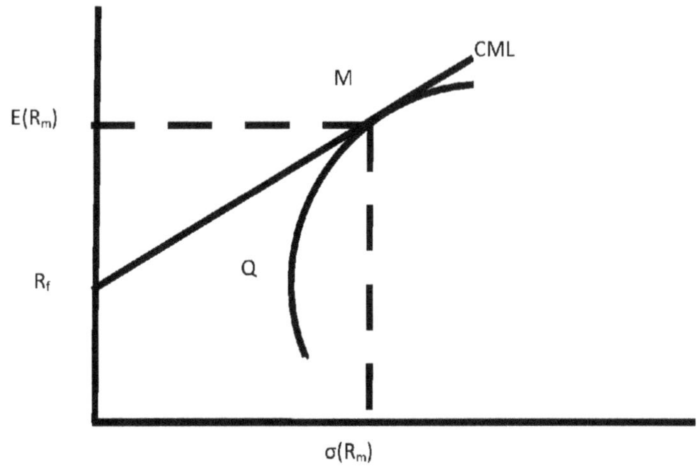

ate decline in risk. However, their investment choices should be aligned across the convex efficiency frontier, in Figure 1 depicted from point Q upwards. All choices below point Q, the so-called minimum variance portfolio, would render investors with comparatively lower returns for the same level of risk. All portfolios below Q on the convex curve and on the right-hand side from the curve offer inferior returns when compared to dominant portfolios on the efficient frontier.

The straight line connecting the risk-free rate (R_f) on y-axis with the market portfolio M is called a capital market line (CML). When all above-mentioned conditions are met investors could invest money only in a risk-free rate when σ, i.e. total risk, is non-extant, aim at the combination of risk-free and risky assets by moving along the upward sloping CML, invest all funds in the market portfolio M or even borrow at R_f and invest proceeds in risky assets, thereby moving further along the upward-sloping line and away from M (Figure 1). Higher returns will be *ex-ante* justified by higher risk and this relationship is captured by the following formula for the CML:

$$E(R_p) = R_f + [(E(R_m) - R_f)/\sigma(R_m)]\sigma(R_p)$$

The term within brackets denotes the slope of the firm and it is a market risk premium in excess of the riskless rate scaled by the unit of risk, the standard deviation of a market portfolio. Higher market risk premium will create a higher risk exposure and, consequently, higher portfolio *p* returns.

Assuming that an investor can invest in asset *i* a *c* amount of money and *(1-c)* in a market portfolio it is possible to partially differentiate the expected return and standard deviation of this portfolio with respect to *c*. Assuming that in equilibrium money will not be invested in any particular asset and all funds will flow to the diversified market portfolio, the final equation is rendered as:

$$E(R_i) = R_f + (\sigma_{im}/\sigma^2_m)[E(R_m) - R_f]$$

where σ_{im}/σ^2_m is the slope of the security market line (SML) and it is more routinely referred to as beta (β_i). Accordingly, expected returns are linear with market risk (β), but not total risk (σ) (Sharpe, 1991).

Figure 2.

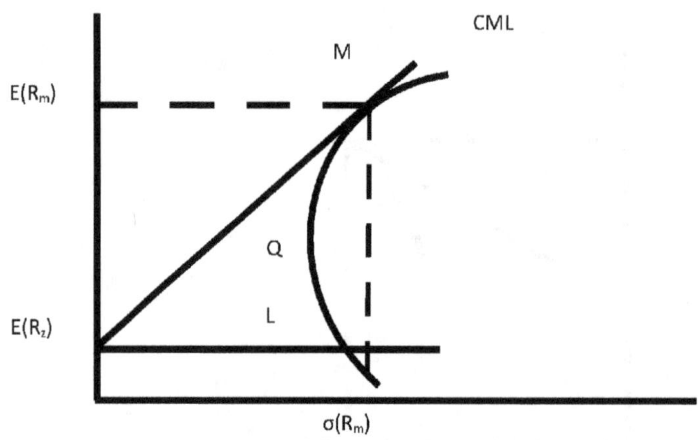

If investors are not able to borrow or lend at the riskless rate Black (1972) offers a solution via the provision of a minimum variance zero-beta portfolio. Unlike the case of Sharpe-Lintner's CAPM, the investors allocate *c* amount of money to a market portfolio and (*1-c*) to the minimum variance zero-beta portfolio. When all investor's wealth is invested in the market portfolio, i.e. when *c* amounts to 100%, the tangential efficient market portfolio M has been selected (Figure 2). Partial derivations of expected returns and standard deviation with respect to *c* and further manipulations provide:

$$[E(R_m)-E(R_{zb})]/\sigma_m = [E(R_j)-E(R_m)]\sigma_m/(\sigma_{jm}-\sigma^2_m)$$

leading to

$$E(R_j) = (1-\beta_j)E(R_{zb}) + \beta_j E(R_m), \text{ subject to } \beta_j = \sigma_{jm}/\sigma^2_m$$

and

$$E(R_j) = E(R_{zb}) + \beta_j[E(R_m) - E(R_{zb})]$$

This is a two-factor model confirming that the CAPM is a linear model and β still explains much of the variation in asset returns. However, this model is valid if there are no constraints in short sales, and a zero-beta portfolio comprises long and short positions, thus reflecting general investment patterns.

TESTABILITY OF CAPM

CAPM faces challenges in empirical tests due to its initial assumptions. It is *ex-ante* valid, but test can be conducted in the *ex-post* environment since the inputs for the former analysis are not observable. The commonly accepted testing procedure comprises two steps. In the initial phase empiricists run a simple regression with the market proxy return used as an independent and a return on any particular asset as a dependent variable:

$$R_{it} = \alpha + \beta i R_{mt} + \varepsilon_{it}$$

The values of these variables are not *ex-ante* assumed, but sourced from secondary data and thus analyzed *ex-post*. The coefficient estimates of market proxy returns are calculated over a period of 36 or more months and the calculation windows move by one period, i.e. one month so as to calculate a series of coefficient estimates. In the second step the expected value of asset *i* is calculated with the coefficient estimates of beta used as independent variables:

$$R_i = \lambda_0 + \beta_i \lambda_i + \nu_i$$

Where λ_0 should equal the risk free rate and λ_i is expected to be close the market premium calculated as $E(R_m) - R_f$. Nevertheless, these claims are not generally purported in studies and regression R^2s are quite low. Therefore, a large amount of return variation is not explained by the inclusion of a single *ex-post* variable. Levy (1983) takes into account differences between *ex-ante* and *ex-post* betas and shows that after small modifications the second step could render an efficient portfolio as long as a range of *ex-ante* betas are used in the evaluations process. Levy and Roll (2010) apply reverse engineering to implement changes in parameters in order to make a market proxy mean-variance efficient. It has been shown that small modifications are necessary to achieve efficiency.

Early CAPM critiques are comprehensively analyzed in Roll (1977). Since the mean-variance efficiency of the market portfolio is the only hypothesis that could be independently tested it is impossible to examine the linear relationship between betas and returns without prior reference to efficiency. In addition, the market proxies[2] do not include all risky individual assets and the assumption about efficiency cannot be easily purported. The linear relationship between betas and returns can be achieved even for inefficient portfolios, while the market equilibrium theory does not make any claims about the expected value of parameters as opposed to simple linear relationships. Portfolios could comprise assets that demonstrate non-linear relationships, but these could be cancelled out cross-sectionally. Finally, it is not clear what is the meaning of non-zero Jensen's alpha, because in CAPM its value is expected to be zero across all aggregated assets. If a positive alpha has been reported it means that the market portfolio is inefficient. All further claims about superior (positive) or inferior (negative) performance could be questioned in the milieu of inefficient portfolios and the inappropriate selection of relevant benchmarks.

The mean-variance or stochastic dominance theory are not useful in making decisions even when a vast majority of economic agents would prefer a specific option vis-à-vis all others. Both theories relate to utility functions, but do not specifically determine the preferred option. Leshno and Levy (2002) modify the stochastic dominance approach so as to exclude the impact of extreme utility functions in the cumulative distribution. The so-called Almost Stochastic Dominance (ASD) theory allows for the ranking of available alternatives, excludes alternative options and creates a link between stock allocations in a portfolio and investments horizons tailored for specific groups of investors.

An important contention point in CAPM discussion is related to the type of distribution necessary to achieve equilibrium. In the mean-variance space initial reference is made to the Gaussian normal distribution, but *ex-post* model tests sample assets from the distribution that is non-normal. Early seminal papers refer to restrictive assumptions and a single investment period, while subsequent studies attempt to include multiple periods, consumption, international assets, alternatives to the mean-variance space and other conditions.

VARIATIONS OF CAPM

Merton (1973) questions strict one-period CAPM requirements and extends the model to multiple periods. Assets are traded continually and the stochastic changes are explained by the Markov process. In addition, investment opportunity sets change in time and investors revise expected returns accordingly. It is evident that the assumption about the exclusion of transactions costs and taxes allows for investors to trade at any point in time and as frequently as possible. However, in the real investment world trading frequencies would vary and aggregated transaction costs could range from being negligible to an important return reducing factor in a portfolio.

Breeden (1979) extends Merton's (1973) methodology in the multi-good and continuous-time framework to obtain a single beta asset pricing model. In this manner the constraints imposed by not being able to recognize multi state variables have been circumvented. The asset beta in this Consumption CAPM is calculated relative to aggregate consumption and is not related to the market portfolio as Sharpe-Lintner-(Black) CAPM. The author manages to find an equilibrium model even if the riskless rate is not available, by calculating expected returns on the zero-beta portfolio relative to the portfolio that does not include returns on assets correlated with aggregate consumption. Campbell (1993) evaluates the problem of extending the one-period CAPM to multiple periods. With an increase in time lengths the stability of parameters is affected, and researchers may be urged to shorten time periods. However, Campbell claims that the variation in the consumption-wealth ratio is small, which allows for the loglinearity in intertemporal evaluations. The market equilibrium reached in this intertemporal CAPM could be tested without consumption data that are measured with errors and inconsistencies in aggregations across time.

Solnik (1974) assumes that the market portfolio comprises value-weighted stocks and a set of risk-free assets collected from countries across the globe. Risk aversions and net foreign investments seem to be the determinants of relative weights in a portfolio. In this model, the final version of the International Asset Pricing Model (IAPM) is quite similar to the initial CAPM, with β representing the international systematic risk exposure of a particular security. However, inconsistencies in setting up utility functions and other assumptions made it impossible to create a comprehensive model (Solnik, 1983). Stulz (1981) introduces varying consumption opportunity sets across countries, while prices of commodities and exchange rates follow an Ito process, and the PPP is applicable to traded goods, only. In this model the expected return is not related to the exchange rate risk.

Major criticism about CAPM claims that beta has weak or non-extant relationship with expected returns and that it may not be the only relevant factor in explaining returns. Pettengill *et al.* (1995) purport that a two-step approach to testing the CAPM includes the reference to realized returns and market proxies, which could lead to the *ex-post* rejection of betas. The suggested Conditional CAPM evaluation separates the beta into two components, i.e. $\rho*\beta i$ if $Rm - Rf > 0$ and $(1-\rho)*\beta i$ if $Rm - Rf<0$. In this manner, large beta portfolios could underperform low-beta portfolios if excess market returns turn negative. Authors also claim that this beta decomposition is historically supported by the fact that the 90-day Treasury bill rates were larger than market returns in more than 40 percent of all observations. Regression results indicate a consistent and positive relationship between beta and expected returns. Jagannathan and Wang (1995) suggest another approach to conditionality by assuming that risk premia vary in time and occasional inaccuracies in *ex-post* CAPM tests indicate varying betas across multiple periods rather than the violation of theoretical assumptions per each period. The expected return on *j*th asset is:

$$E[R_{jt}|I_{t-1}] = \theta_{0t-1} + \theta_{1t-1}\beta_{jt-1}$$

with β_{jt-1} calculated as $\beta_{jt-1} = Cov(R_{jt}, R_{mt}|I_{t-1})/Var(R_{mt}|I_{t-1})$, I_{t-1} representing the investment set available to investors at the end of the previous period, θ_{0t-1} being the conditional expected return on the zero beta portfolio and θ_{1t-1} representing the conditional market risk premium. The authors introduce two types of unconditional betas:

$\beta_j = Cov(R_{jt}, R_{mt})/Var(R_{mt})$, i.e. market beta and

$\beta^{\theta}_j = Cov(R_{jt}, \theta_{1t-1})/Var(\theta_{1t-1})$, a so-called premium beta

and claim that as long as betas are not linked via linear function unconditional returns could be calculated as:

$$E(R_{jt}) = \alpha_0 + \alpha_1\beta_j + \alpha_2\beta^{\theta}_j$$

Grauer (1978) questions the validity of the mean-variance space in providing the best support for CAPM and compares it against additional five utility-based models, such as square root, logarithmic, generalized logarithmic, negative one power and negative five power. All models are supportive for linearity and a positive relationship between risk and return. However, the last assumption about no restriction in riskless borrowing and lending is not supported. Kandel and Stambaugh (1995) question the assumption that as long as the market proxy lies on the efficient frontier that relation between expected returns and betas will be linear. OLS regressions can indicate that there is a linear relationship even though the market proxy may be inefficient, or linearity may not be confirmed even though there is a strong assumption about efficiency. In order to circumvent these constraints, the authors suggest the use of GLS regressions and confirm there is a linear relationship between expected return in betas when market proxies are efficient. Linearity weakens as the market portfolio moves away from the efficient frontier. The repackaging of assets within the portfolio allows for a removal of the market portfolio towards the efficient frontier while the linear relationship in the mean-beta space gradually strengthens until it finally reaches the highest point concurrently with the full efficiency of the market proxy.

CHALLENGES FOR CAPM

The multitude of restrictive conditions associated with CAPM led to the provision of alternative models. Ross (1976) suggested a model that explains the random rate of return on *j*th asset:

$$\tilde{r}_j = E\left(\tilde{r}_j\right) + b_{j1}\tilde{\delta}_1 + \ldots + b_{jk}\tilde{\delta}_k + \tilde{\varepsilon}_j$$

where $E\left(\tilde{r}_j\right)$ is the expected return on asset *j*, various *b* are factor loadings, i.e. sensitivity of the *j*th asset's returns to one of the factors ranging from 1 to k, while $\tilde{\varepsilon}_j$ is a zero mean noise representing the unsystematic risk of the *j*th asset. The Arbitrage Pricing Theory (APT) distinguishes between expectations that could be identical for all agents *ex-ante*, and anticipations for each factor, which may be divergent. The model allows for the creation of an arbitrage portfolio as the number of assets in a portfolio becomes very large and no wealth is being used in the process. For instance, agents could dispose of some assets and use the derived income to purchase others. In the process of arbitrage portfolio creation, it is necessary to eliminate not only the unsystematic, but also the undiversifiable systematic risk. Keeping investment changes at a low level, a large number of assets and making sure that the weighted sum is zero for the systematic risk components, i.e. all b factor sensitivities, will achieve these goals. Ross (1976) indicates that an increase in the number of assets will reduce the importance of the unsystematic risk term $\tilde{\varepsilon}_j$, but an increase in the risk aversion as the wealth of an agent becomes larger provides a counter effect that will allow for noise to persist in this model.

If CAPM establishes a simple relationship between the expected return and a single market-based factor, it is meaningful to explore whether other factors could be identified. Fama and French (1992) analyze the cross-sectional variation in average returns in the US from 1963 until 1990 with respect to market beta, size, book-to-market (B/M) ratios, earnings-to-price (E/P) ratios and leverage. Betas have weak or non-extant relationship with returns when other factors are included in the model. The coefficient estimates of size and book-to-market ratios are significant, and assume most of the explanatory power away from E/P and leverage. When stock markets have been analyzed concurrently with bond markets, the significance of the market proxy is evident in justifying the discrepancy between returns on stocks and one-month bills. The persistency of size and book-to-market variables in explaining stock returns is reconfirmed, and jointly with the market proxy their impact on returns can be extended to bond markets. Nevertheless, the inclusion of a term premium and a default premium eliminates the importance of stock market factors in explaining bond returns (Fama and French, 1993).

The search for explanations shedding light on occasional anomalies documented in contravention of CAPM postulates prompted Fama and French (1996) to regress a set of variables on a portfolio *i*th risk premium:

$$R_i - R_f = \alpha_i + \varsigma_i(Rm - Rf) + \lambda_i SMB + \varphi_i HML + \varepsilon_i$$

where SMB implies the discrepancy between the return on a portfolio of small stocks and the return on a portfolio comprising large stocks, and HML indicates the difference between the return on a portfolio that includes high-book-to-market stocks and the return on a portfolio of low-book-to-market stocks. The selection of variables in this multifactor models was influenced by findings published in previous papers, since the omission of leverage and earnings ratios due to rather poor explanatory power documented earlier, is noticeable. The three-factor model appropriately explains the average return of 25 portfolios made by combining five quintiles of size and book-to—market (B/M) rankings. Only portfolios in smallest size and smallest B/M intersections had non-zero excess returns, in addition to the largest size and smallest B/M quintile cell. The authors then allocate assets to ten portfolios, in accordance with ten deciles calculated for B/M, earnings-to-price (E/P), cash-flow-to-price (C/P) and five-year-sales-rank, and conclude that the suggested multifactor model explains the average returns for most of these portfolios, including the sales-rank. The latter result is important, since it is the only variable not derived from stock data. DeBondt and Thaler's (1985) claim that past winners will underperform in the future, and that past losers will become future winners is examined in conjunction with findings suggested by Jegadeesh and Titman (1993) and Asness (1995) that for short periods of up to one year, the momentum prevails. Rouwenhorst (1998) examines the short-term momentum in twelve European countries, and concludes that in the short-term periods of up to one year the one-month difference between winner and loser portfolios amounts to one percent. However, when companies are sourced from winning and losing industries, the momentum strategy is more successful than in the case of the selection of individual stocks. The best results are in the initial month and the difference dissipates until the end of the one-year period (Moskowitz and Grinblatt, 1999). Fama and French confirm that depending of the period selection (i.e. prior to or after 1963) the reversal story is valid for longer periods of time to varying extent. The reversal pattern is much stronger in the period prior to 1963. It has been found that in both long-term and short-term periods the loadings on HML and SML are quite strong for past losers. While in the long-term this relationship explains the reversal, it fails to capture the short-term momentum story.

By referring to the discounted dividend growth model Fama and French (2013) link profitability and investments to the market-to-book equity price. An increase in a firm's earnings, i.e. the proxy for profitability, would be related to an increase in the expected return. In addition, an investment in book equity would be converted to lower expected returns. The suggested five-factor model is an extension of the three-factor model:

$$R_i - R_f = \alpha_i + \varsigma_i(Rm - Rf) + \lambda_i SMB + \varphi_i HML + \nu_j RMW + \chi_j CMA + \varepsilon_i$$

with RMW as a difference between the returns on a portfolio with robust profitability and the returns on a portfolio with weak profitability, and CMA representing a difference between the returns on a portfolio of low (conservative) investment stocks and the returns on a portfolio with high (aggressive) investment stocks. The five-factor model is evaluated with the addition of the two decades of datasets as opposed to the previous three-factor study. Following various combinations of factors in the analysis, the authors conclude that the HML can be omitted, since its impact is fully accounted for by other four factors. The four-factor model without HML performs as satisfactorily as the initially outlined five-factor model.

The rigidity of CAPM assumptions led to a plethora of studies where some of these assumptions are relaxed. An important breakthrough to the extant body of knowledge has been made by the introduction of the asymmetric information in the decision-making process, not only by individual economic agents by also companies.

INTRODUCING LIQUIDITY CONSIDERATION INTO FINANCIAL SCIENCE

So far we have explained a family of general asset pricing models that do not get into calculus the fact that actors may have available information set less than complete. In various fields of economic sciences, particularly in the field of finance, various forms of dilution of the omniscience assumption were frequently studied issue. We daresay that such discussions are as old as economic science itself. There is a clue:

When Walras sent his classic work devoted to general equilibrium theory to Henri Poincaré, Poincaré commented that Walras makes two critical assumptions:

...you regard men as infinitely selfish and infinitely farsighted. The first hypothesis may perhaps be admitted in a first approximation, the second may call for some reservations (quoted in Minsky, 1995).

Thus, the assumption of perfect information was never considered as granted. But it was a sacrifice that academia was ready to accept in order to reach mathematically elegant solutions for complex economic problems. In contemporary times, as was the case in past times when economic science was given contours of an exact science, it is a dominant style of writing. However, occasionally, pendulum swung back to the other side and voices that claim that the perfect knowledge assumption reduces economic interactions to the level that real economic life in nothing more than a futile ground overpowers the voices that would rather stick to the old tradition. However, theories and models that explicitly incorporate dilution of omniscience assumption are rarely as elegant and complete as economic mainstream theories and models.

From the very beginning we would like to address reader attention on some concepts that at first glance may be seen as distinct phenomena: liquidity, uncertainty, and asymmetric information. The concepts appeared in different times, and have been cornerstones of flourishing intellectual debates for a long, and that continue up to contemporary times.

Let us start with liquidity. It is a concept that can be most easily understood. Put it simply, it is easy with which an asset can be traded. However, the concept has multiple dimensions. According to Kyle (1985, p. 1316) "market liquidity" is a slippery and elusive concept, in part because it encompasses a number of transactional properties of markets. These include "tightness" (the cost of turning around a position over a short period of time), "depth" (the size of an order flow innovation required to change prices a given amount), and "resiliency" (the speed with which prices recover from a random, uninformative shock). Although at first glance the first two dimensions show no direct link to informational features of asset, it is not the case with the third one.

In the very root liquidity is an informational phenomenon. In the informationally complete market (everyone knows everything) there is no need for money. Any asset may serve the roles of money, and there is no need for institutions that are inevitably important for modern economies (e.g. financial intermediaries, etc.). Gorton and Pennacchi (1990) have developed a notion of security liquidity based solely on asymmetric information. According to the authors, a liquid security has the characteristic that it can be traded by uninformed agents without loss to insiders. It means that a less informed trader aware of possibility to trade with better informed may react either asking for price concession in order to take trade offer, or give up from the trade. In the first case, transaction is accomplished but the price will absorb asymmetric information effect. If a trader operates with an incomplete set of information, and is aware of that, he or she might be reluctant to trade. If widespread, such situation will make trade less frequent or less likely to take place, and in its extreme a market may ultimately disappear. In theory this possible outcome is known as 'no trade equilibrium', or market autarchy (Glosten and Milgrom, 1985). We will return to this point latter in this chapter.

INVESTMENT DECISION MAKING UNDER CONDITIONS OF RISK 'OR' UNCERTAINTY

Any discussion of informational impediments to market efficiency and investment process should start with prominent ancestors of what we have established today as asymmetric information paradigm. The first contribution to the research of uncertainty phenomenon is Knight's distinction between insurable and non-insurable risk. In his thesis (1921, pp. 21-22) he wrote: "uncertainty must be taken in a sense radically distinct from the familiar notion of risk, from which it has never been properly separated. The term 'risk', as loosely used in everyday speech and in economic discussion, really covers two things which, functionally at least, in their causal relations to the phenomena of economic organization, are categorically different ... The essential fact is that 'risk' means in some cases a quantity susceptible of measurement, while at other times it is something distinctly not of this character; and there are far-reaching and crucial differences in the bearings of the phenomenon depending on which of the two is really present and operating. It … appear that a measurable uncertainty, or 'risk' proper, … is so far different from an unmeasurable one that it is not in effect an uncertainty at all". As well known, Knight offered an explanation of all entrepreneurial profit (and consequently the same explanation for an existence of firm) as a kind of award for exposing to pure uncertainty. The risk situations can be insured so that they cannot be priced in competitive markets the way that increases entrepreneurial award.

For a long time since Knight's pioneering attempt, academia has been trying to draw the line between the notions of risk and uncertainty. What we know for sure, now as we knew before, is that the boundary is elusive one. If we quote Knight (1921, p. 46) "while a single situation involving a known risk may be regarded as 'uncertain', this uncertainty is easily converted into effective certainty; for in a considerable number of such cases the results become predictable in accordance with the laws of chance, and the error in such prediction approaches zero as the number of cases is increased". It is the essence of insurance business, or 'raison d'être' of insurance companies.

Nevertheless, it was equally agreed long time ago (Samuelson, 1963, p. 113) that no matter how large the number in the sample, in every actuarial situation of mathematical probability, we are left with a finite sample, so "…in the appropriate limit law of probability there will necessary be left an epsilon of uncertainty even in so-called risk situations". Therefore, despite of diversification or actuarial probabilities, we have always to deal with uncertainty. This remark has great importance for the attempt to create a difference of risk and uncertainty in the economics of investment and decision-making.

It is empirical fact that investors seldom know accurately what most securities are worth. They undertake analysis to form as precise as possible estimates. However, this process may differ in that the same information may imply different estimates for different investors. There may not be enough available information to assign a reliable probability measure on all security prices (opposite to CAPM assumptions). Uncertainty will exist about the identity of the major factors that will influence the future path of prices of a given security. Uncertainty reduces to return variance only in the case where the distribution is restricted to a particular form whose corresponding parameters are known to everybody (Kane, 1999). Moreover, casual empiricism suggests that investors seldom bother to make themselves maximally informed. Since information is costly, investors will undertake gathering and processing information as long as benefits of this activity exceed costs. Opposite to traditional asset-pricing models, which assume frictionless markets without imperfections associated with costly information, in real life investment process investors have to deal with frictions of that kind. An investor who is not indifferent to risk may value the complete resolution of uncertainty more than a risk-neutral investor. According to Mehrez et al. (1984) there must be a premium related to incomplete knowledge, that one should not confuse with the conventional risk premium, since the latter stems from subjective averseness to risk while the former reflects the objective cost imposed by imperfect knowledge.

Although Knight's work did not even mention liquidity, he actually laid ground for future research in that field, by pointing out crucial difference between risk and (subjective) uncertainty phenomena, and its implications on market functioning. Shortly afterwards the notion of liquidity has taken place of the notion of uncertainty, and researchers have started using liquidity as a superficial manifestation of hard-to-operate notion of uncertainty.

Liquidity premium was an argument used by Keynes in his seminar work in order to explain the very essence of risk free interest rate. He set up two assets investment universe with investors choosing between default risk-free interest-bearing asset and zero-return money. The implication of the model was that investors have liquidity preference, or readiness to stick to the money, since they are not certain about future path of prices of interest bearing asset, or they fear that positive return may turn into (capital) losses. In the equilibrium, the zero-return asset which holds its value through time will be demanded by investors since the required return for the asset with uncertain value includes a liquidity premium. A couple of sentences derived from the 'General theory', we are of opinion, are exclusively able to express Keynes' (1936, p. 240) view. "The liquidity-premium … is partly similar to the risk-premium, but partly different; – the difference corresponding to the difference between the best estimates we can make of probabilities and the confidence with which we make them". By contemplating about the role of expectations in the process of economic decision making, he wrote: "The state of long-term expectations, upon which our decisions are based, does not solely depend on the most probable forecast we can make. It also depends on the confidence with which we make this forecast – on how highly we rate the likelihood of our best forecast turning out quite wrong. If we expect large changes but are very uncertain as to what precise form these changes will take, then our confidence will be weak" (Keynes, 1936, p. 148). Investment activity is always forward looking one. Investment return is what should be realized in future. If investors are not completely certain, or confident in their forecasts, that must influence their decision making.

This element of Mr. Keynes analysis is frequently misidentified with some other elements, or simply neglected. For example, one of his followers, Tobin, offered explanation for liquidity preference on the basis of investors' risk aversion. According to Tobin's interpretation, within the two-asset class model, investor will demand zero-return riskless asset (money) since risk-averse investors must be compensated for investing in risky interest bearing alternative. He stated (Tobin, 1958, p. 70): "when he [Keynes, added] refers to uncertainty in the market, he appears to mean disagreement among investors concerning the future of the rate rather than subjective doubts in the mind of an individual investor". We have found some points referring to Keynes's liquidity preference and asset pricing modelling in Woodward contribution (1983, p. 356) that matched with our point of view. Author admits that at least part of what Hicks and Keynes had in mind as a source of the liquidity premium was that the far future was inherently more uncertain that the near future, a proposition few of us would dispute.

These influencing ideas published decades ago, again are actualized recently. For instance, Holmström and Tirole (1996, p. 187) agree that "given incomplete insurance, assets will command liquidity premia (even though all agents are risk-neutral). Such liquidity premia correspond to risk premia in standard asset-pricing models, but the empirical implications can be rather different", and in the same paper later, "… liquidity premium on the asset depend on what the asset delivers conditional on the productive sector experiencing a high liquidity shock … While a liquidity premium is a form of risk premium, its structure is different from that seen in standard asset-pricing models. In particular, how the asset behaves when liquidity is abundant is less relevant than how it behaves when liquidity is tight."

MARKET MICROSTRUCTURE THEORY AND ASSET PRICING

Keynes's enlightening ideas, published nearly a century ago, inspired many authors. The idea that there is a spectrum of assets, which can be classified in the continuum from perfectly liquid to ultimately illiquid, further is developed in Davidson (2002). According to the author, an asset with perfect liquidity is the one able to convert (sell) into cash on the spot market where a market maker guarantees firm spot price expressed in money units. It follows an inspiring notion that such an asset will hold the full liquidity as long as the market maker has enough money at hands to support his given guarantee, or as long as investors believe that he will be able to do so. The author uses the word market maker in more general sense, so that any intermediary fits into his notion of market maker.

The institution of organized financial markets, opposite to what is believed out of academic circles, is not able to generate liquidity; per se. Davidson (2002) forceful analogy portrays liquidity generating financial markets as two-edged sword. In good times they make investment process easy, but in bad times they will bring additional instability to the system. Indisputably, financial markets are valuable invention. Markets are good since they make real investments that are fixed for the community to look liquid from the angle of an individual investor. However, the bad thing is that it only looks like that. Namely, as long as financial markets operate orderly, investors will believe that they have a fast-exit option that should be activated whenever they are not satisfied with the investment. In some extent, asset liquidity is possible to increase by organizational design of modern traded markets. It is called endogenous liquidity.

In the next section, we will review the basic results of the intellectual efforts of the market microstructure theory. This strand of economic literature appears in late 70's and focuses on organizational design of contemporary markets, but has equally forceful implications for the asset pricing.

Market microstructure theory brought back into the research focus the nexus between asset liquidity and its price. However, this time the issue was enlightened from the different angle. What was common for majority of researchers that tried to explain what influence asset liquidity might have on the price of financial assets from the market microstructure milieu is their focus on the transaction costs. Existence of transaction costs, which may appear as asymmetric information costs (e.g. adverse selection costs), costs of turning around position and other kinds of transaction costs, diminishes equilibrium value of assets. According to theory, this is why even a risk-neutral agent would demand return that has to compensate him for those extra costs (Amihud and Mendelson, 1986). The focus on the transaction costs as an observable liquidity dimension probably comes along with efforts to test empirically influence of asset liquidity on its price.

For instance, in his comprehensive empirical study, Lesmond (2005) found that in majority of emerging markets, rather high return on stock market investments (which corresponds to depressed stock prices), in some occasions even eighty percent annually, fully corresponds to low liquidity. Market liquidity assessed on the basis of bid ask spread varies from one percent in case of Taiwan to even nearly fifty percent in case of Russian stock market. Similarly, Amihud and Mendelson (1986, 2003) assigned large share of cross-sectional variation in securities return to the liquidity differences among the various kinds of financial and real assets, and markets. All the same, in a frequently cited paper, Amihud and Mendelson (1991) found the difference in bid-ask spread solely able to explain differences in rates of return of long term and short term governmental securities. On the same way, Shen and Starr (1998) found the conventional measure of risk (return volatility) unable to explain the return differences once the bid ask spread appears into the regression model. A rationale offered by authors is on the line with above argumentation. Namely, assets with different liquidity will trade with different bid-ask spread. When we shift to the stock markets this regularity is not as clear as in the case of markets for governmental securities. For instance, Madhavan (2000) found bid-ask spread as a proxy for asset liquidity less informative, and called for more sophisticated measures of liquidity.

The crucial feature of any financial market is the way that the role of providing liquidity is distributed among actors. It is in the very design of financial markets. Trading itself is a process of providing and absorbing liquidity, or buying and selling it. In quote driven markets, dealers are actors solely responsible for providing liquidity, since they create opportunity for other traders to trade, by standing ready to accept a trade proposal that comes from investors' community. Order-driven markets operate without dealers. Trade will take place with no dealer intervention, among traders themselves which will either place or take an offer to trade, in any specific case. Traders that submit standing limit order offer liquidity to other traders while traders that submit marketable limit orders or market orders will take offered liquidity (Harris, 2003). At the end, so called hybrid market structure combines both liquidity providing mechanisms. Hybrid markets either impose dealer role in order driven structure, or allow some traders to compete directly with dealers, changing that way pure order or quote driven structure, respectively. The very choice between different market structures depends on 'availability' of actors that are ready to create liquidity or sell liquidity insurance to other actors. However, the availability of actors that are ready to provide liquidity on the market is determined by informational reasons (Grossman and Miller, 1988). A trader that is ready to postpone execution of its trade demands better price that the trader which wants to execute trade immediately. The price concession belongs to the trader that creates liquidity (dealer or speculator). It is compensation for holding position open till the trade order arrives from the other side of the market, and the trade circle is accomplished. By holding position open for some time the trader exposes himself to risk. The asset price (or value of the position) may change either because of non-informative trade (utilitarian trading interest) takes place and moves the price away from fundamentals, or because new information arrivals bring the price to the new fundamental value. If the dealer is forced to trade with better informed counterparty, which possesses new information that is not yet available to the dealer, the dealer will ex post learn that the executed trade was mistake; loss will be inevitable. In order to avoid trading with better informed a rational dealer will quote less aggressively, increasing the ask (offer) quote and decreasing the bid quote for the amount high enough to compensate him for the perspective losses. Thus, bid-ask spread will include an informational component, known as adverse selection component in addition to other costs like costs of processing and executing orders, cost of financing position, and even costs of oligopolistic dealer market structure.

If informational disturbances are too high, it may even prevent establishing regular market. Namely, if traders are aware of possibility to trade with better informed they will be reluctant to trade and consequently their hesitation will influence transaction properties of market, diminishing market/asset liquidity.

Because of transaction cost financial markets behave like a network. They are susceptible to special sort of network externality, known as 'order flow externality'. From the pure theoretical point of view, the existence of transaction costs prevents traders to trade continuously. From the empirical point, high transaction cost will make transactions less frequent, even sporadic, and probably less balanced. Less frequent trade or less active markets will in turn further increase the transaction cost. Traders will find balancing inventory/position less likely, the position will longer stay open, and consequently the cost of financing inventory and position risk will be higher. Some traders will be forced to leave the market and circle will be closed when because of fewer traders the market become less competitive.

From market microstructure theory we know that risk-averse dealers when selling the asset will command premium above buying (bid) price (Stoll, 1978, O'Hara, 2004). They demand to be compensated for holding position open till accomplishing round trip trade. In this tradition, bid-ask spread is simply market given award for taking inventory risk. It is crucial argument in so-called inventory models (Garman, 1976, Stoll, 1978, Amihud and Mendelson, 1980, Ho and Stoll, 1981). In new generation of models, information models (Milgrom and Stokey, 1982, Copeland and Galai, 1983, Easley and O'Hara, 1992) a dealer must quote ask price above the bid price in order to protect himself against better informed counterparty, which will trade if the dealer quotes are posted so that new market price (determined on the basis of information that dealer is not aware of) stays away of quotes. In both cases, dealer will record losses if unable to simultaneously buy and sell, faced with imbalance in order arrival. In inventory models order arrival process is stochastic, opposite to the case of information models, which assume that a dealer, by making quoting mistakes trigger loss-making trade with better informed counterparty.

We see that bid ask spread as the best proxy for dealership market liquidity can be seen as both as risk premium and a premium related to asymmetric information. The same conclusion holds for order driven markets where similar determinants are identified (Cohen et al. 1981). Theory opts for one or another depending on how much it relies on perfect information assumption. Nevertheless, mainstream theory operates with the concepts of risk and asymmetric information, trying to combine both influences in explanations of investors' decision making, and consequently market equilibrium. It is quite unusual that theory operates with some other informational concepts that are more close to genuine subjective uncertainty. A rare exception is Muranaga and Shimizu (2000) paper. In that study, the authors found that the level of confidence with which investors made their decisions influences assets liquidity. If investors underestimate risk, then they will be more active traders, consequently market 'depth" will increase, and vice versa. Moreover, the level of risk-aversion of market participants has identified as negatively connected to market liquidity. In this paper, levels of confidence and uncertainty are defined as divergence in investors' opinions, rather than subjective uncertainty. However, the divergence in investors' opinions is a consequence of the divergent perceptions of riskiness.

In order to summarize, we would say that followers of traditional models experimented with many variables that could possibly make the core models (CAPM) able to more fully fit real markets data. As expected, richer, more sophisticated models that add some more variables are better performing ones. However, the list of variables merely complies with those that are considered to be core determinants of asymmetric information. For instance, small capitalization stock differs from large capitalization stocks not only in terms of available utilitarian trading interest (existence of large number of shareholders) but also in terms of coverage by stock analysts, or generally the level and accuracy of information provided. Thus the size puzzle may indicate importance of asymmetric information (or liquidity) in asset pricing.

It seems that real life reconciles two strands of literature that rely on the different intellectual tradition. Perfect market models regress financial assets return solely on risk feature of assets, leaving no space for liquidity differences. However, it must be place for both.

Clear distinction between risk and liquidity is an academic issue which is not given definite theoretical answer, yet. Firstly, it is because risk (price volatility) goes hand in hand with liquidity. With no variations in price, there is no element on which traders have to disagree. Whatever measure of informational disturbances we take it will exist if the asset price is changeable. Secondly, even such measures of liquidity like bid-ask spread, contain both influences, meaning that they are elastic on variation in both risk and liquidity. We have seen that even in the ambience of perfect information dealers will command bid-ask spread.

Traditionally, market microstructure microscope is placed over the attributes of individual assets. Just a few theoretical and almost no empirical papers are devoted to studying either common liquidity determinant, or their empirical manifestations (a rare example is Chordia et al. (2000)). Therefore, a promising field of research could be studies of correlated movements of individual assets' liquidity.

There are also valuable but isolated attempts to explore financial market equilibrium from the intellectual tradition of asymmetric information paradigm (Holmström and Tirole, 2001). In contrast to the logic of traditional asset pricing models based on perfect markets, corporation are not able to raise funds on the capital market up to the level of their expected income, and the corporate sector need a cushion against liquidity shock (Holmström and Tirole, 1996, 1998). Financial asset that serve as the cushion will command liquidity premium. Thus, the model belongs to market imperfections models, because it relies on influence of non-pledgeable part of future income, derived solely from asymmetric information nature of financial markets.

CONCLUSION

Although there is a bulk of literature that is dealing with the models built on dilution of 'omniscience' assumption, little has been changed in traditional asset-pricing models. Since appearance of Sharpe (1964) path breaking paper, the traditional model (CAPM), thanks to many contemporary upgrades of them (CCAPM, ICAPM), still is a main reference point, or a cornerstone of modern finance literature. The choice of investment portfolio is directed toward optimization between statistically defined risk and observable return of a universe of available investments, while the equilibrium assets pricing is determined simply by copying the superior investment strategy, in the setting of rational and homogeneous agents (in all aspects but the degree of risk-affinity), where information is common knowledge (everyone knows everything).

An avalanche of empirical studies followed in order to test if the real life fits to the model-predicted outcomes. Despite of large and systematic CAPM pricing errors, the models based on separation of diversifiable and non-diversifiable risk continue to play an important role both in business community and amongst academics. For academics that stand up in defense of beta world-wide documented cross-section anomalies of securities return (e.g. the size effect, the earnings-yield effect, the market-to-book effect and many others), taken by opponents to be inconsistent with the traditional models, are stimuli to further rearranging the basic model, specifications and choice of data etc.

The recent advancement in market microstructure theory brought about a new momentum in exploring asset pricing modeling and risk-reward nexus on financial markets. Researchers assigned large share of cross-sectional variation in securities return to the liquidity differences among the various kinds of financial and real assets, and markets. For example, the size (stock market capitalization) is a good proxy for stock liquidity, meaning that the size effect, as some others can be plausibly linked to the differences in liquidity. It is now well accepted that both very market design and presence of asymmetric information amongst actors help in explaining liquidity differences, with both elements being largely mutually determined. This is why rather frequent re-designs of market clearing mechanism in emerging markets provided effects not even close to that of leading markets.

REFERENCES

Amihud, Y., & Mendelson, H. (1980). Dealership market. *Journal of Financial Economics*, *8*(1), 31–35. doi:10.1016/0304-405X(80)90020-3

Amihud, Y., & Mendelson, H. (1986). Asset pricing and the bid-ask spread. *Journal of Financial Economics*, *17*(2), 223–249. doi:10.1016/0304-405X(86)90065-6

Amihud, Y., & Mendelson, H. (1991). Liquidity, maturity and the yields on US government securities. *The Journal of Finance*, *46*(4), 1411–1426. doi:10.1111/j.1540-6261.1991.tb04623.x

Amihud, Y., & Mendelson, H. (2003). The liquidity route to a lower cost of capital. In J. M. Stern & D. H. Chew Jr., (Eds.), *The revolution in corporate finance* (pp. 70–88). Blackwell Publishing.

Asness, S. C. (1995). *The power of past stock returns to explain future stock returns.* Working paper. Goldman Sachs Asset Management.

Black, F. (1972). Capital market equilibrium with restricted borrowing. *The Journal of Business, 45*(3), 444–455. doi:10.1086/295472

Breeden, T. D. (1979). An intertemporal asset pricing model with stochastic consumption and investment opportunities. *Journal of Financial Economics, 7*(3), 265–296. doi:10.1016/0304-405X(79)90016-3

Campbell, Y. J. (1993). Intertemporal asset pricing without consumption data. *The American Economic Review, 83*(3), 487–512.

Chordia, T., Roll, R., & Subrahmanyam, A. (2000). Commonality in liquidity. *Journal of Financial Economics, 56*(1), 3–28. doi:10.1016/S0304-405X(99)00057-4

Cohen, K., Maier, S., Schwartz, R., & Whitcomb, D. (1981). Transaction costs, order placement strategy, and existance of the bid–ask spread. *Journal of Political Economy, 89*(2), 287–305. doi:10.1086/260966

Copeland, T., & Galai, D. (1983). Information effects on the bid–ask spread. *The Journal of Finance, 38*(5), 1457–1469. doi:10.1111/j.1540-6261.1983.tb03834.x

Davidson, P. (2002). *Financial markets, money, and the real world.* Cheltenham, UK: Edward Elgar Publishing. doi:10.4337/9781843765585

DeBondt, F. M. W., & Thaler, R. (1985). Does the stock market overreact. *The Journal of Finance, 40*(3), 793–805. doi:10.1111/j.1540-6261.1985.tb05004.x

Easley, D., & O'Hara, M. (1992). Adverse selection and large trade volume: The implications for market efficiency. *Journal of Financial and Quantitative Analysis, 27*(2), 185–208. doi:10.2307/2331367

Fama, F. E., & French, K. R. (1992). The cross-section of expected returns. *The Journal of Finance, 47*(2), 427–465. doi:10.1111/j.1540-6261.1992.tb04398.x

Fama, F. E., & French, K. R. (1993). Common risk factors in the returns on stock and bonds. *Journal of Financial Economics, 33*(1), 3–56. doi:10.1016/0304-405X(93)90023-5

Fama, F. E., & French, K. R. (1996). Multifactor explanations of asset pricing anomalies. *The Journal of Finance, 51*(1), 55–84. doi:10.1111/j.1540-6261.1996.tb05202.x

Fama, F. E., & French, K. R. (2013). *A five-factor asset pricing model.* SSRN Working Paper No. 2287202.

Garman, M. (1976). Market microstructure. *Journal of Financial Economics, 3*(3), 257–275. doi:10.1016/0304-405X(76)90006-4

Glosten, L., & Milgrom, P. (1985). Bid, ask, and transaction prices in a specialist market with heterogeneously informed traders. *Journal of Financial Economics, 14*(1), 71–100. doi:10.1016/0304-405X(85)90044-3

Gorton, G., & Pennacchi, G. (1990). Financial intermediation and liquidity creation. *The Journal of Finance, 45*(1), 49–71. doi:10.1111/j.1540-6261.1990.tb05080.x

Grauer, R. R. (1978). Generalized two parameter asset pricing models: Some empirical evidence. *Journal of Financial Economics*, *6*(1), 11–32. doi:10.1016/0304-405X(78)90018-1

Grossman, J. S., & Miller, H. M. (1988). Liquidity and market structure. *The Journal of Finance*, *43*(3), 617–633. doi:10.1111/j.1540-6261.1988.tb04594.x

Harris, L. (2003). *Trading and exchange: market microstructure for practitioners*. New York: Oxford University Press.

Ho, T., & Stoll, H. (1981). Optimal dealer pricing under transactions and return uncertainty. *Journal of Financial Economics*, *9*(1), 47–73. doi:10.1016/0304-405X(81)90020-9

Holmström, B., & Tirole, J. (1996). Modeling aggregate liquidity. *The American Economic Review*, *86*(2), 187–191.

Holmström, B., & Tirole, J. (1998). Private and public supply of liquidity. *Journal of Political Economy*, *106*(1), 1–40. doi:10.1086/250001

Holmström, B., & Tirole, J. (2001). LAPM: A liquidity-based asset pricing model. *The Journal of Finance*, *56*(5), 1837–1867. doi:10.1111/0022-1082.00391

Jagannathan, R., & Wang, Z. (1995). The conditional CAPM and the cross-section of expected returns. *The Journal of Finance*, *51*(1), 3–53. doi:10.1111/j.1540-6261.1996.tb05201.x

Jegadeesh, N., & Titman, S. (1993). Returns to buying winners and selling losers: Implications for stock market efficiency. *The Journal of Finance*, *48*(1), 65–91. doi:10.1111/j.1540-6261.1993.tb04702.x

Kandel, S., & Stambaugh, R. (1995). Portfolio inefficiency and the cross-section of expected returns. *The Journal of Finance*, *50*(1), 157–184. doi:10.1111/j.1540-6261.1995.tb05170.x

Kane, S. (1999). What happened to the utility functions? Imprecise expectations of security prices. *International Review of Financial Analysis*, *8*(2), 165–175. doi:10.1016/S1057-5219(99)00014-9

Keynes, J. M. (1936). *The general theory of employment interest and money. The collected writings of John Maynard Keynes* (Vol. 7). London, UK: The Royal Economic Society.

Knight, F. (1921). *Risk, uncertainty and profit*. Cambridge, MA: Houghton Mifflin Company, The Riverside Press.

Kyle, A. (1985). Continuous auction and insider trading. *Econometrica*, *53*(6), 1315–1335. doi:10.2307/1913210

Leshno, M., & Levy, H. (2002). Preferred by "all" and preferred by "most" decision makers: Almost stochastic dominance. *Management Science*, *48*(8), 1074–1085. doi:10.1287/mnsc.48.8.1074.169

Lesmond, A. D. (2005). Liquidity of emerging markets. *Journal of Financial Economics*, *77*(2), 411–452. doi:10.1016/j.jfineco.2004.01.005

Levy, H. (1983). The capital asset pricing model: Theory and empiricism. *The Economic Journal*, *93*(369), 145–165. doi:10.2307/2232170

Levy, H. (2010). The CAPM is alive and well: A review and synthesis. *European Financial Management, 16*(1), 43–71. doi:10.1111/j.1468-036X.2009.00530.x

Levy, M., & Roll, R. (2010). The market portfolio may be mean-variance efficient after all. *Review of Financial Studies, 23*(6), 2464–2491. doi:10.1093/rfs/hhp119

Lintner, J. (1965). The valuation of risk assets and selection of risky investments in stock portfolios and capital budgets. *The Review of Economics and Statistics, 47*(1), 13–37. doi:10.2307/1924119

Madhavan, A. (2000). Market microstructure: A survey. *Journal of Financial Markets, 3*(3), 205–258. doi:10.1016/S1386-4181(00)00007-0

Markowitz, H. (1952). Portfolio selection. *The Journal of Finance, 7*(1), 77–91.

Mehrez, A., Regev, U., & Spivak, A. (1984). An analysis of risky financial decisions. *Managerial and Decision Economics, 5*(1), 19–24. doi:10.1002/mde.4090050105

Merton, C. R. (1973). An Intertemporal capital asset pricing model. *Econometrica, 41*(5), 867–887. doi:10.2307/1913811

Milgrom, P., & Stokey, N. (1982). Information, trade, and common knowledge. *Journal of Economic Theory, 26*(1), 17–27. doi:10.1016/0022-0531(82)90046-1

Minsky, H. (1995). Financial factors in the economics of capitalism. *Journal of Financial Services Research, 9*(3-4), 197–208. doi:10.1007/BF01051746

Moskowitz, J. T., & Grinblatt, M. (1999). Do industries explain momentum? *The Journal of Finance, 54*(4), 1249–1290. doi:10.1111/0022-1082.00146

Muranaga, J., & Shimizu, T. (2000). *Expectations and market microstructure when liquidity is lost.* Bank of Japan.

O'Hara, M. (2004). *Market microstructure theory.* Cambridge, MA: Blackwell Publishers.

Pettengill, N. G., Sridhar, S., & Mathur, I. (1995). The conditional relation between beta and returns. *Journal of Financial and Quantitative Analysis, 30*(1), 101–116. doi:10.2307/2331255

Roll, R. (1977). A critique of the asset pricing theory's tests. *Journal of Financial Economics, 4*(2), 129–176. doi:10.1016/0304-405X(77)90009-5

Ross, A. S. (1976). The arbitrage theory of capital asset pricing. *Journal of Economic Theory, 13*(3), 341–360. doi:10.1016/0022-0531(76)90046-6

Rouwenhorst, K. G. (1998). International momentum strategies. *The Journal of Finance, 53*(1), 267–284. doi:10.1111/0022-1082.95722

Samuelson, P. (1963). Risk and uncertainty: A fallacy of large numbers. *Scientia, 98*, 108–113.

Sharpe, F. W. (1964). Capital asset prices: A theory of market equilibrium under condition of risks. *The Journal of Finance, 19*(3), 425–442.

Sharpe, F. W. (1991). Capital asset prices with and without negative holdings. *The Journal of Finance*, *46*(2), 489–509. doi:10.1111/j.1540-6261.1991.tb02671.x

Shen, P., & Starr, R. (1998). Liquidity of the treasury bill market and the term structure of interest rates. *Journal of Economics and Business*, *50*(5), 401–417. doi:10.1016/S0148-6195(98)00012-5

Solnik, H. B. (1974). An equilibrium model of the international capital market. *Journal of Economic Theory*, *8*(4), 500–524. doi:10.1016/0022-0531(74)90024-6

Solnik, H. B. (1983). International arbitrage pricing theory. *The Journal of Finance*, *38*(2), 449–457. doi:10.1111/j.1540-6261.1983.tb02251.x

Stoll, H. (1978). The supply of dealer services in securities markets. *The Journal of Finance*, *33*(4), 1133–1151. doi:10.1111/j.1540-6261.1978.tb02053.x

Stulz, M. R. (1981). A model of international asset pricing. *Journal of Financial Economics*, *9*(4), 383–406. doi:10.1016/0304-405X(81)90005-2

Tobin, J. (1958). Liquidity preference as behavior towards risk. *The Review of Economic Studies*, *25*(2), 65–86. doi:10.2307/2296205

Woodward, S. (1983). The liquidity premium and solidity premium. *The American Economic Review*, *73*(3), 348–361.

ADDITIONAL READING

Barucci, E. (2003). *Financial markets theory: equilibrium, efficiency and information*. London, UK: Springer-Verlag. doi:10.1007/978-1-4471-0089-8

Bebczuk, R. (2003). *Asymmetric information in financial markets: introduction and applications*. Cambridge, UK: Cambridge University Press.

Black, F. (1995). Estimating expected return. *Financial Analysts Journal*, *51*(January–February), 168–171. doi:10.2469/faj.v51.n1.1873

Black, F., & Litterman, R. (1992). Global portfolio optimization. *Financial Analysts Journal*, *48*(September–October), 28–43. doi:10.2469/faj.v48.n5.28

Blake, D. (2002). *Financial market analysis*. Chichester, UK: John Wiley and Sons.

Chen, N. F., Roll, R., & Ross, A. S. (1986). Economic forces and the stock market. *The Journal of Business*, *59*(3), 383–403. doi:10.1086/296344

Choudhry, M. (2003). *The bond & money markets: strategy, trading, analysis*. Oxford, UK: Butterworth – Heinemann.

Cohen, K., Maier, S., Schwartz, R., & Whitcomb, D. (1986). *The market microstructure of securities markets*. Englewood Cliffs, NJ, US: Prentice–Hall.

De Jong, F., & Rindi, R. (2009). *The microstructure of financial markets*. Cambridge, UK: Cambridge University Press. doi:10.1017/CBO9780511818547

Elton, J. E., & Gruber, J. M. (1995). *Modern portfolio theory and investment analysis*. New York, US: John Wiley and Sons.

Engel, C. (1992). The risk premium and the liquidity premium in foreign exchange markets. *International Economic Review*, *33*(4), 871–879. doi:10.2307/2527147

Fabozzi, J. F., Modigliani, F., Jones, J. F., & Ferri, G. M. (2002). *Foundations of financial markets and institutions*. Upper Saddle River, New Jersey, US: Prentice Hall.

Fama, F. E. (1970). Efficient capital markets: A review of theory and empirical work. *The Journal of Finance*, *25*(2), 383–417. doi:10.2307/2325486

Fama, F. E. (1991). Efficient capital markets: II. *The Journal of Finance*, *46*(5), 1575–1617. doi:10.1111/j.1540-6261.1991.tb04636.x

Fama, F. E. (1995). Random walks in stock market prices. *Financial Analysts Journal*, *51*(January–February), 75–80. doi:10.2469/faj.v51.n1.1861

Grinblatt, M., & Titman, S. (2002). *Financial markets and corporate strategy*. New York, US: McGraw–Hill.

Grossman, J. S., & Stiglitz, E. J. (1980). On the impossibility of informationally efficient markets. *The American Economic Review*, *70*(3), 393–408.

Hansch, O., Naik, N., & Viswanathan, S. (1998). Do inventories matter in dealership markets? Evidence from the London Stock Exchange. *The Journal of Finance*, *53*(5), 1623–1656. doi:10.1111/0022-1082.00067

Hicks, J. (1939). *Value and capital: an inquiry into some fundamental principles of economic theory* (2nd ed.). Oxford, UK: Clarendon Press.

Ho, T., & Stoll, H. (1983). The dynamics of dealer markets under competition. *The Journal of Finance*, *38*(4), 1053–1074. doi:10.1111/j.1540-6261.1983.tb02282.x

Jacobs, B., & Levy, K. (1988). Calendar anomalies: Abnormal returns at calendar turning points. *Financial Analysts Journal*, *44*(November–December), 28–39. doi:10.2469/faj.v44.n6.28

Jensen, M. (1978). Some anomalous evidence regarding market efficiency. *Journal of Financial Economics*, *6*(2-3), 95–101. doi:10.1016/0304-405X(78)90025-9

Johnson, T. (2008). Volume, liquidity, and liquidity risk. *Journal of Financial Economics*, *87*(2), 388–417. doi:10.1016/j.jfineco.2007.03.006

Kahneman, D., & Tversky, A. (1979). Prospect theory: An analysis of decision under risk. *Econometrica*, *47*(2), 263–291. doi:10.2307/1914185

Keim, B. D., & Ziemba, T. W. (2000). *Security market imperfections in world wide equity markets*. Cambridge, UK: Cambridge University Press.

Lehmann, N. B. (2003). What we measure in execution cost measurement: Guest editorial. *Journal of Financial Markets*, *6*(3), 227–231. doi:10.1016/S1386-4181(03)00005-3

Madhavan, A. (1992). Trading mechanisms in securities markets. *The Journal of Finance*, *47*(2), 607–642. doi:10.1111/j.1540-6261.1992.tb04403.x

Mossin, J. (1966). Equilibrium in a capital asset market. *Econometrica*, *34*(4), 768–783. doi:10.2307/1910098

Pagano, M. (1989). Trading volume and asset liquidity. *The Quarterly Journal of Economics*, *104*(2), 255–274. doi:10.2307/2937847

Pagano, M., & Röell, A. (1992). Auction and dealership markets: What is the difference? *European Economic Review*, *36*(2-3), 613–623. doi:10.1016/0014-2921(92)90119-H

Roberts, H. (1959). Stock–market „patterns" and financial analysis: Metodological suggestions. *The Journal of Finance*, *14*(1), 1–10.

Roll, R. (1984). A simple implicit measure of the effective bid–ask spread in an efficient market. *The Journal of Finance*, *39*(4), 1127–1139. doi:10.1111/j.1540-6261.1984.tb03897.x

Roll, R. (1988). R^2. *The Journal of Finance*, *43*(3), 541–566.

Roll, R., & Ross, A. S. (1984). The arbitrage pricing theory approach to strategic portfolio planning. *Financial Analysts Journal*, *40*(May–June), 14–26. doi:10.2469/faj.v40.n3.14

Rothschild, M., & Stiglitz, E. J. (1976). Equilibrium in competitive insurance markets: An essay on the economics of imperfect information. *The Quarterly Journal of Economics*, *90*(4), 629–649. doi:10.2307/1885326

Rubinstein, M. (2002). Markowitz's "portfolio selection: A fifty–year retrospective. *The Journal of Finance*, *57*(3), 1041–1045. doi:10.1111/1540-6261.00453

Sharpe, F. W. (1995). Risk, market sensitivity, and diversification. *Financial Analysts Journal*, *51*(January–February), 84–88. doi:10.2469/faj.v51.n1.1863

Shleifer, A. (2000). *Inefficient markets: an introduction to behavioral finance*. Oxford, UK: Oxford University Press. doi:10.1093/0198292279.001.0001

Siegel, J. (2002). *Stocks for the long run*. New York, US: McGraw–Hill.

Spulber, D. (1999). *Market microstructure: intermediaries and the theory of the firm*. Cambridge, UK: Cambridge University Press. doi:10.1017/CBO9780511625930

Stiglitz, J. (1987). The causes and consequences of the dependence of quality on price. *Journal of Economic Literature*, *25*, 1–48.

Stoll, R. H. (2000). Friction. *The Journal of Finance*, *55*(4), 1479–1514. doi:10.1111/0022-1082.00259

Stoll, R. H. (2001). Market microstructure. Working paper 01–16, Financial Market Research Center.

Stoll, R. H. (2006). Electronic trading in stock markets. *The Journal of Economic Perspectives*, *20*(1), 153–174. doi:10.1257/089533006776526067

Tversky, A., & Kahneman, D. (1974). Judgment under uncertainty: Heuristics and biases. *Science. New Series*, *185*(4157), 1124–1131.

Van Horne, J., & Parker, G. (1967). The random–walk theory: An empirical test. *Financial Analysts Journal*, *23*(November–December), 87–92. doi:10.2469/faj.v23.n6.87

Whitmore, G. A. (1970). Diversification and the reduction of dispersion: A note. *Journal of Financial and Quantitative Analysis*, *5*(2), 263–264. doi:10.2307/2329850

Wihlborg, C. (1991). Arbitrage, equilibrium and market efficiency: A parable. *Journal of Economic Behavior & Organization*, *15*(2), 297–301. doi:10.1016/0167-2681(91)90034-U

KEY TERMS AND DEFINITIONS

Asset Liquidity: A feature of an asset or market on which the asset is traded that is represented by the easy with which the assets is traded. An asset is more liquid if it is more certainly realisable at short notice without loss. The liquidity is usually measurable by various concepts of transaction costs.

Bid-Ask Spread: The difference between the bid and ask price quoted by a dealer or autonomously formed difference between current best priced sell and buy limit orders in the order book of a continuous auction market. It is used as a good proxy for market liquidity.

CAPM: Also known as capital assets pricing model, it is a single factor general equilibrium model that explains return of any asset, financial or real, as determined by its sensitivity to the market return.

Diversification: An investment strategy that relies on pulling multiple types of asset (or conducting different business activities) in order to make investment outcome less sensitive to specific (idiosyncratic) risk.

Market Portfolio: A virtual or real portfolio that is consisted of all assets available to investors on specific market, or globally.

Portfolio Investment: A process of selection of different securities and other investments in order to achieve investment goals, usually to increase return for the given level of risk, or to decrease the risk for a given level of return.

Size Puzzle: An empirical regularity not explainable by the traditional asset pricing models, i.e. small capitalization stocks are traded with a premium over large capitalization stocks.

ENDNOTES

1 Accordingly, the CAPM model is routinely called Sharpe-Lintner or Sharpe-Lintner-Black models.

2 Market proxies could be efficient portfolios, while market portfolios could be inefficient. Alternatively, market portfolios may be efficient, but sampled assets would not be allocated to an efficient portfolio (Roll, 1977)

Chapter 2
Application of Markowitz Portfolio Theory by Building Optimal Portfolio on the US Stock Market

Martin Širůček
Mendel University in Brno, Czech Republic

Lukáš Křen
Mendel University in Brno, Czech Republic

ABSTRACT

This chapter is focused on building investment portfolios by using the Markowitz Portfolio Theory (MPT). Derivation based on the Capital Asset Pricing Model (CAPM) is used to calculate the weights of individual securities in portfolios. The calculated portfolios include a portfolio copying the benchmark made using the CAPM model, portfolio with low and high beta coefficients, and a random portfolio. Only stocks were selected for the examined sample from all the asset classes. Stocks in each portfolio are put together according to predefined criteria. All stocks were selected from Dow Jones Industrial Average (DJIA) index which serves as a benchmark, too. Portfolios were compared based on their risk and return profiles. The results of this work will provide general recommendations on the optimal approach to choose securities for an investor's portfolio.

INTRODUCTION

Investing in capital markets is one of the main activities of large number of economic subjects. This activity was particularly driven by development of information technology as well as deregulation and globalization, which is typical of the current financial markets. The development of information technology has enabled even small retail investors, who generally do not have the appropriate knowledge and experience, to take advantage of the direct purchase or sale of securities on the capital market. Driven by different motives, investors allocate their available resources to the assets and through selected invest-

DOI: 10.4018/978-1-5225-0959-2.ch002

ment strategies they seek to derive maximum value from invested funds and at the same time eliminate the threat of losses.

Different models for assets valuation describing the relationship between risk and return on the given investment can be used as a tool to support investment decision-making.

One of the most common methods in designing strategies and building portfolios is the Modern Portfolio Theory (MPT). Although it is based on simplifying assumptions, it can be successfully used in portfolio analysis for explaining the relationship between the return and risk of individual portfolio components. The Capital Market Theory, which is closely related to the MPT, then came up with the Capital Asset Pricing Model (CAPM), which extended the existing theory by an equilibrium view of the asset market. In spite of the fact that the capital asset pricing model rests on simplifying assumptions and has been tested many times since its inception in the 60s, but its general applicability was not confirmed, it is currently among the most widely used models and can be used to manage investment strategies and build investment portfolios. The model is based on the equilibrium between the risk and return, or more precisely the risk (represented by beta coefficient) of a specific title is directly proportional to the return achieved on the given investment.

It is these findings about this approach and the model, or its principle (i.e. the idea of equilibrium of return or loss stemming from the risk of a specific investment) that are the reasons for examining its functionality on real data and are used to achieve the objectives of this paper.

The aim of the present paper is to define, on a selected sample of US stocks, the most suitable method for optimal portfolio compilation using the Markowitz Portfolio Theory. That is meaning whether it is appropriate to favour stocks with high or low beta coefficient or whether it is preferable to use a random selection of each stock.

Therefore, the aim of this paper is to verify or answer the research question whether the optimal portfolio compiled in accordance with the Portfolio Theory brings investor an optimal ratio of return to the given risk. Within this basic research question, following research sub-questions can be set out regarding the assumptions and the basic idea of the CAPM model:

- High values of beta coefficient guarantee higher returns on stock titles.
- Random selection of securities in the portfolio provides satisfactory return at an acceptable level of risk.

Defined research questions or empirical analysis of functionality of the CAPM model is based upon knowledge as well as criticism of this issue, which is given in the following chapter. Achieved results of this paper support the arguments against the model and provide investors with recommendation on how to properly compile portfolio regarding its profitability and risk, and whether higher values of beta indicator actually "guarantee" higher valuation.

LITERATURE REVIEW

Just like other areas of economics, the theory of financial markets has a rich history. The firm foundation theory is an approach better known as the determination of the intrinsic value of stock, which is an output of fundamental analysis (Malkiel, 2012). Williams (1938) developed this technique and, thanks to the work by Graham & Dodd (2008), it founded its way even among investors on Wall Street. Although the fundamental analysis has been losing its importance recently and investors rather make their decisions based on subjective and psychological preferences, even instinctively, to a long-term investor (not a speculator) it is still crucial in combination with the modern portfolio theory.

Criticizers of the firm foundation theory focus on psychological analysis; they examine the investor as part of a collective investment game, in which the determinant of behaviour is human psyche. Keynes (1936) expressed the idea that in a way that it makes no sense to calculate the intrinsic value, but it is worth analysing the likely behaviour of a group of investors in the future. Investors can be divides into players and speculators, and investigates their behaviour in the short term, in which, prices are determined primarily by psychological reactions (Kostolany, 1989).

In a comprehensive form, the efficient market theory was introduced by Fama (1965). He concluded that asset markets behave randomly and there is no correlation between the current and past price movements. Asset prices react sharply, precisely and immediately on each new price-sensitive information. On such market, all investment strategies fail, and no investor is able to achieve any above-average long-term yield. Such described behaviour of markets is called the random walk. A distinction can be made between weak, moderate and strong form of efficiency4 according to how new messages are absorbed by the market. The theory, however, has been a subject to sharp criticism, Lo & MacKinlay (2002) demonstrated inertia of prices on the market or inadequate response to newly released reports. Stock prices react to unexpected information in an inadequate manner (over reactive capital market) and also mentions the occurrence of anomalies5 on the markets (Haugen, 1999). Musílek (2011) summarizes that the advanced liquid stock markets behave quite effectively. It is necessary to consider them economically efficient, as new information is not absorbed immediately; in the long run, however, above-average returns cannot be achieved. Less developed and illiquid markets, behave inefficiently, although this inefficiency gradually decreases (Musílek, 2011). Pástor & Veronesi (1999) point out that efficiency together with liquidity of stock markets changes and there are further significant changes in the investment environment, which may make the absorption of new information more difficult. Malkiel (2012) indicates that markets can be highly effective, even if errors occur. Fama himself said at the conference held at the University of Chicago that markets can somehow behave irrationally, thus admitted the non-existence of a perfect financial market (The Wall Street Journal, 2004). This position is now occupied by the vast majority of economists.

Harry Markowitz (1952) is at the origins of the modern portfolio theory, which is sometimes referred to as Markowitz portfolio theory. In 1990, the author was awarded the Nobel Prize in economics for his work. Such optimal portfolio can be build using the Markowitz model that will have less risk than the weighted average of risks of individual securities included in the portfolio, while preserving the given profitability. The risk was thus diversified between the assets constituting the portfolio. This portfolio is located along the efficient frontier, and other portfolios will be omitted by the investor.

Markowitz model assumed a selection of different securities, which are subject to the risk. In the theory of capital markets, the investor may also include a risk-free asset in the portfolio whose rate of return is certain. Musílek (2011) lists three methods for determining the rate of return on a risk-free asset. You can use a rate of return on treasury bills (T-bills) or long-term government bonds (duration of the bond should equal the duration of the intended security). The third method is to consider the current rate of return on T-bills for the first investment period; for future years the investment is based on forward rates according to the shape of the yield curve. For the expected rate of return of a portfolio it can be established that:

$$\overline{r_p} = w_z \overline{r_z} + (1 - w_z) r_f ,$$

where:

w_z = weight of risk (equity) component of the overall portfolio,

$\overline{r_z}$ = mean profitability of risk (equity) component of portfolio,

r_f = rate of return of a riskless asset.

Furthermore, it is possible to formulate the variance (risk) as:

$$\sigma_p^2 = w_z^2 \sigma_z^2$$

where:

σ_z^2 = variance of risk component of portfolio.

As Figure 1 shows, investors can combine efficient portfolios from the efficient frontier with a risk-free asset. Portfolios lying on the line joining points r_f and M represent the best achievable combinations of return and risk when investing in a portfolio of risk-free and risky assets, or the combination thereof. Risk-free asset utilization contributes to reduction the risk while maintaining the required rate of return. Portfolios lying on the intersection are also referred to as lending, as investors in T-bills lend money to the state. Borrowing portfolios, which in turn lie between points M and E, may be achieved by a less risk-averse investor so that he or she will borrow at the risk-free rate and the funds acquired in such way are invested in a risky portfolio. As mentioned by Reilly & Brown (2012), investors use leverage to achieve a higher rate of interest compared to the portfolio along the Markowitz's efficient frontier (the difference between the portfolios E and D).

Should it not be possible to borrow funds at a risk-free rate, the efficient frontier would be formed by the abscissa leading from r_f to M as well as curve from M to D. Sharpe (2000) calls the half line from r_f to E to r_f the Capital Market Line (CML).

The capital market line only provides an optimized relationship for the expected return and risk of efficient portfolio, and does not differentiate between unique and systematic risk of individual securities. To express the relationship between the expected rate of return and the systematic risk of an investment instrument or portfolio, we use the Capital Asset Pricing Model (CAPM), which was independently created by Sharpe (1964), Lintner (1965), Treynor (1962), Mossin (1966).

The basic idea behind the capital asset pricing model is that the overall risk may be split into a systematic (non-diversifiable) risk, which indicates the sensitivity of securities to the general market fluctuations, and unsystematic (diversifiable) risk, which is influenced by factors associated with a particular economic entity. In valuation of a security or portfolio, this theory does not take into account the overall risk, but only that part of the risk which cannot be eliminated by diversifying (Malkiel, 2012). Thus, if

Figure 1. Capital Market Line
Source: Reilly, Brown (2012)

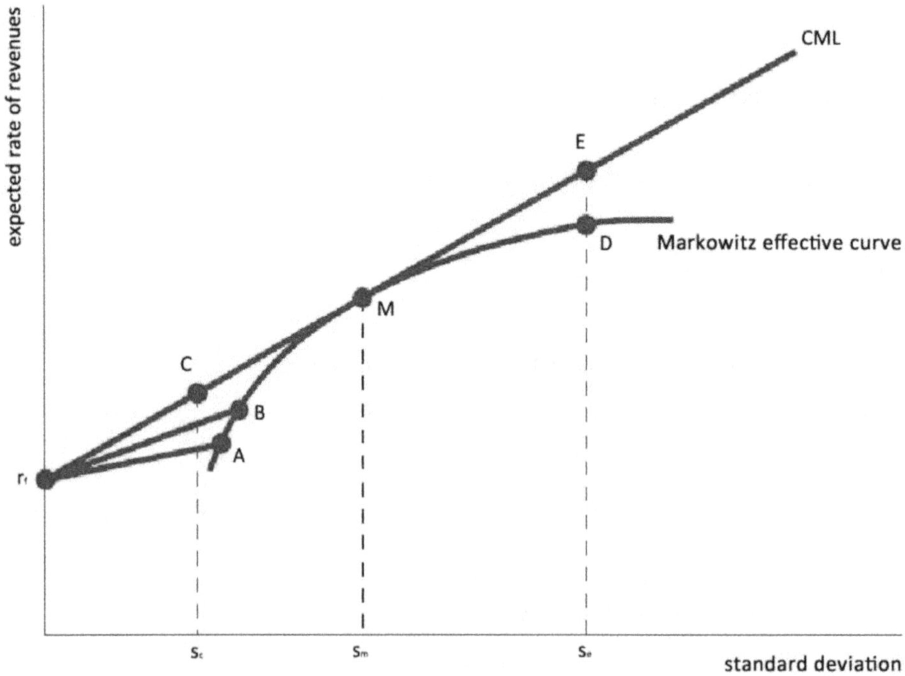

the investor wants to achieve higher long-term profitability, he or she must increase the level of non-diversifiable portfolio risk. From the above mentioned facts, the sensitivity of investment instruments to market developments can be expressed by a coefficient beta. The relationship between the expected return and systematic risk is then expressed by the following equation:

$$\overline{r_i} = r_f + \beta_i(\overline{r_m} - r_f)$$

This relationship is also the equation of a security market line (SML), showing a positive correlation between expected rate of return and systematic risk (or beta factor).

Securities and portfolios from the security market line correspond to correctly priced securities with an equilibrium rate of return. The more the securities are placed to the right on the line, the greater the difference is between the rate of return of the instrument and the risk-free asset (Veselá, 2007). This difference is then a reward in the form of a premium for the systematic risk.

The difference between SML and CML is in the process of how the risk is measured, if bz using beta coefficient or standard deviation (Reilly & Brown, 2012). The consequence is that SML can be applied only to a fully diversified portfolio.

Beta factor expresses a comparison between the movement in prices of individual instruments and that of the whole market. As mentioned above, mathematically it expresses the size of a systematic risk. Broad market index is assigned a value of 1. The higher the beta of a security, the more its price changes on average compared to the rest of the market. The opposite is true for the low value of this

Figure 2. Security market line
Source: Reilly, Brown (2012)

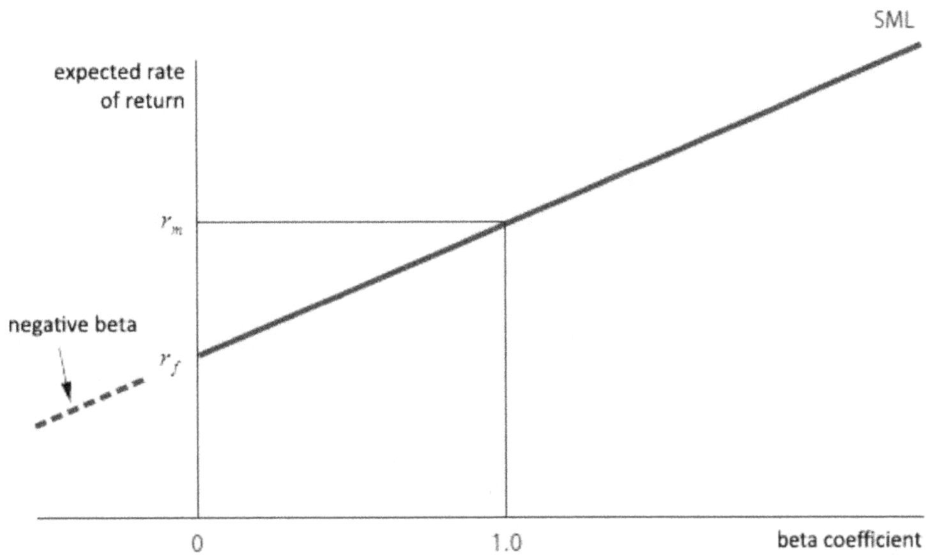

factor. Securities with high beta values are sometimes also referred to as aggressive investments, while instruments with low beta can be called defensive investments.

The space above the line includes undervalued securities and portfolios that bring higher yields than the level of systematic risk. In other words, the real rate of return of investment instruments is higher than the equilibrium rate of return for a given risk.

Markowitz model showed how investors should behave when compiling optimal portfolios. The Capital Market Theory explains the valuation of assets using this model and is based on the concept of effective diversification. The CAPM was and is used due to its simplicity and clarity of the input data. This simplicity, or simplifying assumption in the model, but only those, is a frequent subject of criticism. For example, Veselá (2007) mentions the distortion in the calculated beta factor by selection of a time period. Beta factors of portfolios and especially individual securities also exhibit considerable volatility. Furthermore, she mentions problems in the derivation of the risk-free interest rate and the actual availability of a risk-free asset to all investors. The practical existence of a relationship between the return and risk was tested by Fama & French (2004). They concluded that higher risk measured by beta coefficient is not necessarily associated with a higher yield. Empirical security market line is then flatter than the theoretical line. The security line may take different shapes due to the existence of different borrowing and lending rates or transaction costs (Liška & Gazda, 2004). The fact that investors may be rewarded even for part of unsystematic risk, which is completely contrary to the spirit of CAPM (Fuller & Wong, 1988). The model also ignores industry factors, taxation, dividend yield or the book value of a company as relevant factors that contribute to the expected yield rate. The level of the risk premium varies not only between securities, but also between countries (Damodaran, 2011). The reason may be different national economic policies and development of national macroeconomic variables. Frequent criticism led many economists to modification of the simple version of CAPM.

The problem is, for example, the question of a risk-free asset. The classic version of CAPM considers the existence of a risk-free asset, which is available to all without exceptions at the same borrowing and lending rates. At the same time, we cannot consider the risk-free asset to be completely risk-free, even if these are government bonds. Because even the issuing state may get into serious trouble caused by inflation or exchange rate changes (Širůček, Šoba, & Němeček, 2014). Black (1972) developed the capital asset pricing model with a zero beta coefficient (zero-beta CAPM) that does not assume the existence of a risk-free asset. If such asset does not exist, then there must be portfolios with a zero-beta factor against the market portfolio. Instead of a risk-free asset, investors then combine portfolios not correlated to the market, which have the lowest risk.

Brennan (1970) contested another assumption - the non-existence of taxes. In his model he considered different tax rates for individual investors and even for income and capital gains. His tax-capital asset pricing model (T-CAPM) bases its calculation of expected rate of return on the beta factor of securities, their dividend yield, and different tax rates. Investors in higher tax groups then due to the impact of taxation may prioritize portfolios with lower dividend yield.

Merton (1973) extended the original CAPM to a multifactorial capital asset pricing model (multi-factor CAPM or M-CAPM). In this model, investors do not take into account only risks associated with the expected rates of return, but also risks affecting the amount of future consumption, such as future income, relative prices of goods or investment opportunities. More beta coefficients then enter into the model, which determine the portfolio's sensitivity to off-market sources of risk

Amihud & Mendelson (1986) respond to the assumption of absence of transaction costs with their capital asset pricing model which contains a premium for illiquidity (capital asset pricing model with illiquidity premium - IP-CAPM). The authors divide the investment instruments into liquid and illiquid. Lower demand for illiquid instruments causes a decline in their price and vice versa the growth in returns. These instruments due to higher transaction costs bring investors a premium for illiquidity. In the short term, the investor should invest into liquid instruments, while illiquid, but more profitable instruments may be an appropriate choice for a long-term strategy.

Another approach is the downside CAPM (D-CAPM), which was tested, for example, by Estrada (2002). This approach stems from the fact that investors are not averse to high variance if the rate of return of a security grows. However, the opposite is true when the market downturns, when investors are highly averse to losses (Malkiel, 2012). Beta in D-CAPM therefore expresses the covariance-variance ratio in the market downturn.

As mentioned in the introduction, the CAPM model despite its criticism is extensively used due to its simplicity in equity analysis, as it is in the case of this paper, which focuses on appropriate ways to build equity portfolio in terms of return and risk.

DATA AND METHODS

The Dow Jones Industrial Average (DJIA) was selected as sample to be examined. This index was selected for the potential diversification across almost all traded sectors and moreover. This index may be viewed as a global market mood indicator (Širůček, 2013a). The reason for choosing the US market is also its share of the global market capitalization, accounts for about 42% of the global market capitalization (Širůček, 2013b). In a price-weighted index; high-priced stock has therefore a greater impact on the value of the index. In the event of a stock split, the split stock has a lower impact on the index value, while the impact of others slightly rises (Siegel, 2011). Compared to capitalization-weighted indices (Standard & Poor's 500), the relative size of the company (market capitalization) does not enter the calculation.

Individual DJIA index stocks were selected and optimal portfolio was set up so as to attain the set objective or evaluate the research questions, using the following four approaches:

- Setting up an optimum portfolio from all stocks included in the index, based on the CAPM model and its maximization task
- Setting up a portfolio of low-beta stocks (generally, beta factor < 1 is considered low)
- Setting up a portfolio of high-beta stocks (generally, beta factor > 1 is considered high)[1].
- Setting up a portfolio using a random stock picking[2].

To determine the weight of stocks selected for the portfolio can be used several approaches. One of the options is to use Lagrange multipliers while applying one or two constraints. The calculation, for example, can be run as a minimization task, while minimizing the risk of changes in the portfolio's rate of return. Use may also be made of the so-called "Wolfe's method", which is the method of quadratic programming. Its disadvantage is the rising number of variables in the calculation (Ševčíková, 2008). To derive the weights, also the CAPM model can be used. Derivation of optimal portfolio weights through the CAPM is based on the maximization task. This is to maximize the angle φ between the security market line (SML) and an imaginary line parallel with x-axis starting from point r_f. The task can be formulated as:

$$f(\overrightarrow{X}) = \tan\phi = \frac{\overline{r_p} - r_f}{\sigma_p} = \frac{\sum_{i=1}^{n} w_i(\overline{r_i} - r_f)}{\left[\sum_{i=1}^{n}\sum_{j=1}^{n} w_i w_j \sigma_{ij}\right]^{1/2}} \longrightarrow MAX$$

Then is necessary within the actual calculation to rank securities in a descending order according to their proportion on the right side of the following expression that reflects excess return on a security in relation to its beta coefficient (Čámský, 2007).

$$C_k < \frac{\overline{r_i} - r_f}{\beta_i}$$

In further derivation required for individual securities, following equation can be drawn:

$$C_i = \frac{\sigma_M^2 \sum_{j=1}^{n} \frac{\overline{r_j} - r_f}{\sigma_{\varepsilon_j}} \beta_j}{1 + \sigma_M^2 \sum_{j=1}^{n} \frac{\beta_j^2}{\sigma_{\varepsilon_j}^2}}$$

From the set of calculated C_i $(i \in k)$ are then selected those that meet the above condition of excess return. The last security meeting this condition is marked as C^* and becomes a portfolio constraint. Now we can proceed to calculate the weights:

$$Z_i = \frac{\beta_i}{\sigma^2_{\varepsilon_i}} \left(\frac{\overline{r_i} - r_f}{\beta_i} - C^* \right)$$

In order to express the actual weights of individual stocks in the portfolio, the following formula may be introduced:

$$w_i = \frac{Z_i}{\sum_{i=1}^{k} Z_i}$$

Daily data from early 1995 to the end of March 2014 entered into calculations, with dividends and any eventual stock splits included. The considered risk-free rate (RFR) of return on three-month US treasury bills (US Government Treasury Bills 3-Month) is 0.05%.

RESULTS

Figure 3 shows annualised returns (vertical axis) and standard deviations (horizontal axis) of individual securities, rates of return the Dow Jones Industrial Average as well as Standard & Poor's 500 as potential benchmarks.

Figure 3. Risk and revenue profile of each asset
Source: Yahoo Finance

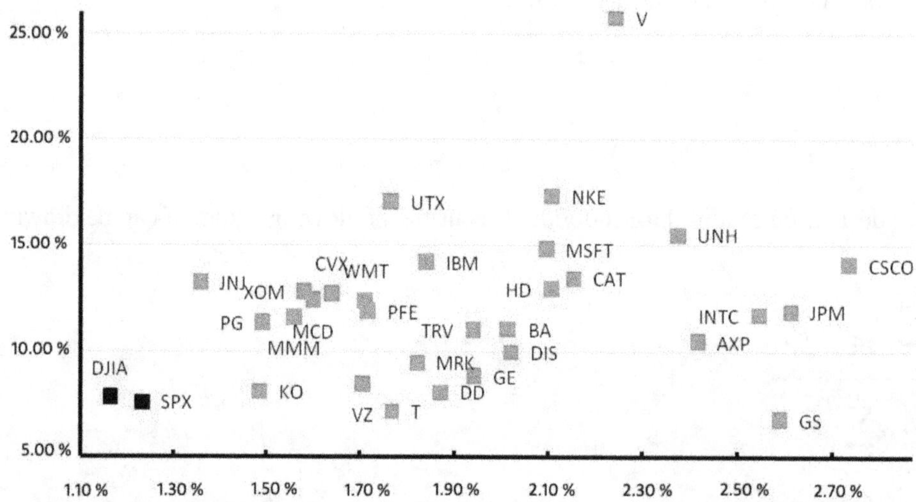

The inclusion of a particular stock title to the portfolio depends on the expected excess return on a security relative to beta coefficient of that security, riskiness of the stock and its beta coefficient. The calculation of the optimal portfolio is shown in the table below.

Stocks were ranked according to the expected excess return relative to their beta coefficients. The last title that meets this condition is Merck & Co. (MRK). Optimal market portfolio of DJIA index thus consists of thirteen titles (see Table 1). The rest of the companies were not included in the portfolio

Other possibilities how to build portfolios is to take into account beta coefficients of individual titles. Two portfolios with five securities each were set up, one consisting of stocks with low beta coefficient and the second consisting of high beta instruments. In the selection of individual titles their sectors were considered, too, so as to avoid, for example, three securities of the same sector within the portfolio. This should contribute to better allocation of risk.

For low-beta portfolio, securities listed in Table 2 were picked.

Given the fact that the portfolio is only made up of several instruments, the excess return condition was not met, and no stock was eliminated from the portfolio. Allocation of weights followed the proce-

Table 1. Weights of securities in an optimal market portfolio

Ticker	$(r_i - r_f)/\beta_i$	C_i	Z_i	w_i
VZ	2.791	0.0013	0.0271	11.47%
V	0.429	0.0479	0.0365	15.08%
MCD	0.353	0.0697	0.0280	11.87%
WMT	0.308	0.0847	0.0216	9.15%
PG	0.282	0.1019	0.0240	10.19%
NKE	0.258	0.1197	0.0170	7.21%
T	0.245	0.1229	0.0079	3.37%
UNH	0.242	0.1313	0.0101	4.27%
JNJ	0.235	0.1485	0.0297	12.59%
KO	0.230	0.1519	0.0116	4.92%
MSFT	0.214	0.1570	0.0097	4.09%
IBM	0.205	0.1619	0.0109	4.64%
MRK	0.178	0.1628	0.0027	1.16%

Source: Yahoo Finance, own calculation

Table 2. Portfolio consisting of stocks with low beta coefficient

Ticker	$(r_i - r_f)/\beta_i$	C_i	Z_i	w_i
VZ	2.7910	0.0013	0.0277	18.51%
V	0.4289	0.0479	0.0438	29.30%
MCD	0.3525	0.0678	0.0371	24.80%
IBM	0.2050	0.0932	0.0269	17.99%
MRK	0.1777	0.1009	0.0141	9.40%

Source : Yahoo Finance, own calculation

Table 3. Portfolio consisting of stocks with high beta coefficient

Ticker	$(r_i - r_f)/\beta_i$	C_i	Z_i	w_i
CVX	0.1171	0.0774	0.0367	71.14%
CSCO	0.1122	0.0821	0.0064	12.41%
BA	0.1058	0.0861	0.0084	16.45%
DIS	0.0757	0.0829		
JPM	0.0623	0.0744		

Source: Yahoo Finance, own calculation

dure specified in the methodology. A procedure identical in terms of the methodology was then applied to the portfolio consisting of high-beta stocks. The results are shown in Table 3.

Due to the high sensitivity to market developments, two securities were removed to optimize the portfolio. But portfolio made up of only three instruments does not provide adequate diversification.

A randomly selected portfolio or more precisely the simulation of randomness when building the portfolio had been put on the computer. To ensure sufficient diversification, the computer randomly selects a number of securities in the portfolio. The minimum possible number of stocks is set at five and the maximum possible number is set at twelve (higher number of stocks does reduce the risk, but diminishes returns). The individual stocks are picked up by computer at random; the method used is combination without repetition. The computer simulation is ensured by the RANDBETWEEN feature. This method provided nine securities in a random portfolio (see Table 4).

To increase its explanatory power, the simulation of a random portfolio setup was repeated. This time the computer picked up eleven stocks. The process of optimization and calculation of weights is shown in Table 5.

Table 4. Random portfolio I

Ticker	$(r_i - r_f)/\beta_i$	C_i	Z_i	w_i
PG	0.2821	0.0308	0.0305	22.95%
UNH	0.2418	0.0519	0.0142	10.67%
JNJ	0.2352	0.0921	0.0429	32.27%
IBM	0.2051	0.1085	0.0192	14.49%
PFE	0.1513	0.1169	0.0080	6.01%
UTX	0.1479	0.1305	0.0181	13.60%
AXP	0.0937	0.1268		
MMM	0.0929	0.0981		
GE	0.0735	0.0970		

Source: Yahoo Finance, own calculation

Table 5. Random portfolio II

Ticker	$(r_i - r_f)/\beta_i$	C_i	Z_i	w_i
NKE	0.2583	0.0397	0.0261	23.34%
T	0.2449	0.0469	0.0129	11.51%
UNH	0.2418	0.0649	0.0166	14.84%
KO	0.2299	0.0754	0.0204	18.28%
HD	0.1447	0.0897	0.0091	8.15%
XOM	0.1368	0.1076	0.0199	17.79%
CVX	0.1171	0.1114	0.0066	5.92%
CSCO	0.1122	0.1115	0.0002	0.17%
TRV	0.0960	0.1088		
DIS	0.0757	0.1017		
GS	0.0343	0.0710		

Source: Yahoo Finance, own calculation

DISCUSSION AND CONCLUSION

In the context of this paper, several portfolios were built and weights of the selected stocks in respective portfolios identified. However, every investor would be interested in the expected rate of return and risk entailed by individual portfolio options. The expected future return may be easily calculated as a scalar product of weights and rates of return of included instruments as follows:

$$\overline{r_p} = \sum_{i=1}^{n} w_i \overline{r_i}$$

where:

w_i = weights of individual securities,

$\overline{r_i}$ = average rates of return on individual securities.

Standard deviation of a multi-component portfolio may be obtained by extracting the root of the matrix product as follows:

$$\sigma_P^2 = (w_1\sigma_1 \quad w_2\sigma_2 \quad \cdots \quad w_n\sigma_n) x \begin{pmatrix} 1 & \rho_{12} & \cdots & \rho_{1n} \\ \rho_{21} & 1 & \cdots & \rho_{2n} \\ \vdots & \vdots & \ddots & \vdots \\ \rho_{n1} & \rho_{n2} & \cdots & 1 \end{pmatrix} x \begin{pmatrix} w_1\sigma_1 \\ w_2\sigma_2 \\ \vdots \\ w_n\sigma_n \end{pmatrix} = (w\sigma)xCx(w\sigma)^T$$

Table 6. Rates of return and risk of resulting portfolios

Portfolio	r_p	σ_p
P1 – Optimal portfolio (according to the CAPM)	14.20%	0.87%
P2 – Portfolio made up from low beta stocks	15.63%	1.20%
P3 – Portfolio made up from high beta stocks	12.60%	1.46%
P4 – Random portfolio 1	13.62%	0.92%
P5 – Random portfolio 2	12.76%	0.89%

Source: Yahoo Finance, FRED, NASDAQ, own calculation

Table 6 shows the calculated expected historic rates of return and risk with a size of one standard deviation.

Results from Table 6 are also shown in Figure 4. The left axis shows the achieved rate of return, the right axis shows the risk incurred.

The optimal portfolio made up of stocks from the entire index range reached the lowest risk rate and, simultaneously, the average rate of return within the examined portfolios. Portfolio made up of securities selected based on their beta factors returned significantly different results. The use of low-beta securities resulted in the second highest rate of return; however, the risk of this portfolio increased, too, being even the second highest amongst the five examined portfolios. The portfolio consisting of high-beta securities generated the lowest returns while incurring high risk. The first random portfolio features the third lowest rate of return and also the third lowest risk rate. Both characteristics of the second random portfolio were slightly lower as compared to the first one, mainly in terms of the rate of return.

Figure 4. Risk and rate of return of selected portfolios
Source: Yahoo Finance, FRED, NASDAQ

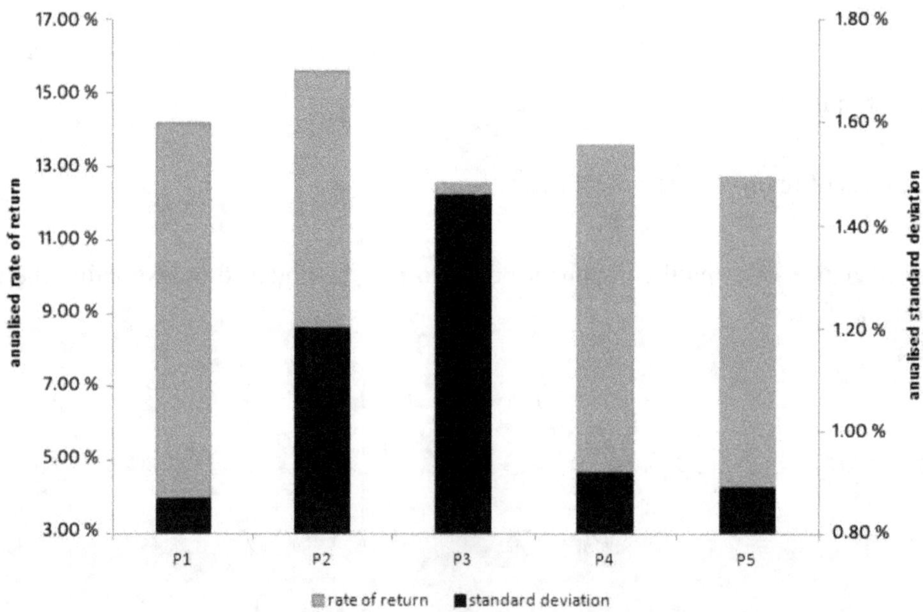

Building a portfolio from securities around the entire index under a restrictive condition that arose in derivation of the maximizing function using the CAPM model, offers one of the best alternatives analysed in this work. The choice of securities is not prejudiced by any subjective views of the investor on individual stock corporations or sectors, and, therefore, the factors decisive for inclusion of a security in the portfolio are solely its historic excess return expressed by the proportion shown on the right side of the aforesaid equation and the risk rate. This result complies with the opinion of Malkiel (2012) and Kohout (2008) who recommend that investors should buy portfolios copying as best as possible the selected index without trying to attempt at active investment strategy, although such portfolio by its broadness somehow lags behind the index. This approach appears to be suitable for common investors who wish to participate in the capital market returns, but find it difficult to go through financial statements of the companies and monitor market trends and events.

One of the research questions examined above was the effect of beta factors of securities on the portfolio's rate of return. Specifically, the idea behind this was that securities with high beta factor should generate higher profits for the investor. Over the period examined in this study and covering close to twenty years, the stocks in the United States did experience two major slumps, but have presently hit their historic highs and despite the ongoing and gradual monetary policy tightening there is still moderate optimism prevailing in the markets. A similar situation may also be encountered in some of the European stock exchanges. Thus, it could be expected that stocks more sensitive to market trends will generate higher rates of return. Still, the results obtained run counter to these assumptions.

The rate of return of the portfolio consisting of low-beta securities outperforms by a large margin the return of the portfolio made up of high-beta securities, by more than three per cent. Still, the risk rate of the former was considerably lower than the risk borne by the second portfolio. A major drop in the rate of return accompanied by a rise in the risk rate disfavours the choice of securities with high beta factors in the investor's portfolio. Similar results were previously arrived at by Fama & French (2004), who argue that higher risk measured by beta coefficient may not be a guarantee for higher returns, or Black, Jensen, Scholes (1972). In their examined sample of stocks, the low-beta stocks achieved better result, which again contradicts the traditional form of the capital assets pricing model. Širůček, Šoba, Němeček (2014) confirm that the link between beta coefficient and return proved to be very weak. According to the results, the model significantly undervalued low beta stocks, which reached considerably higher returns than would match their beta. In the case of stocks in the group with higher beta factor, both an undervaluation and very often also overvaluation was demonstrated.

Based on the above findings the choice of high-beta securities may not be recommended to an investor who wishes to allocate available funds in capital markets over long-term investment horizons. Nevertheless, instruments with high beta factors may be an interesting choice for speculators who can only settle for a few selected companies given the expected market growth and excess return. Investment horizon of these investors would probably reach a maximum of several years and the success of this strategy would furthermore depend on the correct estimates of the periods of partial growth in the stock markets. However, a study undertaken by Pioneer Investments and Ibbotson Associates (2013) goes to show that the portfolio performance is largely, by as much as 92%, affected by assets allocation, which means by ensuring sufficient diversification. Other factors such as market timing, choice of stocks and other similar efforts made by the investors have an almost negligible share in the overall portfolio performance. The study also mentions the portfolio re-balancing as an important factor playing a major role in active risk reduction. Even though this has been based on historic rates of return, which might introduce a certain error into the following recommendations, securities with high beta factors may not be taken for a secure choice if the investor wishes to achieve high returns. Conversely, investors thinking about long-term investments should select low-beta stocks.

The first random portfolio returned slightly worse results both in terms of the expected returns and risk compared to the first calculated tangency portfolio. The second random portfolio generated very similar results. To start with, it should be stressed that no investor should follow this way of managing the securities. If need be, for example in the event of a major market slump and a necessity to reduce the positions or rebalance the positions if the prices of some of the stocks go up, managing such a portfolio would be most likely highly difficult, and as a result of unformulated strategy the investor would have to do with a passive investment strategy.

As regards a random portfolio, the investor does not have guaranteed quality stocks that could possibly be obtained through a detailed analysis and no optimal diversification is guaranteed, either. Thus, such a random choice may result in excessive allocation of invested funds, for example, into just two sectors of the entire economy, which may strongly impact on the profitability and in particular, elevate the risk rate of such a portfolio. Although this does not happen very often on average, there may be portfolios in specific cases composed of, for instance, high-beta securities, which were mentioned above as portfolios suitable for speculators and not for investor thinking more along long-term lines. Furthermore, as stated by Cohen & Pogue (1968), an investor managing a random portfolio composed of a large number of securities would be forced to make a huge number of partial calculations despite the sophisticated computer technologies available today, but by buying the entire index, the investor could easily avoid this problem. Nevertheless, Malkiel (2012) offers several examples demonstrating that the average fund performance did not differ too much from the returns of randomized portfolios.

The results of portfolios developed in this study by a random selection from amongst the available stocks compared to the tangency portfolio from the entire index indicate a relatively high performance of US stock markets. However, this conclusion may not be adopted on the basis of two created portfolios, as this result might be explained as a stroke of luck. The conducted analyses did not aim to confirm nor refute efficient market behaviour. Still, the random portfolio setup did have another major benefit. Although these were randomly selected securities, parameters of the resulting portfolio did not differ too much from the other portfolios. The random portfolios particularly feature a lower risk rate. These results positively show that the final portfolio parameters are to the largest extent affected by the optimal allocation of assets carried out in this study on the basis of a calculation derived from the capital assets pricing model. Other factors such as an active selection of individual stocks and market timing have a substantially lower effect on the portfolio performance.

For the purpose of further analyses, it would be advisable to change the sample stocks and conduct similar calculations in a market other than the American stock market. As repeatedly highlighted above, the stock prices in the United States reach their maxima, similarly to European markets. Therefore, it might be interesting to set up a portfolio from stock corporations listed for example in any of the developing markets, or, potentially, combine securities from several countries.

SUMMARY

The paper deals with the application of Markowitz's portfolio theory on a specific sample of stocks. American DJIA index was selected for the analysis. As part of applying the Markowitz's theory, several options to select available stocks for the portfolios were used. Individual examined portfolio options were built upon the defined research questions, which were based on the literature review and criticism of the model. Thus, a summary tangency portfolio was set up, which could include all securities contained in the index. As part of the maximization task under the given constraint thirteen stocks were included in the portfolio. Crucial parameters determining whether the relevant security should be included in the portfolio are its risk rate and the amount of excess return. This portfolio was the broadest amongst the examined portfolios and was also characterized by the lowest risk rate; its rate of return could be taken as average compared to the other options.

To verify the research question whether securities with higher beta coefficients bring higher returns, two portfolios were set up. The first one included low-beta stocks, the second, on the contrary, high-beta stocks. The portfolio consisting of low-beta stocks generated satisfactory returns; nevertheless, its risk rate was above average compared to the other portfolios. Thus, selecting the lowest-beta stocks entailed a relatively high risk rate of the entire portfolio. As the portfolio was made up of five stocks, the investor would be likely to achieve a better rate of return/risk profile by conducting an in-depth analysis and replacing some of the securities. Conversely, a portfolio made up of higher-beta stocks achieved the worst results compared to the other options. Once optimized, the resulting portfolio consisted of three stocks only, which is definitely not an optimal option. Thus, the aforesaid research question was not confirmed; high-beta securities do not guarantee higher return for the investor.

In the next steps, random portfolios were developed. Naturally, this approach may not be recommended to investors in principle. Such portfolios face a risk of the investor including highly risky and, at the same time, no-yield securities in the portfolio through a random choice. Likewise, there is a potential allocation of funds into the same or similar sectors, which further increases the risk. Such portfolio would also become very hard to manage as the investor would have no investment strategy at hand and the choice of stocks would be left up to the random draw made by the computer. The results of random portfolios did not differ too much from the first examined tangency portfolio of the entire index. The greatest benefit of developing a random portfolio is the demonstration of optimal assets allocation as the crucial factor affecting the resulting characteristics of each portfolio in the greatest extent.

Results of the paper can be summarized into two findings. First, the relationship between the expected rate of return and the beta coefficient is not so prominent and straightforward as Sharpe and Lintner expected. Second, beta coefficient alone is not sufficient to explain the expected returns, or high beta coefficient does not guarantee higher returns and also other indicators should be taken into account, such as market capitalization or the ratio of book value to market value of stocks (B/M) as indicated by Fama and French (2004) or P/E ratio as indicated by Široček, Šoba, and Němeček (2014).

REFERENCES

Amihud, Y., & Mendelson, H. (1986). Asset Pricing and the Bid-Ask Spread. *Journal of Financial Economics*, *17*(2), 223–249. doi:10.1016/0304-405X(86)90065-6

Black, F., Jensen, M., & Scholes, M. (1792). *The Capital Asset Pricing Model: Some Empirical Tests.* Praeger Publishers: Studies in The Theory of Capital Markets. Retrieved June 2, 2014, from http://ssrn.com/abstract=908569

Brennan, M. J. (1970). Taxes, Market Valuation and Corporation Financial Policy. *National Tax Journal*, *23*(4). Retrieved from http://www.albany.edu/faculty/faugere/PhDcourse/BrennanCAPM.pdf

Čámský, F. (2007). *Určení optimálního portfolia.* Retrieved May 5, 2014, from www.derivat.sk/files/2007%20jan-jun/HotJan2007Camsky2.doc

Cohen, K., & Pogue, J. (1968). *Some Comments Concerning Mutual Fund Vs. Random Portfolio Performance.* Sloan School of Management. Retrieved May 15, 2014, from http://dspace.mit.edu/bitstream/handle/1721.1/49022/somecommentsconc00cohe.pdf

Damodaran, A. (2011). *The Little Book of Valuation: How to Value a Company, Pick a Stock and Profit.* John Wiley & Sons.

Estrada, J. (2002). Systemic Risk In Emerging Markets: The D-CAPM. *Emerging Market Review, 3*(4). Retrieved February 10, 2014, from http://www.sciencedirect.com/science/article/pii/S1566014102000420

Fama, E. (1965). Random Walks in Stock Market Prices. *The Journal of Business, 38*(1), 34. doi:10.1086/294743

Fama, E., & French, K. R. (2004). The Capital Asset Pricing Model: Theory and Evidence. *The Journal of Economic Perspectives, 18*(5). Retrieved from http://www1.american.edu/academic.depts/ksb/finance_realestate/mrobe/Library/capm_Fama_French_JEP04.pdf

Fred. (2014). *Federal reserve economic data – FRED – St. Louis Fed.* Federal Reserve Bank of St. Louis. Retrieved June 3, 2014, from http://research.stlouisfed.org/

Fuller, R. J., & Wong, G. W. (1988). Traditional versus Theoretical Risk Measures. *Financial Analyst Journal, 44*(2). Retrieved May 8, 2014, from http://www.jstor.org/stable/4479102

Graham, B., & Dodd, D. L. (2008). Security Analysis (6th ed.). McGraw-Hill.

Haugen, R. A. (1999). The New Finance: The Case Against Efficient Markets (2nd ed.). Prentice Hall.

Keynes, J. M. (1936). *The general theory of employment, interest and money.* Harcourt.

Kohout, P. (2008). Investiční strategie pro třetí tisíciletí (5th ed.). Praha: Grada Publishing.

Kostolany, A. (1989). Und was macht der Dollar? Im Irrgarten d. Währungsspekulationen. Aktualisierte Taschenbuchausg. München: Heyne.

Lintner, J. (1965). The Valuation of Risk Assets and the Selection of Risky Investments in Stock Portfolios and Capital Budgets. *The Review of Economics and Statistics, 47*(1), 13. doi:10.2307/1924119

Liška, V., & Gazda, J. (2004). *Kapitálové trhy a kolektivní investování.* Praha: Professional Publishing.

Lo, A. W., & MacKinlay, A. C. (2002). *A Non-Random Walk Down Wall Street.* Princeton, NJ: Princeton University Press.

Malkiel, B. G. (2012). *Náhodná procházka po Wall Street* (10th ed.). Praha: Pragma.

Merton, R. C. (1973). An Intertemporal Capital Asset Pricing Model. *Econometrica, 41*(5), 867. doi:10.2307/1913811

Morkowitz, H. (1952). Portfolio Selection. *The Journal of Finance, 7*(1). Retrieved from http://onlinelibrary.wiley.com/doi/10.1111/j.1540-6261.1952.tb01525.x/pdf

Mossin, J. (1966). Equilibrium in a Capital Asset Market. *Econometrica, 34*(4), 768. doi:10.2307/1910098

Musílek, P. (2011). *Trhy cenných papírů* (2nd ed.). Praha: Ekopress.

Nasdaq - Revenue and EPS Summary. (2014). *NASDAQ Stock Market*. Retrieved May 6, 2014, from http://www.nasdaq.com/quotes/revenue-eps.aspx

Pástor, Ľ., & Veronesi, P. (1999). Technological Revolutions and Stock. *The American Economic Review, 99*(4). Retrieved from http://www.jstor.org/stable/25592515

Pioneer Ibbotson Asset Allocation Series. (2013). *Pioneer Investments Global Asset Management*. Retrieved May 11, 2014, from http://us.pioneerinvestments.com/misc/pdfs/brochures/pio_ibb.pdf

Reilly, F. K., & Brown, K. C. (2012). Investment Analysis & Portfolio Management (10th ed.). Mason, OH: Cengage Learning.

Ševčíková, B. (2008). *Metody výpočtu vah (podílů) cenných papírů v portfoliu*. Brno: Přírodovědecká fakulta Masarykovy univerzity.

Sharpe, W. F. (2000). *Portfolio Theory and Capital Markets* (1st ed.). New York: McGraw-Hill.

Sharpe, W. F. (1964). Capital Asset Prices: A Theory of Market Equilibrium under Conditions of Risk. *The Journal of Finance, 19*(3). Retrieved June 1, 2014, from http://www.jstor.org/stable/2977928

Siegel, J. (2011). *Investice do akcií: Běh na dlouhou trať*. Praha: Grada Publishing.

Širůček, M. (2013a). *Působení peněžní nabídky na akciové trhy*. Brno: Provozně ekonomická fakulta Mendelovy univerzity v Brně.

Širůček, M. (2013b). *Impact of Money Supply on Stock bubbles*. Brno: Acta Universitatis Agriculturae et Silviculturae Mendelianae Brunensis.

Širůček, M., Šoba, O., & Němeček, J. (2014). CAPM Validity on the US Stock Market. *Trends Economics and Management, 8*(18), 87-100.

Treynor, J. L. (1962). *Towards a Theory of Market Value of Risky Assets*. Unpublished Manuscript.

Veselá, J. (2007). *Investování na kapitálových trzích*. Praha: Aspi.

Wall Street Journal. (2004, October 18). As Two Economists Debate Markets, The Tide Shifts: Belief in Efficient Valuation Yields Ground to Role Of Irrational Investors. *Wall Street Journal*. Retrieved June 1, 2014, from http://www.wsj.com/articles/SB109804865418747444

Williams, J. B. (1938). *The Theory of Investment Value*. Cambridge, UK: Harvard University Press.

Yahoo Finance – Stock Center. (2014). *Yahoo Finance*. Retrieved May 6, 2014, from http://finance.yahoo.com/stock-center/

ENDNOTES

1 These two approaches are based on criticism of CAPM model by Fama and French (2004).

2 The approach is based on the theory of efficient markets, where asset prices react to new price-sensitive information and investment strategies fail.

Chapter 3
Do Judgmental Factors Lead to a Good Decision on Investing in a Currency or Mislead the Financial Player?
An Application in Turkey

Aykan Akincilar
Gazi University, Turkey & Celal Bayar University, Turkey

ABSTRACT

Since decision on making an investment in exchange rate is one of the main problems faced by financial players acting in markets around the world, it is extensively discussed in the literature. In this study, it is investigated whether judgmental factors affect the decision in behavioral environment or not, and, if such an effect exists, its impact is whether positive or negative. In order to achieve that purpose, multi-criteria decision making approach is integrated with time series analysis approach which leads to clearly question the existence and direction of such an impact if it exists. The proposed model is applied to the Turkish market, indicating that judgmental factors prevent the financial player from misleading which is caused by considering solely profitability criterion. Thus, it is demonstrated that judgmental factors have a positive impact on the decision regarding exchange rate selection problem. Ultimately, it is demonstrated that the proposed integrated model provides accurate and reliable results.

1. INTRODUCTION

Forecasting financial time series such as stock prices or exchange rates, is important to investors and governments (Leu et al. 2009). According to Panda and Narasimhan (2007), two main reasons are assumed why financial players should analyze exchange rate movements. First, financial players need to be sure about monetary policies in the country, of which matter can be made possible by understanding movement of exchange rates. The second reason is that exchange rate is a financial asset, and thus, is a

DOI: 10.4018/978-1-5225-0959-2.ch003

potentially valuable source of timely information about economic and financial conditions. Consequently, by understanding the movement of exchange rates better, the financial players are able to extract relevant information about such conditions in a country and so to forecast the future values of the exchange rates more accurately, which leads to gain profit more robustly.

In traditional forecasting and/or decision making processes, it is believed that considering judgmental factors mislead the analyzer since it causes non-objectiveness. Thus, objective forecasting techniques are employed to forecast the movement of exchange rates in a market. Since those techniques produce objective results, they are so popular and are considered of reliable methods. In that point, the question that whether profitability is the only one criterion while handling an investment problem should come to mind. Indeed, it is a very fair question. In author's opinion, in order to make an accurate decision in a particular market, judgmental factors should also be considered as entirely as possible. Because the current status of the market, political relations of the country with the others, some particular events like war, natural disasters, large-scale sport events have significant effect on the market. If a financial player can properly consider those factors, it is clear that the assets can be managed more efficiently. However, objective forecasting techniques have a significant weakness which is that judgmental factors affecting the market are hard to consider in those techniques.

On the other hand, multi-criteria decision making tools are the tools that have a great potential to assess –and even roughly forecast– the movement of exchange rates and so the market. Those tools are capable of making decisions analytically by incorporating different and conflicted criteria in a single model. The more qualified model a decision maker develops; the more accurate results is expected to be obtained. Maybe the most important disadvantage of those tools is that although they are analytical methods, significant personal and/or group influences may be occured, which leads to subjectivity. As a result, those influences may mislead the decision maker when they are solely considered.

At the present time, many researchers biased to develope models which consider judgmental factors. So, many studies have already been conducted about such nature in literature. A study by Blair et al. (1987) may be among the first to demonstrate that expert judgments could be used in exchange rate forecasting. And then, based on that paper, Blair et al. (2002)'s work was published.

Ulengin and Ulengin (1994) also studied a similar approach in exchange rate forecasting with factual criteria, such as interpretations of central bank, related interest rates, and comparison options with other forecasting methods. Autoregressive integrated moving average (ARIMA), vectoral autoregressive (VAR), Bayesian VAR (BVAR), restricted VAR (RVAR) and the analytic hierarchy process (AHP) were compared as forecasting methods, with BVAR winning against the other methods. As a contribution to the debate of those factual criteria, Marinkovic (2014) investigated the effectiveness of official interventions by the National Bank of Serbia (NBS) in the RSD/EUR market, which is also adopted as a criterion in this chapter.

Following these pure method approaches, Ince and Trafalis (2006) proposed a hybrid model to eliminate the disadvantages of parametric and non-parametric methods. In the first step, ARIMA and VAR were used to obtain the number of inputs and, in the next step, artificial neural network (ANN) and support vector regression (SVR) were applied to gain the forecasts of the analyzing pars. According to performance criteria, namely mean square error (MSE) and mean absolute error (MAE), SVR provided the best outcomes. As a result, in comparing their model with pure methods, the authors claimed that a hybrid model could provide better forecasts.

Onkal et al. (2003) focused on judgment accuracy. In their work, judgment accuracy of professionals and amateurs were compared based on a case study of foreign exchange rates. The authors' motivation was process-performance paradox, which tells that the people who have high knowledge often fail to achieve highly accurate judgments. One-day and one-week ahead forecasts of both 40 professionals and 57 sophisticated amateurs were compared in deterministic and probabilistic environments. According to the results of that work, despite forecast environment strongly affects judgment accuracy, professional accuracy usually surpasses amateur accuracy although many amateurs outperform many professionals.

Similar to previously discussed paper, Leitner and Schmidt (2006) proposed a procedure for systematic comparison of professional exchange rate forecasts with the judgmental forecasts of novices. Differently from Onkal et al. (2003)'s work, they found that professional forecasters in foreign exchange rate markets were not able to beat naive forecasts. Forecasts of both professionals and novices were generated based on EUR/USD exchange rate in three different forecast horizons and were evaluated based on mean error (ME), MSE and MAE.

One of the other study adopting judgmental forecasting for predicting exchange rate movements is Pullock et al. (2005)'s work. In their work, some performance qualifiers were developed, and, a procedure based on those measures was proposed in order to identify specific strengths and weaknesses of judgment in the context of directional probability currency forecasting.

In Brandl et al. (2006)'s work, a genetic algorithm (GA) based forecasting tool was developed. The proposed model was utilized to obtain daily forecasts of EUR/USD par and those forecasts outperformed the benchmark forecasts on all probability levels.

Thomson et al. (2013) examined the influence of trend direction and strength on judgmental exchange rate forecasting performance and consistency. The performance on ascending trends was found to be superior to that on decending trends, and the performance on intermediate trends was found to be superior to that on strong trends. However, the consistency of forecasts was still found to be poor.

Lin et al (2014) evaluated possible effects of group-based adjustments to economic forecasts of tourism demand in the manner of accuracy improvement of forecasts. The Delphi method was used to aggregate experts' judgmental adjustments and a range of error measures and statistical tests were employed to evaluate forecast accuracy. Their findings showed that the forecasts after experts' adjustments did not always lead to improvement in accuracy.

Gonul et al. (2009) and Gonul et al (2012)'s works can also be added to this short glance at the literature. For a more sophisticated review, the audiences are refered to Lawrence et al. (2006), Leitner and Leopold-Wildburger (2011) and Goodwin et al.'s (2011) works. In addition, another remarkable work is Fildes and Goodwin (2013)'s editorial paper, in which forecasting support system (FSS)s were described.

When the literature has been glanced in a more comprehensive manner, it can easily be seen that, an FSS –maybe a decisision support system (DSS) rather than FSS– which also allows the financial player to make a choice among alternative currencies to invest on while considering both objective forecast values and judgmental factors is a strong requirement. It is hoped that this chapter might contribute to fill some part of this gap. In order to achieve this, a model incorporating both objective forecasts obtained by an appropriate non-causal time series analysis method and judgmental criteria, was developed. According to the results of case study, the developed model prevents the financial player investing on wrong currency.

This chapter is organized in the following way: methodology is explained in section 2, followed by the experimental results in section 3, and the conclusion appears in section 4.

2. METHODOLOGY

Exchange rate forecasting is a subject frequently discussed in the literature (Box and Jenkins 1976). Economical models, autoregressive (AR), autoregressive moving average (ARMA), and autoregressive integrated moving average (ARIMA) models are a few of the widely-known methods used in exchange rate forecasting. The ARIMA model, also known as the Box-Jenkins model, was first introduced by Box and Jenkins (1976) and applied successfully in many areas up till today. Generally, economic time series are not linear and their mean and variance can change over time. To overcome this difficulty, autoregressive conditional heteroskedastic (ARCH) and generalized autoregressive conditional heteroskedastic (GARCH) models have been developed by Engle (1982) and Bollerslev (1986) respectively, applied extensively in the related literature (Leu et al. 2009). On the other hand, Baillie et al. (1996) and Bollerslev and Wright (2001) have proved that AR models show better results than some GARCH-based models. Furthermore, literature shows that vector autoregressive (VAR), as well as ANN methods have been applied to exchange rate forecasting studies (e.g. El Shazy and El Shazy 1997; Gencay 1999; Panda and Narasimhan 2007).

In order to obtain forecast values, some the non-causal time series analysis methods are applied. In addition, the analytic network prrocess (ANP), which is proposed by Saaty (2001), is employed to incorporate objective and judgmental criteria in the decision process. The proposed model, which achieves this incorporation, is described in detail in this section.

2.1. Obtaining Objective Forecast Values

The objective forecast values are obtained by utilizing some non-causal time series analysis methods, namely moving averages (MA), single exponential smoothing method (SESM) (Brown 1963), Holt's method (HM) (Holt 2004) which is also known as double exponential smoothing method, Winter's method (WM) and autoregressive integrated moving average (ARIMA) (Box and Jenkins 1976) method.

In the proposed model, all of the obtained forecast values are stored for the assessment process which is described in the next sub-section.

2.2. Evaluating Forecast Values

In recent years, non-statistical performance criteria such as mean absolute percentage error (MAPE), root mean square error (RMSE), and MAE have been used frequently to evaluate forecast performance (Song and Li 2008). According to Chu (2009), there is no universally preferred measure of estimation for accuracy, and experts often disagree on which measure to be used. The most well-known measures, in this respect, include mean error (ME), mean percentage error (MPE), MAPE, MSE and RMSE. The ME and MPE measures are not very useful because positive errors are canceled by negative errors. It means that the residuals absorbe the others with opposite sign. Since the significant part of the residuals have been generally absorbed, the mean is always close to zero, which misleads the decision maker. MAPE is used widely, and probably accepted as the basic measure. Additionally, it should be noted that absolute error methods are more appropriate than the squared error methods according to Witt and Witt (1991) and many other researchers. Again according to Witt and Witt (1991), the most important advantage of MAPE criterion may be its meaningfulness by itself due to expressing residuals in an absolute ratio form with the observation value while the others are not meaningful by themselves.

In order to evaluate the accuracy of forecasting models, MAPE, RMSE and MAE performance criteria are used. While MAPE and RMSE are considered as the core performance criteria, MAE is considered as the complementary to those. In the literature, the most extensively considerable advantages of these methods listed as being ease-of-use, time efficiency in application, software availability, and wasting little memory in computers while running (Akincilar, 2011).

The formulations of those performance criteria are given here:

$$MAPE = \frac{1}{n}\sum_{t=1}^{n} \frac{|\varepsilon_t|}{Y_t} \tag{1}$$

$$RMSE = \frac{1}{n}\sqrt{\sum_{t=1}^{n} \varepsilon_t^2} \tag{2}$$

$$MAE = \frac{1}{n}\sum_{t=1}^{n} |\varepsilon_t| \tag{3}$$

where n is the number of observations, Y_t is observation value in period t, ε_t is residual in period t.

Thus, according to the assessment based on MAPE, RMSE, and MAE criteria, the forecasting model which represents the par in the best way is determined. And then, the forecasting model which overcomes the others based on performance criteria is employed in the next steps of the proposed model. In other words, the forecast values obtained by the forecasting model which represents the par in the best way is used as *objective forecast value* for each par. The demonstration of comparison of forecasting methods based on performance criteria can be found in Tables 1-3.

Table 1. The performance criteria of models for $/TL

	Models	MAPE	RMSE	MAE
MA	MA(14) Model	1.504090	0.032863	0.021600
	MA(7) Model	1.165850	0.025298	0.016680
	MA(5) Model	1.022830	0.022361	0.014620
	MA(4) Model	0.935302	0.020445	0.013361
	MA(3) Model	0.848101	0.018547	0.012105
	MA(2) Model	0.756452	0.016583	0.010776
*	MA(1) Model	*0.672630*	*0.014765*	*0.009572*
SESM	α=0.2	1.124360	0.024495	0.016110
	α=0.5	0.782759	0.017205	0.011166
	α=0.7	0.708118	0.015556	0.010083
*	α=0.999	*0.673778*	*0.014799*	*0.009587*
HM	α=0.2 ; γ=0.2	1.136920	0.024698	0.016260
	α=0.6 ; γ=0.1	0.749876	0.016492	0.010681
	α=0.9 ; γ=0.2	0.715784	0.015524	0.010183

continued on following page

Table 1. Continued

	Models	MAPE	RMSE	MAE
	α=0.9 ; γ=0.1	0.697554	0.015199	0.009928
*	α=1.0 ; γ=0.005	*0.675892*	*0.014832*	*0.009619*
WM	α=1.0 ; γ=0.005 ; δ=0.5 ; SL=5	0.718404	0.015133	0.010186
	α=1.0 ; γ=0.005 ; δ=0.2 ; SL=5	0.718404	0.015133	0.010186
	α=1.0 ; γ=0.005 ; δ=0.9 ; SL=5	0.718404	0.015133	0.010186
	α=1.0 ; γ=0.005 ; δ=0.001 ; SL=25	0.672125	0.014731	0.009559
	α=1.0 ; γ=0.005 ; δ=0.001 ; SL=100	0.670922	0.014318	0.009520
*	α=1.0 ; γ=0.005 ; δ=0.001 ; SL=300	*0.629090*	*0.013153*	*0.008910*
ARIMA	ARIMA(1,1,0)	0.673299	0.014765	*0.009581*
	ARIMA(0,1,1)	0.673299	0.014765	*0.009581*
	ARIMA(1,1,1)	0.676424	0.014764	0.009583
	ARIMA(2,1,1)	0.673783	0.014763	0.009588
	ARIMA(1,1,2)	0.673835	0.014763	0.009589
	ARIMA(2,1,0)	0.673574	0.014764	0.009585
	ARIMA(0,1,2)	0.673556	0.014765	0.009584
*	ARIMA(2,1,2)	*0.673158*	*0.014717*	0.009585

Table 2. The performance criteria of models for €/TL

	Models	MAPE	RMSE	MAE
MA	MA(14) Model	1.410860	0.038987	0.026940
	MA(7) Model	1.063640	0.029833	0.020330
	MA(5) Model	0.946437	0.026833	0.018102
	MA(4) Model	0.879027	0.024515	0.016806
	MA(3) Model	0.801476	0.022494	0.015305
	MA(2) Model	0.722300	0.020273	0.013764
*	MA(1) Model	*0.639410*	*0.018028*	*0.012169*
SESM	α=0.2	1.044220	0.009055	0.019920
	α=0.5	0.736415	0.020712	0.014049
	α=0.7	0.671896	0.018894	0.012800
*	α=0.999	*0.639248*	*0.018028*	*0.012166*
HM	α=0.1 ; γ=0.9	1.656220	0.047117	0.031830
	α=1.0 ; γ=1.0	0.910315	0.026268	0.017293
	α=1.0 ; γ=0.9	0.868708	0.025100	0.016502
	α=1.0 ; γ=0.5	0.749206	0.021587	0.014245
	α=1.0 ; γ=0.2	0.686773	0.019748	0.013060
*	α=1.0 ; γ=0.005	*0.649431*	*0.018708*	*0.012354*
WM	α=1.0 ; γ=0.005 ; δ=0.2 ; SL=5	0.649541	0.018111	0.012349

continued on following page

Table 2. Continued

	Models	MAPE	RMSE	MAE
	α=1.0 ; γ=0.005 ; δ=0.5 ; SL=5	0.649541	0.018111	0.012349
	α=1.0 ; γ=0.005 ; δ=0.001 ; SL=50	0.635872	0.017748	0.012101
*	α=1.0 ; γ=0.005 ; δ=0.001 ; SL=300	*0.604349*	*0.016248*	*0.011482*
	α=1.0 ; γ=0.005 ; δ=1.0 ; SL=300	*0.604349*	*0.016248*	*0.011482*
ARIMA	ARIMA(1,1,0)	0.639033	0.018018	0.012162
	ARIMA(0,1,1)	0.638989	0.180180	0.012161
	ARIMA(1,1,1)	0.638590	0.018015	0.012154
	ARIMA(2,1,1)	0.638278	0.018000	0.012148
	ARIMA(1,1,2)	0.638292	*0.017999*	0.012147
	ARIMA(2,1,0)	0.638292	0.018003	0.012149
	ARIMA(0,1,2)	0.638294	0.018004	0.012149
*	ARIMA(2,1,2)	*0.638182*	*0.017999*	*0.012146*

Table 3. The performance criteria of models for £/TL

	Models	MAPE	RMSE	MAE
MA	MA(7) Model	1.129240	0.039497	0.028260
	MA(5) Model	0.992537	0.034943	0.024487
	MA(4) Model	0.919791	0.032373	0.023052
	MA(3) Model	0.839430	0.029682	0.021044
	MA(2) Model	0.752639	0.026758	0.018867
*	MA(1) Model	*0.658949*	*0.023643*	*0.016540*
SESM	α=0.2	1.098750	0.038859	0.027490
	α=0.5	0.770431	0.027331	0.019324
	α=0.7	0.699234	0.024880	0.017536
*	α=0.999	*0.659179*	*0.023643*	*0.016546*
	α=1.0 ; γ=0.7	0.810872	0.029189	0.020367
	α=1.0 ; γ=0.5	0.757843	0.027295	0.019031
	α=1.0 ; γ=0.2	0.696607	0.024980	0.017489
*	α=1.0 ; γ=0.005	*0.660710*	*0.023707*	*0.016588*
WM	α=1.0 ; γ=0.005 ; δ=0.2 ; SL=5	0.673927	0.023896	0.016911
	α=1.0 ; γ=0.005 ; δ=0.7 ; SL=5	0.673927	0.023896	0.016911
	α=1.0 ; γ=0.005 ; δ=0.1 ; SL=50	0.653738	0.023259	0.016930
	α=1.0 ; γ=0.005 ; δ=0.001 ; SL=150	0.634086	0.022159	0.015874
*	α=1.0 ; γ=0.005 ; δ=0.001 ; SL=300	*0.604068*	*0.021000*	*0.015110*
ARIMA	ARIMA(1,1,0)	0.657555	0.023625	0.016507
	ARIMA(0,1,1)	0.657506	0.023624	0.016507

continued on following page

Table 3. Continued

	Models	MAPE	RMSE	MAE
*	ARIMA(1,1,1)	*0.657444*	0.023611	*0.016505*
	ARIMA(2,1,1)	0.657671	*0.023594*	0.016512
	ARIMA(1,1,2)	0.657465	*0.023594*	0.016507
	ARIMA(2,1,0)	0.657765	*0.023594*	0.016514
	ARIMA(0,1,2)	0.657785	*0.023594*	0.016514
	ARIMA(2,1,2)	0.657462	*0.023594*	0.016507

2.3. Constructing the Decision Model

As discussed in the previous section, it seems that taking into account the judgmental criteria in a decision problem has a potential to provide more accurate and reliable results. Criteria such as bias of the decision maker, market conditions, reliability, and political factors which are entirely judgmental and/or behavioral should be incorporated in the decision model after the most suitable forecasting model for each series has been determined. In addition, dependencies among the defined criteria also need to be considered, because a model which includes such relations can represent the problem in a more transparent way. Thus, Figure 1 demonstrates the hierarchy of the decision problem, followed by the related explanations.

Here, the explanations for the criteria and the sub-criteria in the proposed hierarchy have been provided:

1. **The Bias of Investor:** An investor or a financial player generally transacts in particular exchange rate. This main criterion focuses on this bias.
    a. **SJ (Self-Judgments):** This sub-criterion indicates the financial player's personal opinions and instincts.
    b. **EO (Expert Opinions):** The expert opinions about the market and its components directly influence the investor's bias.
    c. **ODF (Other Distinctive Functions):** This sub-criterion contains the other elements affecting the investor's bias.
2. **Market Conditions:** This main criterion determines the economic balances of the market in which the financial player transacts. Changes in the economic balances can excessively impact the movement of the exchange rates.
    a. **SP (Speculations):** Speculations in the market influence transactions of the investor. Even though this effect is for a short-term, the scope of this impact is generally wider.
    b. **TV (Trading Volume):** The trading volume is an important factor for an investment decision.
    c. **USFR (Monetary Policies of the US Federal Reserve):** The monetary policies adopted by the US Federal Reserve influence the value of USD globally.
    d. **EUCB (Monetary Policies of the European Central Bank):** The monetary policies of the European Central Bank influence the value of EURO globally.
    e. **CM (Capital Movements):** Any capital movement in the market can have an impact on the movement of the exchange rate.

Figure 1. Hierarchy of decision problem

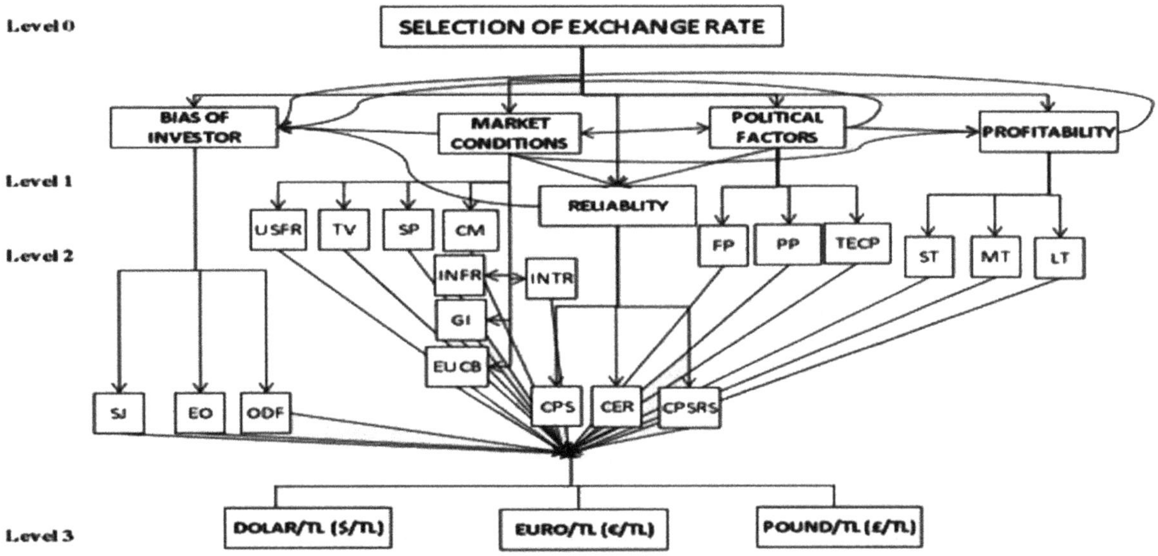

   f. **INTR (Interest Ratio):** The interest ratio of the foreign currencies and TL in Turkey affect transactions of financial players.
   g. **INFR (Inflation Ratio):** The inflation rate in Turkey influences the exchange rates.
   h. **ICBRT (Interventions of by the Central Bank of Republic of Turkey):** As interventions of the Central Bank of Republic of Turkey influence all foreign currencies, the value of TL is also affected by these interventions.
3. **Reliableness:** This main criterion indicates the confidence of the investor in stability of the components of the market.
   a. **CPS (Confidence in Political Stability):** Political stability is crucial for the value of all foreign currencies and TL.
   b. **CER (Confidence in the Exchange Rate):** Since stability in related exchange rate is highly desired, confidence in these rates is an important factor influencing decisions.
   c. **CPSRS (Confidence in the Political Stability of the Related State):** Similar to the stability in the exchange rate, confidence in the political and economic stability of the corresponding state has significance for financial players.
4. **Political Factors:** Domestic and foreign policies of Turkey as well as the external political factors significantly influence both TL and other exchange rates in this country.
   a. **FPT (the Foreign Policies of Turkey):** Mid-term and long-term foreign policies implemented by Turkey impact financial markets.
   b. **PPRS (the Political Power of the Related State):** The political power of the nations of the related exchange rate directly influences the movement of the pars.
   c. **TECP (the Turkey-European Community Proceedings):** Proceedings impact market trends as well.
5. **Profitability:** Profitability of the related exchange rate is one of the most outstanding factors in the exchange rate selection problem.

a. **ST (Short-Term Profitability):** This sub-criterion expresses profit of the related exchange rate in 15 days from the transaction.
b. **MT (Mid-Term Profitability):** This sub-criterion expresses the profit of related exchange rate in 30 days after the transaction.
c. **LT (Long-Term Profitability):** This sub-criterion expresses the profit of related exchange rate in 60 days from the transaction.

The open form of relations among the criteria has been provided in Figure 2, where C1 indicates the bias of the investor, C2 indicates the market conditions, C3 is for reliabilities while C4 is for political factors, and C5 is for profitability. In Figure 2, it is indicated that C2 and C4 have influence on C5 while C5 has an influence on only C1. By considering these relations, the model is expected to become more reliable.

2.4. Integration of the Objective Forecast Values to the Decision Model

As it can be seen in Figure 1, the last criterion is *profitability*, which stands for integrating the objective forecast values to the entire decision model. The forecast values are evaluated for all ST, MT, and LT senarios as described before. And the profitability of those forecasts are then calculated by the equation $P = \left| Y_t - \hat{Y}_{t+s} \right|$ where P indicates the expected profit/gain from the transaction, Y_t indicates the last value observed, and $\hat{Y}_{t+s}$ is forecast value after s terms. P is calculated for each par and for each senario, namely ST, MT, and LT. Thus, objective profitability values are obtained by using analytic forecasting methods instead of expert opinions. To make profit, decisions on *to buy* or *to sell* is required which is entirely dependent on the relationship between forecast value and last observation value. The financial player's decision should be *to buy* transaction if $\hat{Y}_{t+s} \geq Y_t$; however, if $\hat{Y}_{t+s} < Y_t$, the decision should be *to sell* transaction.

All the decisions on *to buy* or *to sell* transactions are assumed that are made correctly. After determining the expected profits, they are evaluated based on pairwise comparisons in the ANP frame for each senario. Thus, the objective forecasting values are able to be incorporated to the decision model.

Figure 2. The open form of the relations among criteria

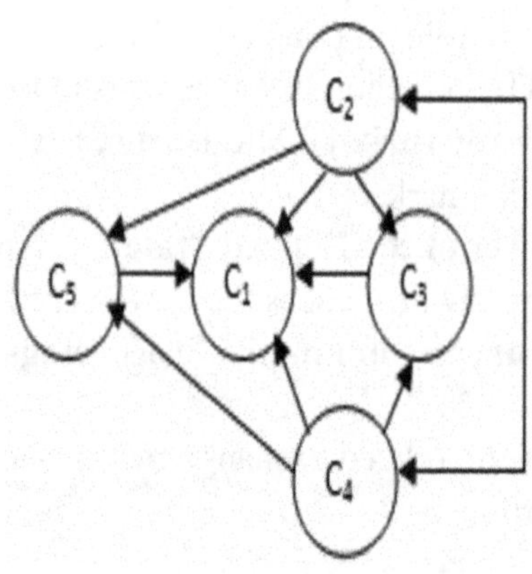

Figure 3. Official daily rates for $ per TL, € per TL and £ per TL

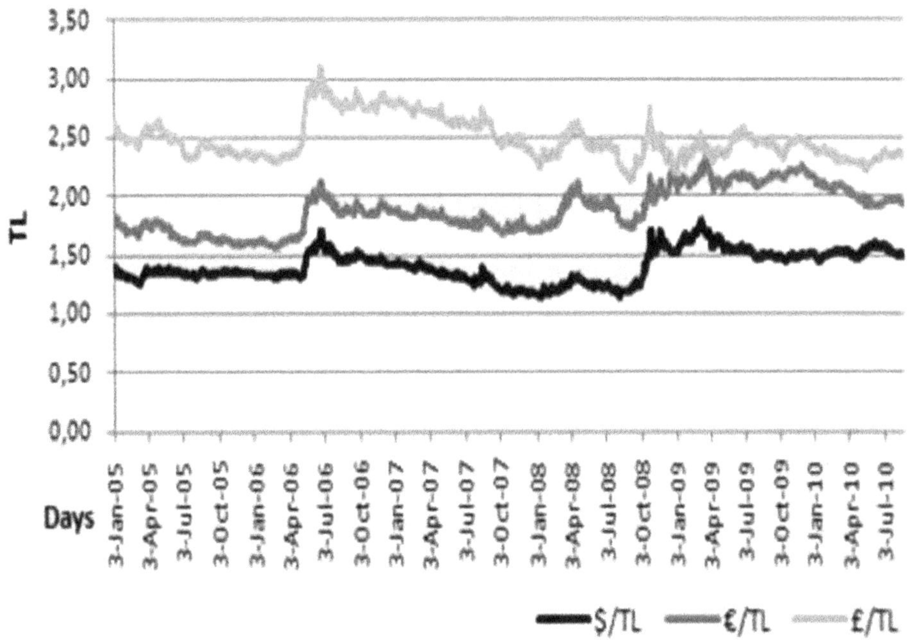

3. EXPERIMENTAL RESULTS

The case study handled in this chapter regards three most common pars in Turkey, namely $/TL, €/TL, and £/TL. In order to obtain forecast values of these currencies, the official daily rates announced by the Central Bank of Republic of Turkey (CBRT) between 01.01.2005 and 18.08.2010 have been used. Figure 3 demonstrates the observations of the exchange rates studied in this paper.

In this section, the experimental results of the case study are provided in three sub-sections; first, forecast values are obtained and, then, those values are integrated to the decision model, and finally, the results obtained by the case study are summarized.

3.1. The Objective Forecast Values

Box-Jenkins approach is one of the most useful forecasting methods also applied to the series in this paper. All of the pure datasets are non-stationary, to be made stationary by the first order difference. The autocorrelation and the partial autocorrelation functions are crucial in order to recognize of the degrees of ARIMA(p,d,q) models. Figure 4 and Figure 5 show these functions instead pertaining to $/TL series and those regarding €/TL and £/TL series are very similar to $/TL series. Despite what can be observed in these figures as the series being theoretically appropriate to the ARMA(1,0) models, various p and q orders are also evaluated for each series.

Various MA, SESM, HM, WM and ARIMA models are applied to each series. The comparisons of the applied models have been tabulated in Table 1-3 for $/TL, €/TL, and £/TL respectively.

Figure 4. Autocorrelation function of $ per TL

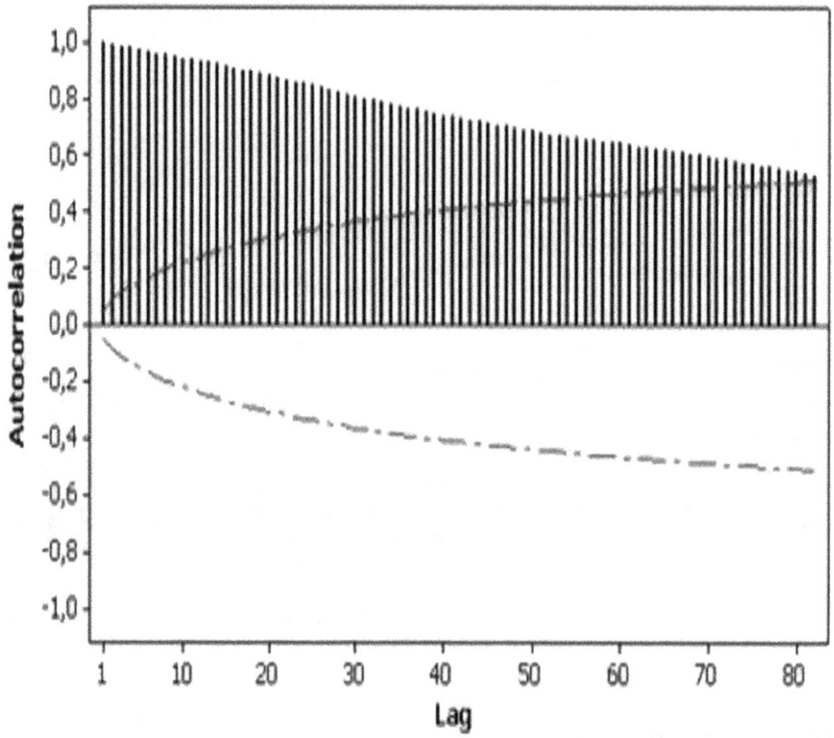

Figure 5. Partial autocorrelation function of $ per TL

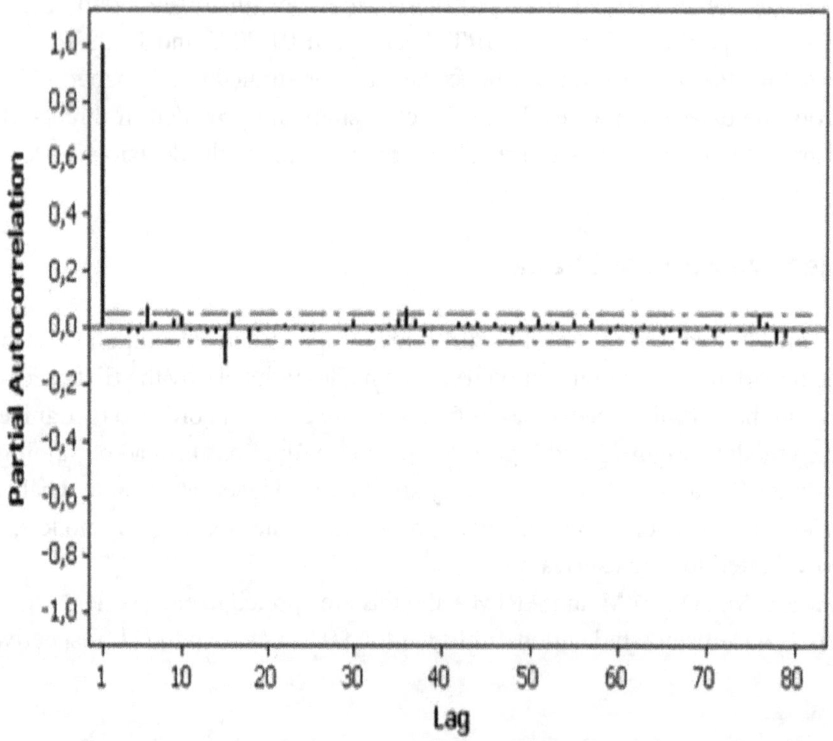

At least two of MAPE, RMSE, MAE or MSE criteria are generally used together due to being non-statistical methods. These methods lack statistical test capability and, therefore, they can neither construct nor test hypotheses. In short, the above criteria can not be used to decide on the accuracy of models, and can only be used for comparing models. In the case study provided here, MAPE, RMSE and MAE criteria are employed.

The most appropriate forecasting model for each method cluster is indicated with an * in the left, and the best performance criteria values are marked in italic type for each cluster in Tables 1-3. As it can be seen in the previous tables, the most accurate forecasting method is Winter's Method with $\alpha = 1.0, \gamma = 0.005, \delta = 0.001$ and $SL = 300$ coefficients for each series.

The values of ST, MT and LT forecasts for 15 days, 30 days, and 60 days, respectively, for each series are shown with MAPE, RMSE, and MAE performance criteria values in Table 4.

3.2. Integration of Forecasts

In order to consider and compare all kind of criteria, i.e. judgmental factors and objective forecast values, a multi-criteria decision making tool, namely the ANP, is employed. In this sub-section, it is described that how the obtained objective forecast values are incorporated to the decision model. Firstly, the decision is to be made as to whether or not *to buy* or *to sell* exchange. This decision is called *transaction decision*, which always has two options, i.e. *to buy* or *to sell*. The upper forecast value than the last observation value of the par indicates a buying transaction, otherwise a selling transaction is indicated for the related par. For instance, ST forecast of $/TL is provided as 1.4896, which is less than the last observation value of 1.4984 on 18.08.2010. The decision should be selling for the ST investment of $/TL. In Table 5, transaction decisions are shown with the estimated profits made. It can be explicitly seen that £/TL is the most profitable par in terms of each investment option, i.e. ST, MT, and LT.

Then, the obtained forecast values and profits made based on those forecast values are integrated to the proposed model as profitability criterion (see Figure 1). According to the integration of judgmental

Table 4. Forecast results

Horizon	Forecast Interval	$/TL Forecasts	MAPE	RMSE	MAE
15 days	18.08.2010 - 13.09.2010	1.4896	1.017371	0.017095	0.015463
30 days	18.08.2010 - 04.10.2010	1.4610	0.851922	0.014732	0.012780
60 days	18.08.2010 - 22.11.2010	1.4378	1.143985	0.019205	0.016547
Horizon	**Forecast Interval**	**€/TL Forecasts**	**MAPE**	**RMSE**	**MAE**
15 days	18.08.2010 - 13.09.2010	1.9147	0.529998	0.012347	0.010257
30 days	18.08.2010 - 04.10.2010	1.8906	1.889416	0.048870	0.037230
60 days	18.08.2010 - 22.11.2010	1.8588	3.512667	0.079994	0.069366
Horizon	**Forecast Interval**	**£/TL Forecasts**	**MAPE**	**RMSE**	**MAE**
15 days	18.08.2010 - 13.09.2010	2.3121	0.697118	0.020661	0.016401
30 days	18.08.2010 - 04.10.2010	2.2620	0.873332	0.023597	0.020395
60 days	18.08.2010 - 22.11.2010	2.2412	0.962142	0.027504	0.022182

Table 5 Transaction decisions for \$/TL, €/TL and £/TL

	Buying or Selling Decision			Profit Made		
	\$/TL	**€/TL**	**£/TL**	**\$/TL**	**€/TL**	**£/TL**
ST	Selling	Selling	Selling	0.0088TL	0.0142TL	0.0281TL
MT	Selling	Selling	Selling	0.0374TL	0.0383TL	0.0782TL
LT	Selling	Selling	Selling	0.0606TL	0.0701TL	0.0990TL

factors with objective forecast values, the pairwise comparison (PC) of the profitability criterion have been provided below for ST, MT, and LT, respectively.

$$\begin{array}{cccc} & \$/\mathrm{TL} & €/\mathrm{TL} & £/\mathrm{TL} \\ \$/\mathrm{TL} & 1.00 & 0.62 & 0.31 \\ €/\mathrm{TL} & 1.62 & 1.00 & 0.51 \\ £/\mathrm{TL} & 3.21 & 1.98 & 1.00 \end{array} \tag{4}$$

$$\begin{array}{cccc} & \$/\mathrm{TL} & €/\mathrm{TL} & £/\mathrm{TL} \\ \$/\mathrm{TL} & 1 & 0.98 & 0.48 \\ €/\mathrm{TL} & 1.02 & 1 & 0.49 \\ £/\mathrm{TL} & 2.09 & 2.04 & 1 \end{array} \tag{5}$$

$$\begin{array}{cccc} & \$/\mathrm{TL} & €/\mathrm{TL} & £/\mathrm{TL} \\ \$/\mathrm{TL} & 1 & 0.86 & 0.61 \\ €/\mathrm{TL} & 1.16 & 1 & 0.71 \\ £/\mathrm{TL} & 1.63 & 1.41 & 1 \end{array} \tag{6}$$

The PCs have been obtained in light of Table 5. Instead of using Saaty scale, the provided profit values in Table 5 are used in order to calculate priorities. For instance, the value 0.62 in Eq.4 becomes to mean the priority of \$/TL to €/TL for ST; and is calculated by the ratio of the provided profits, which can be demonstrated as $\frac{0.0088}{0.0142} = 0.62$. According to the PC of the profitability criterion, £/TL alternative wins against \$/TL and €/TL when the alternative weights are estimated.

3.3. Results of the Case Study

The forecasting model which has $\alpha = 1.0, \gamma = 0.005, \delta = 0.001$ and $SL = 300$ coefficients overcomes the other models for each series. This can be presented as the first distinguishing result of the case study. Secondly, £/TL seems to provide the biggest profit, which means that £/TL is the most profitable alternative according to the calculated expected profits.

One of the results of the study is the realization of the great similarity between the last observation value and the next observation value. In Tables 1-3, this result can be realized easily when HO, SESM, HM and WM model clusters are analyzed. The most appropriate model for HO cluster is HO(1) for all pars while the most appropriate model for SESM, HM and WM are $\alpha = 1.0$ models for all pars. This is a proof that exchange rates handled in this study generally vary minutely for the given intervals.

Calculated values of MAPE, RMSE, and MAE of forecasts are very low. Only MAPE of £/TL for LT is 0.0351 while all MAPE values of the other pars are about 0.01 for all forecast horizons. As Witt and Witt (1991) indicate that models which have MAPE value lower than 0.1 are highly appropriate to the relevant series; the forecast values provide high properness.

Table 6 demonstrates the local and global weights of criteria and alternatives obtained by the questionnarie administrated to a group of academicians. The highest priorities have been marked in italic type for the criteria and the alternatives seperately.

As it can easily be seen in Table 6, while €/TL is the superior alternative among $/TL and £/TL although £/TL is found as the most profitable one, profitability is the most important criterion for the participants by a value of 0.406. Of being the most important criterion for profitability is expected because the intention of all financial players is to gain profit. Following profitability, the market conditions and political factors are mostly weighted by an equal value of 0.259 each. The bias of investors and reliability can be ruled out because of their weak priorities.

The most locally weighted sub-criterion for each criterion is indicated by the sign * at the top right of the local weights column and the first three sub-criteria most weighted globally have been indicated in italic type characters in the global weights column in Table 7. Thus, the capability of viewing the most important criteria and probably ruled out criteria can be presented as another advantage of the proposed model. The most preferential sub-criterion is ST profitability, which has a weight 0.263. Next, PPRS and ICBRT have weights of 0.162 and 0.106, respectively. SJ, CER and CPSRS may be ruled out by the decision maker for their very low weights of 0.004, 0.005, and 0.005, respectively.

Although the forecast values seem reliable and accurate, it is realized that most of the transaction decisions mislead the financial player when the real values are checked. Table 8 demonstrates whether the transaction decision fails or not based on the real values of pars. The failed transaction decisions are indicated as '-' while the correct ones are indicated as '+'. When Table 8 is glimpsed, it is easy to see

Table 6 Global weights of the criteria and the alternatives

Criteria	Global Weights
Bias of Investor	0.038
Market Conditions	0.259
Reliableness	0.038
Political Factors	0.259
Profitability	*0.406*
Alternatives	**Global Weights**
€/TL	*0.445*
$/TL	0.250
£/TL	0.305

Table 7 The local and global weights of the sub-criteria

Sub-Criteria	Local Weights	Global Weights
SJ	0.099	0.004
EO	0.537*	0.020
ODF	0.364	0.014
SP	0.054	0.014
TV	0.113	0.029
USFR	0.160	0.041
EUCB	0.160	0.041
CM	0.047	0.012
INTR	0.028	0.007
INFR	0.028	0.007
ICBRT	0.410*	*0.106*
CPS	0.714*	0.027
CER	0.143	0.005
CPSRS	0.143	0.005
FPT	0.136	0.035
PPRS	0.625*	*0.162*
TECP	0.238	0.062
ST	0.648*	*0.263*
MT	0.229	0.093
LT	0.122	0.050

that transaction decisions related to €/TL par explicitly overcome the transaction decisions related to other two pars in terms of accuracy. Indeed, none of the forecast values captures the right direction of the transaction decision, i.e. *to buy* or *to sell*, except of €/TL par. It should be noted that the proposed decision model captures this point as coming up with result of that €/TL is the most weighted par and should be the first option to invest on. Eventhough £/TL is the most profitable one according to the calculated expected profits, €/TL par wins against the other pars as a conclusion by the constructed decision model. This provides us a novel result which is that considering the judgmental criteria besides profitability in such a financial investment problem lead the financial players to get more accurate and reliable results. In other words, analytically considering judgmental criteria in the decision model prevents financial players from wrong decisions caused by solely considering forecast values even though they seem accurate. This may be the most significant contribution of the proposed model.

Additionally, by the proposed model, hybridization replaces pure methods, thus confirming the view of other experts regarding the advantage of hybrid approaches over pure ones. This hybridization is required for the integration of objectively obtained forecast values with the criteria such as political factors, market conditions, reliability and bias of investor, which highly and positively influence the decision of the financial player. This is because a financial player certainly needs to consider the factors affecting the decision instead of only profitability. Since market conditions and political factors promote €/TL in

Table 8 Accuracy of transaction decisions for $/TL, €/TL and £/TL

	To Buy or To Sell Decision		
	$/TL	**€/TL**	**£/TL**
ST	-	-	-
MT	-	+	-
LT	-	+	-

the proposed model, it is the final decision despite £/TL being the most profitable par according to the objective forecast values.

While the integration of objective forecast values with intangible criteria is the most remarkable advantage of the proposed model, on the other hand, objectivity probably lacks for the other criteria of the model since the weight of the criteria can vary by the participants of the questionnaire. By this reason, great care should be given when selecting experts or academicians.

Since the proposed model evaluates all of the ST, MT and LT investment options, the decision maker has no obligation to make an investment of ST, MT, or LT. In other words, a financial player is free to choose any horizon for the selected par. This flexibility can be announced as another advantage of the proposed model.

The dependency among criteria is also considered in the proposed model, thereby contributing to more reliability and accurateness. This is because the weight of alternatives along with the criteria and sub-criteria vary with the dependency matrix. This dependency matrix can remain unchanged if no global event occurs such as a natural disaster, economic melt-down, war, or civil unrest.

The integration of forecast values into the proposed model in this work leads to provide an objective evaluation of the profitability criterion instead of a subjective one by individuals, since such subjectivity can cause incorrect and/or biased results.

4. DISCUSSIONS AND CONCLUSION

In this chapter, a novel model, which is a strong candidate to fill the gap of considering judgmental criteria objectively in a decision of investing on exchange rates, is proposed. The most distinguishing feature of this work is to develop a model, which is capable of incorporating objective forecast values and judgmental criteria, and, thus it leads the financial player to more accurate and reliable decisions.

Also, the proposed model is highly flexible and can be easily updated for different series, "other time intervals, and forecast horizons. This is because any and all probable factors and conditions can be incorporated into the developed model. In this case, the model needs revising each time by nature of pairwise comparison which is too easy to calculate in today's software and hardware potentiality. Thus, another significant advantage of the proposed model is the ease in application. Similarly, it is possible to promote the proposed model by evaluating other forecasting methods such as VAR, BVAR, RVAR, ARCH and GARCH. In addition, ANN may be considered as a non-parametric method besides these parametric methods.

Exchange rate selection is obviously the type of decision making under uncertainty. To model uncertainty, fuzzy set theory and or grey theory may be suggested for the next research effort.

REFERENCES

Akincilar, A., Temiz, I., & Sahin, E. (2011). An application of exchange rate forecasting in Turkey. *Gazi University Journal of Science*, *24*(4), 817–828.

Baillie, R. T., Bollerslev, T., & Mikkelsen, H. O. (1996). Fractionally integrated generalized autoregressive conditional heteroskedasticity. *Journal of Econometrics*, *74*(1), 3–30. doi:10.1016/S0304-4076(95)01749-6

Blair, A. R., Nachtmann, R., Olson, J. E., & Saaty, T. L. (1987). Forecasting foreign exchange rates: An expert judgment approach. *Socio-Economic Planning Sciences*, *21*(6), 363–369. doi:10.1016/0038-0121(87)90010-3

Blair, A. R., Nachtmann, R., Saaty, T. L., & Whitaker, R. (2002). Forecasting the resurgence of the US economy in 2001: An expert judgment approach. *Socio-Economic Planning Sciences*, *44*(3), 114–121. doi:10.1016/j.seps.2010.03.002

Bollerslev, T. (1986). Generalized autoregressive conditional heteroskedasticity. *Journal of Econometrics*, *31*(3), 307–327. doi:10.1016/0304-4076(86)90063-1

Bollerslev, T., & Wright, J. H. (2001). High-frequency data, frequency domain inference, and volatility forecasting. *The Review of Economics and Statistics*, *83*(4), 596–602. doi:10.1162/003465301753237687

Box, G. E. P., & Jenkins, G. M. (1976). *Time Series Analysis: Forecasting and Control*. San Francisco: Holden Day.

Brandl, B., Keber, C., & Schuster, M. G. (2006). An automated econometric decision support system: Forecasts for foreign exchange trades. *Central European Journal of Operations Research*, *14*(4), 401–415. doi:10.1007/s10100-006-0013-8

Brown, R. G. (1963). *Smoothing, forecasting and prediction of discrete time series*. Englewood Cliffs: Prentice-Hall.

Chu, F. L. (2009). Forecasting tourism demand with ARMA-based methods. *Tourism Management*, *30*(5), 740–751. doi:10.1016/j.tourman.2008.10.016

El Shazy, M. R., & El Shazy, H. E. (1997). Comparing the forecasting performance of neural networks and forward exchange rates. *Journal of Multinational Financial Management*, *7*(4), 345–356. doi:10.1016/S1042-444X(97)00018-2

Engle, R. F. (1982). Autoregressive conditional heteroscedasticity with estimates of the variance of the United Kingdom inflation. *Econometrica*, *50*(4), 987–1008. doi:10.2307/1912773

Fildes, R., & Goodwin, P. (2013). What we know, what we need to know. *International Journal of Forecasting*, *29*(2), 290–294. doi:10.1016/j.ijforecast.2013.01.001

Gencay, R. (1999). Linear, non-linear and essential foreign exchange rate prediction with simple technical trading rules. *Journal of International Economics*, *47*(1), 91–107. doi:10.1016/S0022-1996(98)00017-8

Gonul, M. S., Onkal, D., & Goodwin, P. (2012). Why should I trust your forecasts? *Foresight: The International Journal of Applied Forecasting*, *27*, 5–9.

Gonul, S., Onkal, D., & Goodwin, P. (2009). Expectations, use and judgmental adjustment of external financial and economic forecasts: An empirical investigation. *Journal of Forecasting*, *28*(1), 19–37. doi:10.1002/for.1082

Goodwin, P., Onkal, D., & Lawrence, M. (2011). Improving the role of judgment in economic forecasting. In M. P. Clements & D. F. Hendry (Eds.), *The Oxford Handbook of Economic Forecasting* (pp. 163–189). Oxford University Press. doi:10.1093/oxfordhb/9780195398649.013.0007

Holt, C. C. (2004). Forecasting seasonals and trends by exponentially weighted moving averages. *International Journal of Forecasting*, *20*(1), 5–13. doi:10.1016/j.ijforecast.2003.09.015

Ince, H., & Trafalis, T. B. (2006). A hybrid model for exchange rate prediction. *Decision Support Systems*, *42*(2), 1054–1062. doi:10.1016/j.dss.2005.09.001

Lawrence, M., Goodwin, P., O'Connor, M., & Onkal, D. (2006). Judgmental forecasting: A review of progress over the last 25 years. *International Journal of Forecasting*, *22*(3), 493–518. doi:10.1016/j.ijforecast.2006.03.007

Leitner, J., & Leopold-Wildburger, U. (2011). Experiments on forecasting behaviour with several sources of information – a review of the literature. *European Journal of Operational Research*, *213*(3), 459–469. doi:10.1016/j.ejor.2011.01.006

Leitner, J., & Schmidt, R. (2006). A systematic comparison of professional exchange rate forecasts with the judgemental forecasts of novices. *Central European Journal of Operations Research*, *14*(1), 87–102. doi:10.1007/s10100-006-0161-x

Leu, Y., Lee, C. P., & Jou, Y. Z. (2009). A distance-based fuzzy time series model for exchange rates forecasting. *Expert Systems with Applications*, *36*(4), 8107–8114. doi:10.1016/j.eswa.2008.10.034

Lin, V. S., Goodwin, P., & Song, H. (2014). Accuracy and bias of experts' adjusted forecasts. *Annals of Tourism Research*, *48*, 156–174. doi:10.1016/j.annals.2014.06.005

Marinkovic, S. (2014). Non-parametric sign test and paired samples test of effectiveness of official fx intervention. *Economic Annals*, *59*(202), 107–130. doi:10.2298/EKA1402107M

Onkal, D., Yates, J. F., Simga-Mugan, C., & Oztin, S. (2003). Professional vs. amateur judgment accuracy: The case of foreign exchange rates. *Organizational Behavior and Human Decision Processes*, *91*(2), 169–185. doi:10.1016/S0749-5978(03)00058-X

Panda, C., & Narasimhan, V. (2007). Forecasting exchange rate better with artificial neural network. *Journal of Policy Modeling*, *29*(2), 227–236. doi:10.1016/j.jpolmod.2006.01.005

Pullock, A. C., Macaulay, A., Thomson, M. E., & Onkal, D. (2005). Performance evaluation of judgemental directional exchange rate predictions. *International Journal of Forecasting*, *21*(3), 473–489. doi:10.1016/j.ijforecast.2004.12.006

Saaty, T. L. (2001). *The Analytic Network Process*. Pittsburgh, PA: RWS Publications. doi:10.1007/1-4020-0611-X_32

Song, H., & Li, G. (2008). Tourism demand modelling and forecasting-A review of recent research. *Tourism Management*, *29*(2), 203–220. doi:10.1016/j.tourman.2007.07.016

Thomson, M. E., Pollock, A. C., Gonul, M. S., & Onkal, D. (2013). Effects of trend strength and direction on performance and consistency in judgmental exchange rate forecasting. *International Journal of Forecasting*, *29*(2), 337–353. doi:10.1016/j.ijforecast.2012.03.004

Ulengin, F., & Ulengin, B. (1994). Forecasting foreign exchange rates: A comparative evaluation of AHP. *Omega*, *22*(5), 505–519. doi:10.1016/0305-0483(94)90031-0

Witt, S. F., & Witt, C. A. (1991). Tourism forecasting: Error magnitude, direction of change of error and trend error. *Journal of Travel Research*, *30*(2), 26–33. doi:10.1177/004728759103000205

KEY TERMS AND DEFINITIONS

Decision Model: A model which evaluates existing alternatives based on predefined criteria and results in selecting, sorting, or eliminating alternatives.

Evaluating Forecast Values: Indicates an assessment process for forecast values based on performance indices, namely MAE, RMSE, and MAPE.

Exchange Rate / Currency / Par: The charge for exchanging currency of one country for currency of another.

Forecasting Model: A model which is based on one of non-causal time series analysis methods with certain parameters.

Integration of Forecasts: Indicates incorporating the objective forecast values of a related currency to the developed decision model.

Judgmental Criteria: Some intangible criteria which have an explicit impact on the goal -investment decision on one of three pars.

Objective Forecasts: Represents forecasts obtained by forecasting models.

Profitability: The state of whether a currency may yield when it is invested in.

Transaction Decision: A decision of *to buy* or *to sell* the related currency in the market.

Chapter 4
The Effects of Prudential Supervision on Bank Resiliency and Profits in a Multi-Agent Setting

Alexandru Monahov
Université Côte d'Azur, CNRS, GREDEG, France

ABSTRACT

This chapter utilizes multi-agent modeling to study the effects of prudential supervision on bank resiliency and profitability within a simulated environment of persistent crisis conditions. It focuses on the stabilizing effect of prudential supervision introduced alongside three "traditional" regulatory instruments: a norm, a market-based CDS insurance mechanism and a tax in the form of a bail-in instrument. The results show that: (1) supervision enhances the regulatory instruments' efficiency, (2) the regulatory norm can postpone the bank's default, but not avoid it, (3) the CDS mechanism only produces positive results on resiliency and profitability if the regulator supervises, and (4) the tax bail-in instrument is the most powerful tool in the regulator's arsenal as it potentiates profitable bank operation under long-lasting crisis conditions.

CHAPTER OVERVIEW

The severe economic recession of 2008 led to an increased focus on the importance of banking sector regulation in preventing crises. The downturn revealed that traditional theoretical and empirical models were ill adapted to crisis conditions and produced flawed results especially at turning points in the economic cycle. As such, the very methodology used in constructing theoretical models came under attack for not having been able to predict or measure the extent of the crisis. Increased attention was therefore devoted to finding alternative methodologies capable of more accurately determining the evolution of macroeconomic indicators.

DOI: 10.4018/978-1-5225-0959-2.ch004

Multi-agent modeling is a relatively new but rapidly growing programming methodology that allows researchers to create virtual economies in which economic agents of various types (customers, enterprises, banks, governments and regulators) are created and interact. In this simulative environment, micro-founded macro-economic aggregates emerge as a result of agent interactions. Since the dissection of the causes leading to the 2008 financial crisis indicated a deficiency in the functioning of prudential instruments, it is of interest to consider the role that irrationality plays in the decisions taken by agents (as the theoretical literature suggests that during crises agent behavior may not be completely rational). Given that traditional modeling techniques cannot incorporate irrationally into the analysis, it is beneficial to perform the analysis in a multi-agent environment which allows for limited rationality and complex behavior such as "sunspots" and "herd instincts".

Furthermore, multi-agent modeling allows different types of reactions (or behaviors) to be assigned to agents based on various criteria thereby allowing for a study of the possible responses to the crisis and a comparison of their efficiency. It is possible to include learning algorithms that allow the agents to improve their decision-making abilities or become better at performing pre-defined tasks. Concurrently, agents can be programmed to change their behavior in innovative (and unscripted) ways to respond to the environmental stimuli that they receive.

In general, multi-agent models comprise a number of strengths over other modeling techniques, the most pertinent ones to our study of the financial sector being: the ability to incorporate individual characteristics within agent groups, to study the interactions between agents within a competitive environment and the possibility of performing robustness checks in the presence of randomness. These advantages allow for a richer analysis than what would be possible in a purely representative agent model.

Within this chapter we will utilize multi-agent modeling to perform an analysis of the effects of prudential supervision on bank resiliency to shocks and the profitability of the bank within different regulatory set-ups. At first, we look at the main reasons leading to the 2008 crisis and present references to the existing literature. We then describe the model, its purpose, structure, agents, their affiliations and accounts. Since this is a programming methodology, we also present the order in which events are executed and in which agents make their decisions. Finally, we delve into analyzing the different regulatory instruments implemented in the presence (and, if appropriate, absence) of regulatory supervision and their effectiveness at preventing the bank's default and ensuring its long-term profitability. We describe in each section the functioning of the instrument and how it is implemented in our model.

At the end, we provide a comparison of the instruments and offer concluding remarks as to the best suited tools for regulating the banking system in conditions of long-lasting crises and elaborate on the bank's adaptation to such harsh operating environments. We also discuss the side-effects of implementing each one of the instruments in the presence and absence of supervision.

1. INTRODUCTION

From a prudential perspective, the 2008 financial crisis highlighted the weakness of the deregulated financial system within an environment of growing risk and convoluted market instruments that failed to achieve their objective of risk diversification. As a consequence of the severe economic recession that followed the 2008 crisis, regulators in western economies and the United States concentrated their focus on the re-regulation of the financial sector. The theoretical and empirical literature largely followed suit. Whereas some researchers focused their attention on traditional prudential tools such as capital requirements and how they may be improved in order to produce a less pronounced restrictive effect on credit and growth, others began to investigate whether alternative instruments and transmission channels could be used to ensure the same objective of risk reduction, but with lesser negative consequences[1]. In this context, increasingly growing attention has been given to the role of prudential supervision both in directly ensuring the regulatory objective of risk reduction, as well as in complementing and increasing the efficiency of other instruments implemented by the regulatory authority.

Indeed, recent papers such as Delis and Staikouras (2011) begin to question the effectiveness of traditional tools such as capital requirements in reducing risk. As an alternative, they focus on the efficiency of prudential supervision in terms of bank audits and sanctions. They find that the usage of such "alternative" tools contributes significantly towards ensuring the stability of the financial system where more "traditional" instruments such as capital requirements falter. Hardy and Nieto (2008) suggest that increased supervisory stringency contributes positively towards risk reduction and therefore improves the stability of the financial system. The prudential effect of supervision is confirmed by Bassett et al. (2012) who conclude that increased supervisory stringency increases the quality of loans by incentivizing banks to lend to relatively risk-free clients. Aside from the direct effect of supervision on risk reduction, the role of prudential supervision in complementing other instruments is also documented in the literature. Ratnovski (2013) finds that it is possible, by means of using "alternative" regulatory methods geared towards increasing transparency in the banking sector, to improve the resiliency of the sector to shocks, as well as to enhance the efficiency of prudential instruments such as the liquidity ratio. Furthermore, Maddaloni and Peydro (2013) argue that reducing supervisory stringency diminishes the risk of a credit crunch appearing under tighter lending conditions resulting from higher capital requirements or liquidity ratio constraints. Their conclusions are of particular interest since they are indicative of supervisory measures and traditional macro-prudential tools coexisting and producing better results when coordinated and utilized together.

The objective of this chapter is to look in more detail at the effects of prudential supervision introduced alongside regulatory instruments in an environment of persistent crisis conditions. We do so within a multi-agent framework that allows us to better integrate the persistent crisis conditions into the model and to study the behavior of the financial sector. Persistent crisis conditions in the model are defined as a situation in which the proportion of high risk clients in the economy remains elevated even after an initial shock, thereby placing a strain on the bank's ability to cope with its clients' defaults. We focus on the effects of different prudential supervision configurations on bank profitability and default rates. The study is conducted in an environment of costly monitoring and informational asymmetry where the bank is unable to gauge the exact risk level of its clients. As such, the model simulates the bank's response and financial situation under long-lasting crisis conditions and determines whether the prudential regulator is able to offset the negative effects of persistent crisis conditions. We focus specifically on crises emerging from the default of the bank's debtors when the bank is faced with severe liquidity shortfalls.

We adapt Diamond's (1984) "Financial intermediation and Delegated Monitoring" framework to a multi-agent setting consisting of the bank, its clients, the prudential regulator (that can coincide with the Central Bank) and, where applicable, an insurance agency that will interact in the economy. We calibrate the model based on IFC data and the data resulting from empirical studies related to the subject.

We put three "classic" visions of regulatory intervention to the test: a simple prudential norm, a tax-subsidy mechanism and a market-based CDS insurance scheme. These instruments will fulfill the prudential objective of the regulator and may be regarded as alternatives to the commonly used prudential measures of the Basel frameworks. We adapt the tax-subsidy mechanism to reflect a "bail-in" instrument, as the one recently proposed to deal with the financial crisis in Cyprus[2]. Whereas it is evident that the bank is always better off when the prudential supervisor intervenes, it would seem that different supervisory techniques are better adapted to various economic conjunctures.

Imposed regulatory norms that include credit-rationing provisions only have temporary stabilizing effects on the economy in crisis situations and inevitably falter and allow the bank to default when the credit rationing becomes more stringent. More advanced monitoring techniques used by the bank can extend the stabilizing effect of the supervisory mechanism to a longer period of time, but with unchanged finality. Still, provided that the bank has access to sufficient market information to formulate a more advanced monitoring plan, the norm's effect may last long enough to steer the bank out of a crisis situation. Of course, such methods bear the advantage of not imposing any burden on the tax-payer, but require that the prudential institution determine an appropriate numerical value for the norm that would balance the risk level undertaken by the bank with the activity-stifling effects of credit rationing.

A market based CDS mechanism curated or supervised by the regulator can serve as an equally powerful tool and may be even better adapted to situations where the bank is able to integrate sufficient information about its clients to formulate advanced monitoring methods. Unlike the norm which imposes the bank to follow a prescription, this mechanism incites the bank to participate with the prospect of cost-reduction. Being market based, the mechanism allows for price fluctuations of the CDS instrument according to the bank's demand. The efficiency of such a system that allows the bank to insure against the risk of its clients' default is highly dependent on the bank's ability to integrate the price structure of the insurance instrument. Under the assumption of limited bank access to information, it is impossible for the bank to accurately deduce the price structure – which leads to inefficient allocation of (CDS purchase) funds. Given its unconstrained access to information in the economy, the supervisor's role is to observe the bank's decision model and to correct it by serving as an intermediary between the bank and the CDS market, guiding the bank's decision towards the optimal level. Indeed, provided that the bank has an advanced client monitoring method, it seems that market-based mechanisms are more efficient at stabilizing the bank's situation and at eliminating the negative effects of the crisis conditions by reducing the bank's costs associated with the defaults of it clients. In fact, the bank can operate at increasing profit under long-term crisis conditions when such a supervisory system is applied. It must be noted, however, that if the bank operates an uninformed monitoring model, the market based method performs worse that even the regulatory norm. This is caused by the bank's inability to correctly allocate resources between its monitoring and CDS-purchasing activities. For the same reason, the sole introduction of a CDS mechanism without regulatory supervision to guide the bank in its CDS purchasing choice results in a worsening of the bank's financial situation.

Finally, the tax-subsidy instrument taking the form of a "bail-in" mechanism in which it is those who benefit from the bank's credit activities that are also expected to contribute towards saving the bank when it encounters difficulties - seems to be the most powerful tool in the regulator's arsenal. The role of the supervisor here is to monitor the bank's financial situation and implement a tax on borrowers when the bank reaches dire conditions. Here, the entirety of the social cost (of the bank's default) is borne by the production sector. This method is efficient under all circumstances and regardless of the complexity of the bank's monitoring method and the underlying informational asymmetries present in the economy. The major drawback, however, of this method is that it imposes a very high cost on the firms' profits, with taxes having, at times, to reach close to 100% of the firm's profits in order to ensure the safety of the financial intermediary. Also, this method creates very high fluctuations both in the bank's revenues, as well as in the instrument itself. This can be a negative factor if the prudential regulator is also the

Central Bank and pursues a concurrent objective of stability in the economy. It is also noteworthy to mention that whereas the efficiency of this method generally allows the bank to continue operating at a profit under conditions of long-term financial crisis (unlike the only temporary effects of the prudential norm), due to the fluctuations caused by the system, the bank risks plunging into negative territory in terms of liquidity and may require additional punctual credit facility interventions from the Central Bank in order to continue operating.

Therefore, we find that prudential supervision serves to improve the financial situation of banks faced with long-lasting crisis conditions. The method of choice, however, depends on the objectives pursued by the prudential regulator, its interactions with the Central Bank and the monitoring efficiency of the banking sector.

The rest of this chapter is structured as follows: Section 1 has provided an introduction into the importance of studying the effects of supervision on the resiliency of the banking sector. Section 2 presents the structure of the model, the various interacting agents, and explains the functioning and processes that determine the dynamics of the model. Section 3 explains the various regulatory set-ups envisaged and provides in-depth simulation results for both the baseline scenario, as well as for the model runs containing prudential supervision. Finally we conclude by presenting the main findings.

2. PURPOSE, AGENTS, AND AGENT VARIABLES

Within the model we will have three "main" types of agents: the firms, the investment bank, the Prudential Regulator and one auxiliary agent: the CDS fund, whose presence is conditional upon the usage of CDS instruments in the Prudential Regulator's toolset. It is noteworthy that in many advanced economies, the Central Bank coincides with the prudential regulator thereby giving the regulator additional tools that can be used in unison. To this matter, Schoenmaker (2011) presents a detailed depiction of the regulatory structure of multiple countries. However, we note that it is not our objective to study monetary policy and the specific instruments associated with it for the purposes of this simulation, and we will only make brief general remarks about it where necessary.

2.1. Purpose

The purpose of this model is to study the extent to which prudential supervision accompanied by regulatory instruments can serve to improve the bank's financial situation in terms of profitability and liquidity, as well as the efficacy of such measures in reducing the number of bank default episodes in the context of long-term and short-term crises.

To define a banking crisis we may look at Northcott (2004) who, in a Bank of Canada Working Paper, states that banking crises represent episodes of either financial institution insolvency or illiquidity. Concurrently, Angkinand and Wihlborg (2005) and Duttagupta and Cashin (2008) propose that banking crises appear when the bank loses most or all of its reserve assets, capital or liquidity. Given the setup of our model, we will be focusing primarily on liquidity issues that the bank may face as a result of the crisis situation. We will therefore define a crisis situation as the instance in which a bank is facing a severe liquidity shortfall and has a client portfolio of doubtful quality. These are the two necessary conditions for a crisis to emerge. With respect to the bank's liquidity, we will allow for the bank to have just enough resources to finance one last group of clients. This condition is required for the model to be able to initialize. However, the presence of lower-quality clients with higher default probabilities in the bank's portfolio will then contribute to a potential further deterioration of the bank's financial standing. This will allow us to introduce prudential supervision under different forms and gauge its overall effectiveness under conditions of both short-term and long-term crises.

The length of a crisis will depend primarily on the behavior of the bank's clients and the risk level of the projects that they decide to undertake. During crises, it is assumed that a significant number of agents have undertaken projects of high risk, thereby compromising the stability of the bank. If, subsequently, the agents tend to rapidly converge towards undertaking projects of moderate or low risk – then we can conclude that we have been faced with a short-term crisis, or a crisis episode. Once the crisis event has passed, the bank should, by means of its regular credit activities, be able to replenish its liquidity reserves and continue operating at a profit. If, on the other hand, we do not see a clear tendency of the agents to converge towards some equilibrium and their project risk levels continue to fluctuate over time, then we are to conclude that the underlying conditions causing the crisis have not dissipated and that we are confronted with a long-term (or enduring) crisis which may have negative long-term effects on the bank's financial indicators or even pose a threat to the bank's existence. We do not delve into the factors that have generated the crisis. Instead, we utilize the dynamics of the firms' project decisions as a consequence of the crisis situation to investigate the bank's behavior. The firm dynamics influence the bank's response to the crisis and allow us to study how the prudential authority can improve the bank's situation by implementing prudential supervision and instruments.

2.2. Firms

The firms in our model represent the bank's clients. True to Diamond's (1984) formulation, each firm requires one unit of bank credit in order to finance a project that has a certain probability of success in the next period. In the event of success, the firm obtains a reward allowing it to reimburse the bank loan and maintain a profit, whereas failure is characterized by a situation in which the firm obtains a reward equal to the loan amount, thus rendering impossible the repayment of the interest on the contracted loan. The structure of the firm's risk-reward configuration is given by:

$$V = \begin{cases} V_H, with\,probability : (1-p) \\ V_L, with\,probability : p \end{cases} \tag{1}$$

where V_H is the "high" reward in the event of success, $V_L = 1$ is the "low" reward in the event of failure, p is the probability of default and $(1\text{-}p)$ is the probability of success.

We notice that, as in Diamond, the bank is able to liquidate the firm if it does not pay back an amount f that at the very least equals the bank's invested unit plus interest spent on crediting the firm. This dispels any attempt of the firm's management to announce earnings lower than the bank's expected payoff f, which depends upon the economy's interest rate R, as well as the default probability p of the project that was undertaken by the firm. As such:

$$f = \frac{R}{p} \Leftrightarrow R = p * f \tag{2}$$

As we can see, this condition reflects the risk neutrality of the bank which expects to obtain, on average, the (base) interest rate R in exchange for crediting a firm's project of p riskiness.

A resulting firm variable is the profit that the firm obtains after paying back the bank's loan. It is expressed as: $\pi_f = V_H - f$ in the case of success, whereas if the firm defaults and is liquidated by the bank, its profit is null $\pi_f = 0$.

In our model, the origins of the crisis that the bank is confronted with stem in part from its client portfolio. We assume that in times of crisis, the bank is confronted with clients of different risk levels, with some significant presence of high-risk project-bearing clients. This means that we must depart from Diamond's framework and divide the clients into multiple risk groups. We find that it is more commonplace to divide bank clients into 3 credit risk-groups: low, medium and high-risk clients, although more detailed classifications also exist. For instance, Experian (2014) and CA Technologies (2014) prefer to use 3 risk groups in their credit risk assessment models and their project risk scores. On the other hand, PricewaterhouseCoopers utilizes a finer categorization totaling 5 risk levels, as described in Gillespie et al. (2010). The theoretical literature also seems more inclined towards the usage of 3 categories. This is best illustrated in an IFC study performed by Dickson and Einstein (2010). For the purposes of our model, we shall retain the 3 group classification as we have no need to delve into the level of precision that a 5 group classification would offer.

With respect to the probability of default variable, we shall calibrate our model based on the data provided in the IFC study. In Table 1, we notice the probabilities of default, which in our model will also determine the firm's reward:

Table 1 presents the probability of default intervals for the bank's low, medium and high risk clients.

Besides the firm's individual probability of default, recognizing the fact that the majority of firms have some sort of linkages with counterparts of various nature (competitors, partners, clients, etc.), as evidenced by Koenig et al. (1979), we introduce a global probability of default calculated as the average of the firms' individual default probabilities. This global variable will influence the individual probability of default by a measure $\varphi \in [0;1]$ whereby a value of $\varphi = 0$ means that the global variable exerts no influence whatsoever on the individual firm's probability of default and an extreme value of $\varphi = 1$ would amount to the individual firm's probability of default value coinciding with the global one.

Deriving from the riskiness of an undertaken project, the reward in case of success (V_H) for each firm will be given by:

$$V_H = \frac{R}{1 - \overline{p}_g} + R * \overline{p}_g \tag{3}$$

Table 1. Client risk-groups classified by probability of default

Risk-Group	Probability of Default (p)	
High	p_h	> 10%
Medium	p_m	1 – 10%
Low	p_l	< 1%

source: Dickson and Einstein (2010)

where $\overline{p}_g$ is the average probability of default for the given group $g = \{h, m, l\}$. And we remind that $V_L = 1$ in all instances of default and for all risk groups.

Depending on their probability of default, each period, the firms will either succeed or default. This reflects a one-period credit maturity that applies throughout the model. In the event of success, the firm is likely not to change project risk groups, but we account for a small chance that the firm manager may voluntarily wish to change project types (for personal reasons, because he believes that firms pursuing other project types are more profitable, etc.). This small chance is determined by a group cohesiveness variable (γ). If the firm defaults, however, a new agent will appear in place of the old one with a potentially different type of project.

2.3. Bank

In our model, the investment bank is the sole source of funding in the economy. It provides entrepreneurs with financing so that they can implement their projects. The bank starts off in a crisis situation with low liquidity reserves and an unsound client portfolio. Our bank acts as an investment bank. Hence to avoid the issues arising from the moral hazard that the bank may manifest as a result of catering both to its investors and acting for its own account, the bank funds clients utilizing only its own resources. This type of modeling approach allowing for a segregation of the bank's investment activities from its deposit unit in order to study more minutely the bank's own investment decisions can be found in papers such as de Walque (2010). By reducing the number of processes and actions to be modeled, this framework presents the advantage of focusing our work on the area of prudential supervision without worrying about adverse selection issues on the bank's behalf, but prevents us from implementing leverage-dependent regulatory tools.

In terms of its activity, the bank undergoes a series of processes through which it manifests its credit, monitoring and corrective actions.

Figure 1 displays the two initial decision processes that the bank undergoes with respect to crediting its new clients and subsequently deciding on the number of clients to monitor, as well as the three potential corrective actions that it may take as a result of Central Bank supervision that it undergoes.

The bank initially finances all of its clients, since it cannot determine which (if any) of its clients undertake high-risk projects.

Subsequently, the bank monitors a portion of its clients. Monitoring is assumed to be costly, as evidenced by the literature on the matter. Booth (1992) confirms Diamond's (1984) assumption of high monitoring costs. However, monitoring allows the bank to recover the unit invested into the client

Figure 1. Bank decision processes

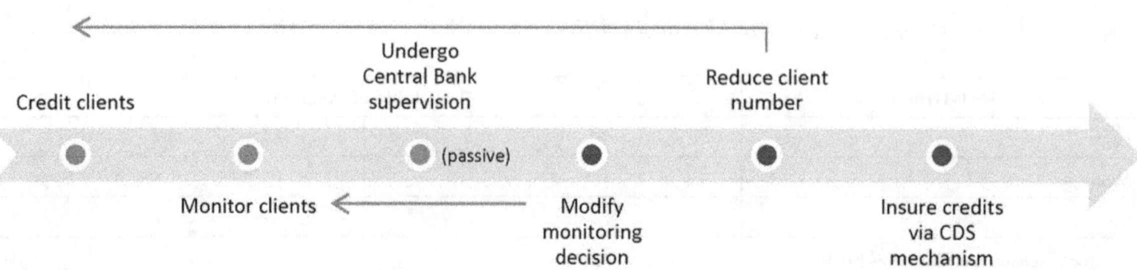

(firm) and to avoid additional costs (such as costs arising from reputation loss, etc.). In fact, the role of monitoring in reducing client default costs is evidenced in multiple studies. Baxter (1967) estimates bankruptcy costs at around 20% of the market value of a client. Stanley and Girth (1971) and Van Horne (1976) later confirm this result. Furthermore, it would seem that financial institutions must also deal with reputation costs arising from the default of their clients. These costs are also proven to be considerable as shown in Infosys (2012) and Deloitte (2014). However just as with bankruptcy costs, they can be reduced via monitoring, as described by Gopalan (2010) and Lin (2011). Furthermore, Vanston (2012) provides evidence that Central Bank supervision may also serve to reduce reputational costs incurred by the bank as a result of its client's default. Finally, Barnett and Harder (2014) argues that banks that do not monitor may be faced with negligence charges in lawsuits initiated by the defaulted clients. The only way of eliminating such costs is for the bank to monitor its client. As we have seen, there is ample incentive for the bank to monitor, however depending on information that the bank has of its clients the decision process may be more subtle. In our model we are able to vary monitoring costs in order to determine their impact on the bank's financial situation and monitoring decision.

The bank disposes of several monitoring techniques that it may use depending on the informational asymmetries associated with the economy in which it operates. If the bank suffers severe informational asymmetries that prevent it from gaining ex-post precise insights into the risk-level of the clients that it credits, then the bank adopts an approximate method of monitoring based largely on the information that it can obtain from the clients that it monitored in the previous period. If informational asymmetries are relaxed and the bank is able to obtain information about a larger portion of its clients, then the bank can implement more advanced monitoring techniques, such as expecting that some clients will remain stable, being more vigilant towards both high-risk and brand-new clients that emerge as a result of firm defaults. These more advanced techniques allow the bank to better adapt to the economic context that it finds itself in and allow for a more efficient usage of the expensive monitoring process.

With respect to agent variables, for our study of the bank's financial standing, we focus on three key indicators that reflect the bank's situation: the number of default episodes, the bank's total liquidity and the ROI (Return-On-Investment). The ROI follows the evolution of the profit variable very closely and we will primarily be using it as a control variable. As such we will refer to it only very briefly. A default episode is defined as being a time period (year) at the end of which the bank has negative liquidity. This indicator is a measure of the length of the bank's distress and, consequently, of the severity of the crisis. For simulation purposes we allow the bank to continue operating even at negative liquidity, but count the period with negative liquidity as a "bank default episode" which would otherwise have led to the failure of the bank and a halt of all its operations. Such an assumption would be justified if the bank had access to some form of external credit (perhaps a credit line of last resort) that it could contract in the event of illiquidity. However, as documented by Allen et al. (2009) as well as by Freixas et al. (2011), it is often the case that during systemic banking crises, financial institutions are unwilling to lend to one another and the interbank market often dries up – thus confronting the individual bank with a lack of external funding options. Still, the bank could be allowed to temporarily continue operating at a loss in the instance in which the Prudential Regulator coincides with the Central Bank and has the option of extending exceptional credit facilities to the afflicted financial institution.

The bank's total liquidity indicator gives us a sense of the bank's capacity to finance new clients and perform the various monitoring and, if required by the regulator, insurance activities. This is our indicator of the financial institution's health. The prudential regulator (usually the Central Bank with regulatory functions) may act upon this variable by providing the bank with stimulus, if such an intervention method is chosen. Finally, the ROI may be of interest since it gives us an indication of the bank's profitability. It is one of the indicators commonly used to compare the performance of both corporate and banking sector entities.

Table 2 presents a sketch of the bank's simplified income statement, including the elements related to the regulator's intervention:

Table 2 details how the bank's profit is formed, by component. As such, it presents the variables that constitute the revenues and expenses of the bank.

As for variables pertaining to the bank's internal processes the bank also chooses the number of clients to monitor within its monitoring function, and if a CDS insurance mechanism is implemented by the regulator, then the bank will also choose the number of CDS units to purchase. On the other hand, if the prudential authority enforces supervision of a regulatory norm regarding the number of clients that the bank must monitor, then the bank will also dispose of a variable that allows it to calculate the number of clients (if any) that it must abandon in order to conform to the norm, subsequently utilizing an internal process to determine which clients to abandon.

2.4 Prudential Regulator

The Prudential Regulator (in the literature, often coinciding with the Central Bank) performs both supervisory and intervention functions. One of the main roles of the regulator is to observe the bank's financial situation, as well as the decisions that it makes in order to ensure its uninterrupted operation. This means that the regulator will be privy to all the internal operations of the bank, its processes and variables. On the other hand, the regulator may also be lead to take corrective action to resolve deficiencies that it observes. Herein lies its second role of actively pursuing the implementation of the chosen regulatory method. We propose three different models of regulatory supervision and intervention that cover the "traditional" intervention mechanisms studied in the literature on market regulation, adjusted

Table 2. Bank income statement

Category	Amount
Revenue	*Total*
Interest (including principal reimbursement) paid by clients (*f*)	
Revenue from monitoring in the event of client defaults	
Regulator's liquidity injections	
Expenses	*Total*
Cost of crediting new clients	
Costs of client defaults - *bankruptcy cost* - *reputation cost* - *negligence cost*	
Monitoring costs	
Insurance costs (if required by the regulator)	
Revenue — Expenses	Profit

for some newer methods of banking crisis resolution circulated within the EU. We provide a brief description of each method here in order to introduce the associated variables and processes and further expand the subject in its appropriate section.

The first regulation method tasks the prudential regulator with supervising the bank's financial variables and determining if the bank may be faced with a problem of illiquidity. If, indeed this turns out to be the case, then the regulator (either by coinciding or by coordinating with the Central Bank) will perform a liquidity injection into the bank to save it. We implement the liquidity injection as a "bail-in" instrument to resemble the EU creditors' proposition in the case of the Cyprus bank defaults of 2014. However in our case we consider a tax on firms' profits. The reasoning behind this is that, as in any bail-in instrument, it is those who benefitted from the activities of the bank that must contribute towards saving the bank, should the financial institution encounter difficulties. And, in the model we present, it is specifically the firms who benefit from bank credit that enables them to obtain profits. Consequently, it is only fair that they support the burden of the bail-in mechanism. The regulator determines the amount of liquidity needed by the bank in order to avoid a default and imposes a tax on firms' profits. This tax is stored in a variable that the regulator will control. The tax evolves in fixed increments. As such, if the regulator raises slightly more money than what is required to save the bank, then the remainder of the taxation proceeds is deposited in a reserve fund. If, after having subjected firms to the maximum imposition level, the regulator is still unable to save the bank, then the regulator will utilize the previously accumulated reserve funds. Finally, if after having depleted its reserves, the regulator is still unable to save the bank, then the bank will be allowed to default.

A second method involves the creation of a CDS insurance market to allow the bank to hedge against the risk of default of its clients. An insurance fund is created and will control the CDS price variable which will depend on the bank's demand for CDS units. The bank, which, as mentioned earlier is confronted with informational asymmetries, is unable to correctly integrate the price structure of the CDS instrument. This opens up the way for the regulator which will now be tasked not only with supervising the bank's financial indicators, but also with overseeing the CDS market and helping the bank to integrate information about the price structure of the CDS tool. The regulator's intervention is performed by a sub-model through which it determines the optimal quantity of CDS units that the bank must demand in order to minimize its costs for any given objective level (in terms of risk reduction). This means that within this supervision method, the regulator obtains an additional variable that stores the optimal quantity of CDS units that the bank must purchase. Furthermore, the prudential authority communicates this value to the bank which corrects its own value of CDS units to purchase.

The third regulatory method involves the implementation of a monitoring norm that constrains the bank to monitor a given number of clients each turn. Failure to do so results in an immediate termination of the bank's activities. In this situation, the norm may be fixed, or it may be enunciated as a percentage of the total number of clients that solicit bank credits. Although time invariant, the norm can be considered as an additional regulator variable that is controllable by the observer and is set at the beginning of the simulation. It must be noted here that a smaller number of clients to monitor reduces the financial strain placed on the bank by the regulator by means of reducing the per client monitoring costs that the bank supports. However, the reduction in the regulatory number of clients to monitor also reduces the efficiency of the method since it increases the chance for non-monitored firm failures to appear. This method could be expanded to include sanctions for non-conformity as opposed to immediate termination, but that would somewhat undermine the strictness of the norm and would allow the bank to disregard regulation as it sees fit – which is contrary to what the regulator hopes to achieve by introducing the norm.

3. MODEL AND SIMULATIONS

Before we can proceed to the simulations, we must first take a look into the scheduling of the various processes described in the first part of the chapter, as their order will impact the functioning of the model.

3.1. Model Structure and Initialization

Initially, in the very first period (t_0), the bank is endowed with sufficient liquidity to finance all of its clients. Optionally, the bank can be bestowed with some extra liquidity above its strict minimal necessity in order to avoid the bank defaulting in the immediately subsequent period as a consequence of a random or chance event. Still the extra cash assigned must be limited in size given the fact that we are modeling a liquidity-constrained bank in the middle of a crisis. If, because of the selected monitoring algorithm, the bank also needs to expend resources on monitoring during the setup phase, then those costs will also be covered.

Clients are generated according to the setup conditions where the observer determines the proportion of low, medium and high risk clients in the economy. The clients determine their desired risk level within the confines of their risk-group which translates into their individual probability of default. Afterwards their actual probability of default is automatically determined based on their individual characteristic, the global default probability and φ.

Finally, the bank credits the new clients and, if required by its algorithm, proceeds to immediately monitor the firms.

The described structure will also be present in the following periods, however a number of new elements will be introduced. Table 3 illustrates the timing of the processes in all subsequent periods and focuses on the bank's monitoring processes, as well as on the regulator's supervision. The line number represents the order in which the events are processed. We begin by determining the project realizations of the firms credited in the previous period and then proceed to operating with the (new) clients that the bank is faced with in the current period.

Table 3 presents the sequence of events that comprise the foundation of the model. These processes are executed in the same sequence within each time period of the model. The events are grouped into 3 categories: one related to processing previous-period information, another to performing current-period actions and a third that comprises auxiliary functions.

This sequence of events will repeat every time step and will allow us to study the dynamics of the system by observing the outcomes of the agents' behaviors under different circumstances. In what follows, we will present in detail the simulation results for each of the three regulatory scenarios and will investigate the effect of different parameter values on the evolution of the system. We will be most interested in varying those parameter values for which there is either limited scientific coverage or for which multiple potential values are suggested by the literature.

3.2. Baseline Scenario and Bank Monitoring

We define the baseline scenario, which will later on be expanded by including regulatory supervision, as a model simulation with no bank monitoring or regulatory intervention, taking place in a system characterized by the parameter values shown in Table 4:

Table 3. Model structure and order of events

Nr.	Event Title	Event Description
Events Related to Previous Period Proceedings		
1.	Project realizations become known to the firms	Some firms (mostly the ones with higher probabilities of default) will go bankrupt (obtaining $V_L < f$), whereas the others will obtain positive rewards such that $V_H > f$.
2.	Statistical data is gathered by the regulator	The regulator now knows information about the defaulted clients, their number, group origins, whether they were monitored by the bank or not, etc.
3.	The bank's financial situation is updated	All non-defaulted clients pay the bank its expected payoff (f), defaulted but monitored clients reimburse the borrowed unit of credit (but without interest) and the bank suffers default penalties for the defaulted and unmonitored clients.
Events Related to the Current Period		
4.	New clients appear - clients are reset - their new risk group is determined (if it changed) - their probability of default is determined	Defaulted clients will be replaced with new clients. Successful firms will tend to undertake new projects of the same risk-level as before. However, some of the successful firms may decide to change risk level for various random internal reasons or (in the case of more advanced firm rationality algorithms) because of external linkages with other firms.
5.	Bank crediting operations	The bank credits its new clients
6.	Bank monitoring occurs	The bank decides how many clients to monitor and (informational asymmetry levels allowing) determines specifically which clients to focus its efforts on.
7.	Regulatory supervision occurs	The prudential authority (or the Central Bank) monitors the bank's situation and determines its viability. If necessary, the regulator intervenes by utilizing the instruments available to it.
8.	Has the bank defaulted?	After all is said and done, we look at whether the bank survived the tribulations of the current period or whether it succumbed to the pressures facing it. We register the eventual default of the bank and either allow the model to continue or stop it (according to our setup).
Auxiliary Processes		
9.	Verification	We verify some of the variables dynamically calculated throughout the model to check for errors.
10.	Plotting and graphs	We display the results of the model within the graphical interface.

Table 4. Baseline scenario parameter values

Parameter	Description	Value	Parameter	Description	Value
N	Number of clients	121	R	Interest rate	1.05
NL	Low-risk clients	30%	k	Initial bank liquidity	12
NM	Medium-risk clients	55%	mc	Cost of bank monitoring	0
NH	High-risk clients	15%	bc	Bankruptcy costs	0.2
φ	Influence of global default rate	0.1	rc	Reputation cost	0.2
γ	Group stability parameter	75%	nc	Negligence cost	0.1

Table 4 presents the parameter values used in the baseline scenario of the model, in which neither bank monitoring, nor regulatory supervision are active.

We select a sufficiently large number of clients for the bank, but not too large in order to limit the simulation time. We assume that the crisis-hit system manifests itself through larger number of high-risk clients and medium-risk clients totaling 15% and respectively 55% of the firm population. This leaves low-risk clients at just under a third of the economy. With respect to the financial indicators such as the interest rates and the bank's costs, we follow Diamond's prescriptions as well as the ones mentioned in the aforementioned literature. We mention that the costs incurred by the bank as a result of client defaults are highest when neither the bank monitors, nor the regulatory institution supervises. These costs will diminish rather significantly, as stated in Gopalan (2010) and Lin (2011), when the bank starts monitoring. Finally, with respect to γ and φ which are indicative of the interaction amongst firms, we assume that firms have a strong tendency to maintain their project risk level in case of success (as evidenced by the group stability parameter) but, at the same time have default rates that are largely uncorrelated (as indicative of the low φ value).

We should note that as a result of our model calibration, the time periods that we study here are, in general, expressed as years. However, given the simulated nature of this economy, one must be very careful with the interpretations attributed to the temporality of the model. Also, with respect to the units of measurement of financial variables, they are similarly abstract, but, for convenience can be thought of as millions of a particular currency.

Let us first look at the results produced by the model under both absence of regulatory intervention, as well as the following client monitoring configurations emanating from the bank: (1) a situation of no monitoring whatsoever (the baseline scenario), (2) a context of low-cost monitoring under heavy informational asymmetry, (3) a situation of costly monitoring under heavy informational asymmetry, and (4) a more advanced monitoring method possible due to diminishing informational asymmetries however maintaining the hypothesis of costly monitoring. In all situations in which monitoring occurs, the costs associated with the client's defaults are automatically diminished for the monitored clients. As such, $rc = 0.1$ and $nc = 0$. What has been described could be visualized graphically in Figure 2.

Figure 2 outlines possible simulation scenarios based on varying the costs associated with monitoring, as well as the informational asymmetries that the bank is faced with.

We must note that whereas monitoring costs (*mc*) represent a parameter value that can be modified by the observer, informational asymmetry is a qualitative measure based on the information that the bank has access to in its monitoring function.

Figure 2. Baseline model simulation under varying informational asymmetry and monitoring costs

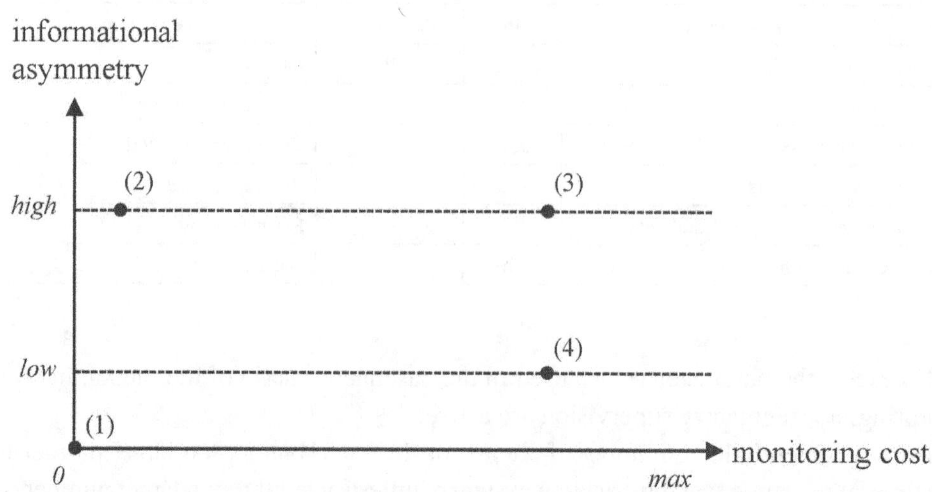

In the first scenario characterized by an absolute absence of monitoring, the firms' behavior is characterized by a significant, although not overly high, attraction towards their risk group, characteristic of entities looking primarily to their internal processes and goals to determine the type of project to undertake. As shown in Figure 3, this results in a rapid decline in the bank's liquidity reserves past the point at which the bank must declare bankruptcy. The bank's average profits lie well below zero, which corresponds to the significant number of high-risk client defaults. The described situation is a consequence of the unstable environment in which low-risk and medium-risk projects compete for dominance, however with a relatively large proportion of high-risk projects in the economy. On average, high-risk enterprises constitute 22.18% of the total number of client submitted projects, within the designated study period.

Figure 3 presents the results of the baseline scenario in the form of the means and standard deviations of the analyzed variables for 100 simulations of the model, over 100 time periods. It reflects the dire situation of the bank in absence of monitoring and regulatory supervision, as bank liquidity declines under conditions of negative profit.

Figure 3. Baseline model simulation without bank monitoring or regulatory supervision

Note: The solid lines represent the mean and the dotted lines denote +/- one standard deviation from the mean, the x-axis denotes time, results are based on 100 repetitions of the simulation.

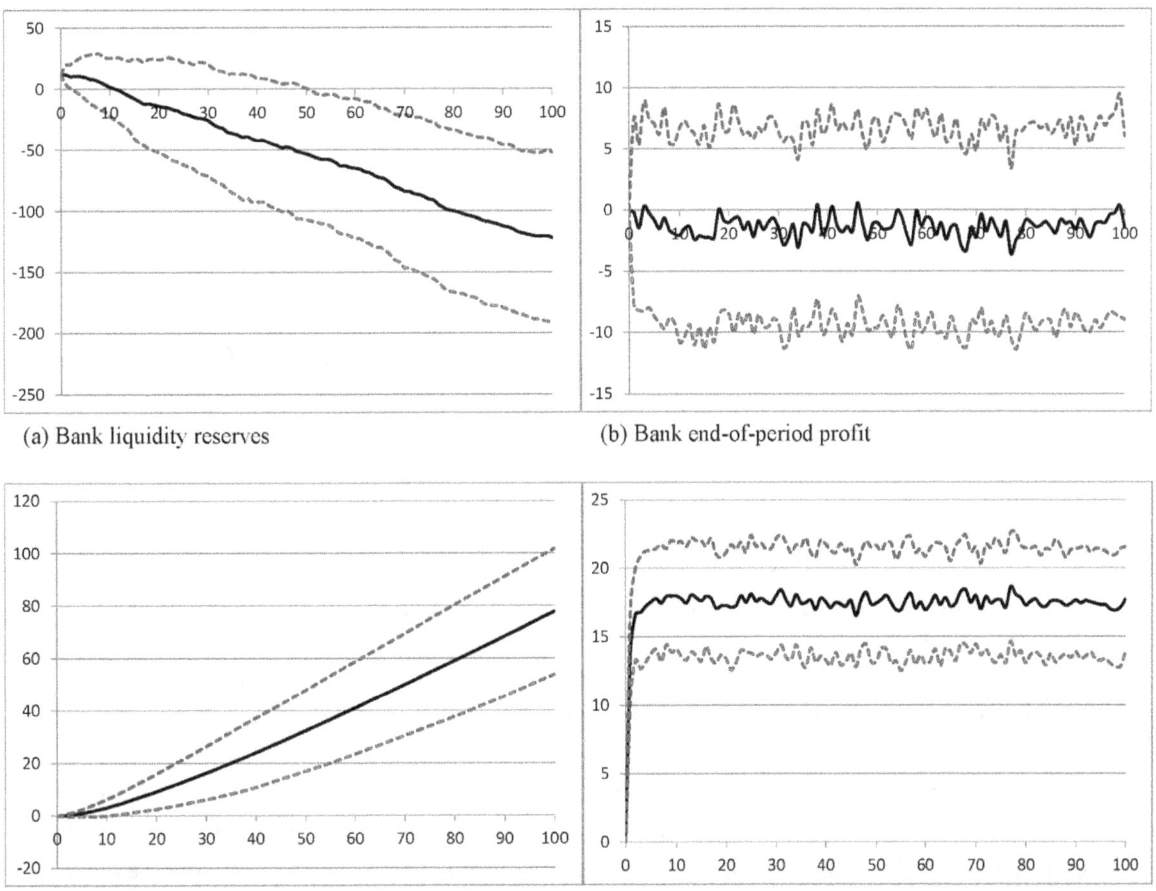

(a) Bank liquidity reserves

(b) Bank end-of-period profit

(c) Number of default episodes

(d) Number of client defaults (all risk groups)

We notice, therefore, that the long-term as well as short-term activity of the bank in these economic conditions is unviable, as by the 7th period, the bank defaults in over 50% of the simulation runs and by the 10th period it defaults in over 2/3 of the total number of repetitions performed. Furthermore, the bank's profits rarely peak above zero, as the bank's expenses generally surpass its income. This underscores the necessity for the bank to monitor its clients in order to reduce default-related costs and recover the invested funds from unsuccessful projects.

As part of a second scenario, we now insert bank monitoring into the equation. We first assume that the environment in which the bank performs its monitoring is characteristic of severe informational asymmetries. As such, the bank is entirely oblivious to the new clients that it faces each period. Besides the absence of any sort of signaling information (that the bank may make use of), the bank is also unable to infer any information regarding the future choices of current clients. These two assumptions amount to the bank operating under conditions of very high uncertainty. Still, the bank has access to general statistics regarding the number of clients and their adherence to the existing risk groups. Given this information, the bank's choice regarding the number of clients to monitor in the current period is based on the proportion of previous period clients from each risk group that the bank detected as part of its monitoring activities. Concurrently, the bank is aware of the value of monitoring a given client group. More precisely, the value of monitoring is equal to the default probability of the given group. As such, the bank monitors that specific group of clients only if the value of monitoring exceeds the cost of monitoring.

$$M_g^c = \frac{C_{g\ t-1}^M}{C_{t-1}^M} if\ \overline{p}_g > mc, where, C_{t-1}^M = \sum_{g=\{h,m,l\}} C_{g\ t-1}^M \tag{4}$$

M_g^c is the percent of clients from group "g" that the bank will monitor in the current period. C_{t-1}^M is the total number of clients that the bank monitored in the previous period, and it is comprised of the sum of clients belonging to each risk group that were monitored in the previous period ($C_{g\ t-1}^M$).

In other words, the bank operates under the assumption that what was characteristic of yesterday still holds true today, and makes corrections to its number of clients to monitor based on the new information that it receives each day (information regarding the previous period).

This monitoring method is highly sensitive to the monitoring costs, since these determine the total number of clients that the bank will decide to monitor. If monitoring costs are low, then the bank will monitor most of its clients and, as such, manage to significantly reduce costs and recover most of its investments in the event of client defaults. However, under the assumption of high monitoring costs, it is conceivable that the bank may only wish to monitor its riskier clients. This, however, coupled with the informational asymmetries that prevent the bank from properly determining which individual clients pose a threat to the bank's operations leads to a deterioration of the bank's financial situation when compared with the baseline scenario.

Indeed, if we look at Figure 4, we notice that in the case of low monitoring costs (the situation corresponding to point (2) in Figure 2), the bank is able to verify a large proportion of its clients, thereby ensuring that most of the defaulted clients are being monitored. This translates into lower expenses for the bank and higher profits which stabilize at a level sufficiently far away from the null value, that even in relatively extreme cases of profits falling at one standard deviation away from the mean value, bank profits remain positive or null. This has a positive effect on the bank's liquidity reserves which progress linearly towards infinity with increasing variability. As can be seen from point (c), the bank does not default in this context. The reason for this highly profitable situation is made clear in point (d) where we see that the number of monitored clients largely surpasses the number of defaulted clients at all points throughout the simulation. Although, because of the asymmetries facing the bank, it is not guaranteed that the monitored clients are also those clients who are defaulting, the odds are in favor of the bank when it comes to monitoring a risky client.

The same favorable situation does, however, not remain true for the scenario in which monitoring costs are high. Indeed, the assumption of costly monitoring has for effect a reduction in the number of monitored clients, given that the value of monitoring condition is not satisfied for all client risk groups. Under these circumstances, monitoring of low-risk and medium-risk clients becomes unprofitable for the bank and the bank reduces its monitoring target. The consequences of this decision can be seen in point (h) where the average number of monitored clients stabilizes at roughly 27 clients (constituting around 22% of the total population). The evolution of the average number of monitored clients is now much closer to that of defaulted clients and indeed can fall below the number of defaulted clients.

This means that the bank is now in a much tougher predicament, as it inadvertently faces the increasing risk of not being able to target the correct clients for its monitoring activities.

The situation translates itself negatively on the bank's profits which now stabilize in negative territory and at lower values that even the base-line scenario containing no monitoring whatsoever. Similarly, the bank's liquidity reserves register a faster drop as the bank now defaults in over 50% of the simulation runs by the 5th period (twice faster than in the case of the baseline scenario). We also see this in point (g) where the average number of default episodes per period is shown to increase linearly, after a short early phase in which the bank's initial reserves stabilize the situation and prevent the bank from failing.

We thus notice that monitoring can provide a way for the bank to reduce costs and recover investments, only under the assumption of reasonably low monitoring costs. Under the assumption of high monitoring costs, however, the process of costly monitoring itself places the bank in a worse off situation that the baseline scenario. As such, it is not recommendable for, nor indeed should it be expected from, a bank to entertain costly monitoring in an environment of high informational asymmetries. Forcing a bank into monitoring would only produce worse results than attainable in its absence.

Figure 4 presents the results of the baseline scenario in the form of the means and standard deviations of the analyzed variables for 100 simulations of the model, over 100 time periods. It shows that, if the assumption of costly monitoring holds true, when bank monitoring occurs under high informational asymmetries, the bank's financial situation is worse off than in the baseline scenario without monitoring or supervision.

In a final monitoring-only scenario, we allow for a decrease in informational asymmetries which allows the bank to better gauge the risk level of it clients. Now, after having monitored its clients, the bank will have enough data regarding their risk level in order to formulate expectations regarding the future risk level of each client. The bank will now be able to target high-risk clients in its monitoring efforts, as well as novice clients who have never yet been credited by the bank. This will allow the bank to better target those client which pose an actual risk and to avoid squandering precious resources on low and medium risk clients. At the same time, since the bank can now accurately target clients based on their previous risk level, we now no longer impose the value of monitoring constraint on the bank and allow it to monitor as many clients as deemed necessary, provided the bank has enough financial resources for the task. The business environment (or the evolution of the clients) remains unchanged.

Figure 4. Baseline model simulation with high informational asymmetry monitoring
Note: The solid lines represent the mean and the dotted lines denote +/- one standard deviation from the mean, the x-axis denotes time, results are based on 100 repetitions of the simulation.

For monitoring costs: mc = 0.05

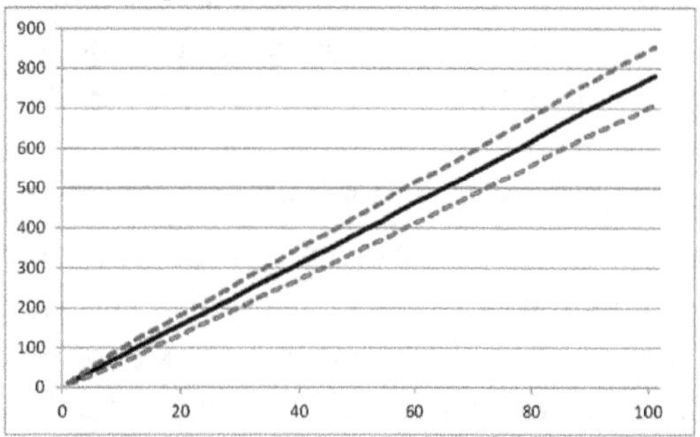

(a) Bank liquidity reserves

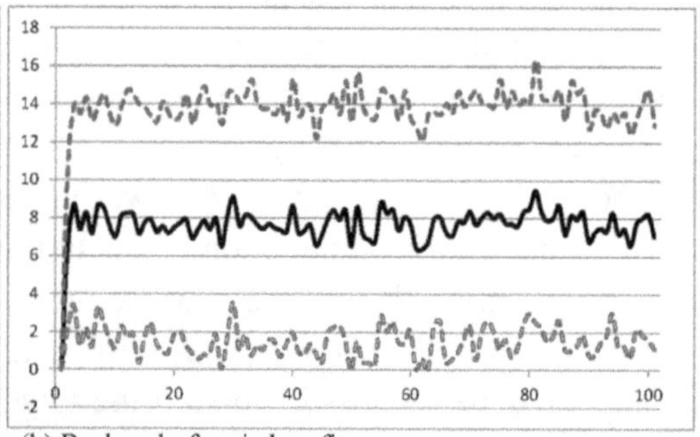

(b) Bank end-of-period profit

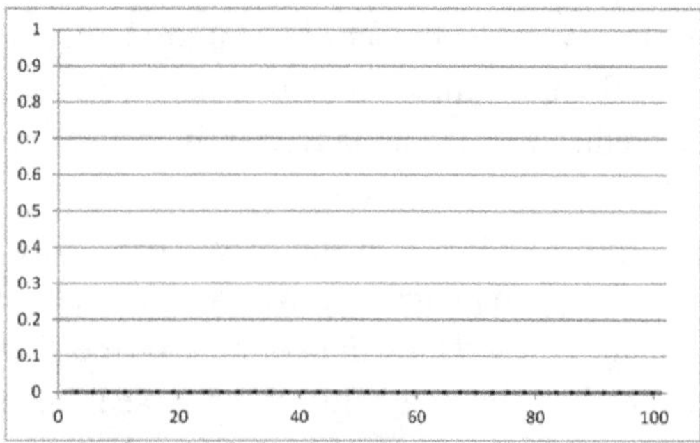

(c) Number of default episodes

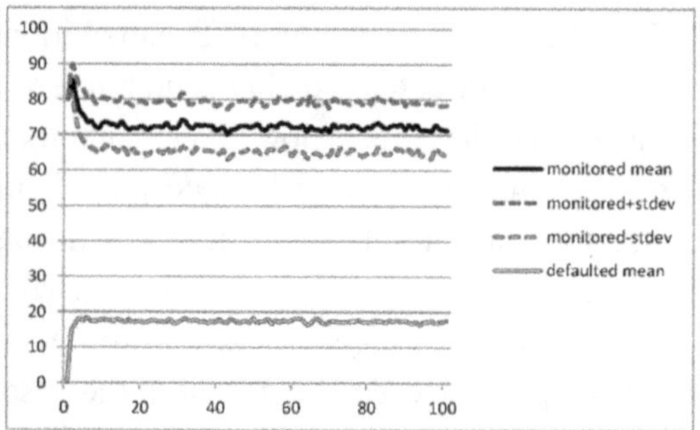

(d) Number of clients monitored and defaulted

For monitoring costs: mc = 0.3

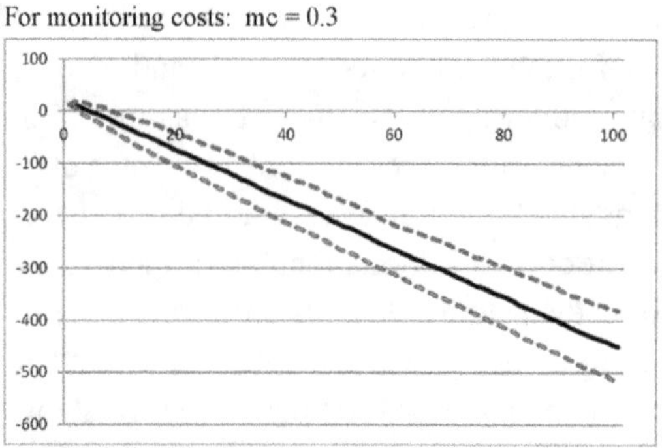

(e) Bank liquidity reserves

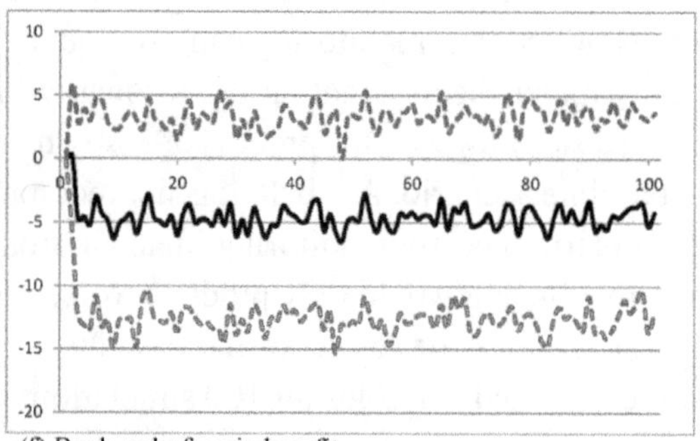

(f) Bank end-of-period profit

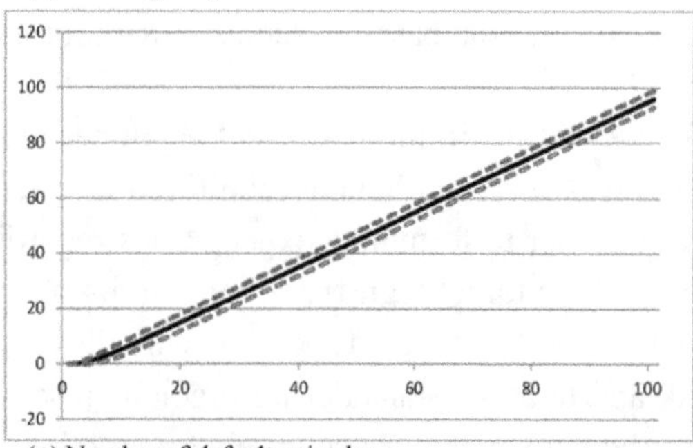

(g) Number of default episodes

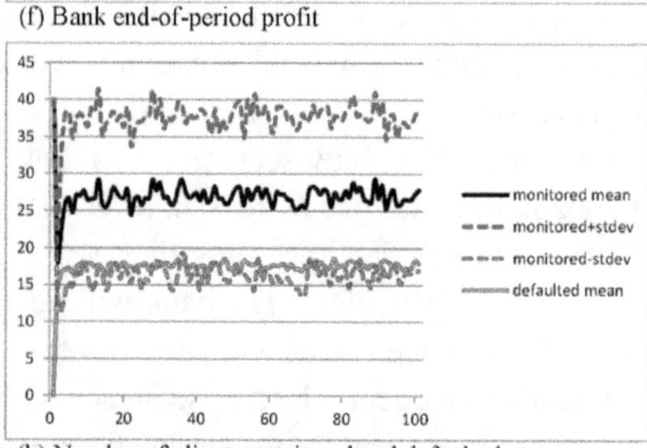

(h) Number of clients monitored and defaulted

We will also assume that the bank operates under costly monitoring conditions and will utilize the same parameter value as before.

Given these conditions, upon first look at the evolution of the bank's financial situation variables, we notice a slight improvement versus the baseline scenario. However, we also remark a significant increase in volatility. Upon closer inspection, we notice that this is because of the duality in the trend of the profits and liquidity indicators. This is best seen in Figure 5, point (b) where we decompose the sample of 100 repetitions into two groups: one containing 47 runs and the other, the remaining 53 ones. In this graph, we notice that in a number of our repetitions, the liquidity indicator, after a short period of volatility (visualized in the average indicator as stagnation, but consisting of both ups and downs, sometimes even in negative territory, symbolizing the default of the financial institution), proceeds to an upward trend of steady growth. This is usually the case when the bank is faced with relatively mild early conditions consisting of lower default rates and/or lower number of high-risk clients. The bank, therefore manages to monitor enough clients in the early periods of its operations to avoid accumulating losses that would send its liquidity reserves below zero. In the event in which the bank faces tougher starting conditions because of higher default rates and a larger numbers of high-risk clients, its initial losses deplete its liquidity reserves rapidly and case the bank's cash to dip below zero, which leaves it in the impossibility of further monitoring its clients, thereby sending it into a vicious circle of losses amounting and not permitting it to monitor. If we had elected to terminate simulation upon bank default, we would interpret this result as the inability of the monitoring process to save the bank in over 50% of our simulation runs.

Figure 5 presents the results of the baseline scenario in the form of the means and standard deviations of the analyzed variables for 100 simulations of the model, over 100 time periods. It shows that when the bank monitors its clients under conditions of low informational asymmetry, the decline in the bank's liquidity is slower, and there is possibility for the bank to avoid default if it is faced with fewer high risk clients initially.

As for the other indicators showing the bank's profits and default rate, we must note that, just as in the case of the bank's liquidity, we can see two separate groups of results, one located roughly between the mean and plus one standard deviation, and the other trend located between the mean and minus one standard deviation. We also notice that the bank is now able to monitor fewer clients than before, while maintaining roughly the same number of clients that were concurrently monitored and that defaulted as in the case of costly monitoring with high informational asymmetry. This amounts to a higher targeting precision for the bank's monitoring process. In other words, the bank monitors fewer clients, but out of those clients who were monitored it finds just as many who defaulted as in the previous scenario. This means that the bank has become better at finding the risky clients.

Indeed, we notice that even by reducing informational asymmetry, the hypothesis of costly monitoring does not allow the bank to ensure its safety – which raises the question of external intervention in the form of prudential supervision and instruments.

Figure 5. Baseline model simulation with costly low informational asymmetry monitoring

For monitoring costs: mc = 0.3

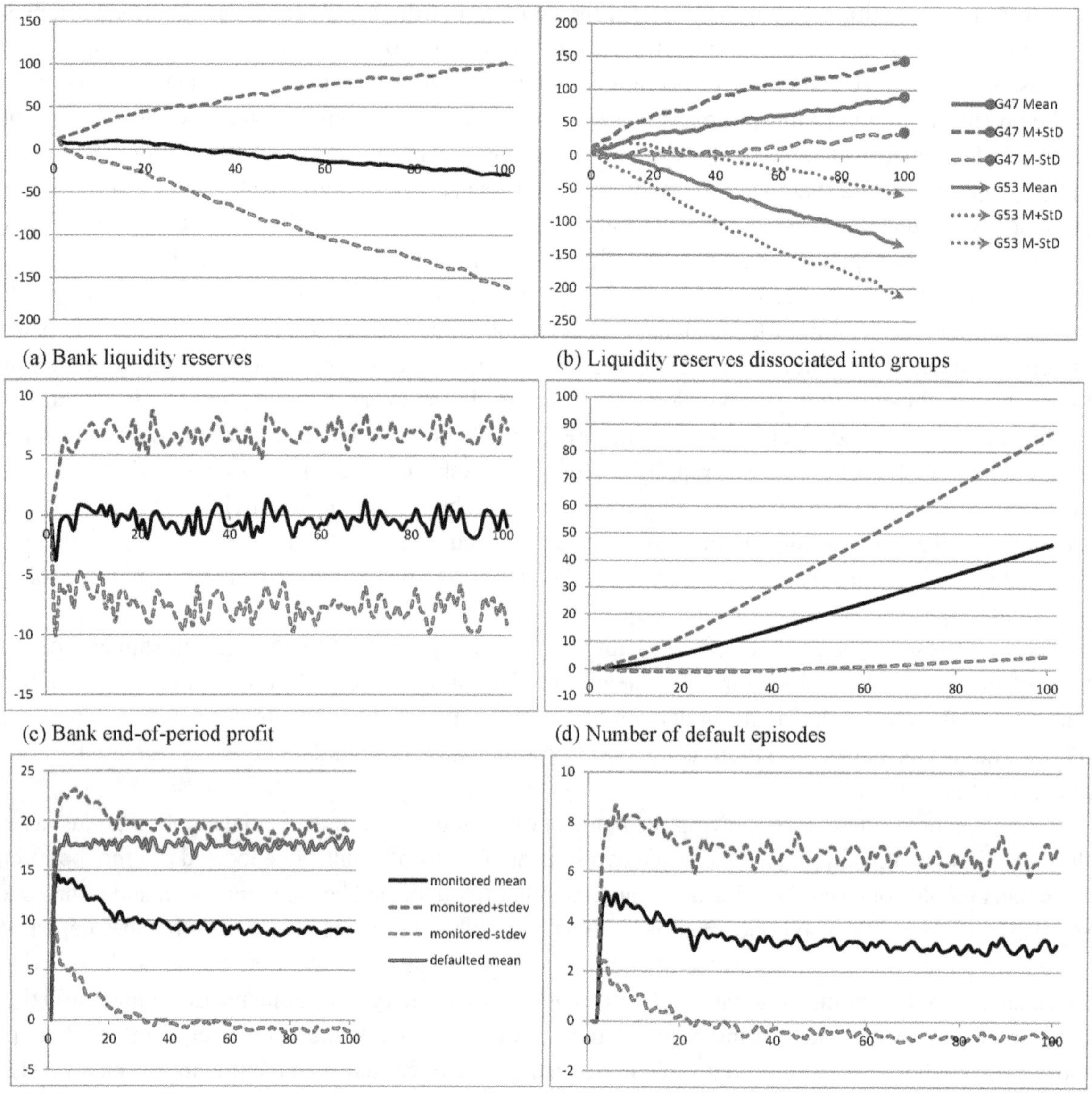

(a) Bank liquidity reserves

(b) Liquidity reserves dissociated into groups

(c) Bank end-of-period profit

(d) Number of default episodes

(h) Number of clients monitored and defaulted

(h) Clients concurrently monitored and defaulted

3.3. Prudential Supervision and Instruments

3.3.1. Supervision with Regulatory Norm

We will first test the efficiency of bank supervision coupled with a regulatory norm imposing the bank to monitor a certain percentage ($m^{\%}$) of its clients[3]. The regulator will supervise the bank in order to ensure that it monitors the appropriate number of clients. To ensure an absolute lack of moral hazard on the bank's side, the bank is made aware that its activities will be terminated in the event in which it fails to comply with the norm. Also, the regulator constrains the bank to have sufficient liquidity for monitoring activities and initially informs the bank that it will not receive any form of credit from the Central Bank. This motivates the bank to try to keep its liquidity reserves above zero for as long as it can, only faltering in the event of impossibility to continue to do so. Beforehand unbeknownst to the bank, if the financial institution does indeed falter, then the Central Bank will either allow it to continue operating (as it has done in our previous simulations by extending a special long term credit facility) or it may alternatively choose to terminate the bank (if such action is specified in the model setup). For the bank to be able to satisfy the requirement of having sufficient cash destined towards monitoring purposes, a special mechanism is introduced: the bank is allowed to abandon some of its clients if it does not have enough money to monitor the percentage of total clients prescribed by the regulator. The bank cannot, however abandon clients that it has already willingly decided to monitor (since this would go against the very purpose of the regulator's intervention). Furthermore, if the bank has negative liquidity, before the bank can monitor the remaining difference of clients between the regulator's norm and its own internally determined optimal number of clients to monitor, it must abandon a sufficient number of clients in order to obtain the required cash to monitor the discrepancy. To give a simple example of the regulatory intervention, if the regulator imposes the bank to monitor an additional 15% of its clients, but the bank only has enough resources to monitor 5% of its remaining clientele, then the bank will be forced to abandon (or not credit) as many clients as required in order to, at the end of the day, be able to monitor the discrepancy. We can view the abandonment process as one of two possibilities: the first of which consists in the bank not crediting its clients before having decided on the number of clients that it will be unable to finance. Such a scenario is consistent with the bank being aware of a monitoring rule set forth by the regulator. A second possibility is one in which the regulator does not immediately inform the bank of the existence of the norm, but will rather discretely inform the bank each time step of the existence (or not) of the regulatory norm. In such a case, the bank will first credit its clients and then have to abandon some of the credited clients. This imposes a recovery rate (*rr*), where $rr \in \left[0;1\right]$, that determines the amount of the initial investment that the bank will be able to recover as a result of abandoning the client. For our simulation purposes we will assume the former case, in which $rr = 1$. Also, we notice that supervision is inseparable from the norm since, in the absence of supervision with threat of liquidation, the bank will never be incited to monitor the number of clients prescribed by the regulator, and the simulation results will revert to the baseline scenario with monitoring.

Figure 6 presents the results of the scenario in which the regulator introduces a norm accompanied by prudential supervision under high informational asymmetries. The results are presented as the means and standard deviations of the analyzed variables for 100 simulations of the model, over 100 time periods. We notice that when informational asymmetries are high, the norm only has a short-term stabilization effect, after which the bank inevitably defaults. Applying this instrument also produces severe credit rationing.

For our simulation, we will therefore fix the two parameters controllable by the observer as follows: $m^{\%} = 0.5$ and $rr = 1$. We note that once fixed, the regulatory percentage can no longer be changed internally by the prudential authority, as it becomes a long term rule. Also, from now on, we will only be referring to the hypothesis of costly monitoring.

As we can notice, in the case of supervision with a regulatory norm and monitoring under high informational asymmetry depicted in Figure 6, by means of the regulatory norm, the supervisor is, on average (however, with relatively low deviation), able to stabilize the bank's financial situation for 11

Figure 6. Supervision with regulatory norm under high informational asymmetry monitoring

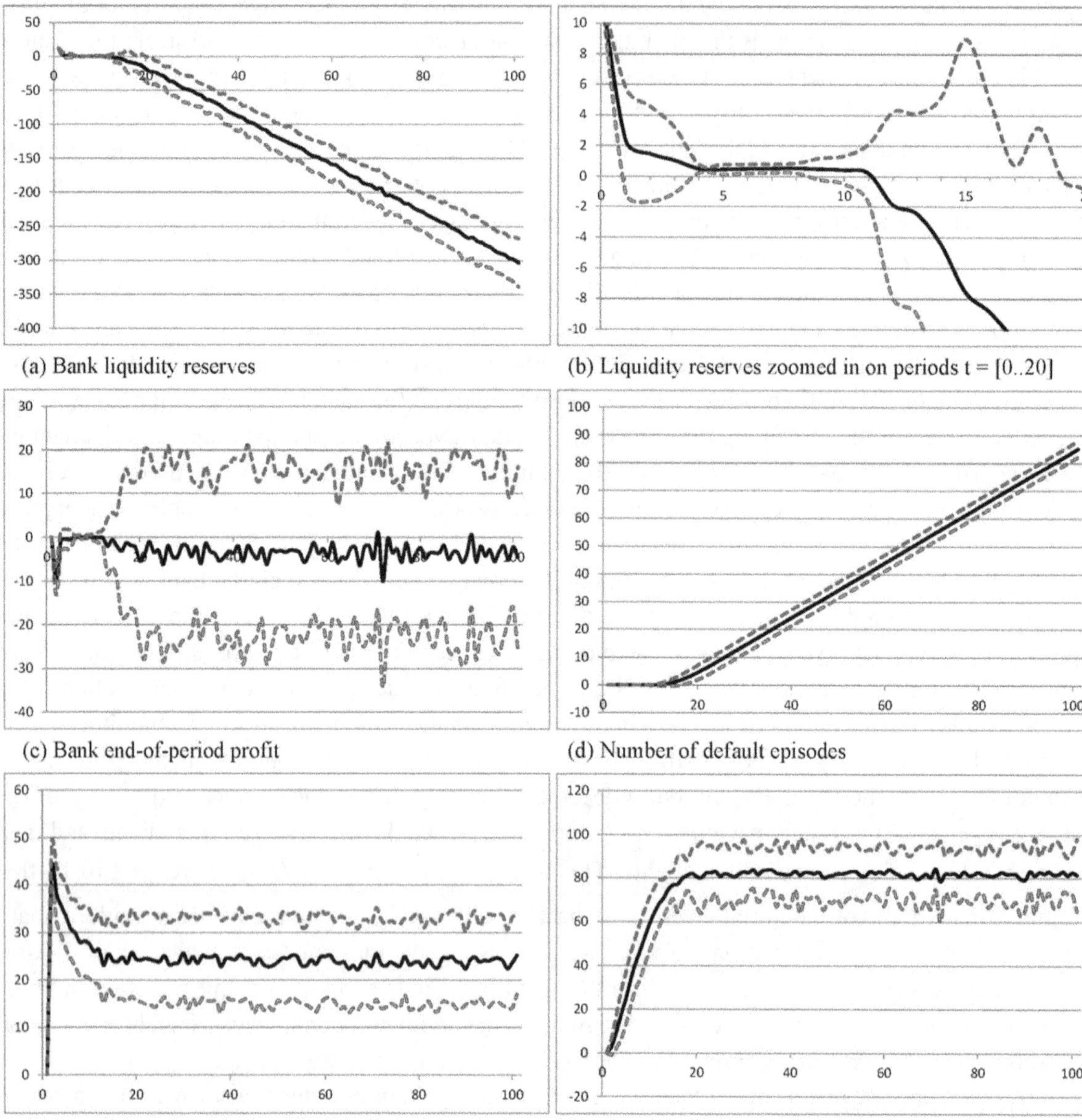

(a) Bank liquidity reserves

(b) Liquidity reserves zoomed in on periods t = [0..20]

(c) Bank end-of-period profit

(d) Number of default episodes

(e) Norm-bank discrepancy regarding clients to monitor

(f) Number of abandoned clients

time periods, after which the negative trend of the bank's financial resources continues, as in the baseline scenario with monitoring. When, as shown in point (b), we zoon into the liquidity graph to focus on what happens at the very beginning of the simulation run, we notice that although the bank's liquidity resources fall as a consequence of the high monitoring costs, they are stabilized by the fact that the bank monitors a larger number of clients and therefore reduces its client-default associated costs. We notice that the bank's liquidity reserves remain low, but positive until period 11, after which they dip irreversibly towards negative infinity.

We also notice that during the period in which the norm is effective, the deviation of indicators is minimal. We notice this both in the very low variance of the bank liquidity indicator, as well as that of the profits and bank default rate indicators. The number of default episodes remains at zero before period 12, which is consistent with the results seen in the bank liquidity indicator graph. We observe an initially higher discrepancy between the norm fixed by the regulator and the number of clients that the bank wishes to monitor on its own, but this discrepancy gradually diminishes and stabilizes, as the bank's internally determined number of clients to monitor also evens out. We notice that the number of clients to monitor decided on by the bank is not the final number of clients that it will monitor, since the regulator will impose the bank to monitor the difference between the norm's prescribed number and that decided on by the bank.

We notice that the bank does not get rid of all of its clients and stabilizes its client abandonment number at a number inferior to the maximum. This is a consequence of the bank's monitoring process which stipulates that the bank always monitors if its monitoring value condition is met. As such, the bank is ready to monitor its internally determined desired number of clients even if it faces default on the short term. This is because, due to the lack of information, the bank expects that by monitoring on the short term it will have long-term benefits in terms of general risk reduction – an expectation rendered unnecessary when the bank gains access to more information and is able to directly form expectations on a client-by-client basis (as in the case of monitoring under low informational asymmetry).

Looking at the situation in which prudential supervision is introduced alongside a regulatory norm and monitoring under low informational asymmetry, as shown in Figure 7, we notice that the stabilizing effect of the norm is much longer. Indeed, we can see in point (a) that after an initially high drop in liquidity owing to losses associated with the bank trying (in the beginning) not to abandon clients (f), the bank's financial situation is stabilized. We notice low volatility in the bank's profit, liquidity and default rate indicators up to around period 40. In this period, the bank facing increasing losses compensates by abandoning clients. Client abandonment produces two positive results: it reduces default-related costs and recovers resources for the bank. This process however is not sustainable, as by roughly period 40 the bank runs out of clients to abandon. This can be seen in point (f). In this monitoring method, the bank obtains enough information to form conclusions on a client by client basis and, thus, its monitoring method is not dependent on the monitoring value condition, but rather on the availability of bank liquidity. As we can see from point (e) by period 10, the bank no longer has enough resources to monitor its clients and the discrepancy between the norm and the number of clients willingly monitored by the bank is maximal. The number of clients effectively monitored by the bank will, however, still coincide with the norm as the bank is forced to abandon clients to meet the norm's requirements. Still, as depicted in point (d), all periods subsequent to time step 10 decrease the revenue obtained by the bank from its monitoring activities, since the bank is forced to abandon an increasingly high number of clients. Also, conditioning regulatory monitoring on available liquidity allows the bank to reduce the number of monitored clients to an extreme – to all but one clients. The finality of the enhanced monitoring method made possible by lower informational asymmetries is that it the regulator was able, through the same norm, to keep the bank running for a period roughly four times larger. This is a positive achievement, as by the time the norm's efficiency wanes away, the crisis conditions of a real (as in non-simulated) economy may dissipate.

Figure 7 presents the results of the scenario in which the regulator introduces a norm accompanied by prudential supervision under conditions of low informational asymmetry. The results are presented as the means and standard deviations of the analyzed variables for 100 simulations of the model, over 100

Figure 7. Supervision with regulatory norm under low informational asymmetry monitoring

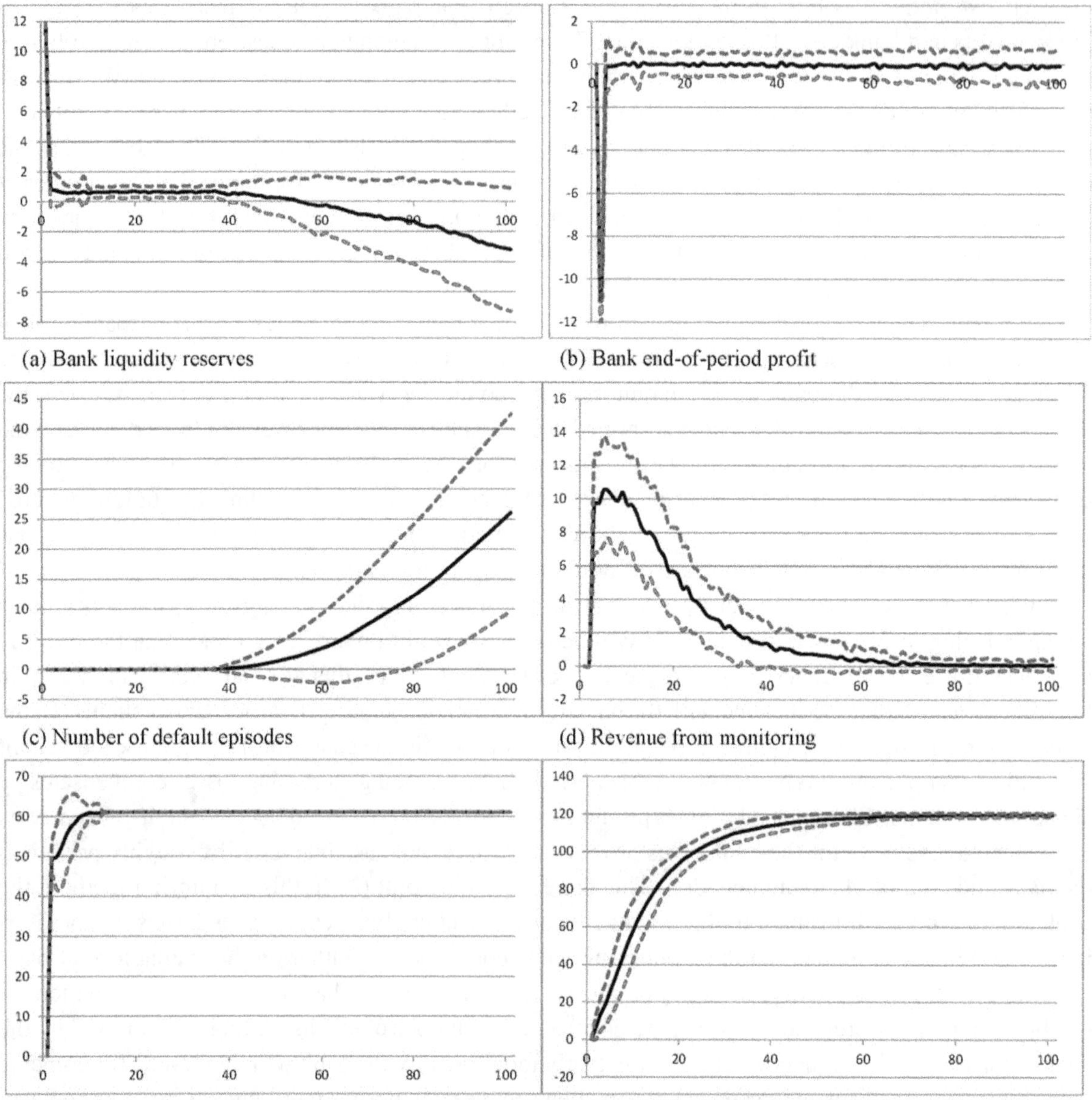

(a) Bank liquidity reserves
(b) Bank end-of-period profit
(c) Number of default episodes
(d) Revenue from monitoring
(e) Norm-bank discrepancy regarding clients to monitor
(f) Number of abandoned clients

time periods. We notice that the stabilization effect of the norm is now more long-lived, but eventually, the bank still defaults. Applying the instrument produces severe credit rationing.

As we have seen from our analysis, the norm is able to postpone the negative effects resulting from the crisis for a certain period of time. Yet this delay is only achievable by means of severe credit rationing, which is introduced as a method of last resort for the bank to use in absence of any other internal or external instruments to fulfill the norm. The duration of the postponement is dependent on the bank's internal processes and its effectiveness at detecting and eradicating risk. However, under persisting crisis conditions, the finality remains the same – the bank eventually is no longer able to compensate and defaults due to a lack of liquidity.

3.3.2. How Supervision Renders a CDS-Market Operational

We again take to the baseline scenario with monitoring and, this time, inquire as to whether market-based regulation would be more efficient at improving the bank's situation. We thus introduce a market-based CDS instrument purchasable by the bank to insure against the risk of client default. We study two scenarios: one in which the regulator simply introduces the CDS mechanism and one in which the regulator actively supervises the market and the bank's actions to help it make optimal decisions. We thereby determine whether supervision improves or hinders the functioning of the market.

The regulator creates an insurance company (which we will refer to as the CDS fund). This CDS fund emits CDS units that the bank can purchase. We model the introduction of our CDS units in a manner that is inspired by Coase's (1960) vision for the distribution of rights on the environment. We similarly create a market structure in which the bank can freely trade, only in our case it is not buying pollution rights, but it's buying insurance rights (i.e. the bank buys the right to not default). The bank decides regarding the number of CDS units that it wishes to purchase. The CDS price is determined and the bank buys the desired number of CDS units, provided that it has sufficient funds to do so. Otherwise, the bank buys as many CDS units as possible within its liquidity constraints. The bank buys CDS units ex-ante, basing its choice only on the information that it has regarding previous period clients. The bank goes to the CDS market to solicit a quantity of CDS units equal to the number of non-monitored and defaulted clients $B_{CDS.D} = C^{M \cap D}$, where $B_{CDS.D}$ is the bank's demand for CDS units and $C^{M \cap D}$ is the number of clients who were both left un-monitored in the previous period and subsequently defaulted. The bank purchases CDS units at a variable price from the CDS fund. One CDS unit insures that the bank obtains R (the risk-free interest rate) from a defaulted client. CDS units are assigned to individual clients, are non-transferable among clients and expire at the end of the period. The money accumulated in the CDS fund is used to pay the bank a total of $B_{CDS.R} = R * C^D$ in the next period (when we find out if the clients that the bank bought CDS units for have defaulted or not). Here, $B_{CDS.R}$ is the bank's reward from purchasing CDS units and C^D is the number of defaulted clients. We now give an example of how the bank's reward functions on a per client basis. If the bank did not monitor the client, then the difference between the per client reward that the bank would have obtained in the event it used the CDS instrument and that in which it didn't use the instrument is: $R - 0 = R$ which is a clear gain for the bank since $R > 0$. However, if the bank did monitor a client and also decided to ensure him (because, for instance, the bank had purchased a very large number of CDS units), then the bank's per client reward would be $R - vl > 0$ since $R > vl$. We notice that the bank still obtains positive gains, albeit smaller than in the previous case.

To implement the described regulatory mechanism, we make two assumptions. The first is that the bank knows the risk-group of all clients after they pay back the bank loan. The second is that the bank does not know the price structure of the CDS instrument. Only the regulator is aware of this price structure.

As such, we must therefore look at the price formation mechanism that exists on the CDS market. Black and Scholes (1973) and Merton (1974) set the basis for relating the pricing of instruments to the key economic determinants of financial distress and the loss given default. Further works expand upon their theoretical models to specific instruments such as CDS. Indeed, if we look at the main theoretical determinants of the CDS premium, as evidenced and verified empirically by Ericsson et al. (2005), we find that the risk-free interest rate plays an important part. In particular, three key variables are mentioned: firm leverage, volatility and the riskless interest rate. In what follows, we will propose a formula that integrates these three components into the CDS price.

First, the CDS insurance fund, in order to ensure its own sustainability establishes a minimum and a maximum price for the CDS units that it offers. The maximum price must correspond to the amount that it will have to pay in the event in which the bank only purchases one CDS unit from the insurer. Since, the damages that the CDS fund must pay to the bank in the event of the default of one client equals the risk-free interest rate, it follows that the maximum price of a CDS unit paid when the bank only purchases 1 unit equals R. The minimum price must allow the CDS fund to pay the promised amount $B_{CDS.R} = R * C^D$ to the bank in the event in which the bank purchases CDS funds to insure all of its clients (C). However, the CDS fund cannot know how many of the bank's current clients will default (since it cannot see into the future), so it must base its decisions on the default statistics of previously credited bank clients. We assume that the fund can obtain these statistics directly from the bank or by some other external means (i.e. ratings agencies, etc.). The formula allowing us to satisfy these two conditions is the following:

$$CDS.P = R - R * \frac{B_{CDS.D}}{C} + CDS.minP * \frac{B_{CDS.D}}{C} \quad (5)$$

$$CDS.minP = R * \frac{C^D}{C}, \quad (6)$$

where $CDS.P$ is the CDS price established on the market based on the bank's CDS unit demand ($B_{CDS.D}$), and $CDS.minP$ is the minimum CDS price that the fund requires from the bank and is based on the number of defaulted clients that the bank registered (C^D). We remind that R also represents the maximum CDS unit price and that C represents the maximum number of buyable CDS units, since the bank will never buy more CDS units than it has clients (which derives from the aforementioned condition that the CDS units expire).

The proposed formula conforms to the literature, as it contains:

- The risk-free interest rate,
- The risk level of firms (this uses C^D to encompass the "volatility" and "firm leverage" indicators that are not directly present in our model, but are prescribed by Ericsson et al. (2009)).

The bank, however, is not aware of this formula, nor is it able to integrate it into its demanded quantity of CDS units announcement decision. This means that the bank, inevitably reaches sub-optimal decisions when it comes to the number of desired CDS units to announce. As a consequence, the CDS price that the bank has to pay is oftentimes larger than the one it would actually have to pay in the event in which it could integrate the price-structure in its decision-making processes. Regulatory supervision should help the bank to overcome this impediment as the supervisor monitors the bank's decision and informs it of the optimal CDS unit quantity that the bank should announce on the market.

Figure 8 shows the per CDS unit purchase price for varying amounts of CDS unit demand on the bank's behalf, on the left axis. We notice that this is a linearly decreasing amount which starts off at the maximal value of $R = 1.05$, as per our model calibration, and descends up until the minimal price point which depends on the number of defaulted clients that the bank was previously faced with (in this exemplifying graph, the minimal CDS unit price is slightly less than 0.2). The graph also shows us the total cost of purchasing the desired amount of CDS units on the right axis. As we can see, this sum increases until a certain point, after which it begins to decrease as the decreasing price allows for savings on the bank's behalf. We, thus, notice that (in this exemplifying graph) any quantity of CDS units demanded by the bank in the interval $B_{CDS.D} \in [23;121)$ is suboptimal since if the bank demands any quantity of CDS units in this interval, due to the price that the CDS fund will fixate, the bank will end up paying more for the desired amount of CDS units than it would pay if it purchased the maximum amount of CDS units purchasable (equal, as per our model specification to $C = N = 121$), which is the optimal CDS demand amount ($B^*_{CDS.D}$) for this interval. We notice that if the bank were to, say, wish to purchase 70 CDS units, then it would end up paying about 37.5, whereas if it purchased 121 CDS units, it would only pay 21. At the same time, all CDS demand choices in the interval $B_{CDS.D} \in [0;23)$ are optimal because the bank would pay less than the total cost for C CDS units.

As we can see, the role of the supervisor is to guide the bank's CDS demand announcement to ensure the optimality of its CDS purchasing decision. The bank should benefit, and the CDS fund should be able to maintain its sustainability (at least, as is the case for most CDS issuing entities, for a while).

Figure 8 shows the price structure of the CDS instrument. It reflects the declining per unit cost of the CDS instrument when the purchased quantity increases. It also shows the total cost for any given solicited quantity of CDS units.

As such, if supervision is introduced to complement the CDS mechanism, the regulator helps the bank to make better CDS buying decisions, by sharing with the bank its knowledge of the CDS price structure. The regulator integrates into the scheme described by Figure 9. We notice that when supervision is introduced, three steps are added in the functioning of the CDS market. Specifically, a feedback

Figure 8. Number of CDS units requested by the bank and total purchase cost

Note: On the x-axis we have the number of clients for whom the bank purchases CDS units; on the left-y-axis we have the price for one CDS unit determined by the CDS fund according to its formula; on the right-y-axis we have the total cost in monetary units for purchasing the respective quantity of CDS units.

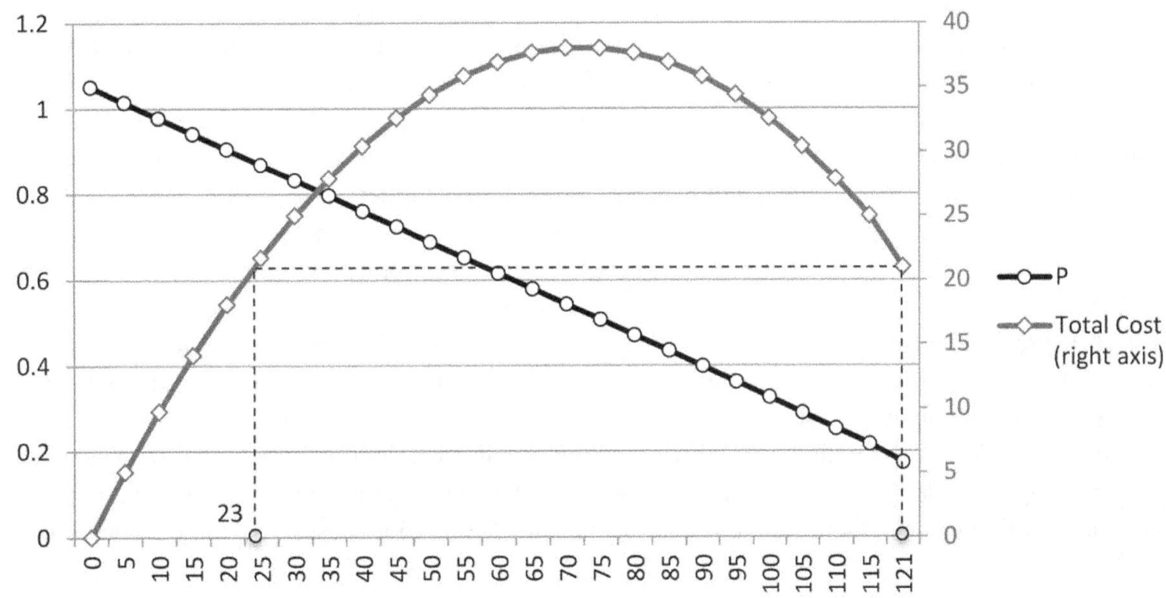

Figure 9. Integrating supervision into the regulatory CDS mechanism

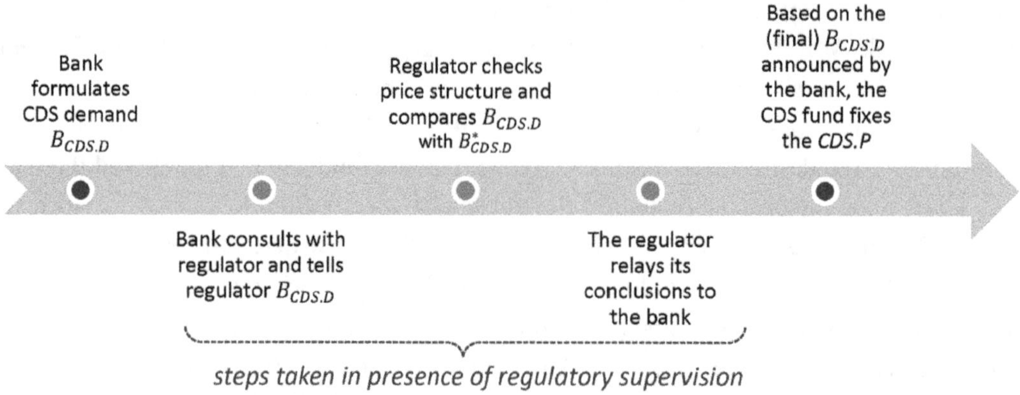

process between the bank and supervisor is inserted which allows the supervisor to inform the bank of the optimal CDS demand for the bank.

Figure 9 explains how supervision is integrated into the model and explains the steps that the regulator takes to ensure that the bank makes the optimal choice regarding the quantity of CDS units to purchase.

Let us now turn our attention to what happens in practice when we apply this new form of regulatory intervention to the baseline scenario with monitoring. We first look at the situation with bank monitoring under high informational asymmetry. In this case, shown in Figure 10, we notice that the monitoring inefficiency characteristic of the difficult to gauge business environment hinders the bank's ability to hedge against risk both when the regulator only introduces a CDS mechanism without supervision, as well as when the added supervisory role is assumed by the regulator. The main reason for this outcome is the high costs of monitoring coupled with the inefficiency of the bank's ability to target risky clients. In absence of supervision, the demand for CDS units expressed by the bank on the CDS market leads to the establishment of a high price equilibrium. This, in turn, rapidly pushes the bank's liquidity reserves into negative territory which no longer allows the bank to participate on the CDS market, thereby rendering the regulatory instrument inactive as the quantity of CDS units purchased by the bank drops to zero, as seen in Figure 10 point (c). A consequence of this is the rapid fall in liquidity (a), profit values stabilizing at negative values (around -3) and a rapidly increasing number of bank defaults (b). As for the CDS fund, since the bank is no longer able to purchase CDS units, the CDS fund's resources freeze. They remain at a positive number since the fund has not yet operated for a sufficiently long time and so it has principally collected resources and thus far hasn't distributed them.

If supervision is introduced, the regulator now monitors the situation on the market and intervenes to guide the bank's CDS demand decision. This allows for a lower price equilibrium to emerge on the CDS market (c-right). This extends the period in which CDS units continue to be purchased by the bank (d-right) since it removes some of the negative pressure on the bank's liquidity reserves. This has for effect a dampening of the rapidity in the bank's liquidity reserve decline (a-right), the stabilization of profits at an initially higher but still negative level, which further declines in time, and an increase in the volatility of the default rate indicator (b-right) signaling that under certain client risk level configurations the bank may avoid default for at least 10 periods. Since the CDS fund is forced to cover the high costs associated with the bank clients' defaults and the bank's CDS unit purchases gradually decline after a

Figure 10. CDS market with (right) and without (left) supervision under high asymmetry monitoring

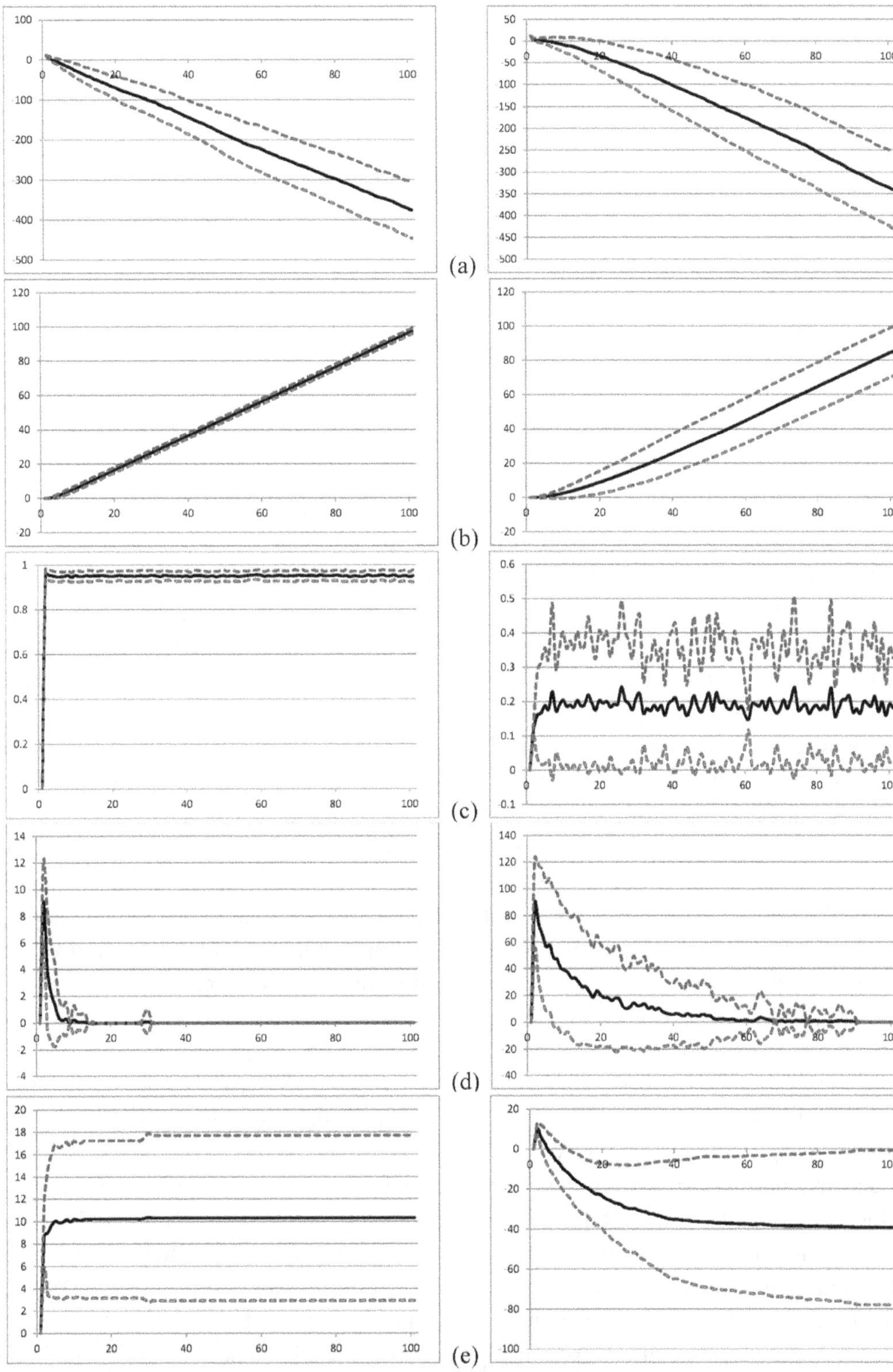

(a) Bank liquidity, (b) Nr. default episodes, (c) CDS.P, (d) CDS units purchased, (e) CDS Fund cash

significantly higher purchase volume (because of liquidity constraints on the bank's side), the CDS fund finds that it does not sell enough insurance units to be able to reimburse the bank for its clients' defaults.

As such, the fund's operations become unsustainable as the reimbursements it faces surpass its revenues. Therefore, under this scenario, the regulator would be faced with the dilemma of saving or letting the fund default very quickly after its introduction.

It is noteworthy to remark that in this monitoring context, the regulator is unable to improve the situation vis-à-vis the baseline scenario regardless of whether supervision is implemented or not. Supervision does help to attenuate the bank's losses, but fails to bring the bank back to profitability.

The next step in our analysis is to investigate the situation in which the regulator introduces a CDS market in presence and absence of supervision when the bank's access to client-related information is improved so that the bank can form anticipations regarding the quality of the clients it will have in the following period. It is expected that the better risk management that the bank is endowed with should lead to an improvement in the bank's situation.

Figure 10 presents the results of the scenario in which the regulator introduces a CDS market under conditions of high informational asymmetry. The results are presented as the means and standard deviations of the analyzed variables for 100 simulations of the model, over 100 time periods. We notice the positive effect that the presence of supervision produces on the bank's resilience, but conclude that high informational asymmetries prevent the bank from operating profitably.

Figure 11 presents the results of the scenario in which the regulator introduces a CDS market under conditions of low informational asymmetry. The results are presented as the means and standard deviations of the analyzed variables for 100 simulations of the model, over 100 time periods. We notice the positive effect that the presence of supervision produces on the bank's resilience, as the bank's profit becomes positive and potentiates profitable bank operations.

We notice that, now, even under lack of supervision, the bank fares better than in the baseline scenario, as both profits and liquidity are higher. Figure 11, point (a) confirms this. Because of the lack of supervision, as before, the price of a CDS unit stabilizes at a high level and the number of CDS units effectively purchased is also low (d). However, this time, it is rather rare for the purchase of CDS units to completely stop thereby rendering the CDS mechanism inactive. Furthermore, now, under the best of conditions, the bank's default is postponed until around period 20 (bottom dashed line in point (b)). Notice that this result obtained in the absence of supervision is a marked improvement over the result obtained when supervision was implemented but in an environment of high asymmetry monitoring. Finally, because there is no supervision to help the bank to integrate the price structure, the CDS fund takes advantage of the situation to improve its financial standing and accumulate resources. Indeed, whereas the bank's default is postponed more than in previous CDS market scenarios, it would seem that the only absolutely safe institution in this economy is the insurance agency (the CDS fund).

When supervision is introduced however, the tables are turned on the CDS fund. Since, the bank's CDS unit demand announcement is influenced by the supervisor which now informs it of the optimal quantity, the price of CDS units stabilizes at a lower point (point (c-right). Now, no longer able to demand exorbitant prices for the CDS instrument it sells because of the regulator's supervision of the market, the fund must content itself with lower revenues. This translates into the lower CDS Fund cash variable depicted in point (e-right). However, we notice that despite the lower values, the fund remains sustainable for a relatively long time – specifically, for approximately 60 periods of our simulation run. We might ask ourselves why this is the case when in the presence of supervision with high asymmetry monitoring, the CDS fund defaulted miserably within five turns of the start of its operations. In fact

Figure 11. CDS market with (right) and without (left) supervision under low asymmetry monitoring

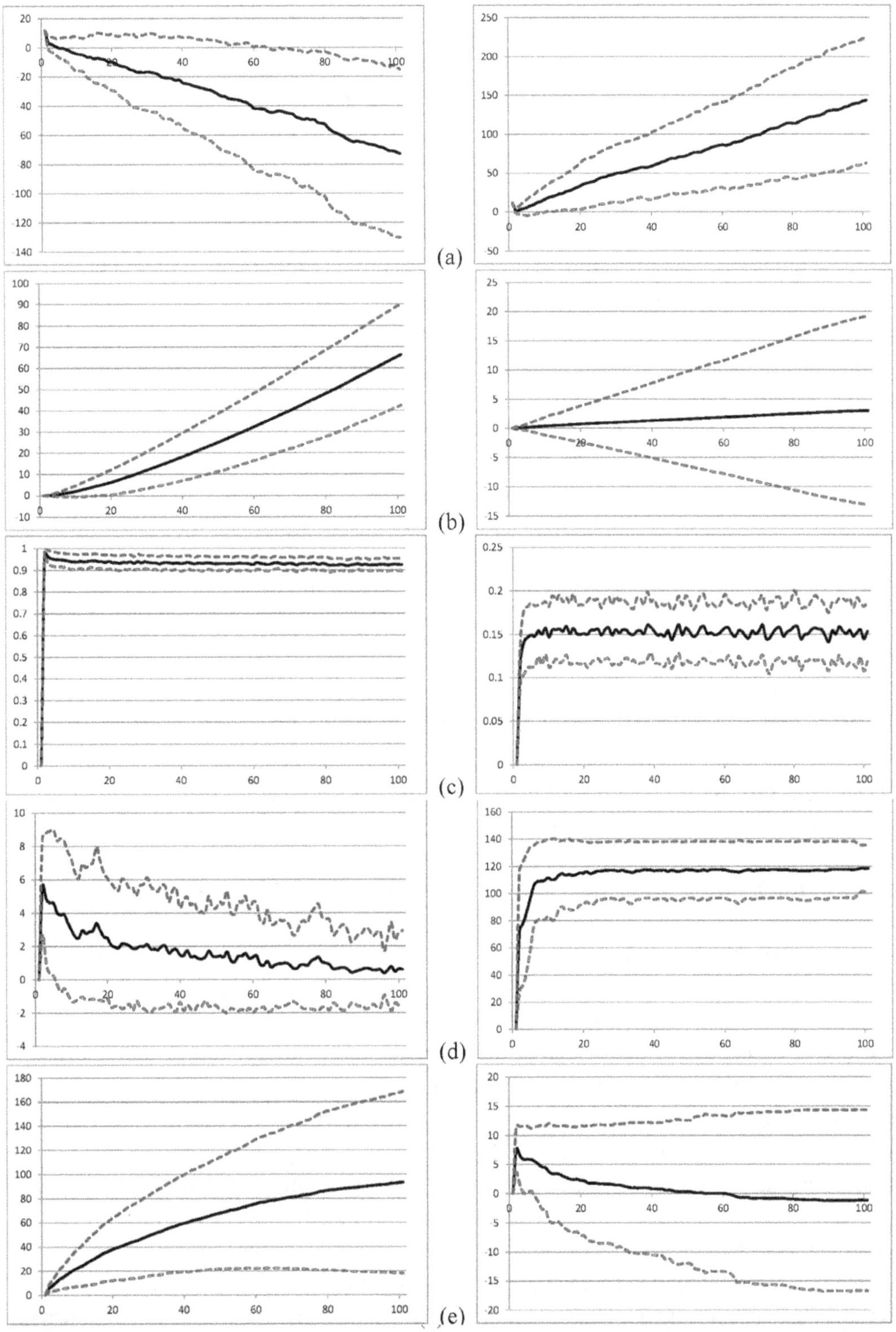

(a) Bank liquidity, (b) Nr. default episodes, (c) CDS.P, (d) CDS units purchased, (e) CDS Fund cash

what changed is that because of the lower liquidity constraints that the bank faces under low asymmetry monitoring, it is able to purchase the entirety of the announced CDS demand quantity (whereas before it was limited by its lack of liquidity). As such, the bank ends up purchasing a very high number of CDS units (d-right). And since CDS unit purchases constitute the revenue of the CDS fund, the insurer is now able to fulfill its obligations for a much longer time. Still, eventually, because of the bank's client defaults, the CDS fund runs out of resources and may need to be saved, or replaced with a new insurance fund. As expected, in this scenario, the bank's liquidity reserves are now largely positive (a-right) and the number of bank default episodes is significantly reduced (b-right). Now, the bank will default only rarely. Still there is significant volatility in the number of default episodes, as the bank is still dependent on the initial configuration in terms of client risk levels. Multiple periods characterized by high upper-risk client density and high client default rates may still cause the bank to default. Regardless of singular incidents, the situation is significantly improved when compared to the baseline scenario. Furthermore, this is the first time that we are able to ensure sustainable (and profitable) bank operations under persistent crisis conditions.

As we have seen, the introduction of a CDS market is not enough to stabilize the financial situation of a bank facing persistent crisis conditions. Not only does is mechanism unable to save bank, but the insurance fund also risks either termination by abandonment or default. The key towards ensuring the sustainability of the bank's operations is to concurrently ensure supervision of the introduced instrument's market, as well as to perform all possible actions towards reducing the informational asymmetry present in the economy. If such steps are taken, then the bank will operate at a profit on the long-term. This is an improvement not only over the baseline scenario, but also over the regulatory norm which manages to stabilize the bank for a shorter time-span, albeit with lesser fluctuations, but, on the other hand, with very severe credit rationing and close to zero profits for the entirety of the duration of the stability period of bank operations. We therefore conclude that a CDS market without supervision will always produce worse results than a regulatory norm. With supervision also in the mix, the CDS market stands a chance of producing better results than the norm, provided that the bank has access to sufficient information allowing it to form anticipations regarding the risk levels of its future clients.

3.3.3. Supervision with Taxation: Can a Bail-In Mechanism Save the Bank?

Our last supervisory set-up includes a tax in the form of a bail-in mechanism. This means that it is those who benefit from the bank's activities that must contribute towards saving the bank. In our model it is the bank's clients (or the firms) who reap the rewards of the bank's operations. As such, the regulator introduces a tax that they must bear. For our tax to be fair, however, the regulator will have to keep in mind two key elements that derive from the bail-in mechanism formulation. The first regards the category of beneficiaries that must be taxed – in our case it is very straightforward that clients of all risk groups who have benefitted from the tax must contribute. And the second is slightly more subtle in that only those clients who were successful must be taxed, thereby excluding from our taxation the defaulted clients. We may ask ourselves why some of the clients should be excluded from the tax. Indeed, why it is those clients who will have led to the crisis that must escape from repairing the damages? The simple answer to this is that we are implementing a punctual tax that only applies in the event of difficulties faced by the bank. As such, the supervisor who will be monitoring the bank's and the firm's situation has no way of knowing which clients will default or even if a tax will be necessary in the given time period. Therefore, since we are not implementing a permanent tax that is collected regardless of the bank's financial state, the supervisor collects the tax from firms ex-post, after the bank will have financed the clients and only when the bank's default will have become imminent. Another consequence of this implementation of the tax is the necessity of supervision of the bank's financial situation by the regulator. In the absence of supervision, the regulator would not be able to coordinate the tax level with the bank's deficit. Furthermore, since the regulator is unable to raise money from defaulted firms, only successful clients can contribute in a bail-in mechanism. This is similar to the European Commission's and ECB's proposals for the Cyprus bail-in scheme whereby only "successful" clients having deposit accounts of more than 100000€ were forced to contribute towards saving the bank. In order to avoid defaulting successful firms, we introduce the bail-in mechanism as a tax on firm profits (and not revenues). The regulator's taxation is dependent on the financial situation of the bank. As such, if the supervisor detects that the bank is in a situation of negative liquidity, immediate action is taken. A tax corresponding to the amount needed to save the bank is raised. The tax is distributed proportionately to all clients' profits. This means that clients from all risk groups have to dedicate the same percentage of their profits towards saving the bank. The regulator calculates which percentage of profits is to be contributed towards paying the tax by the process depicted in Figure 12. As we can see, the loop which will determine the tax contains an increment size (A) which will be responsible for the accuracy of the tax value. An increment value of A = 0.05 means that the regulator would jump from tax size 0% to 5% to 10%, etc. If the bank were to need, for instance a tax of 12% of firm profits to be saved, then the regulator would collect 15% and the remaining 3% would go towards establishing (or replenishing) the reserve fund.

Figure 12 presents the steps followed by the regulator in the bail-in scenario.

Figure 12. Bail-in mechanism tax determination process

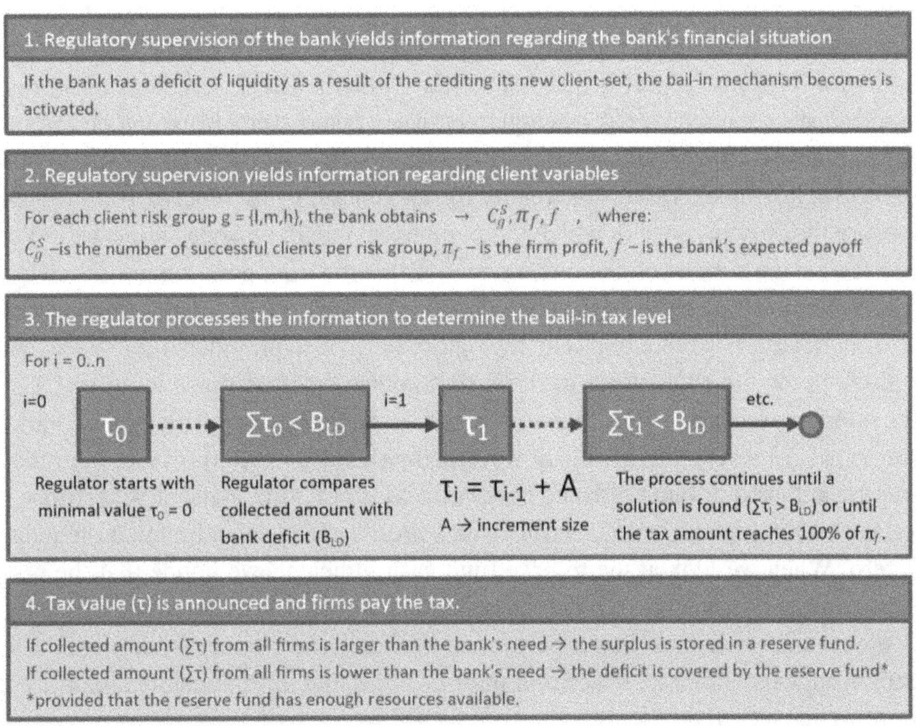

Larger values of A allow for larger reserve fund accumulations, but also more rapid simulation run times. On the contrary, lower values of A allow for more precise taxation, but slow down the accrual of funds in the regulator's reserve.

For simulation purposes we will maintain a relatively large value of A = 0.05 which allows the reserve fund to play a role in saving the bank in the event of a 100% tax on firm profits not being enough to replenish the bank's liquidity reserves.

Figure 13 presents the results of the scenario in which the regulator introduces a bail-in mechanism under conditions of high informational asymmetry. The results are presented as the means and standard deviations of the analyzed variables for 100 simulations of the model, over 100 time periods. We notice the positive liquidity levels maintained by the bank even under the harsh conditions of high asymmetries. Also, we notice the decline in the number of default episodes.

Now that we are aware of the functioning of the bail-in mechanism, we can investigate its effects on the bank's financial standing and compare the results with the other supervisory implementations that we have discussed. At the same time, it is also interesting to investigate what will transpire as a result of the prudential instrument with the firms' profits. We would like to know whether saving the bank can be achieved with moderate levels of taxation or if we must jeopardize the welfare of the firms to save the bank. This, naturally, raises the issue of striking a balance between keeping the productive sector sheltered from regulatory interventionism in the form of over-taxation and ensuring the continuity of the banking sector's activities.

In the event in which the bail-in mechanism is introduced in a context of great difficulties for the bank to obtain information about its future clients, the high costs and monitoring inefficiency lead to, on average, a higher liquidity deficit than the regulator can compensate for via the bail-in mechanism, point (d) in Figure 13. Indeed, even with a tax of 100% of the firm's total profits, the regulator is at times incapable of saving the bank. Unfortunately, due to our representation of averages and standard deviations, we cannot remark the cases in which the tax constitutes 100% of firm profits. This is the case because it is very rare that for any given time period (t) all 100 of our model repetitions should produce the same result of a 100% tax on profits decided by the regulator. There is, in fact, a very great volatility of the regulatory instrument which risks swinging between 0 and 100% from one period to the next, as depicted by the upper and lower bounds of the possible interval at one standard deviation from the mean. Indeed graph (e) slightly misrepresents the reality by not including the peaks of 100% which, under this configuration, are the only instance in which the number of default episodes indicator (c) can increase. Still, when we look at the number of defaults, we realize that the bank now defaults much less often than in the previous scenarios. Indeed, only the CDS market with supervision could produce better long-run results in terms of default risk reduction. The regulatory norm also provided highly efficient short-term default risk relief, but in the end faltered as the final number of default episodes after 100 time periods surpassed the number produced by the taxation method. The generally positive bank liquidity reserves shown in point (a) also attest to this. We do, however, remark that the liquidity reserves initially increase, but afterwards are attracted towards zero and have good odds of falling in negative territory, as the lower bound is well below zero. When looking at the bank's profits (b), we also find that the indicator fluctuates around zero. When we look at the reserve fund cash indicator, we notice that the reserve fund is continually expanding (it is on a slowly increasing trend). We would expect to see this if the regulatory instrument were continuously used. Since, because of the bank's heightened instability, this is indeed the case, we confirm our expectations. However, it must be notes that this indicator cannot rise indefinitely, as there is only so much firm profit to tax.

Figure 13. Supervision with bail-in mechanism in high asymmetry environment

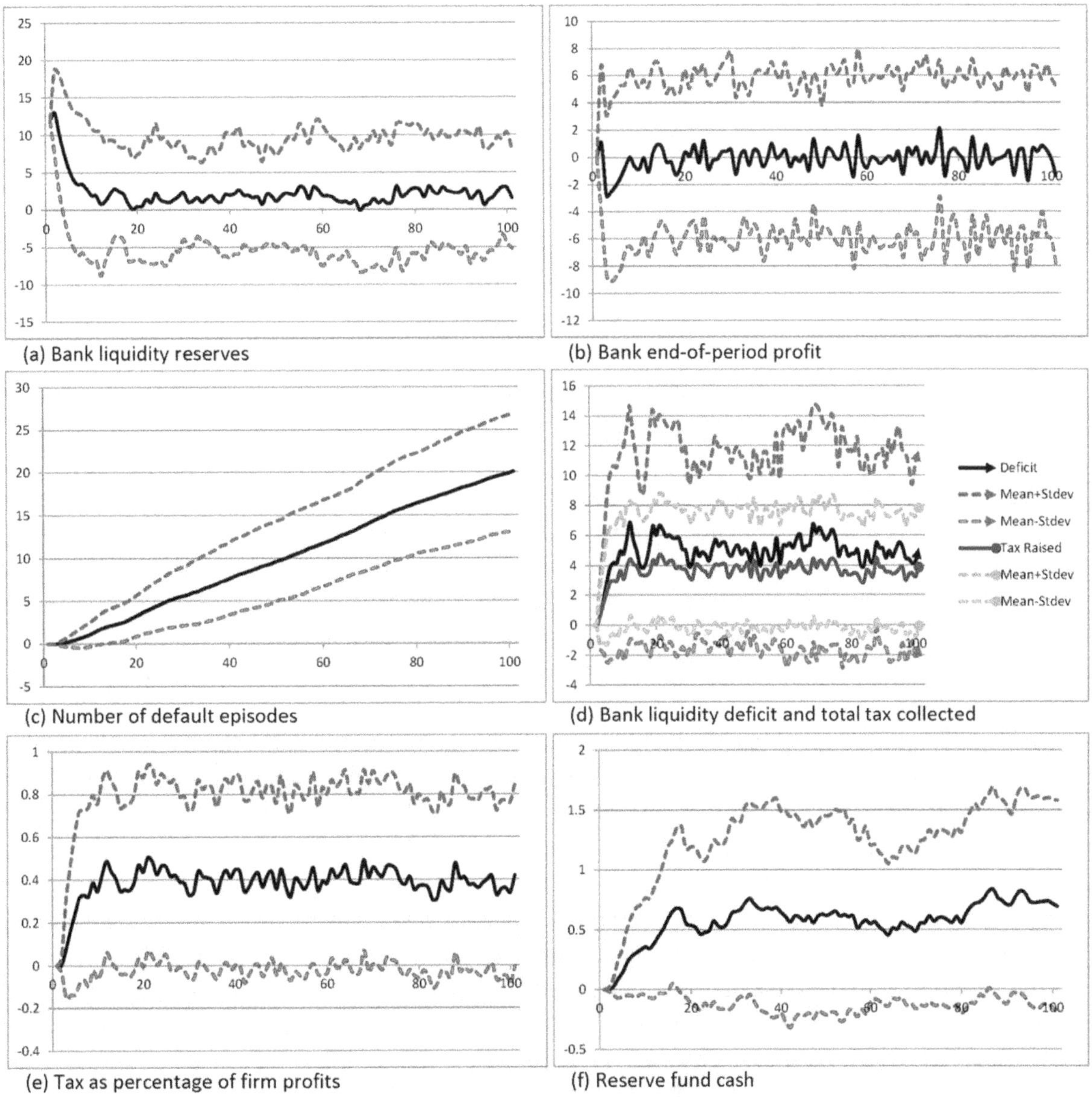

We now switch to the bail-in mechanism introduced in an environment of low informational asymmetry, whereby the bank can extract more information about its clients, thereby enhancing its monitoring method. In this instance, the higher monitoring efficiency, as before leads to lower scarce resources being wasted and therefore reduces the bank's overall expenses. This means that crisis control on the supervisor's behalf becomes a lot more manageable. As we can see from Figure 14, point (d), it is now the case that the bank's deficit is almost always identically matched by the regulator's instrument, as sufficient resources can be collected via the tax. We also notice that the bank's deficit tends to have a higher volatility than that of the instrument which is a welcome finding. In the previous bail-in mechanism scenario, we noticed that the regulatory instrument manifested very high volatility and would therefore be proscribed if the prudential authority coincided with the Central Bank and promoted a concurrent stability objective. In this case, as evidenced by both point (d) and (e), we observe much lower volatility in the prudential tool, and indeed, we see periods in which volatility is reduced to zero, as the instrument is at very low percentage values or is left completely unused. We notice a more intense usage at the beginning of the simulation period, as the bank faces the severe liquidity shortage that is characteristic of the crisis environment. However, as the supervisor manages to stabilize the bank's situation, the bank is able to accumulate resources and, eventually, no longer necessitates the regulator's intervention. In order to confirm this, we extend the model simulation period to 1000 and look at the instrument's usage levels. We notice that by period 200, the instrument ceases to be used which denotes that the bank has managed to push through the crisis and can now continue to operate individually, without external help, even under persistent crisis conditions. Indeed, the riskiness of the new clients that the bank will be facing will not have changed, but, due to the increasing reserves, the bank's ability to withstand client default related shocks will have increased pat the point at which the bank no longer faces any risk of failure. To confirm this, we also find, in point (g), that the bank's liquidity deficit will have permanently gone down to zero by period 200.

Figure 14 presents the results of the scenario in which the regulator introduces a bail-in mechanism under conditions of low informational asymmetry. The results are presented as the means and standard deviations of the analyzed variables for 100 simulations of the model, over 100 time periods. We notice the positive profits, liquidity and close to null default rate of the bank. Furthermore, when we run this scenario over 1000 time periods, we notice that given the improvement in the bank's financial situation, regulatory intervention becomes completely unnecessary after around 200 time periods, even under persistent crisis conditions.

Finally, we remark that the bank's liquidity reserves (a) are on an increasing trend and stay positive throughout the simulation run. The number of default episodes (c) is less than 0.4 which is the lowest value seen so far and which means that, on average, the bank will default 0.4 times over the simulation period. This is the best result so far, with the exception of the low monitoring cost baseline scenario which is deemed unlikely by the literature. As for the reserve fund (f), it increases up to a point after which a small correction occurs after period 60 when the last significant incidence of liquidity deficits occurs. Afterwards, the fund remains largely stable, as the usage of the bail-in mechanism declines.

We, therefore, have seen that under conditions of costly monitoring, the bail-in mechanism, implemented as a tax on bank clients, is the strongest possible tool. It manages to stabilize the bank's situation and significantly reduce the number of bank defaults in an environment where informational asymmetries are predominant. The cost, however, is felt in terms of two major shortcomings of this method: the high tax levels that firms must incur (sometimes having to cede the entirety of their profits in order to save the bank), as well as the very high volatility of the prudential instrument. If it is possible to increase the bank's access to information by means of policies conductive of market transparency, then it is the bail-in mechanism not only stabilizes, but also ensures long-term bank operation sustainability at positive profits and increasing liquidity reserves. The more fortunate economic climate diminishes the negative effects of the regulatory instrument by reducing its fluctuations, as well as by significantly lessening the burden placed on the production sector.

Figure 14. Supervision with bail-in mechanism in low asymmetry environment

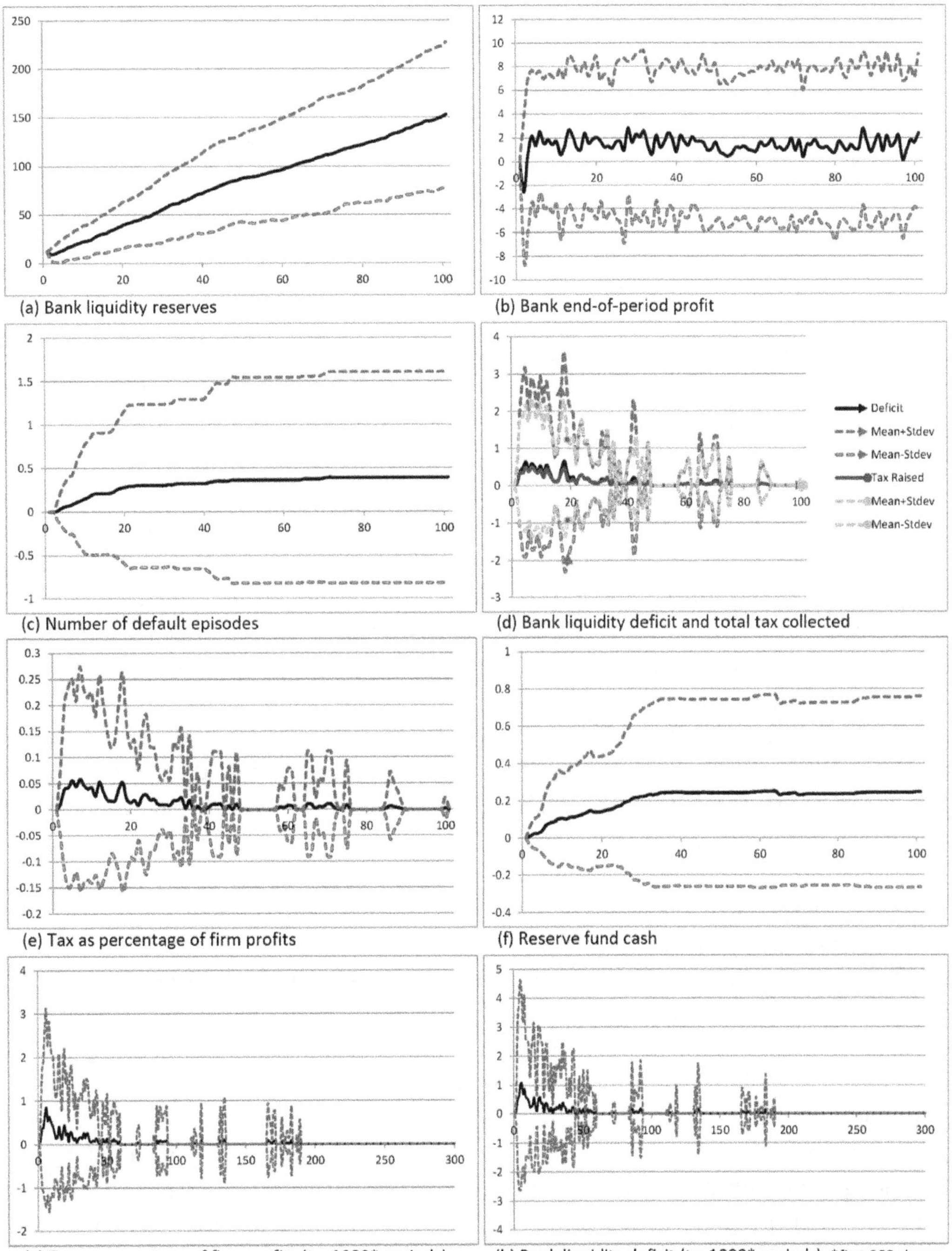

(a) Bank liquidity reserves

(b) Bank end-of-period profit

(c) Number of default episodes

(d) Bank liquidity deficit and total tax collected

(e) Tax as percentage of firm profits

(f) Reserve fund cash

(g) Tax as percentage of firm profits (t = 1000* periods)

(h) Bank liquidity deficit (t = 1000* periods) *first 300 shown

4. CONCLUSION

In this chapter, we have studied the effectiveness of prudential regulation in terms of supervision coupled with three different regulatory tools: a norm, a CDS insurance market and a bail-in mechanism taking the form of a tax on bank clients. Taking as given the both theoretically stipulated, as well as empirically verified hypothesis of costly monitoring, we placed the bank in an environment of high informational asymmetry where its client monitoring abilities are severely hindered by its inability to obtain sufficient information about its clients. We then relaxed this constraint to allow for more market transparency and saw that the bank generally fared better, as the increased availability of client information allowed it to engage in more efficient monitoring activities. Still, we noticed that without regulatory intervention, the bank was eventually drawn into a bankruptcy situation at some point of our simulation run. As such, in order to ensure the bank's sustainability, we resorted to utilizing prudential instruments coupled with supervision. We started with a norm that imposed the bank to monitor a fixed proportion of its clients. The initial simulation results were promising, as the bank's financial situation was stabilized, but we noticed increasing credit rationing throughout the period of stability. Indeed, at the point at which credit rationing reached critical levels, the bank finally faltered and its liquidity reserves turned negative with a long-term trend towards negative infinity. This meant that saving the bank was now out of the question. The only difference that the informational asymmetry environment made was that of the length of the default postponement, with lower asymmetry levels allowing the bank to operate for a longer period of time under conditions of almost-zero, but positive profitability. We then turned to a more advanced market-based instrument – a CDS fund. In this scenario, the regulator introduced a supplementary agency, a CDS fund, which allowed the bank to purchase CDS to insure against the risk of its clients' default. Introduced without supervision, the CDS market would crash leaving behind not only a defaulted bank, but also a failed CDS-emitting agency. When the regulator, however, decided to concurrently become involved in supervising the market by calculating both the amount of resources required for the CDS-fund to survive, as well as the quantity of CDS units needed by the bank in order to avoid failure, we noticed a stabilization of the CDS market. When information was scarce, the CDS fund failed to compensate for the bank's monitoring inefficiencies, which lead to the survival of only the fund. When access to information was facilitated, the bank was able to make good use of the extra instrument available for it to efficiently manage its client risk levels. Indeed, in an environment of transparency, the CDS market produced better results than the regulatory norm. Finally, we introduced a tax-based instrument in the form of a bail-in mechanism that saw the regulator taxing the bank's clients in the event of difficulties encountered by their creditor. Here, we noticed the strength of taxation as the instrument was both able to handle environments devoid of information, and shone when asymmetries were rooted-out of the economy. Indeed, in the latter case, the taxation instrument proved that it was able to protect the bank sufficiently long enough for the financial institution to be able to stand on its own in an environment of persistent crisis. We noticed that after a lengthy period of intervention, the bank was eventually able to operate without external intervention and returned to long-term profitable activity. All in all, we have seen instruments with a very good short term effect, but with nefarious consequences on credit rationing, as well as efficient market instruments dependent, however, on particular set-ups and economic conditions. However, our results suggest that the tax remains a very powerful instrument that the regulator can use to reach a desired outcome. Furthermore, by means of a bail-in mechanism, it is those who benefit from the bank's activities that contribute towards saving the institution, and not the tax-payer. Not without its own faults, however, the tax requires fluctuations in the regulatory instrument, as the prudential authority must constantly adjust the instrument to the ever changing financial landscape. Also, the bail-in part of the mechanism raises the question of whether the regulator does well to sacrifice the profitability of the productive sector in order to save the financial institution, in particular, when it is the productive sector who is the beneficiary.

REFERENCES

Agenor, P., & da Silva, L. (2011). *Macroprudential Regulation and the Monetary Transmission Mechanism*. Working Papers Series 254. Central Bank of Brazil, Research Department.

Allen, F., Carletti, E., & Gale, D. (2009). Interbank market liquidity and central bank intervention. *Journal of Monetary Economics*, *56*(5), 639–652. doi:10.1016/j.jmoneco.2009.04.003

Angkinand, A., & Wihlborg, C. (2005). *Deposit insurance coverage, credibility of non-insurance and banking crisis*. Center for Law, Economics and Financial Institutions at CBS (LEFIC), Copenhagen Business School, Working Paper, (2005-010).

Barnett, K., & Harder, S. (2014). *Remedies in Australian Private Law*. Cambridge University Press.

Bassett, W. F., Lee, S. J., & Spiller, T. W. (2012). *Estimating changes in supervisory standards and their economic effects*. Federal Reserve Board, Finance and Economics Discussion Series (FEDS).

Baxter, N. D. (1967). Leverage, risk of ruin and the cost of capital. *The Journal of Finance*, *22*(3), 395–403.

Benigno, G., Chen, H., Otrok, C., Rebucci, A., & Young, E. (2012). Financial crises and macro-prudential policies. *Journal of International Economics*, *89*(2), 453–470. doi:10.1016/j.jinteco.2012.06.002

Black, F., & Scholes, M. (1973, May - June). The pricing of options and corporate liabilities. *Journal of Political Economy*, *81*(3), 637–654. doi:10.1086/260062

Booth, J. R. (1992). Contract costs, bank loans, and the cross-monitoring hypothesis. *Journal of Financial Economics*, *31*(1), 25–41. doi:10.1016/0304-405X(92)90010-U

Cashin, P. A., & Duttagupta, R. (2008). *The anatomy of banking crises*. IMF Working Papers.

Coase, R. H. (1960). The problem of social cost. *The Journal of Law & Economics*, *3*, 1–43. doi:10.1086/466560

de Walque, G., Pierrard, O., & Rouabah, A. (2010). Financial (In)Stability, Supervision and Liquidity Injections: A Dynamic General Equilibrium Approach. *Revue Economique et Sociale*, *120*(549), 1234–1261.

Delis, M. D., & Staikouras, P. K. (2011). Supervisory Effectiveness and Bank Risk. *Review of Finance*, *15*(3), 511–543. doi:10.1093/rof/rfq035

Deloitte. (2014). *2014 global survey on reputation risk*. Deloitte Touche Tohmatsu.

Diamond, D. W. (1984). Financial intermediation and delegated monitoring. *The Review of Economic Studies*, *51*(3), 393–414. doi:10.2307/2297430

Dickson, J., & Einstein, A. (2010). On measures for illustrating credit risk assessments: The case of heat maps, risk matrices and cubes. *IFC Bulletin*, *25*, 365.

Ericsson, J., Jacobs, K., & Oviedo, R. (2009). The determinants of credit default swap premia. *Journal of Financial and Quantitative Analysis*, *44*(01), 109–132. doi:10.1017/S0022109009090061

Ewing, J. (2015, March). A Fragile Recovery. As Cyprus Recovers From Banking Crisis, Deep Scars Remain. *New York Times*, pp. B2, B7.

Experian. (2014). Credit Risk Management For Small Businesses. *Business Credit Risk.*

Freixas, X., Martin, A., & Skeie, D. (2011). Bank liquidity, interbank markets, and monetary policy. *Review of Financial Studies*, *24*(8), 2656–2692. doi:10.1093/rfs/hhr018

Gertler, M., & Kiyotaki, N. (2010). *Financial Crises, Bank Risk Exposure and Government Financial Policy*. Princeton University Press.

Gillespie, B., Hackwood, J., & Mihos, C. (2010). *Managing credit risk for global commodity producers.* PricewaterhouseCoopers.

Gopalan, R., Nanda, V., & Yerramilli, V. (2011). Does poor performance damage the reputation of financial intermediaries? Evidence from the loan syndication market. *The Journal of Finance*, *66*(6), 2083–2120. doi:10.1111/j.1540-6261.2011.01692.x

Gumbel, P. (2013, March 25). Cyprus Rescue: The Destruction of a Tax Haven. *Time*.

Hardy, D. C., & Nieto, M. J. (2008). *Cross-Border Coordination of Prudential Supervision and Deposit Guarantees*. IMF Working Paper WP/08/283.

Infosys. (2012). *Needed, A Holistic Approach to Reputation Risk Management in Banks*. Building Tomorrow's Enterprise.

Lin, H. & Paravisini, D. (2011). *What's bank reputation worth? The effect of fraud on financial contracts and investment.* The Effect of Fraud on Financial Contracts and Investment.

Maddaloni, A., & Peydro, J. (2013). *Monetary Policy, Macroprudential Policy and Banking Stability: Evidence from the Euro Area*. ECB Working Paper Series No. 1560.

Merton, R. C. (1974). On the pricing of corporate debt: The risk structure of interest rates. *The Journal of Finance*, *29*(2), 449–470.

Northcott, C. A. (2004). *Competition in banking: A review of the literature*. Working Paper. Bank of Canada.

Petroff, A. (2013, June 27). Europe bank rescue plan would hit investors.CNN Money.

Ratnovski, L. (2013). Liquidity and transparency in bank risk management. *Journal of Financial Intermediation*, *22*(3), 422-439.

Schoenmaker, D. (2011). Financial Supervision in the EU. Forthcoming. In G. Caprio (Ed.), *Encyclopedia of Financial Globalization*. Elsevier Amsterdam.

Snyder, M. (2013, September). Cyprus-Style Wealth Confiscation Is Now Starting To Happen All Over The Globe. *Global Research.*

Stanley, D. T., & Girth, M. (1971). *Bankruptcy: Problem, process, reform.* Brookings Institution Press.

Technologies, C. A. (2014). *Project Risk Score Calculation.* CA Clarity PPM Cookbook.

Van Horne, J. (1974). *Fundamentals of Financial Management.* Prentice Hall.

Vanston, N. (2012). *Trust and reputation in financial services. Driver Review DR30. Foresight.* Government Office for Science.

ENDNOTES

1 see Agenor and da Silva (2011), Gertler and Kiyotaki (2010), Benigno et al. (2012) for examples of prudential instruments such as Loan-to-Value (LTV) ratios, liquidity and reserve requirements.

2 The bail-in mechanism was proposed by the European Commission and the ECB to deal with the banking sector crisis in Cyprus in March 2013 (see Ewing (2015) and Gumbel (2013) who reported on the issue). Since then, the idea of using bail-in instruments has become more widespread in Europe, as evidenced by the European Bank Rescue Plan (see Petroff (2013)) and the ongoing efforts of tracking down various bail-in style rescue plan implementations, similar in nature, but sometimes differing in scope or instrumentation from that of Cyprus (see Snyder (2013)).

3 We refer here to the initial clients that request credit from the bank and not to the remaining number of clients after the bank's abandonment procedure. We enforce this specification since our objective is for the bank to monitor and obtain information about its clients, so that it may use this information to make future decisions. As such, the target number of clients to monitor will be invariable, as long as the total population of clients is fixed.

Chapter 5
Measuring Governance:
The Application of Grey Relational Analysis on World Governance Indicators

Vesna Jankovic-Milic
University of Niš, Serbia

Marija Džunić
University of Niš, Serbia

ABSTRACT

The governance concept has become very popular in recent decades and in this regard has increased interest in measuring its quality. The most widely used measures of governance are World Governance Indicators, which represent composite perceptions-based indicators, published by World Bank Institute. There are six composite indicators and the data for constructing those indicators are obtained from 32 individual data sources. The objective of this chapter is to highlight the applicability of Grey Relational Analysis in the ranking of EU countries according to the governance quality. The Grey Relational Analysis entails calculation of Grey relational grade for governance quality. The final stage of the Grey Relational Analysis procedure involves ranking of EU countries according to Grey relational grade and their comparison with ranks obtained from World Bank Institute. The full contribution of Grey Relational Analysis arises on this stage, where ranks of countries have been changed.

INTRODUCTION

In recent years, we have witnessed a growing interest of both academics and policy-makers in defining "good governance" and measuring the quality of governance, which especially accounts for developing countries. Since the mid-1990's, a large number of quantitative governance indicators have been developed for the purpose of decision-making and policy recommendations.

Significant effort has been invested in defining the concept of governance. Broadly speaking, governance could be defined as group decision-making about resolving shared problems. Governance reflects how governments make important decisions, how they relate to the citizens and determine whom to

DOI: 10.4018/978-1-5225-0959-2.ch005

involve in the decision-making process, as well as how the governments render account (Graham et al, 2003). World Bank's definition of good governance accentuates the manner in which power is exercised in the management of a country's economic and social resources for development (World Bank, 1992). Kaufman, Kraay, & Mastruzzi (2010), offer a definition between too broad and too narrow explanations, defining governance as the traditions and institutions by which authority in a country is exercised. This includes the process by which governments are selected, monitored and replaced, the capacity of the government to effectively formulate and implement sound policies; and the respect of citizens and the state for the institutions that govern economic and social interactions among them.

There are several reasons for the popularity of governance concept in recent decades and for the growing interest in measuring its quality: the increase of international investment flows to developing and "emerging" economies (in other words, the increase of risk exposure of the investors' assets); end of the Cold War, followed by a growing interest of developed countries' governments and aid agencies to promote economic and social development in developing countries; failed policy reform (the so-called "Washington Consensus"), promoted through conditional lending by financial organizations to developing countries; and the recognition of the importance of formal and informal institutions for economic growth and development, as suggested by new institutional economics (Oman & Arndt, 2010).

The most widely used measures of governance are World Governance Indicators (hereafter WGI), which represent composite perceptions-based indicators, published by World Bank Institute[1]. The aggregate indicators are based on several hundreds of cross-country indices that measure different aspects of governance. There are six composite indicators covering 215 economies for the period 1996-2013 (Kaufmann, Kraay, & Mastruzzi, 2010):

- **Voice and Accountability:** The indicator that captures the extent to which citizens participate in selecting governments, as well as basic citizen rights and freedoms – freedom of association, expression and media;
- **Political Stability and Absence of Violence:** Includes measures of likelihood that governments will be violently overthrown;
- **Government Effectiveness:** A dimension that reflects the quality of public services as well as government credibility in public policy implementation;
- **Regulatory Quality:** Relates to the ability of governments to create and implement sound policies;
- **Rule of Law:** Indicates the quality of contract enforcement, property rights and formal institutions in a country; and
- **Control of Corruption:** Captures the agents' perceptions of different forms of corruption and state-capture.

The data for constructing the aggregate indicators are obtained from 32 individual data sources - survey respondents, private firms and households, public and non-government organizations. These variables are organized into six broad dimensions, using the Unobserved Components Model. The main advantage of this model is that it can quantify the precision of both individual sources of data and country specific aggregate indicators, by constructing the margins of error. The size of the standard errors of estimates of governance implies that the precise rankings of countries based on governance data cannot be offered, but the aggregate indicators allow sorting the countries into broad groups according to the level of governance quality.

The objective of this chapter is to highlight the applicability of Grey Relational Analysis (GRA) in the ranking of EU countries according to quality of governance, based on World Bank Institute data about six governance indicators (dimensions) in 2013. Grey Relational Analysis is an aspect of Grey Systems Theory. The aim of Grey Relational Analysis is to quantify the overall influence of various dimensions and their relations, known as the whitening of dimensions relation. The essence of this analysis is the relationship between two series. The calculation of Grey Relational Coefficients (GRC) represents the basis of this analysis. The third part of the Grey Relational Analysis procedure involves ranking of EU countries according to Grey relational grade and their comparison with ranks obtained from World Bank Institute Report.

The obtained results will indicate the contribution of the Grey Relational Analysis application in explaining the relations between the dimensions of governance quality in the EU countries. The findings will be aimed at pointing out the dimensions of governance quality that should be improved.

BACKGROUND

Defining Governance

A growing interest of scholars and policy makers in studying governance in the last decade stems from the assumption that "good governance" or "quality of government" is one of the crucial determinants of the economic development and social welfare. Much of the economic and political research in recent years has indicated that a large share of socio-economic problems in modern economies is caused by ineffective and dysfunctional government institutions. However, the literature on this issue has still not offered a clear and unambiguous definition of the concept of governance. The main cause of imprecisions is the tendency to identify this term with a number of related concepts, such as bureaucratic efficiency, rule of law (secure property rights), accountability, democracy and quality of institutions, which resulted in constructing too broad definitions of governance. According to these definitions, governance embraces a number of heterogeneous concepts, which are often considered as separate dimensions of governance. Some research frameworks analyse individual dimensions, and some focus on the analysis of all dimensions jointly. Another problem arises from the functionalist definitions of governance which imply that good governance is what leads to economic growth, causing tautological conclusions and problems of differentiating the concept itself from its effects. One of the main issues of contemporary research in political economy has therefore been to address the task of defining the concept of governance.

The broadest definitions of governance are based on neo-institutional theory that emphasizes the importance of institutions for socio-economic development (North, 1990; Olson, 1996). After questioning the theories that physical capital accumulation is the key determinant of economic growth, economists have pointed out to the importance of politics and institutions for growth and development, which led to the emergence and development of the research on governance. The ideas that secure property rights and contract enforcement are necessary preconditions for growth and prosperity has inspired a large number of authors to explore the link between institutional quality and economic performance. A series of theoretical and empirical works explore different aspects of institutional quality: absence of corruption (Mauro, 1995), bureaucratic efficiency (Alesina, 1998), security of property rights (Knack & Keefer, 1995). The main problem with these definitions is that it is hard to make a distinction between the elements of the governance concept and their developmental outcomes.

International institutions have also tended to define governance in a broad sense. World Development Report (World Bank, 2002) defines governance as "rules, enforcement mechanisms, and organizations", which is criticized for covering "almost anything" (Kaufmann & Kraay, 2008). A bit more specific definition of good governance accentuates the manner in which power is exercised in the management of a country's economic and social resources for development (World Bank, 1992). In the World Bank's governance and anti-corruption strategy (World Bank, 2007b), governance is explained as "the manner in which public officials and institutions acquire and exercise the authority to shape public policy and provide public goods and services". UNDP's definition of governance implies

the exercise of economic, political, and administrative authority to manage a country's affair at all levels. It comprises mechanisms, processes and institutions, through which citizens and groups articulate their interests, exercise their legal rights, meet their obligations and mediate their differences (UNDP, 1997).

The World Bank Institute (WBI), taking on a complex task of developing indicators for measuring governance, defines this concept as

...the traditions and institutions by which authority in a country is exercised. This includes the process by which governments are selected, monitored and replaced; the capacity of the government to effectively formulate and implement sound policies; and the respect of citizens and the state for the institutions that govern economic and social interactions among them. (Kaufman et al., 2010, p.4).

Political economy approach to defining governance points out two alternative groups of explanations: the first relates to the extent to which governments are responsive to citizens and provide them with basic services, while the second focuses on the institutions that determine the incentives of government decision makers. This field of research introduces the problem of non-benevolent politicians, acting in their self-interest (rent-seeking), instead of the general interest of the society. In this sense, governance was mostly explained through the impact of secure property rights, credible government, efficient bureaucracy, voice, accountability and democracy on growth and development (Keefer, 2004).

The WBI definition has been criticized by Rothstein and Teorell (2008), primarily because it is "as broad as any other definition of politics" and it does not distinguish between the access to power and the exercise of power. The authors argue that access to power, as the input size of the relation between government and its citizens, should be regulated by the principle of political equality that enables impartial treatment of any individual entering the political process. They accentuate the need for impartiality on the output side of the political system, in the exercise of public power, in implementing the public policy. Therefore, the authors define quality of governance as "the impartiality of institutions that exercise government authority" (Rothstein & Teorell, 2008, p.1). The argument behind this definition is that principle of impartiality excludes any kind of special relations or personal preferences of public servants in exercising government power, such as clientilism, discrimination, nepotism, patronage, etc. Especially, corruption, which is most often referred to as the abuse of public power, is also explained as disruption of the impartiality principle in public office. The authors insist that such definition of governance does not include the content of public policies and is not related to the size of the government, but should be understood as a procedural norm.

Fukuyama (2013) criticizes the emphasis on power-checking institutions (democratic accountability and rule of law) instead in power-deploying institutions – the state. He defines governance as "a government's ability to make and enforce rules, and to deliver services, regardless of whether that government is democratic or not" (p.4). The author excludes democracy from the definition of governance based on the claim that an authoritarian regime can also be well governed, while democracies can be mal-administered. After evaluating four broad approaches to quality of governance (procedural, input, output and bureaucratic autonomy measures), Fukuyama concludes that the quality of government is a product of interaction between capacity and autonomy. Capacity relates to both resources and the level of education and professionalization of public servants. The autonomy of bureaucracy does not imply total subordination of public servants to the demands of the citizens, nor a complete isolation from their political principals. The proper degree of autonomy is between total autonomy and total subordination.

GOVERNANCE AND GROWTH

A vast amount of empirical research has been conducted with the aim to prove that "good governance" matters for economic growth. This line of research has moved the focus from human and physical capital to the quality of government institutions as determinants of economic development. The main cause for the flourishing of the literature on governance and growth has been the interest of international institutions in exploring the causes of low economic growth in underdeveloped countries, especially during the transition process in the 1990's. Governance has thus been placed at the center of the research agenda and has become a necessary input for creating policy prescriptions.

Since the empirical literature is grounded on theoretical underpinnings, the conceptual vagueness of the governance term has instigated the investigations of the impact of heterogeneous governance dimensions on economic outcomes. The pioneer work in this area represented an investigation of more general notion of quality of institutions and its effects on growth. For example, based on the data from 97 countries and the period of 15 years, Knack and Keefer (1995) found that secure property rights and the level of contract enforcement represent a significant determinant of economic growth and investment. In their cross-country analysis, the authors find a positive correlation between the measures of institutional quality and average growth rates. Measuring the extent to which institutional factors – corruption, red tape and the efficiency of the judicial system affect economic growth, Mauro (1995) finds that corruption lowers investments and growth. Acemoglu et al. (2001) document a strong effect of institutional quality on economic performance, measured as income per capita. By using the mortality rates of European settlers as an instrument for institutional quality, the authors indicated that European colonization policies (setting up "extractive" institutions) have determined the quality of institutions in colonized states. Using the same instrument for measuring institutional quality, Rodrick et al. (2004) find that institutions "trump" the effects of geography and trade integration on income, indicating that an increase in institutional quality for one standard deviation induces a 6.4 – fold difference in per capita incomes. Using the expression "social infrastructure" to explain differences in institutions and government policies across 127 countries, Hall and Jones (1999) document a powerful relation between output per worker and measures of social infrastructure (corruption, trade impediments, contract enforcement, government interference in production). According to their results, differences in capital accumulation, productivity and therefore output per worker are dependent on the institutions and government policies that determine the economic environment.

Besides affecting economic growth, different governance aspects have been proved to be significant determinants of other economic and social outcomes. For example, Rothstein (2005) addresses the causality problem of the relation between governance quality and social capital, claiming that social trust and networks are determined by governance, rather than the other way round.

Interest in Measuring Governance

Although academic interest in governance research originates from the mid XX century, exploring the link between governance and economic development has been induced by the apparent government failures in developing countries, during the last decades of the century. Departing from the standpoint that physical capital availability or the economic policy measures are predominant factors of economic development, the common wisdom focuses on non-policy characteristics of government performance (property rights, bureaucratic efficiency, rule of law, etc.) and its impact on economic growth and development (Keefer, 2004).

Based on the maxim that "you can only manage what you can measure", there has been an increasing interest in developing different governance indicators. According to Arndt and Oman (2006), there are four sets of phenomena that drive the interest in measuring governance. The first one refers to the rising interest of international investors in developing countries and emerging markets (Oman, 2000). As the amount of foreign direct investment in developing countries has multiplied 15 times since the early 1980's, the amount of investors' assets exposed to risk has grown in the same proportion. As developed countries entered the competition arena for attracting foreign investment, the investors' perceptions of policy credibility and governance quality have become the main determinants of their investment decisions. Arnt and Oman also emphasize the importance of ending the "Cold War" and later on the dissolution of Soviet Union for promoting the importance of governance. In addition, failed policy reform, the so-called "Washington Consensus," promoted through conditional lending by financial organizations to developing countries and the recognition of the importance of formal and informal institutions for economic growth and development, as suggested by new institutional economics (Oman, Arndt, 2010) have added to the increasing interest to measuring governance. Governance indicators have started to be widely used for the purposes of tracking progress and monitoring the reform process implemented by developing countries' governments.

The key moment for expansion of use of governance indicators was the adoption of 1997 World Development Report (World Bank, 1997), where the role and the effectiveness of the state have been emphasized. Later on, Governance and Anticorruption Strategy (World Bank, 2007b) stressed the importance of monitoring and measuring different areas of governance. From that moment on, an array of different indicators has been developed for this purpose (Anderson, 2009).

Economist Intelligence Unit (EIU) has compiled a set of expert opinion indicators, with the aim to assess the risk of foreign investors, such as "the pervasiveness of corruption within the public sector" or "the effectiveness of state institutions in formulating and executing policy". International Country Risk Guide also offers monitoring corruption in the public sector as well as institutional strength and quality of bureaucracy. Unlike these risk rating agencies, Freedom House Countries at the Crossroads (FHCC) provides indicators of judiciary, protection of property rights and media independence, while Country Policy and Institutional Assessment (CPIA) measures the quality of regulatory environment, property rights budget and financial management. Open Budget Index (OBI) and Global Integrity Index (GII) have appeared as the result of the efforts to improve the existing expert opinion indicators and to affect governments' transparency and accountability. The OBI provides the assessment of government budget and financial activities, while the GII assesses the existence and effectiveness of anti-corruption mechanisms that promote public integrity. Public Expenditure and Financial Accountability (PEFA) represents an indicator aimed to support the reform in the fields of public expenditure, procurement and financial accountability of governments.

Besides expert opinion indicators, different dimensions of governance are measured through surveys, such as Executive Opinion Survey (World Economic Forum), Enterprise Surveys (World Bank) or Global Corruption Barometer (Transparency International). The WEF survey includes governance-related questions about the perception of judicial independence, reliability of property rights and corruption. The World Bank's Enterprise Surveys focuses on measuring the characteristics of business environment, interactions with the state (licenses, inspections and labor regulations), corruption and financial performance of enterprises. Global Corruption Barometer is a public opinion survey aimed at exploring the perceptions and experience of corruption.

All mentioned governance indicators serve their purpose in different ways. Some of them are criticized for the lack of transparency in design, for frequent changes, subjectivity, circularity, small sample size or limited time frames. An assessment of these various indicators based on several criteria (clarity, transparency, temporal and strategic relevance, as well as usefulness for constructive dialogue) can be found in Anderson (2009). However, governance indicators that have caused the most criticisms and have suffered the most intensive public scrutiny are aggregate indicators, such as Worldwide Governance Indicators (World Bank Institute) and Corruption Perception Index (Transparency International). These aggregate indicators comprise a large number of other indicators, in order to form a single index or a number of sub-indices. The following chapter will analyze the World Governance Indicators (WGI) in detail.

World Governance Indicators

World Governance Indicators (WGI) represent the result of the efforts directed at creating a systematic approach in measuring governance, since they aggregate a large set of indicators of various aspects and dimensions of governance. The creation of these indicators has been motivated by the fact that scholars, policy makers and aid donors have reached an understanding that governance matters for economic development, which is why an urgent need for a wide set of empirical measures of governance has appeared, that would enable comparison across countries as well as over time. Therefore, WGI represent a contribution to the empirical base for the research on governance, with the aim to improve the possibilities for measuring the progress of individual countries, understanding the effects of good/bad governance on economic development and exploring the causes of governance failures.

WGI actually represent a long-term research project of the World Bank Institute, initiated by a group of researchers (Daniel Kaufmann, Aart Kraay, Pablo Zoido-Lobatón and Massimo Mastruzzi). They have first been published in 1996, every other year until 2002, since when they have been released annually. WGI report on six dimensions of governance in 215 countries, and are based on 32 different data sources (surveys of households and firms, commercial business information providers, non-government organizations and public sector organizations)[2]. Therefore, WGI are a rich research dataset, summarizing the views of citizens, enterprises and experts from private, public and non-government sectors about the quality of governance.

Collecting data on governance indicators draws on an operational WBI definition of governance, earlier mentioned in this paper, as "the traditions and institutions by which authority in a country is exercised". As this conceptualization of governance includes three different areas (process by which governments are selected, capacity of the governments to implement sound policies and respect for the institutions that govern economic and social interactions), two broad measures of governance are constructed to correspond to each area, resulting in six measures (dimensions) of governance, covered by the WGI (Kaufmann et al., 2010). For the first area, the following two governance indicators are constructed:

1. **Voice and Accountability:** An indicator of the extent to which citizens are able to participate in selecting their government, including the freedom of expression, association and media.
2. **Political Stability and Absence of Violence/Terrorism:** Indicates the likelihood of political instability, violence and terrorism.

The following two indicators relate to the capacity of government to formulate and implement sound policies:

3. **Government Effectiveness:** A measure of the quality of public services, the quality and the independence of the civil service, the quality of policy formulation and implementation and the credibility of the government's commitment to such policies.
4. **Regulatory Quality:** Measure the ability of the government to formulate and implement sound policies and regulations that permit and promote private sector development.

Finally, as aggregated measures of the respect of citizens and the state for the institutions that govern economic and social interactions among them, two indicators have been constructed:

5. **Rule of Law:** Measures agents' confidence in the rules of society (quality of contract enforcement, property rights, the police, courts), as well as the likelihood of crime and violence.
6. **Control of Corruption:** An indicator of the extent to which public power is exercised for private gain, including both petty and grand forms of corruption, as well as "capture" of the state by elites and private interests.

These six broad measures of governance are highly correlated and mutually interdependent, which allows space for different choice of variables that fall into individual dimensions and different ways of organizing the empirical measures of governance. It is very important to stress that governance indicators are exclusively relied on the perceptions of different respondents (individuals and domestic firms, multilateral development agencies, non-government organizations, commercial business information providers) and therefore include a significant degree of subjective judgment, which is a source of potential measurement error. However, the creators of WGI point out several reasons for why they believe that perceptions data have particular value in measuring governance (Kaufmann et al., 2005): all the agents base their actions on perceptions, there aren't any alternative measures of some areas of governance other than perceived views of the agents (for example, on corruption) and perceptions data most precisely depict the *de facto* reality. Still, there are a large number of potential problems underlying the use of perception data: imprecision, systematic biases, "halo effects", correlated perceptions errors.

Another important issue related to WGI is the way how a large number of empirical proxies are aggregated into six broad dimensions of governance. Combining different measures from different sources on the same dimension enables the creation of a composite indicator that summarizes the points of view and opinions of diverse groups of respondents. Although the individual variables are rescaled (0-1), their scores across countries are not directly comparable, due to the differences in the reference groups.

Constructing six aggregate measures enables the adjustment of such differences and allows meaningful comparisons across countries.

Starting from the assumption that each individual data source provides an imperfect signal of a deeper underlying notion of governance that cannot be observed directly, the creators of WGI apply a specific method of data sources aggregation that would overcome the signal extraction problem. As the main goal of the aggregation is to isolate informative signal of governance from individual sources and combine them into an aggregate indicator, the method of choice was the Unobserved Components Model (UCM) (Kaufmann et al., 2009). This way, aggregate indicators become more informative than the individual data sources. The procedure of the aggregation begins with rescaling of the data and constructing weighting averages. Determination of weights is based on the assumption that the correlations between different data sources are the sign of their common but unobserved signal of governance, so higher correlations imply higher precision of data sources on a certain dimension of governance, so these sources are assigned greater weights. In other words, the weights are determined on the basis on the estimates of the UCM on the precision of data sources.

This specific aggregation procedure enables the calculations of explicit margins of error that reflect the unavoidable uncertainty in measuring governance, thereby providing an estimate of the precision of the indicators values. The creators of the WGI argue that margins of error have declined over time and have been significantly smaller than the margins of error of individual sources. Still, they urge the users of these indicators to take into account these margins of error when making comparisons across countries and over time, in the sense that when the confidence intervals overlap, there are no significant differences in governance between countries/time periods. Confidence intervals are calculated as the country's score plus/minus 1.64 times of its standard error. This implies that the precise rankings of countries based on governance data cannot be offered, but the aggregate indicators allow sorting the countries into broad groups according to the level of governance quality.

Critics of the Use of Composite Perception-Based Indicators

The advantage of composite indicators is reflected in the fact that they reduce a large number of different sources to a single number (the so-called point score), enabling comparisons across countries and over time. However, the immanent imprecision of these indicators is very often underestimated and not taken into account, which represents a serious cause of concern.

There is a vast amount of literature that criticizes the WGI on different basis. One line of critics accentuates the lack of a normative definition of what constitutes "good" or "bad" governance that informs or guides the scoring system and ranking of countries (Oman, Arndt, 2010). The authors argue that country scores are procedural outcomes, that reflect the process of aggregating subjective perceptions, and are not determined by a normative theory on how to distinguish between "good" and "bad" governance. The same authors criticize the fact that household surveys have been given lower weights compared to firm surveys and expert opinions, implying the existence of a "hidden bias". Questioning the transparency of the WGI, the authors conclude that these indicators should not be used for automatic decision-making and urge users to rely on more specific indicators that come from transparent and theoretically founded sources.

Kurtz and Shrank (2007) provide a detailed critique of measuring governance with WGI, starting with the argument that perceptions-based measures of governance are seriously flawed, since they are biased many ways. They rely mostly on the perceptions of a certain type of respondents - business people (anti-regulation bias is, for example, common in business surveys). Also, cross-country surveys are subject to cultural biases, reflected in different attitudes on the same governance dimension. Another argument against the use of WGI as reliable measure of governance relates to the fact that perceptions on governance are the result of the short-term economic performance rather than fundamental differences in institutional quality. Finally, they argue that there is no empirical evidence that confirms the effect of governance on growth.

There are opinions that, although WGI declaratively measure distinct concepts and various aspects of governance, they in fact measure the same broad concept – "they appear to say the same thing, with other words" (Langbein, Knack, 2008). In other words, each index only reflects the perceptions of quality of governance more broadly, instead of discriminating among different aspects of governance. They criticize the way of determining the content of individual indexes on purely conceptual grounds, instead by empirical methods, such as factor analysis.

According to Fukuyama (2013), WGI represent highly inadequate measure of governance, since they treat sovereign nations as units of analysis, not taking into account the enormous variations in the quality of governance within countries, by specific government functions or regions.

Based on the analyzed strengths and weaknesses of governance indicators, it is clear that, since measuring governance is extremely important, the usefulness of the indicators should be subject to continuous monitoring and scrutiny.

The Concept of Grey Relational Analysis

Special attention in this chapter is paid to Grey Relational Analysis (GRA). Grey Relational Analysis is a part of Grey Systems Theory. This concept originated in 1982 in China. The basis for the development of this theory was the fact that for some systems, especially complex ones, such as economic, social, agricultural, industrial, environmental and biological, it is impossible to provide a complete information system (or full information).

It is interesting to describe the system with the help of color as white, black and gray. In system theory, a system can be defined by the color that represents the amount of clear information about that system (Kayacan, Ulutas, Kaynak 2010, 1785). The presence of incomplete information in the literature is marked as "gray". The word "black" represents unknown information, "white" for completely known information, and „grey" for those information which are partially known and partially unknown (Chen et al., 2006, 234).

With the development of Grey System Theory, its application is becoming more widespread. During the last two decades, the Grey System Theory has been developed rapidly and caught the attention of many researchers. It has been widely and successfully applied to various systems (Kayacan, Ulutas, Kaynak 2010, p. 1787). The application of Grey System Theory is generally associated with Eastern countries. In the 1990's, this theory began to be investigated at universities in Japan, China and Australia. In 1996, Chinese Grey System Association – CGSA (Chinese Grey System Association) was created. Expansion of this theory in Western countries is resulting in the publication of journal titled "The Journal of Grey System" in 1989 in England.

There are several aspects for the theory of Grey system (Cui, Dang, Liu 2009, p. 84):

- Grey generation
- Grey modelling

- Grey prediction
- Grey decision
- Grey control
- Grey relational analysis (GRA): Quantifying the influences of various factors and their relations, which is called the whitening of factor relation

The essence of Grey Relational Analysis is the relationship between two series. GRA is a quantitative analysis that explores the similarity and difference of development trends among elements used to measure the relation among elements (Huang & Lin, 2009, p. 1132). Calculation of Grey relational coefficients (GRC) represents the basis of Grey Relational Analysis. The calculation procedure for these coefficients implies firstly normalization of the analyzed data, so that they are reduced to the same scale. In this case, there is no normalization because the WEF data are already normalized (reduced to a scale from -2.5 to 2.5). According to the Grey relational methodology, parameter values in the selected sample are compared with reference series. Elements which are necessary for the calculation of the Grey relational coefficients may be generally represented as follows:

X_0 is a referential series with k entities, while x_1, ..., x_N are the data series which are compared with referential series.

$$x_0 = \left[x_0(1), x_0(2), \ldots, x_0(j), \ldots, x_0(k)\right]$$
$$x_1 = \left[x_1(1), x_1(2), \ldots, x_1(j), \ldots, x_1(k)\right]$$
$$\vdots$$
$$x_1 = \left[x_j(1), x_j(2), \ldots, x_j(j), \ldots, x_0(k)\right]$$
$$\vdots$$
$$x_N = \left[x_N(1), x_N(2), \ldots, x_N(j), \ldots, x_N(k)\right]$$

In this case, the referential series consists of maximum values of $N = 6$. Each country in the sample represents separate series.

The absolute difference (Δ_{0i}) of the compared series and the referential series should be obtained by using the following formula:

$$\Delta_{0i}(j) = | x_0(j) - x_i(j) \qquad (1)$$

and the maximum and the minimum difference should be found.

Grey relational coefficients (γ_{0i}) between the series being compared with the referential series for the *j-th* value, i.e. in this case the pillar, is obtained by the following formula:

$$y_{0i}(j) = \frac{\Delta \min + \Delta \max}{\Delta_{0i}(j) + \Delta \max} \qquad (2)$$

Where $\Delta\max = \max\max\Delta_{0i}(j), \Delta\min = \min\min\Delta_{0i}(j)$

Grey relational grade (Γ_{0i}) for each series x_i can be calculated by summarising GRC weighted values.

$$\Gamma_{0i} = \sum_{j=1}^{k} w_j \gamma_{0i} \tag{3}$$

The final value of Grey relational grade represents the average value of grades obtained from the equation (3). The higher value of the Grey relational grade means that the corresponding parameter is closer to optimal (Hasni, Tabatabaei, Amiri, 2012, p. 83). Optimal parameter is defined target value of variable of interest.

In this chapter Grey Relational Analysis will be applied on data provided by World Bank Institute. Variable of interest are values of six indicators (dimensions) of governance quality in EU countries. By application of Grey Relational Analysis it is possible to determine the level of governance quality in EU countries by identifying deviation from target values. Target values are the highest values of the indicators on the global level.

Information base are values of six worldwide governance indicators for EU countries in 2013. These data are presented in the Table 1.

The measures of governance are presented in units of a standard normal distribution, with mean zero, standard deviation of one, and running from approximately -2.5 to 2.5, with higher values corresponding to better governance.

Minimal score in observed countries is -0.293, while the maximum score is very close to up margin in the scale, i.e. 2.411. Extreme scores for all indicators, as well as a corresponding country, are presented in the Table 2. It can be noticed that Scandinavian countries have highest scores, while the minimum values are recorded in Balkan countries.

The procedure of calculating the Gray Relations Coefficients and the ranking of countries in the sample (EU coutries) according to GRC values implies a number of steps. At the beginning of the analysis, determination of target values must be performed. As mentioned, target values are the maximum values of observed indicators on the global level. Target values for all indicators and corresponding countries are presented in Table 3.

The next step of the Grey Relational Analysis involves calculation of distances between target values and observed values of indicators. Absolute values of distances are presented in Table 4.

Based on the determined deviations, using the formula (2), values of Grey Relational Coefficient for each indicator within each country are calculated. The main purpose for their calculation is to express the relation between actual and ideal values of indicators. It is necessary to stress that a higher value of the Grey Relational Coefficient entails less deviation from the target values (Table 5).

Bearing in mind that the higher value of grey relational coefficients represents the strong relational degree between the reference (target) value and given value of indicator, based on the Grey Relational Coefficient values, it is possible to analyze the critical indicators for improving the quality of governance in the observed countries. In order to obtain a better insight into the position of each EU country according to governance performance, as well as to establish a comparative advantage in relation to other countries, ranking has been made. Comparative review of countries ranks according to World Bank Institute and Grey Relational Coefficients is presented in the Table 6.

Table 1. Worldwide Governance Indicators for EU countries

Country	Voice and Accountability	Political Stability and Absence of Violence/ Terrorism	Government Effectiveness	Regulatory Quality	Rule of Law	Control of Corruption
Austria	1.464	1.343	1.566	1.478	1.829	1.507
Belgium	1.370	0.917	1.590	1.291	1.403	1.630
Bulgaria	0.318	0.176	0.153	0.519	-0.137	-0.293
Croatia	0.475	0.614	0.689	0.440	0.265	0.107
Cyprus	0.966	0.518	1.351	0.911	0.998	1.236
Czech Republic	0.958	1.053	0.876	1.087	1.002	0.190
Denmark	1.682	0.947	1.971	1.802	1.873	2.411
Estonia	1.094	0.725	0.984	1.429	1.165	1.109
Finland	1.585	1.359	2.168	1.849	1.926	2.192
France	1.201	0.424	1.470	1.148	1.398	1.303
Germany	1.408	0.927	1.518	1.551	1.615	1.778
Greece	0.654	-0.198	0.449	0.617	0.438	-0.107
Hungary	0.732	0.779	0.644	0.888	0.563	0.288
Ireland	1.312	0.878	1.465	1.579	1.721	1.538
Italy	0.935	0.510	0.452	0.769	0.357	-0.037
Latvia	0.736	0.573	0.882	1.027	0.746	0.266
Lithuania	0.918	0.922	0.824	1.131	0.791	0.364
Luxembourg	1.610	1.332	1.616	1.762	1.788	2.115
Netherlands	1.584	1.117	1.767	1.766	1.809	2.046
Norway	1.759	1.332	1.865	1.655	1.968	2.286
Poland	0.973	0.948	0.708	1.048	0.785	0.548
Portugal	1.041	0.741	1.227	0.787	1.033	0.916
Romania	0.291	0.153	-0.073	0.589	0.106	-0.203
Slovak Republic	0.936	1.100	0.777	0.915	0.446	0.058
Slovenia	0.982	0.866	1.001	0.607	0.969	0.702
Spain	0.966	0.015	1.146	0.931	0.996	0.814
Sweden	1.673	1.127	1.890	1.890	1.954	2.286
United Kingdom	1.317	0.483	1.471	1.766	1.673	1.681

Source: http://info.worldbank.org/governance/wgi/index.aspx#reports

According to both criteria, the best ranked country among EU countries is Norway. It can be noticed that, for Norway, Regulatory Quality can be extracted as a critical indicator, because according to the values of this indicator Norway in on the sixth place. Bulgaria and Romania are the lowest ranked countries among EU countries.

If we compare ranks of countries obtained by World Bank Institute data and Grey Relational Coefficients, it can be concluded that there are almost no differences. For this reason, and also in order

Table 2 Extreme values of indicators

Indicator	Minimum	Maximum
Voice and Accountability	0.291 (Romania)	1.759 (Norway)
Political Stability and Absence of Violence/Terrorism	-0.198 (Greece)	1.359 (Finland)
Government Effectiveness	-0.073 (Romania)	2.168 (Finland)
Regulatory Quality	0.440 (Croatia)	1.890 (Sweden)
Rule of Law	-0.137 (Bulgaria)	1.968 (Norway)
Control of Corruption	-0.293 (Bulgaria)	2.411(Denmark)

Source: Authors` preview

Table 3 Target values

Indicator	Value	Country
Voice and Accountability	**1.759**	Norway
Political Stability and Absence of Violence/Terrorism	**1.9**	Greenland
Government Effectiveness	**2.168**	Finland
Regulatory Quality	**2**	Singapore
Rule of Law	**1.968**	Norway
Control of Corruption	**2.411**	Denmark

Source: Authors` preview

to highlight the real contribution GRA to the governance quality analysis, it is necessary to calculate weighted values of Grey Relational Coefficients, so-called Grey relational grades.

The determined weights should be assigned to each indicator. In literature and in practice, however, there are many approaches in their determination. Most of them can generally be classified into two main categories: objective and subjective approach (Ma, 1999). An objective approach in weights determination is based on objective information and includes the use of mathematical or statistical methods, such as (Randjelovic et al., 2013):

- Principal component method
- Regression analysis
- Correlation analysis
- Data envelopment analysis
- Entropy

Principal component analysis and more specifically factor analysis groups together the attributes (variables) that are collinear to form a new factor or attribute capable of capturing as much of common information of those attributes as possible. This method of multivariate analysis provides more options for determining the weights of attributes, i.e. variables in factor analysis. The first possibility occurs during designing the correlation matrix. Another possibility for weights determination appears at the higher step in the process of factor analysis. At this phase, it is possible to construct the weights from matrix of

Table 4 Distances between observed and target values

Country	Voice and Accountability	Political Stability and Absence of Violence/ Terrorism	Government Effectiveness	Regulatory Quality	Rule of Law	Control of Corruption
Austria	0.295	0.557	0.602	0.522	0.139	0.904
Belgium	0.389	0.983	0.578	0.709	0.565	0.781
Bulgaria	1.441	1.724	2.015	1.481	2.105	2.703
Croatia	1.285	1.286	1.479	1.560	1.703	2.304
Cyprus	0.793	1.382	0.817	1.089	0.970	1.175
Czech Republic	0.802	0.847	1.292	0.913	0.966	2.220
Denmark	0.077	0.953	0.197	0.198	0.095	0.000
Estonia	0.665	1.175	1.184	0.571	0.803	1.302
Finland	0.175	0.541	0.000	0.151	0.042	0.219
France	0.559	1.476	0.699	0.852	0.570	1.108
Germany	0.352	0.973	0.650	0.449	0.353	0.633
Greece	1.106	2.098	1.719	1.383	1.530	2.517
Hungary	1.027	1.121	1.524	1.112	1.405	2.123
Ireland	0.447	1.022	0.703	0.421	0.247	0.873
Italy	0.825	1.390	1.717	1.231	1.611	2.448
Latvia	1.023	1.327	1.286	0.973	1.222	2.145
Lithuania	0.842	0.978	1.344	0.869	1.177	2.047
Luxembourg	0.149	0.568	0.553	0.238	0.180	0.296
Netherlands	0.176	0.783	0.401	0.234	0.159	0.365
Norway	0.000	0.568	0.303	0.345	0.000	0.125
Poland	0.786	0.952	1.460	0.952	1.183	1.863
Portugal	0.718	1.159	0.941	1.213	0.935	1.495
Romania	1.468	1.747	2.241	1.411	1.862	2.614
Slovak Republic	0.823	0.800	1.391	1.085	1.522	2.353
Slovenia	0.778	1.034	1.167	1.393	1.000	1.709
Spain	0.794	1.885	1.022	1.069	0.972	1.597
Sweden	0.087	0.773	0.278	0.110	0.014	0.125
United Kingdom	0.442	1.417	0.697	0.234	0.295	0.729

Source: Authors` calculation

factor loadings, given that the square of factor loadings represents the proportion of the total unit variance of the variable which is explained by the factor. Notice that different methods for the extraction of principal components imply different weights. The rest of the variance not explained by the listed factor or factors, i.e. the difference between the total variance and squared values of factor loadings is valued as a specific variance, unique for each variable.

Table 5 Grey relational coefficients

	Voice and Accountability	Political Stability and Absence of Violence/ Terrorism	Government Effectiveness	Regulatory Quality	Rule of Law	Control of Corruption
Austria	0.833	0.994	0.788	0.802	0.938	0.784
Belgium	0.790	0.857	0.795	0.736	0.788	0.812
Bulgaria	0.505	0.690	0.527	0.549	0.500	0.523
Croatia	0.533	0.780	0.602	0.535	0.553	0.565
Cyprus	0.649	0.758	0.733	0.630	0.685	0.729
Czech Republic	0.647	0.896	0.634	0.675	0.686	0.574
Denmark	0.950	0.865	0.919	0.950	0.957	1.046
Estonia	0.688	0.806	0.654	0.784	0.724	0.706
Finland	0.894	1.000	1.000	0.976	0.980	0.968
France	0.724	0.738	0.762	0.692	0.787	0.742
Germany	0.807	0.859	0.775	0.831	0.857	0.848
Greece	0.570	0.629	0.566	0.567	0.579	0.542
Hungary	0.588	0.820	0.595	0.625	0.600	0.586
Ireland	0.767	0.846	0.761	0.843	0.895	0.791
Italy	0.640	0.756	0.566	0.598	0.567	0.549
Latvia	0.589	0.770	0.635	0.659	0.633	0.583
Lithuania	0.636	0.858	0.625	0.687	0.641	0.595
Luxembourg	0.908	0.990	0.802	0.929	0.921	0.943
Netherlands	0.893	0.916	0.848	0.931	0.930	0.922
Norway	1.000	0.990	0.881	0.876	1.000	1.000
Poland	0.651	0.865	0.606	0.665	0.640	0.619
Portugal	0.671	0.810	0.704	0.602	0.692	0.674
Romania	0.500	0.686	0.500	0.562	0.531	0.532
Slovak Republic	0.641	0.911	0.617	0.631	0.580	0.559
Slovenia	0.654	0.842	0.658	0.565	0.678	0.641
Spain	0.649	0.662	0.687	0.635	0.684	0.658
Sweden	0.944	0.919	0.890	1.000	0.993	1.000
United Kingdom	0.768	0.751	0.763	0.931	0.877	0.824

Source: Authors` calculation

Table 6 Ranked values of World Government Indicators – comparative review

Country	Voice and Accountability		Political Stability and Absence of Violence/ Terrorism		Government Effectiveness		Regulatory Quality		Rule of Law		Control of Corruption	
	R1	R2	R1	R2	R1	R2	R1	R2	R1	R2	R1	R2
Austria	7	7	2	2	8	8	9	9	5	5	10	10
Belgium	9	9	12	11	7	7	11	11	11	11	8	8
Bulgaria	26	26	24	23	27	26	26	26	28	28	27	27
Croatia	25	25	18	17	23	23	27	27	26	26	22	22
Cyprus	17	17	20	19	13	13	19	19	16	16	12	12
Czech Republic	18	18	7	7	19	19	14	14	15	15	21	21
Denmark	2	2	9	8	2	2	3	3	4	4	1	1
Estonia	13	13	17	16	17	17	10	10	13	13	13	13
Finland	5	5	1	1	1	1	2	2	3	3	3	3
France	12	12	23	22	11	11	12	12	12	12	11	11
Germany	8	8	10	9	9	9	8	8	10	10	6	6
Greece	24	24	27	26	26	25	23	23	24	24	25	25
Hungary	23	23	15	14	24	24	20	20	22	22	19	19
Ireland	11	11	13	12	12	12	7	7	8	8	9	9
Italy	20	20	21	20	25	25	22	22	25	25	24	24
Latvia	22	22	19	18	18	18	16	16	21	21	20	20
Lithuania	21	21	11	10	20	20	13	13	19	19	18	18
Luxembourg	4	4	3	3	6	6	5	5	7	7	4	4
Netherlands	6	6	5	5	5	5	4	4	6	6	5	5
Norway	1	1	3	3	4	4	6	6	1	1	2	2
Poland	16	16	8	8	22	22	15	15	20	20	17	17
Portugal	14	14	16	15	14	14	21	21	14	14	14	14
Romania	27	27	25	24	28	27	25	25	27	27	26	26
Slovak Republic	19	19	6	6	21	21	18	18	23	23	23	23
Slovenia	15	15	14	13	16	16	24	24	18	18	16	16
Spain	17	17	26	25	15	15	17	17	17	17	15	15
Sweden	3	3	4	4	3	3	1	1	2	2	2	2
United Kingdom	10	10	22	21	10	10	4	4	9	9	7	7

R1 – Rank according to WB
R2 – Ranked values of GRC

In this case, variables entered in the Principal Component Analysis are indicators related to the governance quality. Squared values of factor loadings (Table 7) represent a proportion of total variance of variables explained by the factor (governance quality in this case).

On the basis of the results related to the Grey Relational Coefficients which are presented in Table 5 and the calculated weights from Table 7, weighted values of the Grey Relational Coefficient, named Grey Relational Grade, for each indicator and country were obtained. The determined values are shown in Table 8.

The Grey relational grade indicates the degree of influence (or in this case, correlation) of particular indicator on governance quality. Therefore, if a particular indicator is more correlated with governance quality or has more influence on it, then the grey relational grade for that indicator will be higher than other Grey relational grades. This is a key advantage of this method over other methods.

Based on Grey relational grades for each indicator presented in Table 8, final Grey relational grade has been calculated as their average value (Table 9). According to final Grey relational grade and average scores of six indicators regarding governance quality, rank list of EU countries has been made. This rank list could be understood as an order of the grey relationship among indicators.

Comparing the ranks of the countries it can be noticed that the application of GRA leads to some changes in the position of countries on the rank list. The biggest change in ranking is related to Spain. This country is, according to average value of scores (World Bank Institute) on the 20th place, while it`s on 17th place according to value of final Grey relational grade.

Based on the results it can be concluded that complete contribution of Grey Relational Analysis comes after weights inclusion. This means that an adequate choice of weights has a great influence on the final results of the Grey Relational Analysis. For this reason, in the application of GRA it is necessary to take care of the method for weights determination.

CONCLUSION

The problem of defining good governance or quality of governance has persisted to the present day, despite the efforts of different scholars and institutions aimed at establishing a clear and unambiguous

Table 7. Weights obtained by Principal Component Analysis

Indicator	Factor Loading	Squared Values of Factor Loadings (weights)
Voice and Accountability	**0.981**	0.962
Political Stability and Absence of Violence/Terrorism	**0.74**	0.548
Government Effectiveness	**0.963**	0.927
Regulatory Quality	**0.941**	0.885
Rule of Law	**0.981**	0.962
Control of Corruption	**0.969**	0.939

Source: Authors` calculation

Table 8. Grey relational grades for EU countries

Country	Voice and Accountability	Political Stability and Absence of Violence/ Terrorism	Government Effectiveness	Regulatory Quality	Rule of Law	Control of Corruption
Austria	0.801	0.544	0.731	0.710	0.903	0.736
Belgium	0.761	0.469	0.737	0.652	0.759	0.762
Bulgaria	0.486	0.378	0.488	0.486	0.481	0.491
Croatia	0.513	0.427	0.559	0.474	0.532	0.530
Cyprus	0.625	0.415	0.680	0.558	0.659	0.685
Czech Republic	0.623	0.491	0.588	0.598	0.660	0.539
Denmark	0.914	0.474	0.852	0.841	0.921	0.982
Estonia	0.662	0.442	0.607	0.694	0.697	0.663
Finland	0.860	0.548	0.927	0.864	0.943	0.909
France	0.697	0.404	0.707	0.613	0.757	0.697
Germany	0.776	0.471	0.719	0.736	0.824	0.796
Greece	0.549	0.344	0.525	0.502	0.557	0.509
Hungary	0.566	0.449	0.552	0.553	0.577	0.550
Ireland	0.738	0.463	0.706	0.746	0.861	0.743
Italy	0.616	0.414	0.525	0.530	0.545	0.516
Latvia	0.567	0.422	0.589	0.584	0.609	0.548
Lithuania	0.612	0.470	0.580	0.609	0.617	0.559
Luxembourg	0.873	0.542	0.744	0.823	0.886	0.886
Netherlands	0.860	0.502	0.787	0.824	0.895	0.866
Norway	0.962	0.542	0.817	0.776	0.962	0.939
Poland	0.627	0.474	0.562	0.589	0.616	0.582
Portugal	0.646	0.444	0.653	0.533	0.666	0.633
Romania	0.481	0.376	0.464	0.498	0.511	0.499
Slovak Republic	0.617	0.499	0.572	0.559	0.559	0.525
Slovenia	0.629	0.461	0.610	0.501	0.653	0.602
Spain	0.625	0.363	0.637	0.562	0.658	0.618
Sweden	0.909	0.503	0.825	0.885	0.956	0.939
United Kingdom	0.740	0.411	0.707	0.824	0.844	0.774

Source: Authors` calculation

concept of governance. It is more or less clear that the concept includes more dimensions, the importance of particular ones being subject to various strands of academic and practitioners' thought.

Assessment of the impact of governance on different economic outcomes calls for establishing a precise method of measuring and the usage of valid indicators of governance. However, conceptual vagueness of the term itself has induced the development of a large number of governance indicators.

Table 9. Comparative overview of ranks for EU countries

Country	Average Score	Rank	GRG	Rank
Austria	1.531	7	0.738	7
Belgium	1.367	11	0.690	11
Bulgaria	0.123	27	0.468	28
Croatia	0.432	24	0.506	25
Cyprus	0.997	14	0.604	14
Czech Republic	0.861	16	0.583	16
Denmark	1.781	4	0.831	4
Estonia	1.084	13	0.627	13
Finland	1.846	1	0.842	1
France	1.157	12	0.646	12
Germany	1.466	8	0.720	8
Greece	0.309	25	0.498	26
Hungary	0.649	22	0.541	23
Ireland	1.415	9	0.710	10
Italy	0.497	23	0.524	24
Latvia	0.705	21	0.553	22
Lithuania	0.825	19	0.574	20
Luxembourg	1.704	5	0.792	5
Netherlands	1.682	6	0.789	6
Norway	1.811	2	0.833	3
Poland	0.835	18	0.575	19
Portugal	0.957	15	0.596	15
Romania	0.144	26	0.471	27
Slovak Republic	0.705	21	0.555	21
Slovenia	0.854	17	0.576	18
Spain	0.811	**20**	0.577	**17**
Sweden	1.803	3	0.836	2
United Kingdom	1.399	10	0.717	9

Source: Authors` calculation

These indicators are based on expert opinions, surveys of business entities, public institution actors and public opinion. Many of them have been criticized for lack of transparency, frequent changes, subjectivity, small sample size or limited time frame. However, governance indicators that have caused the most criticisms and have been subject to the most intensive public scrutiny are aggregate indicators, such as Worldwide Governance Indicators, that comprise data from more than 30 sources, aggregating them into 6 broad dimensions of governance (voice and accountability, political stability and absence of violence, government effectiveness, regulatory quality, rule of law and control of corruption). These indicators represent a rich research dataset, summarizing the views of citizens, enterprises and experts from private, public and non-government sectors about the quality of governance, enabling the ranking of the countries according to different dimensions of governance, as well as their comparison over time.

Although World Governance Indicators offer a single point score as a result of aggregating a large number of different data sources, they have been criticized on many grounds: lack of a normative definition on what constitutes good governance, assigning larger weights to expert opinions compared to household surveys, the biases caused by the perception-based data, cultural biases, but also for many methodological concerns. The aggregate indicators allow sorting the countries into broad groups according to the level of governance quality, but the precise rankings of countries based on governance data cannot be offered. The analysed strengths and weaknesses of governance indicators imply that the usefulness of the indicators should be subject to continuous monitoring and scrutiny.

Grey Relational Analysis is a comparative method which can be applied in social, economic, financial, scientific, technological, agricultural, industrial, transportation, ecological, and other systems. This method can be used in order to analyze systems which are very complex or determined with larger number of parameters which are not possible to define with great precision. In this chapter, Grey Relational Analysis is used in order to analyze the quality governance in EU countries. The analysis included six indicators: Voice and Accountability, Political Stability and Absence of Violence/Terrorism, Government Effectiveness, Regulatory Quality, Rule of Law and Control of Corruption. According to data of World Bank Institute for 2013, the maximum values of these indicators at the global level are related to the EU countries (Norway, Finland and Denmark). This fact has a direct impact on the results of the analysis, i.e. the ranking of the EU countries according to values of Grey relational coefficients. Principal Component Analysis served in this chapter as the basis for weights determination in Grey relational grade calculation. Ranking of countries based on the Grey relational grades, show that there is a change in the ranks compared to the World Bank Institute data, especially in the case of Spain. In this regard, in some future research Grey relational analysis can be applied to each governance indicator individually, bearing in mind that they are created as composite indicators.

REFERENCES

Acemoglu, D., Johnson, S., & Robinson, J. (2001). The Colonial Origins of Comparative Development: An Empirical Investigation. *The American Economic Review*, *91*(5), 1369–1401. doi:10.1257/aer.91.5.1369

Alesina, A. (1998). The Political Economy of High and Low Growth.*Annual World Bank Conference on Development Economics 1997*. Washington DC: World Bank.

Anderson, J. H. (2009). *A Review of Governance and Anticorruption Indicators in East Asia and Pacific*. World Bank.

Arndt, C. & Oman, C. (2006). *Uses and Abuses of Governance Indicators*. OECD Development Center Study.

Calderón, C., & Chong, A. (2000). Causality and Feedback between Institutional Measures and Economic Growth. *Economics and Politics*, *12*(1), 69–81. doi:10.1111/1468-0343.00069

Chen, Z., Chen, W., Chen, Q., & Chen, M. (2006). Trend Relational Analysis and Grey-Fuzzy Clustering Method. *Proceedings of the 2006 SIAM International Conference on Data Mining*, (pp. 234-245). doi:10.1137/1.9781611972764.21

Cui, J., Dang, Y., & Liu, S. (2009). Study on Novel Property of Some Grey Relational Analysis Models. *Journal of Grey System*, *12*(2), 83–88.

Evans, P., & Rauch, J. E. (1999). Bureaucracy and Growth: A Cross- National Analysis of the Effects of 'Weberian' State Structures on Economic Growth. *American Sociological Review*, *64*(5), 748–765. doi:10.2307/2657374

Fukuyama, F. (2013). *What Is Governance?* Center for Global Development Working Paper 314.

Graham, J., Amos, B., & Plumptre, T. (2003). *Principles for Good Governance in the 21st Century. Policy Brief no 15.* Ontario, Canada: Institute on Governance.

Hall, R. E., & Jones, C. I. (1999). Why Do Some Countries Produce so Much More Output per Worker than Others? *The Quarterly Journal of Economics*, *114*(1), 83–116. doi:10.1162/003355399555954

Hasni, H., Tabatabaei, A., & Amiri, G. (2012). Grey Relational Analysis to Determine the Optimum Process Parameters for Open-End Spinning Yarns. *Yournal of Engineered Fibers and Fabrics*, *7*(2), 81–86.

Huang, Y., & Lin, C. (2009). Constructing grea relational analysis model evaluation of tourism. *Journal of Information and Optimization Sciences*, *30*(6), 1129–1138. doi:10.1080/02522667.2009.10699931

Jankovic-Milic, V., & Jovanovic, S. (2014). Application of Grey relational analysis in considering competitiveness of the South Eastern Europe countries. In B. Krstic (Ed.), *Determinants of improving the competitiveness of national economies and enterprises* (pp. 45–65). Nis: Faculty of Economics.

Kaufmann, D., & Kraay, A. (2008). Governance Indicators: Where Are We, Where Should We Be Going? *World Bank Research Observer*, *23*(1), 1–30. doi:10.1093/wbro/lkm012

Kaufmann, D., Kraay, A., & Mastruzzi, M. (2005). *Governance Matters IV: Governance Indicators for 1996-2004.* Policy Research Working Paper No. 3630. Washington, DC: World Bank.

Kaufmann, D., Kraay, A., & Mastruzzi, M. (2009). *Governance Matters VIII: Aggregate and Individual Governance Indicators for 1996-2008.* World Bank Policy Research Working Paper No. 4978. Washington, DC: World Bank.

Kaufmann, D., Kraay, A., & Mastruzzi, M. (2010). *The Worldwide Governance Indicators: Methodology and Analytical Issues.* Policy Research Working Paper Series 5430. The World Bank.

Kayacan, E., Ulutas, B., & Kaynak, O. (2010). Grey system theory-based models in time series prediction. *Expert Systems with Applications*, *37*(2), 1784–1789. doi:10.1016/j.eswa.2009.07.064

Keefer, P. (2004). *A Review of the Political Economy of Governance: From Property Rights to Voice.* World Bank Policy Research Working Paper No. 3315. Washington DC: World Bank.

Keefer, P., & Knack, S. (2002). Polarization, Politics and Property Rights: Links between Inequality and Growth. *Public Choice*, *111*(1-2), 127–154. doi:10.1023/A:1015168000336

Knack, S., & Keefer, P. (1995). Institutions and Economic Performance: Cross Country Tests Using Alternative Institutional Measures. *Economics and Politics*, *7*(3), 207–227. doi:10.1111/j.1468-0343.1995.tb00111.x

Kurtz, M. J., & Schrank, A. (2007). Growth and Governance: Models, Measures and Mechanisms. *The Journal of Politics*, *69*(2), 538–554. doi:10.1111/j.1468-2508.2007.00549.x

Langbein, L., & Knack, S. (2008). *The Worldwide Governance Indicators and Tautology: Causally Related Separable Concepts, Indicators of a Common Cause, or Both?* World Bank Policy Research Working Paper 4669. Washington, DC: World Bank.

Ma, J., Fan, Z., & Huang, L. (1999). A Subjective and Objective Integrated Approach to Determine Attribute Weights. *European Journal of Operational Research*, *112*(2), 397–404. doi:10.1016/S0377-2217(98)00141-6

Mauro, P. (1995). Corruption and Growth. *The Quarterly Journal of Economics*, *110*(3), 681–712. doi:10.2307/2946696

North, D. (1981). *Structure and Change in Economic History*. New York: W.W. Norton.

North, D. (1990). *Institutions, Institutional Change and Economic Performance*. Cambridge, UK: Cambridge University Press. doi:10.1017/CBO9780511808678

Olson, M. Jr. (1996). Big Bills Left on the Sidewalk: Why Some Nations are Rich and Others Poor. *The Journal of Economic Perspectives*, *10*(2), 3–24. doi:10.1257/jep.10.2.3

Oman, C. (2000). Policy Competition for Foreign Direct Investment: A Study of Competition Among Governments to Attract FDI. OECD Development Centre.

Oman, C. P., & Arndt, C. (2010). *Measuring Governance*. Policy Brief no 39. OECD Development Centre, OECD. doi:10.1787/9789264181083-en

Randjelovic, D., Stankovic, J., Jankovic-Milic, V., & Stanković, J. (2013). Weight Coefficents Determination Based on Parameters in Factor Analysis. *Metalurgia International*, *18*(3), 128–132.

Rodrik, D., Subramanian, A., & Trebbi, F. (2004). Institutions Rule: The Primacy of Institutions over Geography and Integration in Economic Development. *Journal of Economic Growth*, *9*(2), 131–165. doi:10.1023/B:JOEG.0000031425.72248.85

Rose-Ackerman, S., & Kornai, J. (Eds.). (2004). *Building a Trustworthy State in Post-Socialist Transition*. New York: Palgrave/Macmillan.

Rothstein, B. (2005). *Social Traps and the Problem of Trust*. Cambridge, UK: Cambridge University Press. doi:10.1017/CBO9780511490323

Rothstein, B., & Teorell, J. (2008). What Is Quality of Government? A Theory of Impartial Government Institutions. *Governance: An International Journal of Policy, Administration and Institutions*, *21*(2), 165–190. doi:10.1111/j.1468-0491.2008.00391.x

Svensson, J. (1998). Investment, Property Rights and Political Instability: Theory and Evidence. *European Economic Review*, *42*(7), 1317–1341. doi:10.1016/S0014-2921(97)00081-0

United Nations Development Programme. (1997) Governance for sustainable human development. UNDP Policy Document.

World Bank. (1992). *Governance and development*. Washington, DC: The World Bank.

World Bank. (1997). *The State in a Changing World—World Development Report 1997*. New York: Oxford University Press.

World Bank. (2002). *Building Institutions for Markets*. Washington, DC: Oxford University Press.

World Bank. (2007a). *Main Report*. Washington, DC: World Bank Group.

World Bank. (2007b). *Strengthening World Bank Group Engagement On Governance And Anticorruption*. Washington, DC: World Bank Group.

ADDITIONAL READING

Acemoglu, D., & Robinson, J. A. (2012). Why Nations Fail: The Origins of Power, Prosperity and Poverty. New York: Crown.

Clague, C., Keefer, P., Knack, S., & Olson, M. (1999). Contract-Intensive Money: Contract Enforcement, Property Rights, and Economic Performance. *Journal of Economic Growth*, *4*(2), 185–211. doi:10.1023/A:1009854405184

Drazen, A. (2000). *Political Economy in Macroeconomics*. Princeton University Press.

Easterly, W., & Levine, R. (2003). Tropics, Germs, and Crops: How Endowments Influence Economic Development. *Journal of Monetary Economics*, *50*(1), 3–39. doi:10.1016/S0304-3932(02)00200-3

Evans, P. (1989). Predatory, Developmental, and Other Apparatuses: A Comparative Political Economy Perspective. *Sociological Forum*, *4*(4), 561–587. doi:10.1007/BF01115064

Holmberg, S., Rothstein, B., & Nasiritousi, N. (2009). Quality of Government: What You Get. *Annual Review of Political Science*, *12*(1), 135–161. doi:10.1146/annurev-polisci-100608-104510

Khan, M. H. (2006, January). Governance and Development. *Paper presented at theWorkshop on Governance and Development organized by the World Bank and DFID in Dhaka.*

Knack, S. (Ed.). (2003). *Democracy, Governance and Growth*. Ann Arbor: The University of Michigan Press.

La Porta, R., Lopez-de-Silanes, F., Shleifer, A., & Vishny, R. (1998). The Quality of Government. *Journal of Law Economics and Organization*, *15*(1), 222–279. doi:10.1093/jleo/15.1.222

KEY TERMS AND DEFINITIONS

Economic Development: An increase in material, political and social well-being of the citizens in a national economy.

Factor Loadings: A measure of correlation between observed variable (indicator) and factor (resulted by Principal Component Analysis). Its squared value indicating the level of explanation of the observed variables by created factor.

Governance: The capacity of the state to impartially govern the society's resources, implement effective policies, provide quality public goods and account for citizens' preferences in the process of political decision-making process.

Grey Relational Analysis (GRA): Quantitative analysis used to measure the relation among elements (series) by exploring the similarity and difference between observed characteristics and optimal characteristics.

Grey Relational Grade: A value generated using the Grey Relational Analysis and which can be used to rank the analysed characteristics of the phenomenon which is the subject of Grey Relational Analysis. Institutional Quality: Security of property rights and contract enforcement.

Principal Component Analysis: The method of multivariate data analysis, which is used to reduce the number of empirical variables, without losing the available information. World Governance Indicators: Composite indicators summarizing the perceptions of citizens, enterprises and experts from private, public and non-government sectors about the quality of governance.

ENDNOTES

1 http://info.worldbank.org/governance/wgi/index.aspx#home_

2 For a detailed overview of underlying data sources, see http://info.worldbank.org/governance/wgi/index.aspx#doc-sources

Chapter 6
Export-Led Recovery in Portugal: Can It Also Sustain Growth?

Gonçalo Carvalho
University of Coimbra, Portugal

Marta Simões
GEMF, CeBER, University of Coimbra, Portugal

António Portugal Duarte
GEMF, CeBER, University of Coimbra, Portugal

ABSTRACT

The recent expansion of Portuguese exports can not only promote post crisis recovery but also accelerate economic growth if the theoretical predictions on the relationship between exports and growth are correct. The export-led growth hypothesis advocates that export expansion is key in promoting long run performance. However, controversies remain on the causal relationship between the variables. We investigate this nexus for Portugal over the period 1970-2012 by estimating a bivariate VAR model with output and exports and applying cointegration, Granger causality and impulse response analysis. The results show a long-run equilibrium relationship between exports and output supporting the export-led-growth hypothesis. We also investigated the growth impact of exports of manufactured and non-manufactured products. The findings point to the existence of a positive impact of manufactured exports on output and a "limiting" effect of non-manufactured exports supporting in this way the view that what a country exports matters for growth.

INTRODUCTION

After joining the European Economic Community (EEC) in 1986, the Portuguese economy enjoyed a phase of sustained economic growth until the early 2000s, recording an annual average growth rate of real GDP per capita of more than 3 per cent (Andrade, Duarte & Simões, 2014). However, since around the year 2000 up to 2010 growth receded to less than 1 per cent a year (accompanied by declining exports

DOI: 10.4018/978-1-5225-0959-2.ch006

performance) and the recent evolution of the Portuguese economy has been strongly affected by the austerity policies recommended by the Troika (the IMF, the European Central Bank and the European Commission) following the sovereign debt crisis, which resulted in Portugal agreeing to a bailout programme in May 2011 and exiting the three year Economic Adjustment Programme in June 2014. The need to reduce the deficit and public debt are the main objectives that have underpinned austerity policies and resulted in a depleted domestic demand and the need to promote exports as a driver of recovery. According to the OECD (2014), p. 4 "The authorities have been implementing a wide-ranging structural reform agenda, which is helping to rebalance the economy towards the export sector." Portugal showed impressive export growth (as high as 10% a year), especially when compared with other Southern European countries like Spain and Italy, with Portuguese exports going from 27 per cent of GDP in 2009 to 39 per cent of GDP in 2013 (Arnold, 2015).

Besides their role as a driver of economic recovery, given the dismal growth prospects faced by the Portuguese economy an even more important question is whether exports have the potential to ignite and sustain economic growth in Portugal. The potential of exports to be the engine of growth is known in the economic literature as the Export-Led Growth (ELG) hypothesis and has given rise to substantial research (Giles & Williams, 2001a; 2001b; Palley, 2011). A fundamental issue that remains open to debate concerns the existence of a feedback relationship between exports and output that implies a Growth-Led-Export hypothesis (GLE) (Kónya, 2006). The ELG hypothesis is justified on the basis that competition in international markets fosters economies of scale and increases efficiency by concentrating resources in sectors in which the country has greater comparative advantage. These positive externalities promote economic growth (Balassa, 1978). On the contrary, the GLE hypothesis advocates that economic growth leads to productivity gains, creating a comparative advantage for the country that facilitates exports (Santos, 2012). Additionally, countries that record high growth rates but have relatively low absorption rates must necessarily export the surplus of goods and services (Mishra, 2011). In any case, the two hypotheses are not mutually exclusive and a reciprocal/feedback relationship between the two variables may exist (Kónya, 2006).

This chapter investigates the dynamics among exports and output over the period 1970-2012 for Portugal. The main aim is to examine whether the expansion of Portuguese exports may constitute an opportunity for its long run macroeconomic performance. For this purpose, we estimate a bivariate VAR model with output and exports and apply cointegration, Granger causality and impulse response analysis to take into account both the ELG and GLE hypotheses. Following the suggestion of several authors according to whom what a country exports matters for growth (Herzer, Nowak-Lehmann & Siliverstovs, 2005; Hausmann, Hwang & Rodrik, 2007), we will also take into account the composition of exports by investigating the separate effects of manufactured and non-manufactured exports on output.

The chapter is organized in three sections, besides the introduction. Section 2 gives an overview of the theoretical and empirical literature on the relationship between exports as a whole and economic growth, and the relationship between the composition of exports and growth. In section 3, we describe the estimation methodology and present and discuss the results obtained. Finally, section 4 contains the main conclusions.

EXPORTS AND ECONOMIC GROWTH: AN OVERVIEW OF THE LITERATURE

There is by now an extensive and rich literature on the relationship between exports and economic growth that has been carefully and thoroughly surveyed by Gilles & Williams (2001a, b), Hausmann, Hwang & Rodrik (2007) and Palley (2011), among others. However, the relationship between the two variables is still controversial, given the lack of consensus in the results obtained. The aim of this chapter is to present an overview of the theoretical and empirical literature on the relationship between exports and economic growth. In the first part, we concentrate on the relationship between aggregate exports and economic growth and in the second part we address the issue of exports composition.

Although we do not explicitly address it in this chapter, we are aware that the nature of exporting activity, in particular which industries, what share of domestic produced value added and which regional destination, is also a potentially important determinant of the economic growth impact of exports. Gkagka and Zarotiadis (2011) constitutes an example of a recent study that tries to distinguish the growth impact of exports according to destination by considering the exports of 15 EU member states over the period 1995-2007 to three different markets: other EU countries, China and the rest of the world. The results obtained indicate that exports destination matters with a positive growth impact of intra-EU exports, a negative growth impact of exports to China and a non-significant impact of exports to the rest of the world. Santos, Ribeiro and Carvalho (2013) also conclude, for a sample of 23 EU members over the period 1995-2010 that higher growth is fostered by export diversification across member states while enlarging destination to less developed and more distant countries has a negative growth impact. The authors also find evidence that export specialization in high value-added products, such as manufactures and high technology, accelerates economic growth. Pistikos and Zarotiadis (2014) deals with the importance of destination for exports performance based on a sample of 19 EU member states over the period 2002-2012. The main concern of the authors is identifying how crises affect intra-EU net exports, concluding that export intensity declined in the crisis period in countries whose main exports destinations were other EU member states that recorded important GDP decelerations or declines after the crisis. On the other hand, EU member states outside the Euro Zone and that were thus able to devaluate their currency were able to increase the respective exports intensity. Finally, the fragmentation of production across different countries makes it increasingly difficult to measure a country's export performance and its contribution to domestic output growth since it is necessary to evaluate the value added that exports create in a given country. A high import content of exports will result in weak linkages between exports and the rest of the economy and thus economic growth.

A slightly different but related issue concerns the importance of competition in domestic markets for export performance. Based on a review of empirical literature, Goodwin and Pierola (2015) claim that intense domestic competition is a pre-requisite to export more. According to the authors, for more productive firms to enter the domestic markets there must be effective competition. In this way, the most productive competitors will gain additional market share, which in turn improves aggregate productivity levels and leads to higher exports levels. This claim is supported, for instance, by empirical studies that find that higher domestic concentration is associated with a smaller domestic share in world output and fewer net exports while other studies obtain a positive relationship between domestic rivalry and export performance. Moreover, Goodwin and Pierola (2015) provide evidence from previous studies that anti-trust policy for input product and services markets contributes to export competitiveness of downstream sectors.

Aggregate Exports and Economic Growth

The idea that international trade is associated with faster economic growth goes as far back as the mercantilist theory that dominated Europe from the 16th to the 18th century and gained a renewed interest with the classical and neo-classical schools of economic thought through the 19th and 20th centuries until today. The Export-Led-Growth (ELG) hypothesis in particular argues that export expansion is a key factor in promoting long-run output growth. Several arguments support this view. From a demand-side perspective, increasing the degree of openness of an economy expands the market, overcoming the effects of a possible deceleration or exhaustion of domestic demand (Herzer, Nowak-Lehmann & Silivestovs, 2005). On the supply-side, export expansion can promote economic growth through an increase in productivity, achieved through three different mechanisms. First, an increase in exports may promote specialization in sectors where a country has greater comparative advantage and lead to a reallocation of resources from (relatively) inefficient sectors to more productive export-oriented sectors (Santos, 2012). Second, exporting requires facing stronger competition, which encourages the exploration of economies of scale and stimulates not only an improvement in product quality, but also the reduction of inefficiency in domestic production (Akbar & Naqvi, 2000). Finally, export growth could positively affect productivity through spillovers effects to the rest of the economy. According to Chuang (1998), the possible sources of spillovers are increased competitiveness, access to more efficient forms of management and organization, labor training, the acceleration of technological progress and increased knowledge of international markets. The Growth-Led-Export (GLE) hypothesis, on the other hand, argues that it is the fact that economic growth enables the development of human and technological capacities by a country that improves efficiency, creating comparative advantages in certain areas, lowering the prices of domestic production and consequently promoting exports (Kónya, 2006).

The early empirical literature from the 1960s and 1970s that examined the exports-economic growth relationship applied the Spearman's rank correlation index to determine the degree of association between exports and growth (Emery, 1967; Kravis 1970; Michaely 1977). This first group of research was followed by a second one that applied cross-country regression analysis (usually ordinary least squares) to estimate an augmented production function that included exports as an independent variable, in addition to investment and human capital accumulation (Balassa 1978; Tyler 1981; Ram 1987). The results from both groups of studies reveal a positive correlation between exports and economic growth. However, as noted by Rodriguez & Rodrik (2001), these studies do not address the problem of endogeneity, questioning the robustness of the results. The methodologies applied do not investigate the cointegration properties of the variables involved, nor the potential bidirectional relationship between exports and growth. More recent studies try to overcome these drawbacks by applying methodologies that better take into account the potential bidirectional relationship such as cointegration techniques, estimating VAR models (or VECM, depending on the results), which treat all variables as endogenous, and applying Granger causality analysis. Overall, this group of empirical studies has obtained four different types of results corresponding to:

1. Support for the ELG hypothesis, that is those that confirm a unidirectional relationship from exports to economic growth;
2. Support for the GLE hypothesis, that is those that confirm a unidirectional relationship from economic growth to exports;

3. Results that indicate a bidirectional relationship between exports and economic growth; and
4. Results that find that the behavior of both variables is independent of one another.

Table 1 contains a summary of some empirical studies (according to the date of publication) that examined the relationship between aggregate exports and economic growth belonging to the last group of studies identified above.

As far as the Portuguese economy is concerned, Oxley (1993) applied stationarity, cointegration and Granger causality tests to Portuguese annual data (log of real GDP and log of real exports), over the period 1865-1985, and found support for the GLE hypothesis. Kónya (2004) considered a sample of twenty-five OECD countries over the period 1960-1998 to study the relationship between real GDP and real exports. The author found support for: the ELG hypothesis in Iceland, Australia, Austria and Ireland; a unidirectional relationship from growth to exports in Canada, Japan, South Korea, Finland, United States and Portugal. As for the case of Luxembourg, Netherlands, Denmark, France, Greece, Hungary and Norway the author found no evidence of causality between the two variables, while for Sweden and the UK he found evidence of a bidirectional relationship.

In light of such varied results, some researchers tried to improve the existing empirical models by taking into account the structure (composition) of exports and its impact on economic growth.

Exports Composition and Economic Growth

The composition of exports is a relevant factor when analyzing the impact of exports on economic growth. Hausmann, Rodrik & Hwang (2006) suggest that the type of exports in which a country spe-

Table 1. An overview of some empirical studies

Author	Period	Sample	Variables	Conclusions
Jung and Marshall (1985)	1950-1981	37 Developing Countries	Real GDP, real GNP, real Exports	ELG hypothesis valid for 4 countries
Dutt and Ghosh (1994)	1953-1991	Israel and Turkey	Real GDP, real GNP, real Exports	ELG hypothesis valid for both countries
Khalafalla and Webb (2001)	1965-1996	Malaysia	Real GDP, real Exports, real Imports	Bidirectional relationship
Kónya (2006)	1951-2004	India	Real GDP, real Exports, real Imports	ELG hypothesis valid
Jordaan (2007)	1970-2005	Namibia	Real GDP, real GDP per capita, real Exports, real Imports	ELG hypothesis valid
Elbeydi, Hamuda and Gazda (2010)	1980-2007	Libya	Real GDP, real Exports,	Bidirectional relationship
Amiri and Gerdtham (2011)	1961-2006	France	Real GDP, real Exports, real Imports	ELG hypothesis valid
Tang and Lai (2011)	1960-2007	Hong Kong, Korea, Taiwan and Singapore	Real GDP, real Exports, exchange rate	ELG hypothesis valid for Singapore and Hong Kong
Mishra (2012)	1970-2009	India	Real GDP per capita, real Exports	GLE hypothesis valid

Source: Authors' own elaboration

cializes has significant effects on subsequent economic performance. Their results show that countries that export goods associated with higher productivity levels grow faster. According to Santos (2012), the probability of developing production and consumption goods associated with more advanced technologies is higher in more developed countries. From a demand-side perspective, this is explained by the higher demand for more innovative goods in wealthy countries. On the supply-side, Grossman & Helpman (1991) argue that the most advanced economies have technological advantages, particularly when it comes to Research and Development (R&D). Thus, the more developed a region is, the higher is its level of technology, production and exports of sophisticated goods and, consequently, the greater the impact on economic growth.

An interesting way forward consisted in analyzing exports taking into account the respective technological intensity. Cuaresma & Wörz (2005) tested the hypothesis of high-tech exports having a stronger impact on productivity for 44 industrialized and developing countries between 1981 and 1997. Applying a random effects model, the authors found that high tech-intensive exports have a significant impact on economic growth in industrialized countries, while low tech-intensive exports have a negative effect on economic growth.

Previous empirical studies have also pointed out the need to distinguish between the impact of primary and manufactured products exports on economic performance. Several authors suggest different arguments to explain why primary products exports may become an obstacle to productivity increases. According to these authors, primary products are not a sustainable source of knowledge spillovers and an increase in exports of such products can draw resources away from the externality-generating manufacturing sector (Herzer, Nowak-Lehmann & Siliverstovs, 2005). In addition, exports of primary products are more likely to suffer from price and volume fluctuations and therefore increasing such exports could lead to greater GDP volatile and macroeconomic uncertainty. In turn, the high volatility and economic uncertainty may affect negatively investments' efficiency.

Ghatak, Milner & Utkulu (1997) examined the ELG hypothesis for Malaysia and the effect of manufactured and primary exports on growth, over the period 1955-1990. Using cointegration and causality techniques, the authors found that aggregate exports Granger-cause economic growth, but not the other way around. This relationship is driven mainly by manufactured exports, given the negative effect of non-fuel primary exports on GDP.

Herzer, Nowak- Lehmann, & Siliverstovs (2005) investigate the impact of primary and manufactured exports on economic growth, in Chile. Using annual time series data from 1960 to 2001, the study applies cointegration techniques and the Granger methodology. The results show unidirectional causality from manufactured exports to economic growth, and the presence of a bidirectional relationship between primary exports and GDP. The main conclusion of this work is that although both types of exports contribute to the Chilean GDP, manufactured exports are especially important because of the increased productivity they provide and therefore induce sustained economic growth. In a similar study, Ngumi, Kimuyu & Gakure (2013) analyzed the influence of manufactured exports on economic growth in Kenya over the period 1970-2007. The authors found a long-run equilibrium relationship between GDP, manufactured and non-manufactured exports, imports and the terms of trade. The results from the causality analysis also point to an independent relationship between manufactured exports and growth. According to the authors, a possible justification for this result is the relative low weight of this type of exports relative to total output of the sector representing on average around 27% of total sectoral output. As to non-manufactured exports, the impact of these on GDP is negative because of the instability of the respective prices.

From this literature overview, it is clear that exports can have a key role on a country's economic performance. Despite the large number of studies that have been conducted to test the ELG hypothesis, the results concerning the direction of causality between exports and economic growth are not consensual depending on the specific country under analysis. Accordingly, this chapter will investigate the direction of causality between exports and economic growth for Portugal, also taking into account the structure of exports, which allows for more specific and detailed results.

DATA, METHODOLOGY, AND RESULTS

This section examines the causal relationship between exports and economic growth in Portugal over the period 1970-2012 within a VAR model with two variables, exports and output. We apply cointegration analysis, Granger causality tests and impulse-response functions to analyze the existence of a long-run relationship, the direction of causality and check how unexpected changes influence growth. VAR models allow us to take into account inter-dependencies and dynamic relationships between variables by explaining the behaviour of the endogenous variables by their own past values. Theoretical predictions point to increased export performance as being able to generate faster growth. However, richer countries also tend to export more. Thus, estimating a single regression with output growth as the dependent variable can lead to misleading results since it does not adequately capture the relationship under analysis if inverse causality applies. In a VAR model all variables are considered as potentially endogenous making this a suitable framework to model interdependent variables as is the case in this study. In summary, we estimate a country-specific model in a VAR-framework with all variables treated as endogenous, which avoids the often arbitrary classification, within a growth framework, of variables as endogenous or exogenous, and the imposition of restrictive specifications on the dynamic adjustment mechanisms inherent in the structural approaches, such as those associated with the estimation of cross-country growth regressions (Gobbin & Rayp, 2008; Frank, 2009). Cointegration, granger causality and an impulse response analysis are used to determine the sign of the association between variables.

Our basic VAR model can thus be generically represented as:

$$X_t = \alpha + \beta_1 X_{t-1} + \beta_2 X_{t-2} + \dots + \beta_p X_{t-p} + \varepsilon_t, \quad (1)$$

with vector X including the variables under analysis:

$$X = \begin{bmatrix} l\_GDP & l\_\exp \end{bmatrix}' \quad (2)$$

where "l" stands for the logarithm; "GDP" is the real Gross Domestic Product at 2005 prices and "exp" refers to real exports of goods and services at 2005 prices, either total or of manufactured or non-manufactured products (the last two variables are considered as a ratio of total exports). All variables were taken from the World Development Indicators database, from the World Bank, with an annual frequency. The evolution of all the series is shown in Figure 4 in the Appendix..

As a preliminary step to investigate the link between exports and growth in Portugal, we test for the order of integration of variables, a necessary condition to perform Granger causality analysis. We examine the unit root properties of the variables by applying the augmented-Dickey-Fuller (ADF) unit root test (see Dickey & Fuller (1979)). This test considers as the null hypothesis (H0) the presence of a unit root in the series against the alternative hypothesis (Ha) that the series is stationary. This can be expressed as, for any series *y*:

$$\Delta y_t = C + \beta T + \delta * y_{t-1} + \theta_1 \Delta y_{t-1} + \theta_2 \Delta y_{t-2} + \ldots + u_t \tag{3}$$

where C is a constant and T a time trend, included according to the characteristics of the series. The test for a unit root is conducted on the coefficient of y_{t-1} in the regression. If the coefficient is significantly different from zero, then the hypothesis that *y* contains a unit root is rejected. Rejection of the null hypothesis implies stationarity. If H0 cannot be rejected for the series in levels, we next apply the test to the first differences of the series (Δ) and so on until the series becomes stationary.

Given the low power of the ADF test in small samples such as ours, we also applied the Kwiatkoswaski, Philliips Schmidt and Shin (KPSS) stationarity test ((Kwiatkoswaski et al., 1992)). This test considers as the null hypothesis that the series is stationary against the alternative of non-stationarity and is used in the literature as a complement to the ADF test. The interpretation of the results of both tests combined is summarized in Table 2. If the series are non-stationarity in their levels, the tests are applied to their first differences to determine the respective order of integration.

If the series are integrated of order one, we next perform cointegration analysis that allows for the identification of long-run relationships between variables and to avoid the problem of spurious regressions. We say that the variables are cointegrated if they have the same order of integration (one, in our case), and if there is a linear combination of the variables that is integrated of order zero. To test the number of cointegration vectors in our model we follow the Johansen procedure (see Johansen & Juselius (1990); Johansen (1995)). If there is no cointegration vector, we can continue to estimate a VAR in first differences in order to perform causality analysis. If there are one or more vectors, we must estimate a Vector Error Correcting Mechanism (VECM) system.

Aggregate Exports and Economic Growth: Estimation of a VECM Model

We begin by analyzing the relationship between output and aggregate exports considering total real GDP and total real exports, respectively, as proxies.

Table 3 contains the results obtained with the ADF and KPSS tests, with constant and trend (CT) for the variables in levels and only with constant (C) for the first differences. The results obtained with the ADF test reveal the presence of a unit root in the variables in levels since the p-value is greater than 0.05; when applied to the variables in first differences the null hypothesis is rejected. For the KPSS test,

Table 2. Possible outcomes of the ADF and KPSS tests combined

KPSS Test	ADF Test	
	Do Not Reject H_0	**Reject H_0**
Do Not Reject H_0	Inconclusive outcome	Stationaraty
Reject H_0	Non-stationary	Inconclusive outcome

Notes: the null hypothesis indicates non-stationarity in the ADF test and stationarity in the case of the KPSS test
Source: Nusair (2003)

Table 3. Results of the ADF and KPSS tests - l_GDP and l_exp

Variable	ADF Test			Teste KPSS					
	Lags	p-value	Rej. H_0	Statiscal Test	Critical Values			Rej. H_0	Conclusion
					10%	5%	1%		
l_GDP	*1*	*0.995*	No	0.19515*	0.122	0.149	0.212	Yes	*NS, I(1)*
Δl_GDP	2	*0.023***	Yes	0.46936**	0.352	0.472	0.720	No	*S, I(0)*
l_exp	*4*	*0.791*	No	0.11462***	0.122	0.149	0.212	No	*IO, I(1)*
Δl_exp	*1*	*4.32e-006****	Yes	0.09251***	0.352	0.472	0.720	No	*S, I(0)*

Note: Δ - series in first differences; Rej. H_0- rejection of the null hypothesis; NS – non-stationary; S - stationary; IO – Inconclusive Outcome. All tests were performed with a maximum of 4 lags. ***, **, * indicate that the coefficients are statistically significant at 1%, 5% and 10% significance levels, respectively. In the KPSS test we reject H_0 if the statistical test is greater than the critical value at the 5% significance level

Source: Authors' own calculations

it is possible to verify that the only variable that is not stationary at a 5% significance level is l_GDP. Comparing the results of both tests, we conclude that a single differentiation is sufficient to make the series stationary, so we can say that both series are integrated of order one, *I*(1).

Since the series are integrated of the same order, *I*(1), the next step is to determine the optimal number of lags to consider in the estimation of the VAR model in order to eliminate the autocorrelation of the residuals. The optimal number of lags corresponds to the minimum value of three information criteria: AIC (Akaike Information Criterion), BIC (Bayesian Information Criterion) and HQC (Hannan-Quinn Criterion). Note that the inclusion of too many lags implies the loss of degrees of freedom (low power tests) and increases the risk of collinearity. However, an estimation with insufficient lags may lead to biased estimates. From the inspection of Table 4 it can be seen that the optimal number of lags is two according to the three criteria used.

We next investigate the existence of a cointegration relationship between the variables, in other words, we determine if there is a long-run equilibrium relationship between the two series. To this end, we use the methodology proposed by Johansen (1995), which applies two statistical tests to determine the number of cointegration vectors: the trace test (λ trace) and the maximum eigenvalue test (λ max). In the trace test, the null hypothesis (H_0) is that the number of cointegration vectors is $r \leq p$, where r is the number of vectors and $p = n - 1$ (where n is the number of variables included). As for the maximum eigenvalue test, the null hypothesis (H_0) is whether there are at most r cointegrating vectors, against the alternative that there are exactly $r + 1$. The cointegration analysis results are shown in Table 5. It can be seen that there is one cointegrating vector since the null hypothesis of both the trace and the maximum eigenvalue tests for the presence of at least one cointegrating vector was not rejected at a 5% significance

Table 4. VAR Lag Selection – l_GDP and l_exp

Lags	Likelihood Log.	P(LR)	AIC	BIC	HQC
1	141.94781		-6.79739	-6.54406	-6.70579
2	152.33208	0.00035	-7.11660*	-6.69438*	-6.96394*
3	153.89839	0.53588	-6.99492	-6.40381	-6.78119

Source: Authors' own calculations

Table 5. Results of the Johansen Cointegration tests- l_GDP and l_exp

Trace Test				λ Max Test			
H_0	H_1	λ Trace	p-value	H_0	H_1	λ max	p-value
r = 0	r > 0	17.190	0.0258	r = 0	r = 1	16.266	0.0218
r ≤ 1	r >1	0.92456	0.3363	r = 1	r = 2	0.92456	0.3363

Notes: The number of lags used was two, determined by the criteria AIC, BIC and HQC
Source: Authors' own calculations

level (p-value greater than 0.05). Thus, the two variables of our VAR model show a long-run equilibrium relationship between them, although short-run deviations can occur relative to this equilibrium.

The cointegration equation between GDP and exports is reported in Table 6. Based on the estimated cointegration vector corresponding to the long-run equilibrium relationship between the variables, we can say that our results confirm the theoretical predictions on the relationship between exports and output for Portugal over the period under analysis with the estimated coefficients presenting the expected sign and also being statistically significant. An increase in exports as a positive long-run effect on output, probably because it enables access to larger markets by the Portuguese economy, with the associated increase in competition that leads to higher efficiency in order for the exporting firms to stay competitive, allowing for the exploration of scale economies. Higher exports seem also to have encouraged technology diffusion and knowledge spillovers that contribute to faster productivity growth

The presence of cointegration between the two variables implies a causality on at least one direction. To determine the direction of causality between the series we proceeded to the estimation of a VECM model, which is identical to a VAR model with variables in first differences. However, the first includes an error correction term, which aims to correct the deviations from the long-run equilibrium through a series of partial short-run adjustments. The VECM model to estimate is given by the following two equations:

$$\Delta l_{GDP} = \beta_0 + \beta_1 \Delta l\_GDP_{t-1} + \beta_2 \Delta l\_exp_{t-1} + \delta_1 EC_{t-1} + \varepsilon_{1t} \quad (4)$$

$$\Delta l_{exp} = \alpha_0 + \alpha_1 \Delta l\_GDP_{t-1} + \alpha_2 \Delta l\_exp_{t-1} + \delta_2 EC_{t-1} + \varepsilon_{2t} \quad (5)$$

where EC are the error correction terms corresponding to the cointegration vector identified before.

When the variables are *I* (1) and cointegrated, Granger causality should be analyzed based on the results of the estimation of the corresponding VECM model, and it can be said that there are two sources of causality: via the lagged differences and via the error correction term. For instance, if the estimated

Table 6. Cointegration Equation – l_GDP and l_exp

Beta	Coefficient	Standard Error
l_GDP	1.0000	0.0000
l_exp	-0.43398	0.034691

Source: Authors' own calculations

coefficient of the error correction term is negative and statistically significant in the equation for l_GDP, this variable is also influenced/caused by l_exp via adjustments / corrections of the deviations from the long-run equilibrium between the variables. Table 7 shows the estimation results for the Δl_GDP equation (equation (4)) and the Δl_exp equation (equation (5)) in our VECM model. According to the estimation results for equation (4), since the estimated coefficient of the error correction term is negative and statistically significant, we can conclude that in the long-run real exports Granger-cause GDP. The fact that the estimated coefficient of lagged exports is not statistically significant indicates the absence of causality in the short-term. In turn, the estimation results for equation (5) indicates that there is no causality from real GDP to exports since the estimated coefficients on lagged GDP and the variable of adjustment to the long-run equilibrium (EC) are not statistically significant in this equation.

From the results above, we can conclude that, in the long-run, there is a unidirectional causal relationship from exports to GDP, which means that the ELG hypothesis is valid. This result contradicts the conclusion of some of the works that analyzed the Portuguese economy, like Oxley (1993) and Kónya (2004), who found results supporting a unidirectional causal relationship from economic growth to exports. However, the period under analysis used in both of these studies are distinct (1865-1985 and 1960-1997, respectively), thus covering quite different institutional and commercial arrangements and so it is not surprising that we found different results.

Finally, we performed impulse response functions analysis that shows how a one standard deviation shock in one of the variables of the model affects the contemporaneous and future values of all endogenous variables in that same model. The impulse response analysis is thus an alternative way of obtaining information regarding the relationships among the variables since these functions allow us to analyse the sign and duration of the reaction of the different variables in the model to an exogenous shock in one of the other variables. The responses of each variable over a 20 year timeframe are shown in Figure 1.

As can be seen, an unexpected shock to exports has a gradual positive effect on GDP over the first 5 periods, reaching a clear long-term equilibrium above the baseline, thus, an increase in exports causes an increase of GDP and the adjustment is quite fast. This effect again confirms the predictions of the theoretical literature since, for instance, exports growth originates productivity gains achieved by a more efficiently reallocation of resources, by creating economies of scale and through the acceleration of tech-

Table 7. Results of the estimation of the VECM Model

	Δl_GDP (4)	**Δl_exp** (5)
Const	1.87723 * (1.944)	−2.14106 (−0.8157)
Δ_l_GDP_1	0.315036 * (1.858)	−0.478711 (−1.038)
Δ_l_exp_1	0.0465734 (0.7366)	0.437380 ** (2.544)
EC	−0.122543 * (−1.933)	0.143444 (0.8322)
R^2	0.299234	0.160202

Notes: ***, **, * indicate that the coefficients are statistically significant at a significance level of 1%, 5% and 10%, respectively. The value in parenthesis corresponds to the t-statistic

Source: Authors' own calculations

Figure 1. Impulse-response functions - l_GDP and l_exp

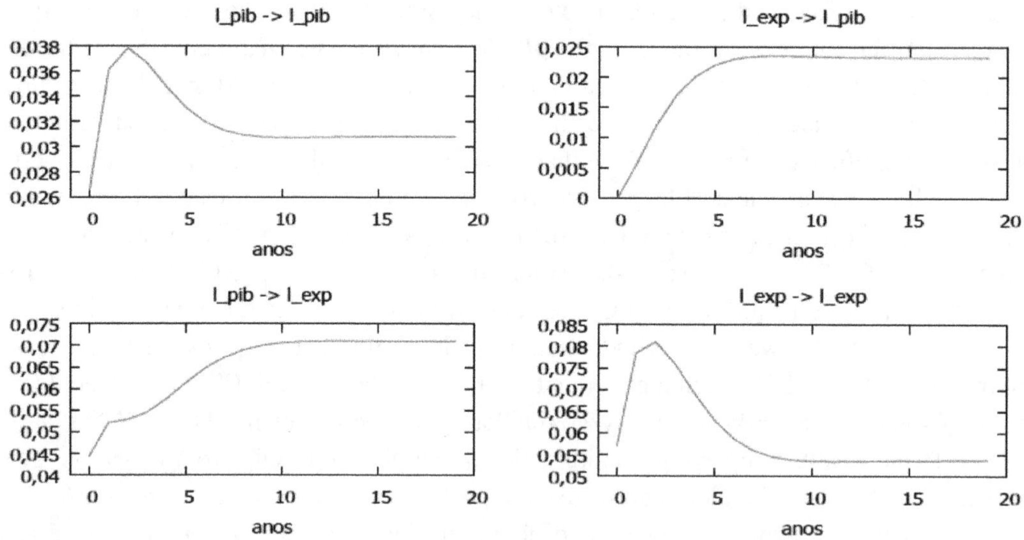

nological progress that promotes economic growth. On the other hand, a positive shock to GDP has an increasingly positive effect on exports, stabilizing after 10 years in a higher equilibrium. This adjustment period is consistent with the modest value of the coefficient associated with the error correction term of the exports equation in the VECM model, which is the speed of adjustment to the long-run equilibrium (see Table 7). According to the theoretical predictions, economic growth promotes exports through the development of human and technological capacities, which cause an increase in efficiency, creating comparative advantages in certain areas and lowering the price of production, in this way improving exports performance. However, this is a lengthy process, which may explain the longer time horizon to reach the long-run equilibrium. On the other hand, the faster adjustment of GDP to a shock to exports reinforces the ELG hypothesis for the Portuguese case.

Exports Composition and Economic Growth: Estimation of two VAR models

This section takes into account the composition of exports, disaggregated into manufactured and non-manufactured products, to analyze its impact on the Portuguese economic growth, replicating the methodology used in the previous section.

To study the relationship between manufactured exports and economic growth, vector X consists of:

$$X = \begin{bmatrix} l\_GDP \\ l\_Manuf \end{bmatrix} \tag{6}$$

where l_Manuf is the ratio of manufactured exports to total exports.

To analyze the causal relationship between non-manufactured exports and economic growth, vector X consists of:

$$X = \begin{bmatrix} l\_GDP \\ l\_NonManuf \end{bmatrix} \tag{7}$$

where l_NonManuf is the ratio of non-manufactured exports to total exports. The evolution of the percentage of manufactured and non-manufactured products in total exports of goods is shown in Figure 5 in the Appendix.

Table 8 presents the results of the stationarity tests - ADF and KPSS - for the new variables l_Manuf and l_NonManuf variables. According to the approach proposed by Nusair (2003), which analyses the combined results of both tests, we conclude that the variables in levels are not stationary for a 5% significance level. When applied to the first differences the tests indicate that these are stationary, since their p-values are lower than 0.05 and their statistical test are lower than the critical value for the% significance level 5. We thus conclude that the series are integrated of order one, $I(1)$.

We next determine the optimal number of lags for each VAR model. According to the results of three information criteria - AIC, BIC and HQC, presented in Tables 13 and 14 of the Appendix, the optimal number of lags is one for both models. We can thus proceed to test for the existence of cointegration relationships between, on the one hand manufactured exports and output and on the other hand non-manufactured exports and output, again using the Johansen (1995) procedure. We report the results in Tables 13 and 14, respectively. As can be seen, the assumption of at least one cointegration vector was not rejected for the two models, at a 5% significance level (p-value greater than 0.05). It can therefore be concluded that there is a long-run equilibrium relationship between each of the exports variables and output.

The cointegration vector for the long-run equilibrium relationship between l_Manuf and l_GDP is presented in Table 15 in the Appendix. The results are consistent with the theoretical predictions. An increase in manufactured exports as a positive long-run impact effect on output, which indicates that an expansion of these type of exports is accompanied by an increase in GDP due to the high added value of such exports. As for the cointegration vector corresponding to the long-run equilibrium relationship between l_NonManuf and l_GDP, presented in Table 16 in the Appendix, the estimated coefficient of non-manufactured exports implies that decreasing the weight of such products in total exports will raise

Table 8. Results of ADF and KPSS tests - l_Manuf and l_nonManuf

Variable	ADF test			KPSS test					Conclusion
	Lags	p-value	Rej. H_0	Estatistical Test	Critical Values			Rej. H_0	
					10%	5%	1%		
l_Manuf	1	0.9779	No	0.21124*	0.122	0.149	0.212	Yes	NS, *I(1)*
Δl_Manuf	1	0.0019***	Yes	0.41379**	0.352	0.472	0.720	No	S, *I(0)*
l_NonManuf	1	0.9673	No	0.19044*	0.122	0.149	0.212	Yes	NS, *I(1)*
Δl_NonManuf	1	0.0145**	Yes	0.31074***	0.352	0.472	0.720	No	S, *I(0)*

Note: Δ - series in first differences; Rej. H_0- rejection of the null hypothesis; NS – non-stationary; S - stationary; IO – Inconclusive Outcome. All the tests were performed considering a maximum of 4 lags. ***, **, * indicate that the coefficients are statistically significant at the 1%, 5% and 10%, significance levels, respectively. For the KPSS test we reject H_0 if the statistical test is greater than the critical value at the 5% significance level

Source: Authors' own calculations

GDP. Several previous studies, Ghatak et al. (1997), Herzer et al. (2005) and Ngumi et al. (2013), found similar results, supporting the argument that, due to the fact that these products are not a sustainable source of positive productivity spillovers and their prices are volatile, higher non-manufactured exports increase macroeconomic instability, which in turn impacts negatively on capital accumulation, and thus GDP.

Again, the existence of one cointegration vector means that there is at least causality in one direction between the variables, but does not allow us to identify the direction of that causality. Contrary to what we have done in the model with aggregate exports, in this case, we will note estimate a VECM model, since the optimal number of lags is one for both models. Thus, using this methodology would lead to an increased loss of information about the dynamics of the variables since the VECM model would just include the error correction term as an explanatory variable. We thus decided to use the strategy proposed by Doan, Litterman, & Sims (1984) which consists on the estimation of a VAR model with the variables in levels and the analysis of the respective impulse-response functions. This strategy is also suggested by Kónya (2004) as an alternative to the VECM methodology when the variables are $I(1)$ and the system is bivariate as is the case of our variables.

The results of the estimation of the first order VAR model with manufactured exports model is documented in Table 11. As shown in equation (6a), given the statistical significance of the estimated coefficient for l_Manuf, it is possible to conclude that an increase in the ratio of manufactured products to total exports Granger-causes real GDP. Using the information from equation (6b), on the other hand, it is possible to conclude that there is no causality from l_GDP to l_Manuf, since the respective lag is not statistically significant in this equation.

Still focusing on manufactured exports, we next estimated the impulse-response functions for a 20-year time horizon. The results are presented in Figure 2. According to these, an unexpected shock to the ratio of manufactured products to total exports of goods causes a progressive increase in l_GDP, which reaches its peak in the sixth year, gradually decreasing from that period onwards. A similar effect, but less intense, is caused by a shock in real GDP in the ratio of manufactured products to total exports of goods.

Table 9. Results of the Johansen Cointegration Tests - l_GDP and l_Manuf

Trace Test				λ max Test			
H_0	H_1	λ Trace	p-value	H_0	H_1	λ max	p-value
r = 0	r > 0	20.044	0.0084	r = 0	r = 1	16.314	0.0213
r ≤ 1	r >1	3.7296	0.0535	r = 1	r = 2	3.7296	0.0535

Notes: The number of lags used was one, determined by the criteria AIC, BIC and HQC
Source: Authors' own calculations

Table 10. Results of the Johansen Cointegration Tests - l_GDP and l_NonManuf

Trace Test				λ max test			
H_0	H_1	λ Trace	p-value	H_0	H_1	λ max	p-value
r = 0	r > 0	18.804	0.0138	r = 0	r = 1	16.780	0.0176
r ≤ 1	r >1	2.0238	0.1549	r = 1	r = 2	2.0238	0.1548

Notes: The number of lags used was one, determined by the criteria AIC, BIC and HQC
Source: Authors' own calculations

Table 11. Results of the Estimation of the VAR Model– l_GDP and l_Manuf

	l_GDP (6a)	l_Manuf (6b)
Const	4.63317** (2.25316)	−0.316356 (2.35757)
l_GDP_1	0.775985*** (0.101705)	0.0306952 (0.106418)
l_Manuf_1	0.238104** (0.0925050)	0.899006*** (0.0967918)
time	0.00403648 (0.00260353)	−0.00118180 (0.00272419)
R^2	0.994015	0.895512

Notes: ***, **, * indicate that the coefficients are statistically significant at a significance level of 1%, 5% and 10%, respectively. The value in parenthesis correspond to the standard errors
Source: Authors' own calculations

Figure 2. Impulse-response functions - l_GDP and l_Manuf

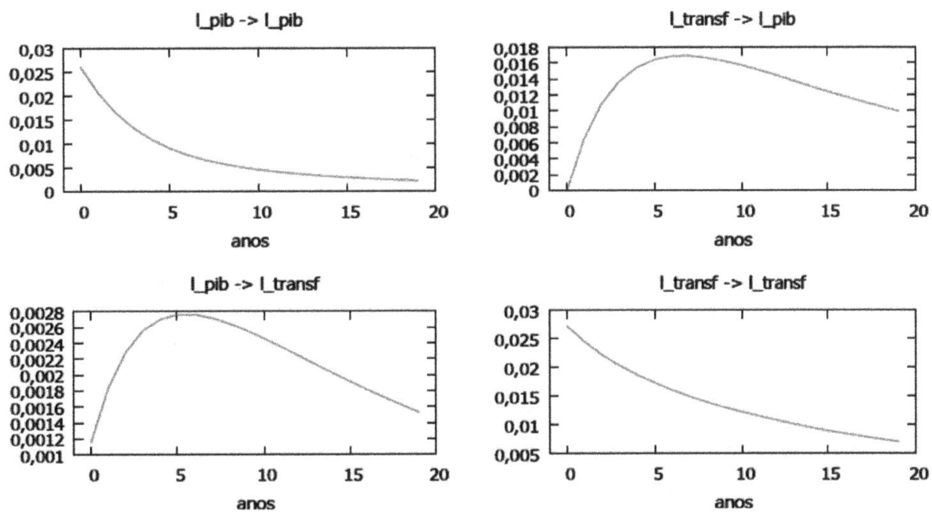

As for the relationship between output and non-manufactured exports, the estimation results for the respective first order VAR model composed of the equation for l_GDP (7a) and l_NonManuf (7b), can be found in Table 12. The statistical significance of the estimated coefficient for l_NonManuf in equation (7a) reveals that the ratio of non-manufactured exports to total exports of goods Granger-causes real GDP. In equation (7b), the absence of statistical significance in the respective lag invalidates the existence of causality from l_GDP to l_NonManuf.

Finally, we estimated the impulse-response functions for the VAR model with non-manufactured exports and output. The results can be found in Figure 3. As can be seen, an unexpected shock to non-manufactured exports a progressive decrease in real GDP that reaches its lowest value in the ninth year after the shock, growing slightly from that period onwards. A similar effect, but less intense, is caused by a shock to real GDP on non-manufactured exports.

Table 12. Outcomes of the VAR Model Estimation – l_GDP and l_NonManuf

	l_GDP (7a)	**l_ *NonManuf* (7b)**
Const	5.97758** (2.50807)	2.64077 (8.54672)
l_GDP_1	0.772077*** (0.0979584)	−0.100114 (0.333812)
l_ *NonManuf*_1	−0.0696456*** (0.0250692)	0.940627*** (0.0854279)
time	0.00421606 (0.00254233)	0.00421341 (0.00866345)
R^2	0.994158	0.913118

Notes: ***, **, * indicate that the coefficients are statistically significant at a significance level of 1%, 5% and 10%, respectively. The value in brackets represent the standard error

Source: Authors' own calculations

Figure 3. Impulse-response functions - l_GDP and l_NonManuf

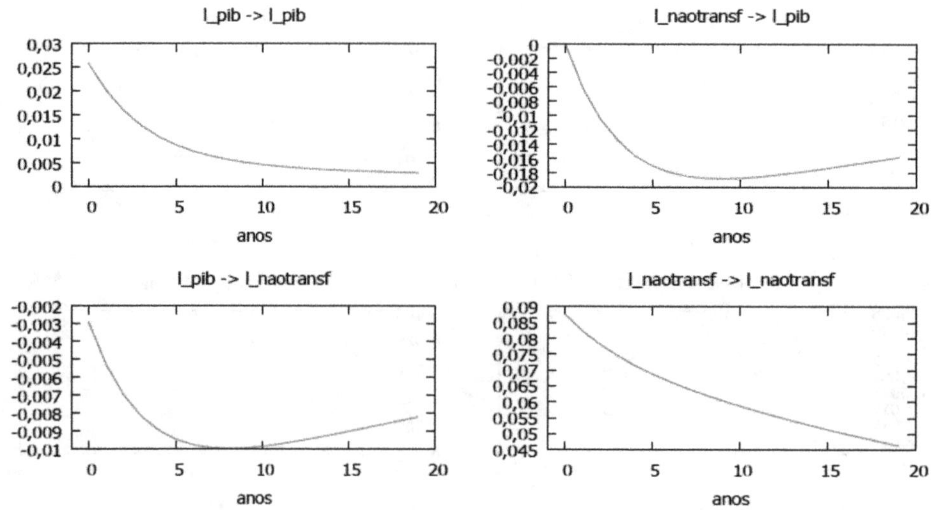

CONCLUSION

The increasing openness to international trade in the second half of the twentieth century is an undeniable feature of the Portuguese economy, especially after the accession of Portugal to the former EEC in 1986. Currently undergoing a recession following the financial and economic crisis that started in the USA in 2007-08 and resulted in the Portuguese sovereign debt crisis in 2011, export promotion appears as a crucial source to achieve sustained economic growth. To aid in the discussion on the role of exports as a driver of economic growth in Portugal, this study examined the causal relationship between exports and output in this country. For this purpose, we estimated a bivariate VAR model with real GDP and exports over the period 1970-2012. We first considered the relationship between aggregate exports and output and afterwards we disaggregated exports into manufactured and non-manufactured products to derive additional insights.

Taking into account the results of the stationarity and cointegration tests, they revealed the existence of a long-run equilibrium relationship between real GDP and overall exports and also between real GDP and exports disaggregated into manufactured and non-manufactured goods. Causality analysis showed a unidirectional relationship from exports of goods and services to GDP validating the Export-led-Growth hypothesis. This result goes in line with economic theory, since exports allow countries to overcome the limitations of its domestic market and contribute to productivity gains by creating economies of scale in sectors where the country has comparative advantage, allowing the countries to specialize in what they do best and thus lead to technological and overall productivity improvements.

Disaggregating exports of goods and services into manufactured and non-manufactured goods showed different effects on output from the two categories. The ratio of manufactured products to total exports of goods has a positive effect on GDP and the opposite applies to the ratio of non-manufactured products to total exports of goods. This result is justified by the fact that exports of non-manufactured products cannot be a sustainable source of spillovers and positive externalities and because this type of products are more likely to suffer from fluctuations in their prices, which may generate macroeconomic instability.

In conclusion, the results from this study indicate that Portugal should use exports, especially of manufactured products, as a strategy to accelerate economic growth and therefore decision makers should provide the institutional and macroeconomic conditions that promote exports (see Arnold, 2015).

In order to derive more precise and accurate policy implications, future research should focus on the identification of the sign of the relationship between more disaggregated types of exports (which industries) and output growth/productivity in Portugal, which can also involve the estimation of multivariate VAR models with a higher number of variables that can help clarify the nature of the relationship. This also applies to the study of the importance of the import content of exports and regional destination for economic growth. As Cardoso, Esteves and Rua (2013), p. 107 highlight: "the effect on domestic production resulting from an increase of the Portuguese exports is certainly lower if it is driven by a product such as fuels (which have a high import content) than tourism (since services related with hotels and restaurants present a low import content)." As for the second issue, the literature seems to agree that market diversification enhances the positive growth impact of exports but more recently research has focused on the importance of particular markets of destination such as more developed countries and regional trade agreements partners. Finally, domestic market competition has been identified as a pre-requisite for the growth enhancing role of exports that deserves further investigation as this can be a particularly important issue for Portugal. According to the OECD (2014), p.6, "… Portuguese exporters continue to be at a potential disadvantage vis-à-vis international competitors across a number of dimensions, notably with respect to access to inputs from non-tradable sectors…" Wider international comparisons applying panel data methodologies could also allow for important generalizations on the relationship under analysis.

REFERENCES

Amiri, A., & Gerdtham, G. (2011). *Relationship between exports, imports and economic growth in France: evidence from cointegration analysis and Granger causality with using geostatistical models. MPRA Paper nº 34190*. University Library of Munich.

Akbar, M., & Naqvi, Z. (2000). Export diversification and the structural dynamics in the growth process: The case of Pakistan. *Pakistan Development Review*, *39*(4), 573–589.

Andrade, J. S., Duarte, A., & Simões, M. (2014). A Quantile Regression Analysis of Growth and Convergence in the EU: Potential Implications for Portugal. *Notas Económicas*, *39*(39), 48–70. doi:10.14195/2183-203X_39_3

Arnold, J. (2015). *Boosting export performance in Portugal.* OECD Economics Department Working Papers, No. 1257. OECD Publishing.

Balassa, B. (1978). Exports and Economic Growth: Further Evidence. *Journal of Development Economics*, *5*(2), 181–189. doi:10.1016/0304-3878(78)90006-8

Cardoso, F., Esteves, P. S., & Rua, A. (2013, Autumn). The import content of global demand in Portugal. *Banco de Portugal Economic Bulletin*, 107-121

Chuang, Y. (1998). Learning by doing, the technology gap, and growth. *International Economic Review*, *39*(3), 697–721. doi:10.2307/2527396

Cuaresma, C. J., & Worz, J. (2005). On Export Composition and Growth. *Review of World Economics. Weltwirtschaftliches Archiv*, *141*(1), 33–49. doi:10.1007/s10290-005-0014-z

Dickey, D., & Fuller, W. (1979). Distribution of the Estimators for Time Series Regressions with a Unit Root. *Journal of the American Statistical Association*, *74*(366), 427–431. doi:10.2307/2286348

Doan, T., Litterman, R., & Sims, C. (1984). Forecasting and Conditional Projection Using Realistic Prior Distributions. *Econometric Reviews*, *3*(1), 1–100. doi:10.1080/07474938408800053

Dutt, S. D., & Ghosh, D. (1994). An Empirical Investigation of the Export Growth – Economic Growth Relationship. *Applied Economics Letters*, *1*(3), 44–48. doi:10.1080/135048594358285

Emery, R. F. (1967). The Relation of Exports and Growth. *Kyklos*, *20*(4), 470–486. doi:10.1111/j.1467-6435.1967.tb00859.x

Frank, M. W. (2009). Income inequality, human capital, and income growth: Evidence from a state level VAR analysis. *Atlantic Economic Journal*, *37*(2), 173–185. doi:10.1007/s11293-009-9172-z

Ghatak, S., Milner, C., & Uktulu, U. (1997). Exports, export composition and growth: Cointegration and causality evidence for Malaysia. *Applied Economics*, *29*(2), 213–223. doi:10.1080/000368497327272

Giles, J., & Williams, C. (2001a). Export-led growth: A survey of the empirical literature and some non-causality results. Part 1. *The Journal of International Trade & Economic Development*, *9*(3), 261–337. doi:10.1080/09638190050086177

Giles, J., & Williams, C. (2001b). Export-led growth: A survey of the empirical literature and some non-causality results. Part 2. *The Journal of International Trade & Economic Development*, *9*(4), 445–470. doi:10.1080/096381900750056867

Gkagka, A., & Zarotiadis, G. (2011). Growth and EU Trade Relations: A case study. *South-Eastern Europe Journal of Economics*, *1*, 1–11.

Gobbin, N., & Rayp, G. (2008). Different ways of looking at old issues: A time-series approach to inequality and growth. *Applied Economics*, *40*(7), 885–895. doi:10.1080/00036840600771106

Goodwin, T., & Pierola, M. (2015). *Export competitiveness: Why Domestic Market Competition Matters. Public Policy for the Private Sector NoteNo. 348, Trade & Competition, World Bank*. GTCDR.

Grossman, G. M., & Helpman, E. (1991). Trade, Knowledge Spillovers, and Growth. *European Economic Review*, *35*(3), 517–526. doi:10.1016/0014-2921(91)90153-A

Hausmann, R., Hwang, J., & Rodrik, D. (2007). What you export matters. *Journal of Economic Growth*, *12*(1), 1–25. doi:10.1007/s10887-006-9009-4

Herzer, D., Nowark-Lehmann, F. D., & Siliverstors, B. (2004). *Export-Led Growth in Chile: Assessing the Role of Exports*. Ibero-America Institute For Economic Research. Discussion Paper No.103.

Johansen, S. (1995). *Likelihood - Based Inference in Cointegrated Vector Autoregressive Models. Advanced Texts in Econometrics*. Oxford, UK: Oxford University Press. doi:10.1093/0198774508.001.0001

Jordaan, A. C., & Eita, J. H. (2007). Export and Economic Growth in Namibia: A Granger Causality Analysis. *The South African Journal of Economics*, *75*(3), 540–547. doi:10.1111/j.1813-6982.2007.00132.x

Jung, W. S., & Marshall, P. J. (1985). Exports, Growth and Causality in Developing Countries. *Journal of Development Economics*, *18*(2), 1–12. doi:10.1016/0304-3878(85)90002-1

Khalafalla, K. Y., & Webb, A. J. (2001). Export-Led Growth and Structural Change: Evidence from Malaysia. *Applied Economics*, *33*(13), 1703–1715. doi:10.1080/00036840010015066

Kónya, L. (2004). Export Led Growth, Growth Driven Exports, Both or None? Granger Causality Analysis On OECD Countries. *Applied Econometrics and International Development*, *4*(1), 73–94.

Kónya, L. (2006). Exports and growth: Granger causality analysis on OECD countries with a panel data approach. *Economic Modelling*, *23*(6), 978–992. doi:10.1016/j.econmod.2006.04.008

Kravis, I. B. (1970). Trade as a Handmaiden of Growth. *The Economic Journal*, *80*(323), 850–870. doi:10.2307/2229902

Kwiatkoswaski, D., Phillips, P., Schmidt, P., & Shin, Y.-J. (1992). Testing the Null Hypothes is of Stationary Against the Alternative of a Unit Root: How Sure Are We That Economic Time Series Have a Unit Root? *Journal of Econometrics*, *54*, 159–178. doi:10.1016/0304-4076(92)90104-Y

Michaely, M. (1977). Exports and economic growth: An empirical investigation. *Journal of Development Economics*, *4*(1), 49–53. doi:10.1016/0304-3878(77)90006-2

Mishra, P. K. (2011). The Dynamics of Relationship between exports and economic growth in India. *International Journal of Economic Sciences and Applied Research*, *4*(2), 53–70.

Ngumi, P., Wambugu, A., Kimuyu, P., & Gakure, R. (2013). Exports and Economic Growth. The case of Kenya. *Prime Journal of Business Administration and Management*, *3*(4), 950–959.

OECD. (2014). *OECD Economic Surveys - PORTUGAL overview*. Paris: OECD Publishing.

OECD. (2014). *Portugal: Deepening structural reform to support growth and competitiveness.* Better Policies Series. OECD.

Oxley, L. (1993). Cointegration, Causality and Export-led Growth in Portugal, 1865-1985. *Economics Letters, 43*(2), 163–166. doi:10.1016/0165-1765(93)90030-G

Palley, T. I. (2011). *The Rise and fall of Export-Led Growth.* Levy Economics Institute of Bard College Working Paper No. 675.

Pistikos, K., & Zarotiadis, G. (2014). Tie or Try: Intra-Eu Trade in Times of Economic Crisis. *Journal of Sociological Research, 5*(1), 126–137.

Ram, R. (1987). Exports and Economic Growth in Developing countries: Evidence from Time Series and Cross Section Data. *Economic Development and Cultural Change, 36*(1), 51–72. doi:10.1086/451636

Rodriguez, F., & Rodrik, D. (2001). Trade Policy and Economic Growth: A Skeptic's Guide to the Cross-National Evidence. In B. Bernanke & K. S. Rogoff (Eds.), *NBER macroeconomics annual* (pp. 261–338). Cambridge, MA: MIT Press.

Santos, P. (2012). *Destination and product structure of exports: Impact on the economic growth of Europe.* Faculdade de Economia da Universidade do Porto.

Santos, P., Ribeiro, A., & Carvalho, V. (2013). *Export-Led Growth in Europe: Where and What to Export?* FEP Working papersNo. 479.

Tang, C.F., & Lai, Y.W. (2011). *The stability of export led growth hypothesis: Evidence from Asia's four little Dragons.* Munich personal Re PEc Archive paper No. 27962.

Tyler, W. G. (1981). Growth and expansion in developing countries some empirical evidence. *Journal of Development Economics, 9*(1), 121–130. doi:10.1016/0304-3878(81)90007-9

APPENDIX

Table 13. VAR Lag Selection – l_GDP and l_Manuf

Lags	Likelihood Log.	P(LR)	AIC	BIC	HQC
1	174.78171		-8.439085*	-8.185753*	-8.347489*
2	178.07738	0.15913	-8.403869	-7.981649	-8.251207
3	180.71643	0.25993	-8.335821	-7.744714	-8.122095

Source: Authors' own calculations

Table 14. VAR Lag Selection – l_GDP and l_NonManuf

Lags	Likelihood Log.	P(LR)	AIC	BIC	HQC
1	127.54181		-6.077091 *	-5.823759*	-5.985494*
2	130.77886	0.16643	-6.038943	-5.616723	-5.886282
3	134.28568	0.13517	-6.014284	-5.423176	-5.800558

Source: Authors' own calculations

Table 15. Cointegration Equation – l_GDP and l_Manuf

Beta	Coefficient	Standard Error
l_GDP	1.0000	0.0000
l_Manuf	-1.4677	0.69207

Source: Authors' own calculations

Table 16. Cointegration Equation – l_GDP and l_NonManuf

Beta	Coefficient	Standard Error
l_GDP	1.0000	0.0000
l_NonManuf	0.51350	0.19668

Source: Authors' own calculations

Figure 4. Ratio of Manufactured and Non-Manufactured Products to Total Exports of Goods

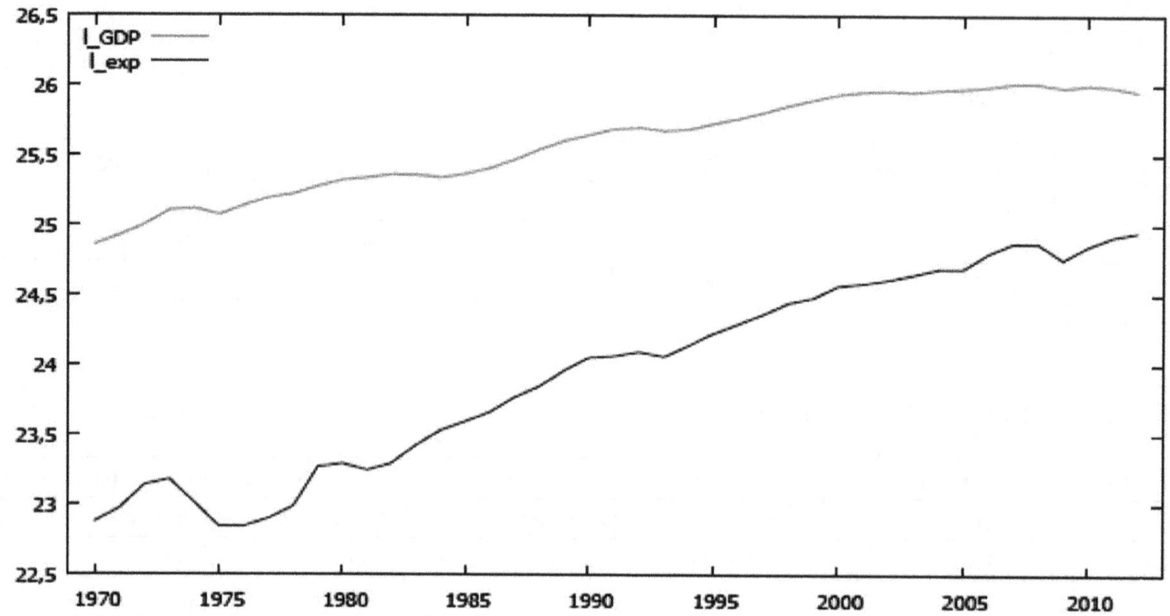

Figure 5. Ratio of Manufactured and Non-Manufactured Products to Total Exports of Goods

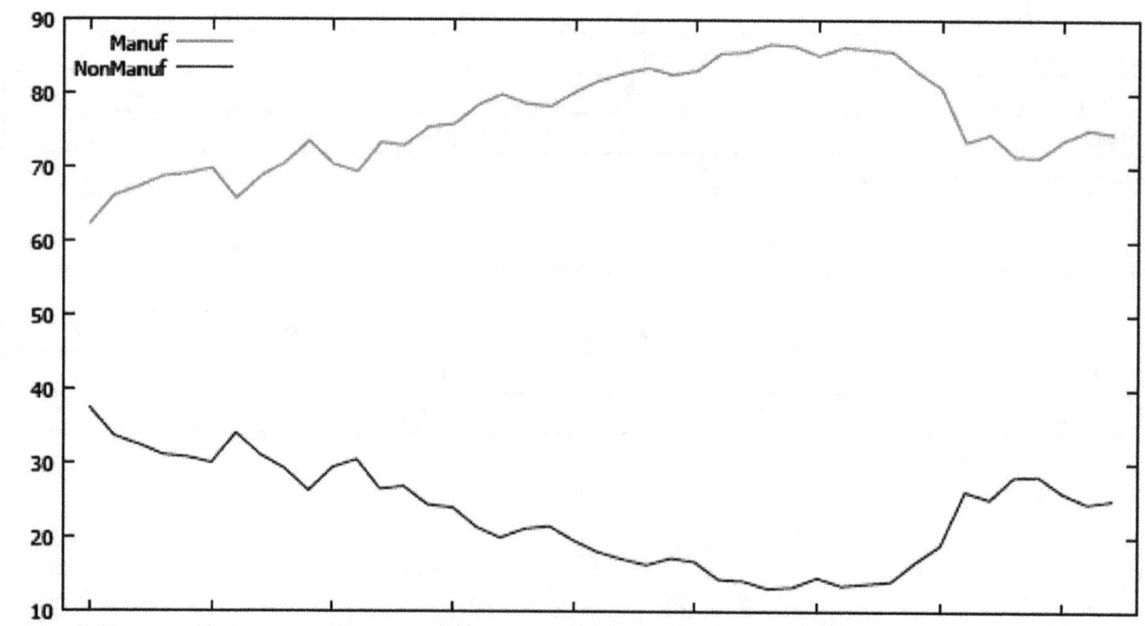

Chapter 7
Modeling Labor Market Flows on the Basis of Sectoral Employment in Europe

Mirko Savic
University of Novi Sad, Serbia

Jovan Zubovic
Institute of Economic Sciences, Serbia

ABSTRACT

By tracking the cross-sectoral distribution of employment growth, it is possible to significantly improve the ability to understand aggregate fluctuations of labor force. Adequate model can provide information which sectors have stronger impact on unemployment-to-employment transitional probability. The main goal of this research is modeling the influence of sectoral employment on outflow rate across Europe during economic crisis. Authors argue that shifts in sectoral demand have strong influence on cyclical variation in unemployment-to-employment transition. Study also uncovers highly linear relationships of outflow rate from unemployment to employment and job flows at sectoral level. Empirical data proved a strong positive correlation between dispersion of employment growth across sectors and outflow rate in Europe. Shifts in demand from some sectors to the others are responsible for significant fraction of unemployment-to-employment transition probability. Reallocation shocks accounted for about 70 to 80 percent variability of outflow rates across Europe, during the 2008-2012.

INTRODUCTION

The importance of sectoral reallocation as a source of labor market flows is well known fact and it is often cited in scientific literature. Sector specific shocks are changing the pattern of labor market demand among sectors. On the basis of relation between different sectors and indicators of unemployment flows it is possible to discover which sectors are more correlated with creation of jobs and leaving the unemployment status during the recent years. By tracking the cross-sectoral distribution of employment growth, and through implementation of robust models of sectoral behavior, it is possible to significantly

DOI: 10.4018/978-1-5225-0959-2.ch007

improve the ability to understand aggregate fluctuations of labor force. This information is very significant for policy makers in order to create labor market policies in efficient way. The econometrical model will provide us with information which sectors have stronger impact on reduction of unemployment throughout Europe in the last several years.

In scientific literature significant number of theoretical models of labor market are trying to explain labor market flows (hires and separations) and job gains and losses at the individual level. Authors are trying different approach, starting from sectoral-level and cross-sectional data to study the relationship between unemployment-to-employment transitional probability and job flows over five years, from 2008 to 2012. The similar approach is possible to find in Davis, Faberman, and Haltiwanger (2011). The five year period is in focus because it covers the period of "great recession" as it was named in the paper from Christiano et al. (2014).

The main goal of the research is to analyze the influence of employment shares across industrial sectors on outflow rate in European countries. Authors argue that shifts in labor demand among sectors, rather than changes in the level of aggregate demand, are the cause of cyclical variation in unemployment-to-employment transition in Europe. This study also uncovers highly linear relationships of outflow rate from unemployment to employment and job flows at sectoral level. Specific implications of the findings will be better policy measures in the field of labour market across different sectors. If we understand how different sectors behave during economic crisis in terms of employment and unemployment, it is possible to develop specific policy measures targeting sectors with greater impact on outflow rates in order to mitigate the negative effects of economic crisis on labor force.

Outflow rate is the measure of how fast an unemployed person can find a payed work (unemployment-to-employment transition). This is actually a probability of unemployed person to find a job, and it corresponds to instantaneous rates of transition on a monthly basis. There is also the inflow rate as a probability for employed person to become unemployed. Both indicators were calculated on the basis of ILO methodology. More on indicators of labor market flows can be found in Elsby et al. (2013), Shimer (2007), or Shimer (2012).

Inflow and outflow rates were designed to overcome simple stock approach and to help in more detailed analysis of labor market fluctuations and to understand the variation of unemployment from two aspects:

1. Employment-to-unemployment (separations); and
2. Unemployment-to-employment (job findings).

These measures of transition from one state to another are useful tool for targeting labor market policies in a specific way at certain subgroups of labor force or tool for adjusting the same policies and recommendations in accordance with domination of one kind of transition over another. Inflow and outflow rates are especially informative when they are analyzed in the context of economic cycles to better understand labor market upturns and downturns.

When it comes to the unemployment dynamics, there are differences in the scientific literature what leads cyclical changes in unemployment: inflows or job findings (outflows). One part of the researchers is claiming that unemployment-to-employment transition dominates and employment-to-unemployment transition has no cyclical impact. These findings were given by King (2011), Hall (2005), Shimer (2007), Shimer (2007), Gali and Blanchard (2008), Gertler and Trigari (2009), etc. According to King, the importance of unemployment-to-employment is very significant: "In summary, the results show that, while vacancies and separations both account for significant fractions of the cyclical fluctuations in unemployment, variation in the rate at which the unemployed exit the labor force can be viewed as the most important cyclical driver of the unemployment rate." (King, 2011).

Opposite statement is that separations (inflow rate) accounts closely or around the half of unemployment variance and leads cyclical variations (Fujita and Ramey (2009), Elsby et al. (2009), Petrongolo and Pissarides (2008), etc.). Most of these findings were based on the data from U.S. labor market. This research relies on the finding of the first group of authors and the focus in this paper will be exclusively on the outflow rate. The cross sectoral volatility series in employment are used to assess the importance of reallocation shocks for unemployment-to-employment transition probability fluctuations.

Elsby et al. (2013) in their research confirmed "counter cyclicality of the employment-to-unemployment transition probability, and the corresponding procyclicality of the unemployment-to-employment transition probability" on the basis of "gross flows" data from the Current Population Study (CPS) in USA. Authors' goal was to test the procyclicality of the unemployment-to-employment transition probability on the basis of the employment shifts across industries in European countries. Econometrical results will give us the possibility to recognize industries with strongest influence on the unemployment-to-employment transition probability in Europe through regression of outflow rate on sectoral employment.

First level of economic activity aggregation comprises three broad sectors: agriculture, industry and services. The textbook case of economic development is that reallocation of jobs is moving from agriculture to industry and to services sector at the end. Since authors would like to capture variation on more detailed level, they decided to focus the analysis on the second level of aggregation. The second level is based on the ISIC classification of sectors (International Standard Industrial Classification of all Economic Activities, Revision 4 (2008)). The main variables are percentages of employed persons in certain sector of total employment. Since broad classification onto three sectors can hide pattern of labor force movements, breakdown onto 19 sectors on the second level will help us in identification of more prosperous economic activities throughout Europe. This kind of analysis can serve as a guide for policy makers in order to improve skill match between labor market supply and demand through educational systems and training programs.

Before econometric analysis authors will conduct descriptive analysis of outflow rates and cluster analysis in order to compare the variations of sectoral employment across European countries and to discover the groups of similar countries. The cluster analysis will be conducted on the basis of differences between two periods. Differences were calculated from the employment shares at the beginning of economic crisis (2008) and with the latest available data (2012) in order to monitor the changes in sectoral structure across countries during the period of five years.

The paper is organized as following: After introduction, in Section 1 authors are giving the overview of the state-of-the-art in the field of labor market flows and cyclicality. In Section 2 authors are presenting the scientific methods implemented in this research and the data. Section 3 presents the results of cluster analysis and econometric models for three kinds of outflow rates. Finally, the last Section is dedicated to discussion and conclusions.

LITERATURE REVIEW

In the field of labor economy, relations between labor market flows and industrial sector from the aspect of cyclicality is the subject in the substantial number of scientific papers (Abraham and Katz (1984), Brainard and Cutler (1990), Barnichon et al. (2011), Corvers and Dupuy (2009), Davis, Faberman, and

Haltiwanger (2006), and especially Davis et al. (2011)Braun et al. (2006), Braun et al. (2007) and many others).

For example, Foster and Poschl (2009) were underlying importance of labor mobility at cross-sectional level for employment flows. Mukoyama (2013) is analyzing the job-to-job transitions in the USA and its cyclicality. Fujita and Ramey (2006) were suggesting that age is important factor and prime-age workers are demonstrating extremely countercyclical behavior while young workers on the other hand have procyclical adjustments. More general, Krusell et al. (2012), in their paper about labor supply and business cycles, are suggesting that it would be useful assessing relations between business cycles and various groups of population.

There are two aspects of looking at the problem of unemployment variations, through aggregate demand and sectoral shifts. Abraham and Katz (1984, p. 1) are suggesting that both explanations for cyclical unemployment have different policy implications and "the degree to which each of these two possible sources contributes to cyclical unemployment is a matter of considerable importance."

On the one hand, Keynesian economists are explaining unemployment through aggregate disturbances as the cause of business cycles, while on the other side business cycle theories are claiming that sectoral shocks and imperfect labor market adjustment are primarily responsible for labor market flows. Brainard and Cutler comment that constant debate "over the causes of unemployment persist in large part because it is difficult to distinguish empirically between unemployment associated with reallocation versus aggregate shocks." (Brainard & Cutler, 1990, p. 1).

Barnichon et al. (2011) were trying to explain Beveridge curve gap in USA through industry decomposition. They were trying to decompose the deviations from the Beveridge curve on the basis of micro data from Job Openings and Labor Turnover Survey (JOLTS). They have found that most of the recent deviations from the Beveridge curve can be explained through shortfalls in hires per vacancy and this phenomenon is spread across all industrial sectors, but especially in the construction, transportation, utilities, leisure, and hospitality.

Davis, Faberman, and Haltiwanger (2006) claim that the labor market flow magnitudes vary substantially across industrial sectors, even if industry groups were defined broadly. There is an example about job flow rates in construction and leisure & hospitality where flow rates are three times larger than in manufacturing. These variations in magnitude and nature of ins and outs of unemployment have significant impact on management of working force, the incidence of unemployment, and the response of unemployment to industry-level shocks.

In other paper from the same authors, there is a statement that "economic and statistical models of worker flow behavior in the cross section can significantly enhance our understanding of aggregate hires, separations, layoffs and quits" (Davis, Faberman, & Haltiwanger, 2011, p. 30).

The last economic crisis had strong impact on the cyclical behavior of unemployment. According to Elsby et al. (2011, p. 2) "The labor market downturn that accompanied the 2007-2009 recession was the most severe experienced in the postwar era, and the subsequent recovery has been tentative and uneven." The same group of authors is claiming that labor demand recovered modestly and it is not enough to generate significant drop of unemployment rate. This is why we have to analyze the labor market flows during great recession to discover which industries had more significant impact on the recovery of labor market in the context of creating efficient employment policies.

Modeling of labor market flows across sectors on the basis of econometrical techniques is in a way standard approach. Shimer argues that "if one wants to understand fluctuations in unemployment, one must understand fluctuations in the transition rate from unemployment to employment, the 'outs of unemployment" (Shimer, 2007). For example, Corvers and Dupuy (2009) were trying to estimate labor demand across sectors and occupations by using the system dynamic OLS techniques. They used the employment data from Labor Force Survey (LFS) of Statistics Netherlands. The major goal was to document the importance of short run dynamics of occupational employment among sectors, although they also estimated long run relations between sectoral and occupational employment. They discovered substantial differences within industries in the importance of intersectoral dynamics. Some sectors are strongly affected by intersectoral dynamics, like agriculture, transport, and banking and insurance, while many manufacturing industries are barely affected by other sectors in the short run.

Many other authors also conducted worker flows analysis but from the perspective of individuals (Blanchard, Diamond, Hall et al. (1990), Fallick and Fleischman (2004), Shimer (2007), Fujita et al. (2007), Fujita et al. (2008), etc.), Mueller (2012). This type of research studies is based on the longitudinal data on the individual employment status and cross-sectional data of employment duration and unemployment spells. The major goal of this studies is estimation of different labor market flows (between jobs, into and out of employment, unemployment, activity, and inactivity).

Large part of scientific sources about labor market flows is focused on the labor market of USA and their cyclicality. It is described and analyzed in details from many aspects. For example, Christiano et al. (2010) were analyzing involuntary unemployment and business cycles. Also, in Cristiano et al. (2013) they were writing about unemployment and business cycles, then Braun et al. (2007) were describing supply and demand shocks and labor market fluctuations, Hall (2005) tried to explain labor market flows in USA over the past fifty years, especially in the periods of crisis, etc.

There is significantly smaller number of papers about labor market flows in Europe. For example, in the paper from Elsby et al. (2008), authors are providing a set of comparable estimates for the inflow and outflow rates from unemployment for 14 OECD countries by using publicly available data collected through labor force surveys. Smith (2010) is examining the importance of job finding and separation in UK on the basis of data from British Household Panel Survey. Perhaps the problem is in the lack of reliable and elaborate data from all European countries. The results from Elsby et al. (2008) showed that among Anglo-Saxon countries inflow rates are contributing to unemployment variations by 20%, while outflow rates are contributing by 80%. In European countries this proportion is approximately 50:50 percent.

SCIENTIFIC METHODS

For the analysis authors were using the KILM comprehensive database of country-level data (Key Indicators of the Labor Market). KILM (8th Edition software) is multi-functional research tool of the International Labor Organization (ILO). Authors have created small panel-data series with 33 European countries over 5 year period (from 2008 to 2012). Data for 2012 were the latest available data.

Indicators of labor market fluctuations (inflow and outflow rates) in KILM database are displayed as estimates of unemployment transitions on monthly basis from employment to unemployment and unemployment to employment. Estimations were done on the basis of data on unemployment spells of different durations (less than one month, less than 3 months, less than 6 months, and less than one year). In the case of duration of less than one month, estimations were conducted following the methodology presented by Shimer (2012).

KILM database also contains weighted estimates of fluctuation rates, which are calculated on the basis of the methodology presented by Elsby et al. (2013). The weighted estimates of labor market flows were implemented when there is no evidence of unemployment duration or duration of less than one month.

Through modeling authors have implemented standard econometrical procedure for panel data series and model selection was based on the Breusch-Pagan test and Hausman test for the selection between fixed and random effects. Authors have created three models using three different indicators of unemployment-to-employment transition probability as dependent variables:

- Outflow rate defined by Elsby et al. (2013) (OutE)
- Outflow rate for unemployment spells of less than 12 months (OutSd12)
- Weighted outflow rate (OutWeighted).

As independent variables authors were using employment shares of 19 out of 22 industrial sectors according to ISIC classification of sectors (International Standard Industrial Classification of all Economic Activities, Revision 4 (2008)).

In order to avoid perfect multicollinearity, three categories were excluded from the analysis: T - Activities of households as employers; undifferentiated goods- and services-producing activities of households for own use; U - Activities of extraterritorial organizations and bodies; X - Not classifiable by economic activity. Also, for these three variables there are differences in national classifications and missing data problem because many countries did not report data for the categories in question. According to KILM (ILO, 2014) employment-by-sector indicators can be different across countries in the case of female employment in armed forces, self-employment and contributing family members. This elimination causes some limitations to this study but does not actually interfere significantly with the results and conclusions because the obtained models cover all major sectors of economic activity.

At the beginning of the analysis authors have done descriptive analysis of outflow rates and non-hierarchical clustering in order to compare the shares of sectoral employment across European countries and to identify the groups of similar countries. The cluster analysis has been conducted on the basis of differences in employment shares between two periods, between 2008 and 2012.

RESULTS

Figure 1 is showing the variations of outflow rate (calculated by Elsby et al. (2013)) since the beginning of economic crisis in 2008 until 2012, which are the latest available data from ILO, across European countries. We can see that unemployment-to-employment transition probability dropped during the five year period for almost all countries. The outflow rate is actually gradually dropping down since the beginning of recession. The only positive exception is Germany where the situation is opposite because outflow rate has grown. In the case of Lithuania data for 2008 were missing but it is easy to notice that indicator in question is also decreasing.

The explanation for Germany probably lies in the substantial flexibility of German labor market, where drop of employment in construction (F) and manufacturing (C) is compensated with growth in other sectors which are more resistant to the influence of economic crisis, like electricity, gas, steam and air conditioning supply (D) where outflow rate has grown from 0.8 in 2008 to 1.0 in 2012. The similar cases are sectors I (accommodation and food service activities), J (information and communication), L

Figure 1. Variation of outflow rate according to Elsby et al. (2013) during five-year period (2008-2012)
Source: Author's own calculations.

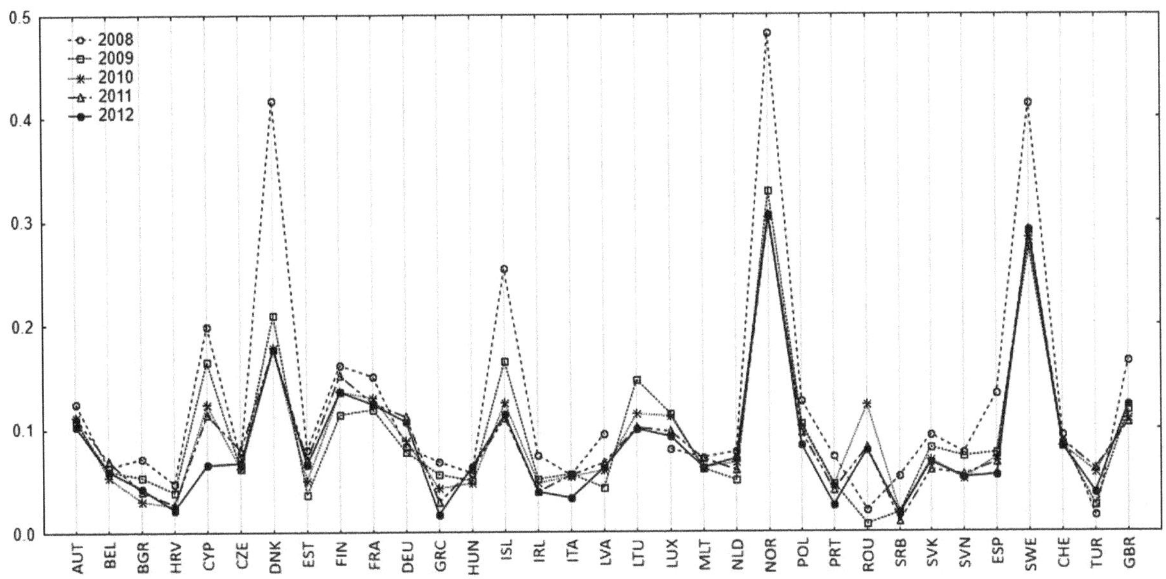

(real estate activities), M (professional, scientific and technical activities), N (administrative and support service activities), P (education), and Q (human health and social work activities).

This graph is showing us that the impact of economic crisis is widespread across entire region and unemployment-to-employment transition probability is showing the similar variations in almost all countries. In Appendix there are two more graphs with outflow rates for the 12 months unemployment spells and for weighted estimates of fluctuation rates. The question is which industrial sectors are significantly influencing the variations of outflow rate?

The next step was to conduct cluster analysis of European countries in the case of employment shares across industrial sectors in order to show variations and to discover groups of similar countries. Results of non-hierarchical clustering are showing four different clusters. Analysis of variance discovered that in the case of 8 out of 19 sectors there are statistically significant differences among clusters:

- A - Agriculture, forestry and fishing
- C - Manufacturing
- F - Construction
- H - Transportation and storage
- I - Accommodation and food service activities
- M - Professional, scientific and technical activities
- P - Education
- S - Other service activities.

Complete results of cluster analysis are presented in the Appendix of this paper. The following picture (Figure 2) is showing the average differences of employment shares between 2008 and 2012 across sectors for each cluster separately.

Figure 2. Average differences of sectoral employment shares between 2008 and 2012 across four clusters
Source: Author's own calculations.

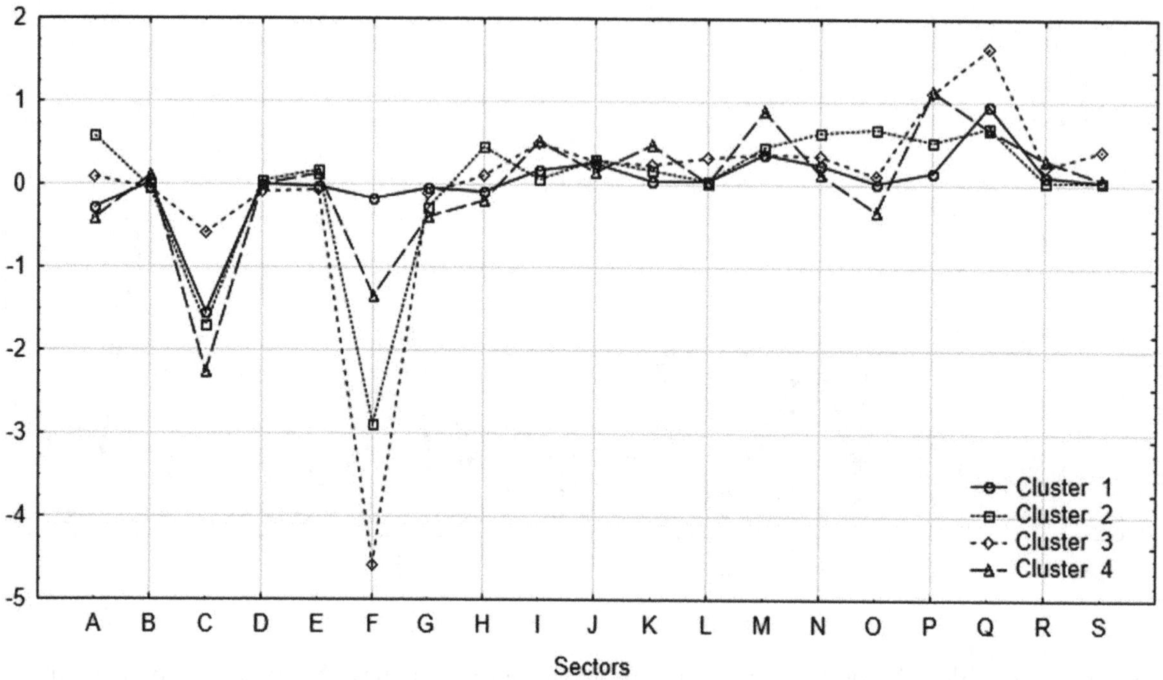

Changes in demand are manifested in the following way across sectors: The biggest "losers" are construction (F) and manufacturing (C). Considerable drop of demand is noticed in agriculture, forestry and fishing (A) but not in all countries, and also in the case of transportation and storage (H) and public administration and defence; compulsory social security (O). Some countries actually had the increase of employment in these three sectors. On the other side, the biggest "winners" where employment moved during the period of crisis are accommodation and food service activities (I), financial and insurance activities (K), professional, scientific and technical activities (M), education (P), human health and social work activities (Q), and other service activities (S).

Cluster 1 is the largest group with 13 countries and it is characterized with smallest differences between two periods when it comes to the employment shares across sectors, which means that in almost all sectors the level of employment shares in 2012 is equal to the level in 2008, with exception of sector C (manufacturing) – largest decrease, and Q (human health and social work activities) were they have increase of employment shares. Cluster 2 is comprised out of five Eastern European countries plus Greece and this cluster has the significant drop of employment shares in sector C (manufacturing) and F (construction) and largest positive movement in the case of sector A (agriculture, forestry and fishing), H (transportation and storage), N (administrative and support service activities), and O (Public administration and defense; compulsory social security). Cluster 3 has five countries and with largest negative difference in the case of sector F (construction), while in many other sectors their performance was above the average. Cluster 4 has five countries with largest negative differences in the case of sectors A (agriculture, forestry and fishing), C (manufacturing), H (transportation and storage), and O (administration and defense; compulsory social security), while they have the increase of employment shares in sectors K (Financial and insurance activities), and M (professional, scientific and technical activities). In general, the conclusion is that employment shares during the five years of recession are shifting from production sectors like agriculture, manufacturing and production towards non-industrial, public sectors like education, health, public administration, etc.

From the aspect of policy measures, the results of cluster analysis are suggesting that in the case of the countries from Cluster 1, for improvement of employment and returning to the levels before economic crisis policy measures must be targeted most of all towards manufacturing sector (C), agriculture, forestry and fishing (A) and construction (F). In the case of Cluster 2, policy measures must be targeting increase of employment in manufacturing sector and construction also. Countries in Cluster 3 have extremely difficult problem in the manufacturing sector, but they can continue to implement the existing policy measures in the case of sector Q (human health and social work activities) because that sectors are in relatively better position after crisis then before. Cluster 4 must target its policy measures towards sectors A, C and F, but they can be satisfied with the situation in sectors M (professional, scientific and technical activities) and P (education). Similar sectors are the problem across clusters, but the magnitude is significantly different. Therefore policy measures in construction must have much stronger impact in countries from clusters 2 and 3, while in the case of the countries from cluster 4 stronger impact must be obtained in the case of manufacturing, even at the expense of some other sectors.

Econometric Model

The results of econometric analysis are presented in the following table (Table 1). The difference among three models is in the choice of dependent variable, which is named in the second row of the table.

On the basis of F-test we can conclude that all three models are good because p-values are very small and less than significance level of 1% (last row in Table 1). More detailed tables were given in the Appendix of this paper. In the case of Model 1 authors have selected pooled OLS estimation because in the case of panel data analysis they have obtained high p-values for Breusch-Pagan test (p=0.124651) and Hausman test (p=0.164783). Heteroskedasticity for Model 1 was not detected (White's test for heteroskedasticity, p=0.233216).

In the case of Model 2 authors have also selected to conduct the pooled OLS estimation because of high p-values for Breusch-Pagan test (p=0.137956) and Hausman test (p=0.20013). The model was corrected because of detected heteroskedasticity (White's test, p=2.89816e-005). The same situation is in the case of Model 3: pooled OLS estimation, Breusch-Pagan test (p=0.130081), Hausman test (p=0.221135) and correction for detected heteroskedasticity (White's test, p=6.61673e-005).

In the case of the Model 1, where authors regressed outflow rate by Elsby et al. (2013) on sectoral employment shares, the conclusion is that employment growth in different sectors has different impact on the probability of unemployed person to find a job. For example, the employment growth of 1% in sector A (agriculture, forestry and fishing) will on average increase the outflow rate for 0.009%. Beside sector A, positive influence on employment probability is also in the case of sectors B, C, F, G, J, L, M, O, and Q. It is interesting that sector K (financial and insurance activities) has negative sign, and it is probably because of different variations in that sector during economic crisis. The largest impact on the growth of unemployment-to-employment transitional probability is in the case of sectors J (information and communication) and L (real estate activities), where 1% of growth will generate approximately 0.06% of outflow probability growth. Overall, the Model 1 is explaining 70.2% of variations in outflow rate across European countries through variations of sectoral employment.

Table 1. Regression estimates for influence of cross-sectoral employment shares on outflow rate across European countries. Source: Author's own calculations.

	Model 1		Model 2		Model 3	
Dependent variable	OutE (Outflow rate (Elsby et al., 2013))		OutSd12 (Outflow rate, d< 12 months)		OutWeighted (Outflow rate, weighted)	
Independent variables	*Coefficient*		*Coefficient*		*Coefficient*	
const	-0.902	***	-0.182	**	-0.139	*
A Agriculture, forestry and fishing	0.009	***	0.003	***	0.002	**
B Mining and quarrying	0.036	**	0.023	***	0.031	***
C Manufacturing	0.006	**	0.003	***	0.002	**
D Electricity, gas, steam and air conditioning supply	-0.036		-0.057	***	-0.055	***
E Water supply; sewerage, waste management and remediation act.	0.026		-0.024	***	-0.019	**
F Construction	0.021	***	0.007	***	0.007	***
G Wholesale and retail trade; repair of motor vehicles and motorcycles	0.020	***	0.010	***	0.009	***
H Transportation and storage	-0.014		-0.001		-0.003	
I Accommodation and food service activities	-0.009		-0.008	***	-0.008	***
J Information and communication	0.061	***	0.018	***	0.019	***
K Financial and insurance activities	-0.014	*	-0.003		-0.005	*
L Real estate activities	0.064	***	0.017	***	0.019	***
M Professional, scientific and technical activities	0.025	***	0.006		0.005	
N Administrative and support service activities	-0.003		-0.003		-0.003	
O Public administration and defense; compulsory social security	0.012	**	-0.002		-0.001	
P Education	0.007		-0.000		-0.002	
Q Human health and social work activities	0.012	***	0.003	**	0.002	
R Arts, entertainment and recreation	-0.019		0.007		0.009	
S Other service activities	0.005		0.000		0.006	
R-squared	0.702		0.814		0.838	
S.E. of regression	0.048		1.779		1.638	
P-value(F)	5.81e-24		5.62e-36		1.57e-39	

Source: authors' calculations based on data from KILM database.
* indicates significance at the 10 percent level
** indicates significance at the 5 percent level
*** indicates significance at the 1 percent level

In the Model 2 authors regressed estimates of outflow rates calculated on the basis of unemployment spells less than twelve months on sectoral employment. Overall, the Model 2 is explaining 81.4% of variations in outflow rate across European countries through variations of sectoral employment.

In the Model 3 there is regression of weighted outflow rate estimates based on the methodology proposed by Elsby et al (2013). This model is very similar to the previous one and there are only two major differences, in the case of two sectors: K (Financial and insurance activities – significant only in Model 3) and Q (Human health and social work activities – significant only in Model 2). The Model 3 is explaining 83.8% of variations in outflow rate across European countries through variations of sectoral employment.

The mutual characteristic of these three models is that employment growth in five sectors does not have any significant influence on the outflow rate: H (transportation and storage), N (administrative and support service activities), P (education), R (arts, entertainment and recreation), and S (other service activities).

According to the values information criteria (Log-likelihood and Akaike criterion), the conclusion is that Model 1 is the best among three models and it describes in the best way relations of sectoral employment shares with outflow rates.

CONCLUSION

Authors have developed econometrical models for evaluation of relationship between outflow rate and cross-sectoral employment. Aggregate fluctuations of unemployment-to-employment transition probability are well captured by empirical specifications about significant cross-sectoral link between worker flows and job flows. Authors showed that cross-sectoral employment contains information that substantially improves our ability to understand the movements in aggregate labor market flows.

Empirical data proved a strong positive correlation between dispersion of employment growth across sectors and outflow rate in Europe. It implies that shifts in demand from some sectors to the others are responsible for significant fraction of unemployment-to-employment transition probability. In the best model (Model 1) variations of sectoral employment shares is explaining 70.2% of variations in outflow rate across European countries.

Econometric analysis in this research actually started from implementation of fixed effects model, which takes into account specific characteristics of every unit of observation, in this case every country. In other words, the focus is on "within" variation inside every country, but the Breusch-Pagan test showed that although every country has its own characteristics, these characteristics are not correlated with coefficients in the model, so the key lies in the overall variations, and not in "within" variations when it comes to the outflow rates.

Authors have concluded that reallocation shocks accounted for about 70 to 80 percent variability of outflow rates across Europe, during the five year period (2008-2012). This results suggests that reallocation of employment has substantial economic importance and significant contribution to fluctuations in unemployment. The largest impact on the growth of unemployment-to-employment transitional probability authors have found in the case of sectors J (information and communication) and L (real estate activities).

Obtained econometrical models are significantly informative in the context of analyzing economic cycles for better understanding of labor market variations and creation of efficient labor market policies.

Further research in the area will be oriented towards cross-cluster analysis and modeling of outflow rates on the cluster level.

This paper represents the contribution in the area of relations between labor market flows and industrial aspect of cyclicality. The added value of this paper lies in the explanation of behavior of different industrial sectors in condition of economic crisis and it is based on the latest available data from country-level KILM comprehensive database. The new information should help policy makers and experts in the area to better understand the phenomena in question.

REFERENCES

Abraham, K. G., & Katz, L. F. (1984). *Cyclical Unemployment: Sectoral Shifts or Agregate Disturbances?* National Bureau of Economic Research Cambridge, Working Paper No. 1410.

Barnichon, R., Elsby, M., Hobijn, B., & Sahin, A. (2011). *Which Industries are Shifting the Beveridge Curve.* Federal Reserve Bank of San Francisco, Working Paper No. 2010-32.

Blanchard, O. J., Diamond, P., Hall, R. E., & Murphy, K. (1990). The Cyclical Behavior of the Gross Flows of U.S. Workers. *Brookings Papers on Economic Activity, 1990*(2), 85–143. doi:10.2307/2534505

Brainard, L. S., & Cutler, D. M. (1990). *Sectoral Shifts and Cyclical Unemployment Reconsider.* National Bureau of Economic Research Cambridge Working Paper No. 3491.

Braun, H., De Bock, R., & DiCecio, R. (2006). *Aggregate Shocks and Labor Market Fluctuations.* Federal Reserve Bank of St. Louis Working Paper No. 2006-004A.

Braun, H., De Bock, R., & DiCecio, R. (2007). *Supply Shocks, Demand Shocks, and Labor Market Fluctuations.* Federal Reserve Bank of St. Louis Working Paper No. 2007-015A.

Christiano, L. J., Eichenbaum, M. S., & Trabandt, M. (2013). *Unemployment and Business Cycles.* National Bureau of Economic Research Cambridge Working Paper No. 19265.

Christiano, L. J., Eichenbaum, M. S., & Trabandt, M. (2014). *Understanding the Great Recession.* National Bureau of Economic Research Cambridge Working Paper No. 20040.

Christiano, L. J., Trabandt, M., & Walentin, K. (2010). *Involuntary Unemployment and the Business Cycle.* National Bureau of Economic Research Cambridge Working Paper No. 15901.

Corvers, F., & Dupuy, A. (2009). *Estimating Employment Dynamics across Occupations and Sectors of Industry.* IZA Bonn Discussion Paper Series No. 4428.

Davis, S. J., Faberman, J. R., & Haltiwanger, J. (2006). *The Flow Approach to Labor Markets: New Data Sources and Micro-Macro Links.* National Bureau of Economic Research Cambridge Working Paper No. 12167.

Davis, S. J., Faberman, J., & Haltiwanger, J. C. (2011). *Labor Market Flows in the Cross Section and Over Time.* National Bureau of Economic Research Cambridge Working Paper No. 17294.

Elsby, M., Hobijn, B., & Sahin, A. (2008). *Unemployment Dynamics in the OECD*. National Bureau of Economic Research Cambridge Working Paper No. 14617.

Elsby, M. W., Hobijn, B., & Sahin, A. (2013). *On the Importance of the Participation Margin for Market Fluctuations*. Federal Reserve Bank of San Francisco Working Paper No. 2013-05.

Elsby, M. W., Hobijn, B., Sahin, A., & Valletta, R. G. (2011). *The Labor Market in the Great Recession: an Update*. Federal Reserve Bank of San Francisco Working Paper Series No. 2011-29.

Elsby, M. W., Michaels, R., & Solon, G. (2009). The Ins and Outs of Cyclical Unemployment. *American Economic Journal. Macroeconomics, 1*(1), 84–110. doi:10.1257/mac.1.1.84

Fallick, B., & Fleischmann, C. A. (2004). *Employer-to-Employer Flows in the U.S. Labor Market: The Complete Picture of Gross Worker Flows*. Finance and Economic Discussion Series Washington Working Paper No. 2004-34.

Foster, N., & Poschl, J. (2009). *The Importance of Labour Mobility for Spillovers across Industries*. The Vienna Institute for International Economic Studies Working Paper No. 58.

Fujita, S., Nekarda, C. J., & Ramey, G. (2007). *The Cyclicality of Worker Flows: New Evidence from the SIPP*. Federal Reserve Bank of Philadelphia Working Paper No. 07-5.

Fujita, S., & Ramey, G. (2006). *The Cyclicality of Job Loss and Hiring*. Federal Reserve Bank of Philadelphia Working Paper No. 06-17.

Fujita, S., & Ramey, G. (2008). *The Cyclicality of Separation and Job Finding Rates*. Federal Reserve Bank of Philadelphia Working Paper No. 07-19/R.

Fujita, S., & Ramey, G. (2009). The Cyclicality of Separation and Job Finding Rates. *International Economic Review, 50*(2), 415–430. doi:10.1111/j.1468-2354.2009.00535.x

Gali, J., & Blanchard, O. (2008). *Labor Markets and Monetary Policy: A New-Keynesian Model with Unemployment*. National Bureau of Economic Research Cambridge Working Paper No. 13897.

Gertler, M., & Trigari, A. (2009). Unemployment Fluctuations with Staggered Nash Wage Bargaining. *Journal of Political Economy, 117*(1), 38–86. doi:10.1086/597302

Hall, R. E. (2005). Employment Efficiency and Sticky Wages: Evidence from Flows in the Labor Market. *The Review of Economics and Statistics, 297*(3), 397–407. doi:10.1162/0034653054638346

Hall, R. E. (2005). *Job Loss, Job Finding, and Unemployment in the U.S. Economy over the Past Fifty Years*. National Bureau of Economic Research Cambridge Working Paper No. 11678.

ILO. (2014). *Key Indicators of the Labour Market (KILM)* (8th ed.). Retrieved July 2, 2014 from Key Indicators of the Labour Market (KILM): http://www.ilo.org/empelm/what/WCMS_114240/lang--en/index.htm

King, T. B. (2011). *Variable Participation and Cyclical Unemployment*. Division of Monetary Affairs, Federal Reserve Board Washington.

Krusell, P., Mukoyama, T., Rogerson, R., & Sahin, A. (2012). *Is Labor Supply Important for Business Cycles*. National Bureau of Economic Research Cambridge Working Paper No. 17779.

Mueller, A. I. (2012). *Separations, Sorting and Cyclical Unemployment*. IZA Bonn Discussion Paper No. 6849.

Mukoyama, T. (2013). *The Cyclicality of Job-to-Job Transitions and Its Implications for Aggregate Productivity*. Board of Governors of the Federal Reserve System Washington, International Finance Discussion Papers No. 1074.

Petrongolo, B., & Pissarides, C. A. (2008). The Ins and Outs of European Unemployment. *The American Economic Review*, *98*(2), 256–262. doi:10.1257/aer.98.2.256

Robert, S. (2005). The Cyclical Behavior of Equilibrium Unemployment and Vacancies. *The American Economic Review*, *95*(1), 25–49. doi:10.1257/0002828053828572

Shimer, R. (2007). *Reassessing the Ins and Outs of Unemployment*. National Bureau of Economic Research Cambridge Working paper series No 13421.

Shimer, R. (2012). Reassessing the Ins and Outs of Unemployment. *Review of Economic Dynamics*, *15*(2), 127–148. doi:10.1016/j.red.2012.02.001

Smith, J. C. (2010). *The Ins and Outs of UK Unemployment*. The University of Warwick, Department of Economics, Warwick Economic Research Papers No. 944.

APPENDIX

Figure 3. Variation of outflow rate (unemployment spells less than 12 months) during five year period (2008-2012)

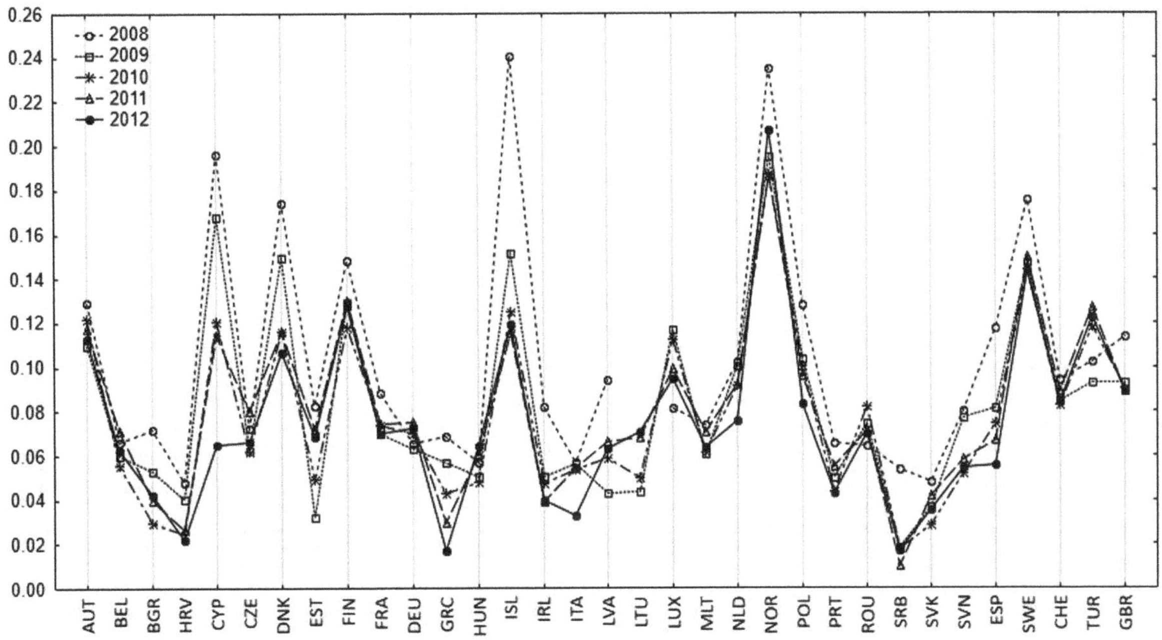

Figure 4. Variation of weighted outflow rate during five year period (2008-2012)

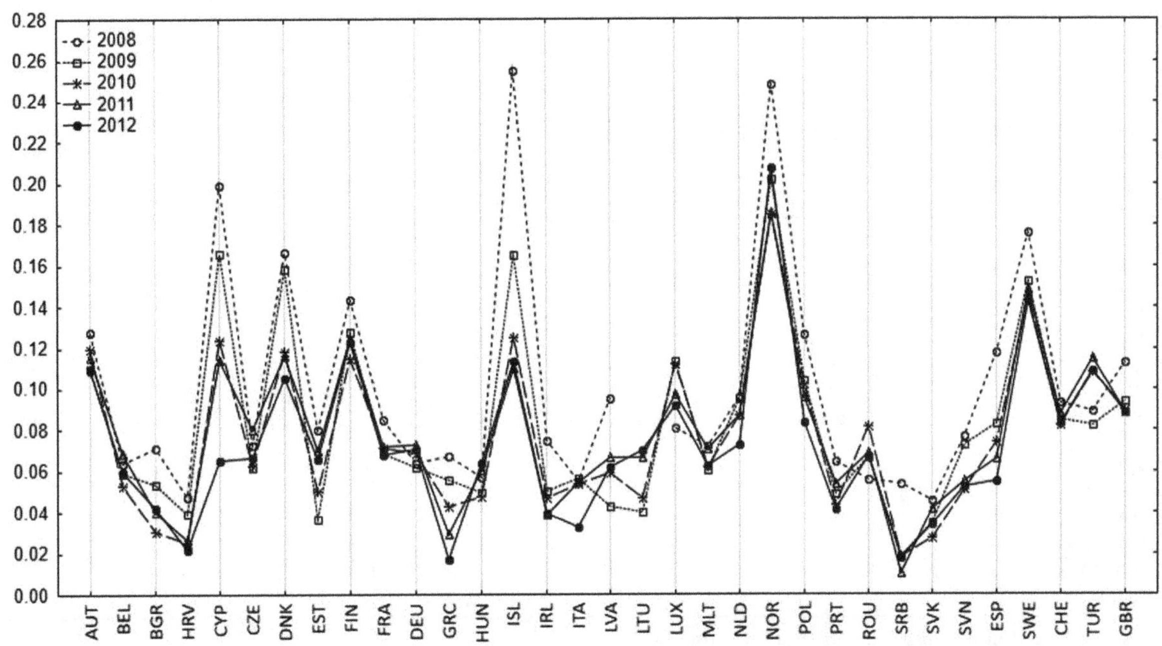

Table 2. Analysis of variance: Testing statistical differences among clusters in the case of employment shares across industrial sectors. Source: Author's own calculations.

Variable	Analysis of Variance					
	Between SS	df	Within SS	df	F	Signif. p
A Agriculture, forestry and fishing	4.045	3	10.465	25	3.221	0.040
B Mining and quarrying	0.075	3	0.544	25	1.144	0.351
C Manufacturing	7.351	3	14.791	25	4.142	0.016
D Electricity, gas, steam and air conditioning supply	0.048	3	0.712	25	0.559	0.647
E Water supply; sewerage, waste management and remediation act.	0.236	3	1.494	25	1.317	0.291
F Construction	81.528	3	10.251	25	66.278	0.000
G Wholesale and retail trade; repair of motor vehicles and motorcycles	0.614	3	16.536	25	0.310	0.818
H Transportation and storage	1.588	3	1.864	25	7.098	0.001
I Accommodation and food service activities	0.956	3	2.609	25	3.055	0.047
J Information and communication	0.061	3	1.691	25	0.300	0.825
K Financial and insurance activities	0.702	3	3.706	25	1.579	0.220
L Real estate activities	0.324	3	2.743	25	0.983	0.417
M Professional, scientific and technical activities	1.115	3	2.992	25	3.107	0.045
N Administrative and support service activities	0.823	3	4.470	25	1.535	0.230
O Public administration and defense; compulsory social security	2.865	3	9.989	25	2.391	0.093
P Education	5.288	3	7.378	25	5.973	0.003
Q Human health and social work activities	3.234	3	12.768	25	2.111	0.124
R Arts, entertainment and recreation	0.212	3	0.880	25	2.012	0.138
S Other service activities	0.567	3	1.467	25	3.221	0.040

Source: own calculations based on data from KILM database.

Table 3. Cluster membership. Source: Author's own calculations

Cluster 1	Cluster 2	Cluster 3	Cluster 4
13 Cases	6 Cases	5 Cases	5 Cases
Distance	Distance	Distance	Distance
AUT 0.498	BGR 0.746	ISL 0.699	CYP 0.574
BEL 0.540	HRV 0.340	IRL 0.489	DNK 0.361
CZE 0.341	EST 0.314	LVA 0.641	MLT 0.366
FIN 0.229	GRC 0.364	PRT 0.484	SVN 0.532
FRA 0.260	HUN 0.412	ESP 0.519	GBR 0.375
DEU 0.212	LTU 0.370		
ITA 0.302			
NOR 0.496			
POL 0.350			
ROU 0.351			
SVK 0.350			
SWE 0.318			
CHE 0.389			

Source: own calculations based on data from KILM database.

Complete Results of Three Econometric Models for Regression of Outflow Rate on Sectoral Employment Shares

Model 1. Pooled OLS, using 143 observations

Included 33 cross-sectional units Time-series length: minimum 3, maximum 5 Dependent variable: OutE (Outflow rate (Elsby et al., 2013))				
	Coefficient	***Std. Error***	***p-value***	
const	-0.902	0.267	0.001	***
A Agriculture, forestry and fishing	0.009	0.003	0.003	***
B Mining and quarrying	0.036	0.014	0.013	**
C Manufacturing	0.006	0.003	0.024	**
D Electricity, gas, steam and air conditioning supply	-0.036	0.026	0.170	
E Water supply; sewerage, waste management and remediation act.	0.026	0.019	0.178	
F Construction	0.021	0.004	0.000	***
G Wholesale and retail trade; repair of motor vehicles and motorcycles	0.020	0.005	0.000	***
H Transportation and storage	-0.014	0.009	0.118	
I Accommodation and food service activities	-0.009	0.006	0.113	
J Information and communication	0.061	0.017	0.000	***
K Financial and insurance activities	-0.014	0.007	0.053	*
L Real estate activities	0.064	0.018	0.001	***
M Professional, scientific and technical activities	0.025	0.007	0.001	***
N Administrative and support service activities	-0.003	0.008	0.674	
O Public administration and defense; compulsory social security	0.012	0.006	0.037	**
P Education	0.007	0.005	0.150	
Q Human health and social work activities	0.012	0.004	0.002	***
R Arts, entertainment and recreation	-0.019	0.019	0.317	
S Other service activities	0.005	0.015	0.760	

Mean dependent var	0.098	S.D. dependent var	0.082
Sum squared resid	0.281	S.E. of regression	0.048
R-squared	0.702	Adjusted R-squared	0.656
F(19, 123)	15.268	P-value(F)	0.000
Log-likelihood	242.644	Akaike criterion	-445.289
Schwarz criterion	-386.032	Hannan-Quinn	-421.209
rho	0.000	Durbin-Watson	1.651

Source: own calculations based on data from KILM database.
White's test for heteroskedasticity, OLS, using 143 observations
Dependent variable: uhat^2, Test statistic: TR^2 = 43.977, with p-value = P(Chi-square(38) > 43.977430) = 0.233

Model 2. Heteroskedasticity-corrected, using 143 observations

Dependent variable: OutSd12 (Outflow rate, d< 12 months (Shimer, 2012))				
	Coefficient	*Std. Error*	*p-value*	
const	-0.182	0.071	0.012	**
A Agriculture, forestry and fishing	0.003	0.001	0.001	***
B Mining and quarrying	0.023	0.006	0.000	***
C Manufacturing	0.003	0.001	0.002	***
D Electricity, gas, steam and air conditioning supply	-0.057	0.01	0.000	***
E Water supply; sewerage, waste management and remediation act.	-0.024	0.008	0.002	***
F Construction	0.007	0.001	0.000	***
G Wholesale and retail trade; repair of motor vehicles and motorcycles	0.010	0.002	0.000	***
H Transportation and storage	-0.001	0.003	0.760	
I Accommodation and food service activities	-0.008	0.002	0.002	***
J Information and communication	0.019	0.006	0.005	***
K Financial and insurance activities	-0.003	0.003	0.208	
L Real estate activities	0.017	0.005	0.002	***
M Professional, scientific and technical activities	0.006	0.004	0.140	
N Administrative and support service activities	-0.003	0.003	0.317	
O Public administration and defense; compulsory social security	-0.002	0.002	0.390	
P Education	-0.001	0.002	0.744	
Q Human health and social work activities	0.003	0.001	0.022	**
R Arts, entertainment and recreation	0.007	0.006	0.260	
S Other service activities	0.000	0.006	0.971	

Source: Author's own calculations

Table 4. Statistics based on the weighted data

Sum squared resid	389.121	S.E. of regression	1.779
R-squared	0.814	Adjusted R-squared	0.785
F(19, 123)	28.305	P-value(F)	0.000
Log-likelihood	-274.483	Akaike criterion	588.966
Schwarz criterion	648.223	Hannan-Quinn	613.045

Table 5. Statistics based on the original data

Mean dependent var	0.082	S.D. dependent var	0.043
Sum squared resid	0.093	S.E. of regression	0.028

Source: own calculations based on data from KILM database.

Model 3. Heteroskedasticity-corrected, using 143 observations

Dependent variable: OutWeighted (Outflow rate, weighted)				
	Coefficient	*Std. Error*	*p-value*	
const	-0.139	0.076	0.070	*
A Agriculture, forestry and fishing	0.002	0.001	0.027	**
B Mining and quarrying	0.031	0.005	0.000	***
C Manufacturing	0.002	0.001	0.039	**
D Electricity, gas, steam and air conditioning supply	-0.055	0.01	0.000	***
E Water supply; sewerage, waste management and remediation act.	-0.019	0.007	0.012	**
F Construction	0.007	0.001	0.000	***
G Wholesale and retail trade; repair of motor vehicles and motorcycles	0.009	0.002	0.000	***
H Transportation and storage	-0.003	0.003	0.355	
I Accommodation and food service activities	-0.008	0.002	0.001	***
J Information and communication	0.019	0.006	0.003	***
K Financial and insurance activities	-0.005	0.003	0.074	*
L Real estate activities	0.019	0.005	0.000	***
M Professional, scientific and technical activities	0.005	0.003	0.140	
N Administrative and support service activities	-0.003	0.002	0.151	
O Public administration and defense; compulsory social security	-0.001	0.002	0.519	
P Education	-0.002	0.002	0.190	
Q Human health and social work activities	0.002	0.002	0.109	
R Arts, entertainment and recreation	0.009	0.006	0.133	
S Other service activities	0.006	0.006	0.303	

Source: Author's own calculations

Table 6. Statistics based on the weighted data

Sum squared resid	330.217	S.E. of regression	1.639
R-squared	0.838	Adjusted R-squared	0.813
F(19, 123)	33.411	P-value(F)	0.000
Log-likelihood	-262.747	Akaike criterion	565.494
Schwarz criterion	624.751	Hannan-Quinn	589.573

Table 7. Statistics based on the original data

Mean dependent var	0.081	S.D. dependent var	0.043
Sum squared resid	0.092	S.E. of regression	0.027

Source: own calculations based on data from KILM database.

Chapter 8
Typologies as Management Tools:
Understanding the Environmental Attitudes and Economic Prospects of Mussel Farmers in Greece

Alexandros Theodoridis
Aristotle University of Thessaloniki, Greece

Panagiotis Angelidis
Aristotle University of Thessaloniki, Greece

Athanasios Ragkos
Alexander Technological Educational Institute of Thessaloniki, Greece

Christos Batzios
Aristotle University of Thessaloniki, Greece

Vagis Samathrakis
Alexander Technological Educational Institute of Thessaloniki, Greece

ABSTRACT

Mussel farming in Greece constitutes an important economic activity for the areas where it is concentrated. This paper presents the results of a survey of mussel producers in Thermaikos Gulf, Northern Greece, where almost 90% of the total mussel production in the country takes place. Using data from a questionnaire survey of 66 mussel producers in the area, a typology is elaborated, by means of which three types of mussel farmers are discerned. "Professionals" are the ones continuing their family tradition, "Newcomers" are those who chose mussel farming as their main occupation and recently invested in the sector and "Aged amateurs" are the oldest and least educated group, members of which plan to pass their farm to younger family members. There is strong evidence that the sampled "Newcomers" achieve considerably higher financial results, however the sample size is not adequate to generalize for all results except for the farm income. When it comes to their environmental attitudes, mussel farmers comply to bans in cases where high toxin concentrates are detected, but they are not convinced about the effectiveness of controls. They discern very clearly between the environmental and regulatory measures necessary to boost the productivity of the sector, but they seem to proclaim by far the latter type of adjustments, including the resolution of location issues. Based on the profile of each cluster and the general results of the sample proposals are made concerning the implementation of the new Common Fisheries Policy.

DOI: 10.4018/978-1-5225-0959-2.ch008

INTRODUCTION

The sea aquaculture constitutes today one of the most dynamic economic activities of the primary sector in Greece. It consists of the fish and mussel farming sub-sectors, whose main characteristic is their intense export orientation. Approximately 80% of Greek fish aquaculture production, principally European seabass (Dicentrarchus labrax) and Gilthead seabream (Sparus aurata) and 90% of Mediterranean mussels (Mytilus galloprovincialis) are exported, mainly to the European market (FAO, 2015; Karagiannis et al., 2013; Theodorou et al., 2011). According to the Greek and European Statistical Authorities, the production of farmed fish in Greece, 95% of which is seabass and seabream, reached up to 90.7 thousand tons in 2013 with a value of 408.5 million €, while mussel production averaged 17,193 tons with a value of 6.7 million € (European Commission, 2014). Today, aquaculture is the leading agricultural sector in Greece, and fisheries constitute a strategic product for the national economy (European Commission, 2014). Apart from the decline in the traditional fishing sector, the rapid growth of aquaculture in Greece in the last three decades can be attributed to the extended and sheltered coastline of the country, the prevailing favorable climatic conditions and the increased demand for fresh marine products of high nutritional value (Theodorou et al., 2010; Theodorou et al., 2011).

Although Greece is one of the largest producers in seabass and seabream in the EU, the country's mussel farming sector has not been developed according to its growth potentials. The Greek mussel sector entails a strong impact on the rural economy, providing employment for a significant part of the local population and producing a high quality product. More than 300 farms, located mainly in the Thermaikos Gulf (North Aegean Sea, Region of Central Macedonia) are engaged in mussel farming. The farms operating in Thermaikos Gulf account for almost 90% of the annual harvest in the country, constituting the main centre of mussel production in Greece (Theodorou et al., 2010; Galinou-Mitsoudi et al., 2006).

The legislative framework for the operation of aquaculture in general, including, of course, mussel production, is the Common Fisheries Policy (CFP). Its basic goal is to ensure that the sectors of fisheries and aquaculture are environmentally, economically and socially sustainable and that they produce healthy food for EU citizens. At the same time, the CFP seeks to promote the dynamics of the fisheries sector and to ensure reasonable standards of living for fishermen and their communities. A basic principal of the CFP in the 2015-2020 period is to ensure the viability of fish stocks over time, through a safe approach which recognizes the impact of human activities in all elements of water and marine ecosystems. It aims at rendering fish fleets more selective in their choice of catches. As a result, CFP promotes regulatory measures for farmers, including mussel producers, whose intentions, needs and basic characteristics should be explicitly recognized in order to understand their dynamics and anticipate their impact on the environment and the growth of the sector. Then, the implementation of relevant measures could become less generalized and more targeted on the particular profiles of farmers, thus significantly increasing their efficiency in the achievement of the strategic goals set by the EU.

The purpose of this paper is to examine the profile and the attitudes of Greek mussel farmers, based on data from a questionnaire survey on a sample of 66 mussel farmers of Thermaikos Gulf. Respondents were categorized into clusters and differences in their economic performance were tested and analyzed. In addition, their environmental attitudes and proposals for the future of the sector were examined, in order to gather valuable information for policy makers, under the light of the new CFP.

THE MUSSEL PRODUCTION SYSTEM

In Thermaikos Gulf, the center of mussel production in Greece, mussel farming is a family-based activity that tries to adopt an entrepreneurial orientation; however, it confronts with serious environmental and institutional problems that jeopardize its development. The environmental issues in the sector stem from the geographical position of the Gulf, as it is influenced by the material inputs of three rivers (Loudias, Axios, Aliakmon), and from the designation of the neighboring area as a Ramsar Convention site. As a result, mussels are produced legally within the Ramsar protected area, facing however institutional restrictions. In addition, mussel farms operate under a strict monitoring system aiming at the timely detection of the potential presence of five types of shellfish toxins (paralytic SP, diarrheic SP, Amnesic SP, yessotoxins, azaspiracid). If the concentration of these toxins exceeds a predetermined threshold level, mussel harvest should stop (Angelidis, 2007); these levels are implied in the Reg. (EC)/853/2004 concerning the monitoring of bivalves. The decision is taken and implemented by the Regional Rural Economy and Veterinary Service. Toxin occurrence in the area has been examined before, for instance Economou et al. (2007) reported massive hospitalization of individuals having consumed mussels, which was due to high concentrations of toxic algae Dinophysis acuminata in the water ofThermaikos Gulf. According to the authors, measures of suspension of mussel harvesting were taken immediately and no sporadic cases or outbreaks were reported in the subsequent period (2000 – 2005).

Concerning the institutional problems, the most important concerns the licensing of farm operation, as due to Ramsar restrictions the on-table production system (pole cultivation) is – not complete - prohibited in the area and legitimate producers only apply the long-line system, although the former exhibits some important benefits (Angelidis, 2007). In general, the current institutional framework and the unsatisfactory organization of relevant public services, seriously hinders the development of the sector and compels active mussel farmers to take "shortcuts" in order to operate successfully their businesses. The final aim is the designation of areas for the proper establishment of mussel farms, where all the necessary controls will be implemented and producers will be able to function without competition from rival users. A part of the Thermaikos Gulf – in Pieria Prefecture - was designated as an Area for Organized Aquaculture Development ("POAY") in 2013, as a result of the implementation of a 2011 Greek law (31722/04-11-2011). This area of 1,208 ha and of 12,000 ton mussel production capacity was the first "POAY" established in Greece, setting the example for the designation of other Greek areas as well. Besides the strategic goals of the designation of the "POAY", including environmental protection and sustainable management of water resources, other goals are also pursued, such as the elimination of bureaucratic complications and restrictions and the development of an integrated development framework for mariculture, within which synergies will be accomplished among actors and policies.

METHODOLOGICAL FRAMEWORK

The Profile of the Survey

The data used for the typological analysis of mussel farmers in the study area were gathered through a survey which took place in 2013-2014. A sample of 66 mussel farmers was surveyed by means of personal interviews in their place of residence and economic activity, all situated in three areas (Chalastra, Kymina and Makrygiallos) of the Thermaikos Gulf region. Respondents were approached by enumerators and answered a set of open-ended and close-ended questions included in a structured questionnaire. The collected data concerned the profile of the head of the farm, technical and economic indicators describing the operation of the production units (expenses, yields, prices, capital endowments, labor requirements) and the opinions and attitudes of mussel farmers concerning institutional and environmental aspects of the sector. Overall, the survey was conducted in a relatively smooth way, as the mussel farmers approached were generally eager to participate. The questionnaire was not very extended, so that it might have caused fatigue issues; on the contrary, several respondents were willing to discuss the issues raised within the survey and to share some of their personal experiences, views and aspirations, further than the survey questions themselves.

Theoretical Background of the Analysis

Established methodological tools were used for the analysis of the survey data. First, the sampled farms were categorized to clusters/groups with common characteristics based on the personal characteristics of their owners, using the Two-Step Cluster Analysis (TSCA) method. TSCA constitutes an extension of a typical cluster analysis aiming at the determination of clusters which share common characteristics based on categorical and/or continuous variables (SPSS, 2002). Then, in order to detect significant differences between the financial results achieved by farms categorized in different clusters, methods of statistical inference for parametric and non-parametric hypotheses testing, such as analysis of variance (ANOVA), Kruskal-Wallis test and Wilcoxon rank sum test (Mann-Whitney U-test), were employed. The non-parametric tests were applied in cases where the assumptions about either variability or the form of the distribution of the population were seriously violated, with or without transformed data (SPSS, 2002). As a final step, a Factor Analysis was used in order to reduce the original set of variables proposing alternative ways for the improvement of the productivity of the sector into a smaller set of uncorrelated components that represent most of the information found in the original variables (Nurošis, 2012).

RESULTS AND DISCUSSION

Farm Typology

The sampled mussel farmers were clustered according to their personal characteristics on the basis of four variables:

1. Level of education;
2. The type of job they do besides mussel farming;
3. Their age; and
4. Whether their parents were also mussel producers.

Table 1 presents the results of the TSCA. It can be seen that the four variables are all significant in the formulation of the clusters and the importance of the typology is fair (slightly over 0.3).

Cluster 1 is the largest, as it includes 25 respondents (37.9% of the total cohort). The common characteristic of the farmers categorized here is that they are all also employed in fisheries and mussel

Table 1. Results of the Two-Step Cluster Analysis (TSCA) – categorization of mussel farmers

	Clusters				
	1	2	3	Total	Importance
Cluster size (%)	25 (37.9%)	20 (30.3%)	21 (31.8%)	66	0.30
Education	25	20	21	66	1.00
Primary School	2	1	21	24	
Secondary School	13	3	0	16	
High School	1	8	0	9	
Technical education	6	5	0	11	
Higher education	3	3	0	6	
Other job	25	20	21	66	0.61
Other	0	9	7	16	
Fisherman	25	3	13	41	
None (Unemployed)	0	8	1	9	
Age (mean)	46.48[a]	46.8[a]	60.43[b]	51.02[c]	0.53
Parents	25	20	21	66	0.46
Yes	19	7	1	27	
No	6	13	20	39	

Note: Values with different superscripts in each row indicate statistical difference between clusters (p-value≤0.05)

production is their main or secondary source of income. Their decision to engage in this activity was largely due to the fact that the business was started by their parents, as 76% of the farmers categorized in this cluster come from a family of mussel producers; nonetheless only 6 out of 19 farmers coming from a family of mussel producers claimed that this was the main factor affecting their decision to undertake the activity, although there was no significant statistical association. Most of them are of low and average educational backgrounds, as the majority attained low secondary education (the compulsory level of formal education in Greece); however a significant percentage of farmers attended some type of higher education, either a University Faculty or a Technical School. They are the youngest farmers among the three groups. Based on the profile outlined here, these farmers can be called "Professionals", as they followed a family tradition, thus inheriting relevant know-how, and are also engaged in fisheries.

Cluster 2 includes 20 farmers (30.3% of the sample). This cluster consists mainly of persons who are not engaged in fisheries alongside with mussel production; they are either employed in sectors other than fishery (45%) or mussel farming is their only activity (40%). In fact, 8 out of the 9 persons stating that mussel farming is their only source of employment are categorized in this cluster. More than two thirds of respondents do not come from mussel-producing families; instead the majority (55%) chose this profession because they wanted to, unlike respondents in other clusters who revealed other motivations behind their decision. Their average age is 46.8 years, which is significantly lower than the sample average (51.02 years). Concerning their education, they attended high school (40%) or some type of post-graduate education (40%), so it can be safely argued that the average participant of this category is fairly educated and of a considerably higher educational level than the typical participant of the remaining two categories. Based on these observations, Cluster 2 is named "Newcomers" because it consists of persons with no prior family know-how about mussel production, who chose this profession as an alternative to unemployment because they felt appealed by it.

Cluster 3 consists of the remaining 21 respondents (31.8% of the sample). These producers are significantly older than the sample average, but also than the producers categorized in the other two groups (mean age 60.43 years). Their level of education is low as none of them proceeded in school after Primary School (six years in Greece). Apart from their low level of formal education, 33% of these producers have not attended any type of formal or vocational training on mussel production, which is the highest rate among the three clusters (the corresponding percentages are 16% for "Professionals" and 25% for "Newcomers"). They initiated their own mussel production business, as only one of them comes from a family previously engaged in mussel farming. The majority are simultaneously employed as fishermen (62%) and only one person claimed to practice mussel farming as their sole activity. Examining their reasons to enter the sector, a significant motivation was detected in the compulsory choice of mussel farming, compared to the remaining two clusters, as their only employment alternative. According to this profile, Cluster 3 is named "Aged amateurs" as they only sought for vocational training at a low degree and their considerable higher age than the sample average indicates that they are going to leave the sector soon. Note, however, that they plan to pass the mussel business to their children after they leave the sector (71% compared to 48% and 40% for the remaining two clusters respectively, although a chi-square test of homogeneity did not reveal a significant difference).

Management Diversities Among Cluster Profiles

Table 2 presents the main financial results achieved by the sampled mussel farms. In absolute numbers, "Newcomers" achieve considerably higher financial results; indeed, their gross output is almost 80% higher than the average gross output of "Professionals" and "Aged amateurs", while the differences between their production costs are much lower. This high gross output of "Newcomers" is justified by their high production. Accordingly, the net profit reflects this difference, with "Professionals" achieving net losses, the "Aged amateurs" achieving profits marginally over zero and the "Newcomers" being the most profitable of all. The farm income exhibits the same pattern, being higher for "Newcomers" and very lower for the remaining two types of farmers. Also, "Newcomers" achieve the highest farm income. The financial results per 100kg of product are also presented in Table 2 in order to make comparisons. Under this basis, the economic performance of "Newcomers" does not exhibit the same extended differences compared to other groups.

Despite the evident differences between the financial results achieved by the average farm of each cluster, the Kruskal – Wallis test did not reveal statistically significant differences. The reason behind this lies in the low sample size, as a survey extended to more mussel farmers would generate the data necessary to account for such differences. Significant differences were only detected between groups, namely "Professionals" and "Newcomers" considering the profit and the farm income they achieve.

Table 3 presents the responses of mussel producers regarding some environmental and territorial issues linked to the operation of their production system. Concerning the implementation of the "POAY", 81.8% of respondents believe that it is an effective solution for the territorial issues of mussel farming; however, a significant part of "Professionals" did not seem convinced by its effectiveness. On the other hand, most of respondents acknowledge the efficiency of controls in order to resolve location issues of mussel farms, but a non-trivial part of "Newcomers" (30%) stated otherwise. It is also interesting to stress that although the vast majority of respondents claims compliance with bans due to marine biotoxins

Table 2. Financial results of the three types of mussel farms

	Clusters						Average	
	1 ("Professionals")		2 ("Newcomers")		3 ("Aged amateurs")			
	Mean (.000€) (S.D.)	**Mean (€/100kg) (S.D.)**	**Mean (.000€) (S.D.)**	**Mean (€/100kg) (S.D.)**	**Mean (.000€) (S.D.)**	**Mean (€/100kg) (S.D.)**	**Mean (.000€) (S.D.)**	**Mean (€/100kg) (S.D.)**
Gross Output	42.75 (53.59)	43.3 (7.8)	76.45 (124.19)	44.0 (11.1)	44.14 (41.04)	40.0 (6.3)	53.40 (79.51)	42.5 (8.6)
Total Costs	45.27 (62.06)	49.2 (15.7)	50.81 (49.27)	41.6 (14.3)	43.11 (37.13)	41.8 (16.1)	46.26 (50.65)	44.5 (15.6)
Net Profit	-2.52^{1} (17.86)	-6.6 (14.7)	25.64^{2} (76.27)	2.2 (16.6)	1.02^{1,2} (8.91)	-1.0 (13.3)	7.14 (44.68)	-2.1 (15.1)
Gross Margin	21.87 (38.53)	17.1 (10.9)	45.00 (89.31)	22.2 (13.8)	19.71 (16.00)	19.4 (9.1)	28.19 (55.53)	19.4 (11.3)
Farm Income	15.16^{1} (17.34)	14.3^{a} (10.1)	47.56^{2} (93.60)	23.2^{b} (11.9)	20.44^{1,2} (23.14)	17.0^{ab} (6.6)	26.66 (55.08)	17.9 (10.3)
Production (.000kg)	96.2 (108.6)		179.4 (316.7)		114.4 (111.4)		127.2 (196.9)	

Note: Values with different superscripts in each row indicate statistical difference between clusters (p-value≤0.05)

presence, there were three out of 66 respondents who did not comply with such bans, two of which were "Professionals". It has to be mentioned here that although 95.5% of respondents comply with the bans, 39.4% of them questioned the results of state laboratories regarding the presence of coliforms and marine biotoxins and 51.5% believe that the ban decisions do not correspond to actual phenomena. Responses about these issues do not vary significantly among clusters. When it comes to harvesting dead mussels, two out of three respondents confirmed it, with no significant variations among clusters; of them, six producers expressed concerns about the deaths being due to the presence of toxics.

As a final step, respondents were asked to state their opinions concerning the amelioration of the performance and productivity of the sector. For this reason, they were asked to agree or disagree with eight proposals and their responses were analyzed using a factor analysis. The frequency analysis of the corresponding variables is presented in Table 4. The most important adjustments are linked to laboratory quality controls (62.1%), the establishment of effective legislative framework (60.6%) and the provision of technical and scientific support (62.1%). Proposals of less importance include the coordination of relevant services – i.e. the simplification of processes which would lead to less bureaucracy – (57.6%) and the resolution of location issues – also related to the implementation of the "POAY" - (51.5%), as well as the establishment of a price observatory in order to improve information flows between markets and producers (48.5%). Interventions to prevent the adverse effects of toxic phytoplankton are of less importance to respondents.

The results of the factor analysis are presented in Table 5. The proposed adjustments are loaded in two factors, which explain 54.96% of the total variance and describe two distinct types of issues affecting the performance and productivity of the sector. Variables describing the effectiveness of ban measures, the establishment of a price observatory and the effective resolution of location issues of mussel farms are loaded in Factor 1 with the highest loadings. In Factor 2, the variables describing the toxic phytoplankton controls exhibit the highest loadings. Hence, Factor 1 concerns structural and regulatory issues, while Factor 2 deals with human health and quality issues.

Table 3. Environmental attitudes of mussel farmers

		Cluster 1 "Professionals" N (% of cluster)	Cluster 2 "Newcomers" N (% of cluster)	Cluster 3 "Aged amateurs" N (% of cluster)	Total N (% of cluster)
Will the "POAY" resolve location issues?	Yes	16 (64.0)	19 (95.0)	19 (90.5)	54 (81.8)
	No	9 (36.0)	1 (5.0)	2 (9.5)	12 (18.2)
Systematic control for the resolution of location issues	Yes	23 (92.0)	14 (70.0)	18 (85.7)	55 (83.3)
	No	2 (8.0)	6 (30.0)	3 (14.3)	11 (16.7)
Compliance with bans of mussel consumption due to marine biotoxins	Yes	23 (92.0)	20 (100.0)	20 (95.2)	63 (95.5)
	No	2 (8.0)	0	1 (4.8)	3 (4.5)
Trust in controls of state laboratories concerning the presence of toxins	Yes	15 (60.0)	12 (60.0)	13 (61.9)	40 (60.6)
	No	10 (40.0)	8 (40.0)	8 (38.1)	26 (39.4)
Do bans correspond to actual phenomena?	Yes	12 (48.0)	10 (50.0)	10 (47.6)	32 (48.5)
	No	13 (52.0)	10 (50.0)	11 (52.4)	34 (51.5)
Harvesting dead mussels	Yes	16 (64.0)	14 (70.0)	14 (66.7)	44 (66.7)
	No	9 (36.0)	6 (30.0)	7 (33.3)	22 (33.3)
Presence of toxins	Yes	1 (4.0)	2 (10.0)	3 (14.3)	6 (9.1)
	No	24 (96.0)	18 (90.0)	18 (85.7)	60 (90.9)
Alternative uses of shells	Recycle	19 (76.0)	17 (85.0)	10 (47.6)	46 (69.7)
	Storage	1 (4.0)	2 (10.0)	1 (4.8)	4 (6.1)
	Burn	5 (20.0)	1 (5.0)	9 (42.8)	15 (22.7)
	Bury	0	0	1 (4.8)	1 (1.5)

FUTURE RESEARCH DIRECTIONS

The most important limitation of this study is the lack of statistically rigorous results which could be generalized to the whole population. The reason behind this lies in the low sample size, as a survey expanded to more mussel farmers would generate the data necessary to account for such differences. However, it is difficult to approach more producers because many of them have issues with the license of operation of their farms, which renders them cautious and uncommunicative towards such surveys. However, the findings of this study provide an indicative image of the sector which can be of use for policy makers and for actors engaged in it.

CONCLUSION

The analytical framework in this paper revealed the existence of three distinct types of mussel farmers in the study area, each one of which requires different approaches and is in need of different structural adjustments and institutional interventions in order to ameliorate their performance. "Newcomers" are the ones achieving the best financial results, partly as a result of their conscious decision to undertake mussel farming and of their relatively high educational level. It can be supported that "Newcomers" are

Table 4. Proposals concerning the productivity of the sector – Descriptive analysis

		Cluster 1 "Professionals" N (% of cluster)	Cluster 2 "Newcomers" N (% of cluster)	Cluster 3 "Aged amateurs" N (% of cluster)	Total N (% of cluster)
Rapid and effective control laboratories	Yes	16 (64.0)	13 (65.0)	12 (57.1)	41 (62.1)
	No	9 (36.0)	7 (35.0)	9 (42.9)	25 (37.9)
Better technical and scientific support	Yes	18 (72.0)	11 (55.0)	12 (57.1)	41 (62.1)
	No	7 (28.0)	9 (45.0)	9 (42.9)	25 (37.9)
Effective and not precautionary bans to actual phenomena	Yes	16 (64.0)	12 (60.0)	12 (57.1)	40 (60.6)
	No	9 (36.0)	8 (40.0)	9 (42.9)	26 (39.4)
Coordination of services to safeguard the legality of farms	Yes	13 (52.0)	12 (60.0)	13 (61.9)	38 (57.6)
	No	12 (48.0)	8 (40.0)	8 (38.1)	28 (42.4)
Rational location of mussel farms	Yes	14 (56.0)	9 (45.0)	11 (52.4)	34 (51.5)
	No	11 (44.0)	11 (55.0)	10 (47.6)	32 (48.5)
Price observatory	Yes	13 (52.0)	10 (50.0)	9 (42.9)	32 (48.5)
	No	12 (48.0)	10 (50.0)	12 (57.1)	34 (51.5)
Effective control of toxic phytoplankton in water	Yes	7 (28.0)	6 (30.0)	6 (24.0)	19 (28.8)
	No	18 (72.0)	14 (70.0)	15 (76.0)	47 (71.2)
Effective control of toxic phytoplankton in mussel flesh	Yes	6 (24.0)	7 (35.0)	5 (23.8)	18 (27.3)
	No	19 (76.0)	13 (65.0)	16 (76.2)	48 (72.7)

Table 5. Proposals concerning the productivity of the sector – Factor analysis (Rotated component matrix)

	Factors	
	1	2
Effective control of toxic phytoplankton in water	0.110	0.945
Effective control of toxic phytoplankton in mussel flesh	0.170	0.928
Effective and not precautionary measures to actual phenomena	0.720	0.245
Rapid and effective control laboratories	0.504	0.080
Price observatory	0.641	0.192
Coordination of services to safeguard the legality of farms	0.607	0.139
Rational location of mussel farms	0.743	0.079
Better technical and scientific support	0.605	-0.049

* VARIMAX rotation method

* Bartlett's test of sphericity (KMO) chi-square = 150.335, p<.000

the ones able to support the growth of the sector, being endowed with the necessary characteristics to promote the sector. They are the ones proclaiming an even stricter monitoring and control system as a prerequisite to the sector's development. On the other hand, "Aged amateurs" achieve lower financial results, while they seem deprived of the necessary characteristics to be the target group of innovative practices and environmental friendly policies - note that a significant part of "Aged amateurs" supports burning mussel shells instead of recycling them (Table 3). Taking into account their age, they are the ones who will be leaving the sector shortly giving their place to younger successors. Finally, "Professionals" do not perform satisfactorily from an economic point of view but they support changes in the regulatory framework. Being the successors of their families' farms, they are endowed with considerable know-how, which constitutes an important asset for the development and expansion of the sector. Policies should support them in capitalizing this experience.

It is clear that mussel farmers clearly discern structural and regulatory issues from hygiene and environmental ones. They prioritize institutional issues for the improvement of their performance; nonetheless, some of these are expected to contribute to the solution of the environmental ones, for instance through the establishment of efficient laboratories in charge of monitoring and control. The qualitative information gathered by the enumerators during the interviews demonstrated that most of the mussel farmers were not dissatisfied from their incomes but mainly from the institutional framework. They were highly preoccupied concerning unexpected changes and uncertainty, while a non-trivial part of respondents thought the resolution of issues relating to quality and control are the most important prerequisites for the development of the sector. A post-analysis examination revealed that these views mainly came from "Newcomers" but also from a small percentage of "Professionals", although the qualitative nature of this information cannot permit robust statistical analyses to be undertaken. Note that the new CFP provides useful tools not only in the institutional aspect but also in the provision of financial support to mussel farmers.

REFERENCES

Angelidis, P. (2007). Shellfish culture in estuary zones and the sanitary restrictions. *Scientific Annals of the Danube Delta Institute*, *13*, 161–174.

Economou, V., Papadopoulou, C., Brett, M., Kansouzidou, A., Charalabopoulos, K., Filioussis, G., & Seferiadis, K. (2007). Diarrheic shellfish poisoning due to toxic mussel consumption: The first recorded outbreak in Greece. *Food Additives and Contaminants*, *24*(3), 297–305. doi:10.1080/02652030601053139 PMID:17364933

European Commission. (2014). *Facts and figures on the Common Fisheries Policy, basic statistical data*. Publications Office of the European Union.

FAO. (2015). *FAO Global Aquaculture Production database updated to 2013*. FAO.

Galinou-Mitsoudi, S., Savvidis, Y., & Dimitriadis, X. (2006). Interaction between mussel culture and hydrodynamics: A preliminary study in the gulfs of Thessaloniki and Thermaikos, Greece. *Journal of Biological Research*, *6*, 139–145.

Karagiannis, D., Vatsos, I., Theodoridis, A., & Angelidis, P. (2013). Effect of culture system on the prevalence of parasites of the Mediterranean mussel *Mytilus galloprovincialis* (Lamark, 1819). *Journal of Hellenic Veterinary Medical Society*, *64*, 113–122.

Norušis, M. J. (2012). *IBM SPSS Statistics 19 Statistical Procedures Companion*. Prentice Hall Inc.

SPSS. (2002). *SPSS Categories 11.5. A Software Package, Version 11.0*. Chicago: SPSS Inc.

Theodorou, A., Viaene, J., Sorgeloos, P., & Tzovenis, I. (2011). Production and marketing trends of the cultured mediterranean mussel Mytilus galloprovincialis Lamarck 1819, in Greece. *Journal of Shellfish Research, 30*(3), 859–874. doi:10.2983/035.030.0327

Theodorou, J., Sorgeloos, P., Adams, C., Viaene, J., & Tzovenis, I. (2010). Optimal farm size for the production of the Mediterranean mussel (Mytilus galloprovincialis) in Greece.*Proceedings of the 15th Biennial Conference of the International Institute of Fisheries Economics and Trade Conference (IIFET 2010).*

Chapter 9
Decision Making under Risk and Uncertainty in the Oil and Gas Industry

Christopher Boachie
Central University, Ghana

ABSTRACT

The energy system studies include a wide range of issues from short term to long term horizons. The decision making chain is fed by input parameters which are usually subject to uncertainties. The art of dealing with uncertainties has been developed in various directions and has recently become a focal point of interest. Decision making is certainly the most important task of Oil and Gas managers and it is often a very difficult one. The purpose of this chapter is to review and investigate the decision making processes under risk and uncertainty of Oil and Gas companies. Questionnaires were distributed to eight Oil and Gas companies in Ghana to solicit their view on decision making under risk and uncertainty. Results indicate that most managers use Maximax, Minimax Regret and Expected Value when making decisions under risk and uncertainty.

1. INTRODUCTION

Oil and Gas are the major source of world's fuel consumption. Most of the Oil and Gas is transported from one location to another through pipelines. Existing pipelines around the globe have been subjected to deterioration due to aging, aggressive environmental factors, inadequate design and improper protection and maintenance. To ensure optimal performance, this often requires extensive maintenance, repair and renewal practices or even replacement of certain components. Integrity of these pipelines is of primary interest to the Oil and Gas companies, governmental agencies, consumers and other stakeholder due to potential adverse consequences related to public health, safety and heavy financial liabilities in case of system failure. Increasing economic development is stipulating the growth of energy demand due to the limited availability of fossil energy, the high cost of renewable technologies and various environmental concerns on energy-related activities; energy systems planning is desired for supporting sustainable re-

DOI: 10.4018/978-1-5225-0959-2.ch009

gional development. However, such planning is associated with various uncertainties that exist in many related impact factors. These uncertainties will affect various processes of energy systems management (Huang et al., 1993). Neglecting them may result in missed information and reduced decision robustness.

Modelling for decision making involves two distinct parties, one is the decision maker and the other is the model builder known as the analyst. The analyst is to assist the decision maker in his/her decision making process. Therefore, the analyst must be equipped with more than a set of analytical methods. Specialists in model building are often tempted to study a problem, and then go off in isolation to develop an elaborate mathematical model for use by the manager (i.e., the decision maker). Unfortunately, the manager may not understand this model and may either use it blindly or reject it entirely. The specialist may feel that the manager is too ignorant and unsophisticated to appreciate the model, while the manager may feel that the specialist lives in a dream world of unrealistic assumptions and irrelevant mathematical language. Such miscommunication can be avoided if the manager works with the specialist to develop first a simple model that provides a crude but understandable analysis.

After the manager has built up confidence in this model, additional detail and sophistication can be added, perhaps progressively only a bit at a time. This process requires an investment of time on the part of the manager and sincere interest on the part of the specialist in solving the manager's real problem, rather than in creating and trying to explain sophisticated models. This progressive model building is often referred to as the bootstrapping approach and is the most important factor in determining successful implementation of a decision model. Moreover, the bootstrapping approach simplifies the otherwise difficult task of model validating and verification processes (Arsham, 1987).

In deterministic models, a good decision is judged by the outcome alone. However, in probabilistic models, the decision maker is concerned not only with the outcome value but also with the amount of risk each decision carries. As an example of deterministic versus probabilistic models, consider the past and the future. One can do nothing to change the past, but everything we do influences and changes the future, although the future has an element of uncertainty. Managers are captivated much more by shaping the future than the history of the past (Ben-Haim, 2001).

Uncertainty is the fact of life and business. Probability is the guide for a good life and successful business. The concept of probability occupies an important place in the decision making process, whether the problem is one faced in business, in government, in the social sciences, or just in one's own everyday personal life. In very few decision making situations is perfect information all the needed facts are available. Most decisions are made in the face of uncertainty. Probability enters into the process by playing the role of a substitute for certainty—a substitute for complete knowledge.

Probabilistic modelling is largely based on application of statistics for probability assessment of uncontrollable events (or factors), as well as risk assessment of your decision. The original idea of statistics was the collection of information about and for the state. The word statistics is not derived from any classical Greek or Latin roots, but from the Italian word for state. Probability has a much longer history. It is derived from the verb to probe meaning to find out what is not too easily accessible or understandable. The word "proof" has the same origin that provides necessary details to understand what is claimed to be true. Probabilistic models are viewed as similar to that of a game; actions are based on expected outcomes. The centre of interest moves from the deterministic to probabilistic models using subjective statistical techniques for estimation, testing and predictions. In probabilistic modelling, risk means uncertainty for which the probability distribution is known. Therefore, risk assessment means a study to determine the outcomes of decisions along with their probabilities. Many decisions have to be made with inadequate information, perhaps because the outcome of a decision is uncertain or because the outcome will occur at some time in the future. Many decisions have more than one criterion. Decision analysis is based on hundreds of years of philosophical and practical thought about uncertainty and decision-making. Yet there remain some important unresolved issues, and each new set of crises presents new puzzles.

Exploration and production of hydrocarbons is a high-risk venture. Geological concepts are uncertain with respect to structure, reservoir seal, and hydrocarbon accumulation. On the other hand, economic evaluations have uncertainties related to costs, probability of finding and producing economically viable reservoirs, technology and oil price. The role of risk and uncertainty in decision-making is a topic that has increasingly attracted the attention of both practitioners and scholars. However, as managers hold widely divergent views on the handling of risk and uncertainty in business situations, with some taking a more analytical approach, whereas others appear to operate on a more intuitive basis. The chapter provides new insights about the theory and practice of decision making under risk and uncertainty from an international perspective to aid knowledge transfer. This research is a useful source of policy relevant information for policy officials at all levels of oil and gas industry. This study does not only seek to review and investigate the decision making processes under risk and uncertainty, promote and extend the advances in decision methodology and theory, but also in application possibilities of decision models in various aspects of business, and techniques for facilitating decision-making. The oil and gas industry is used as a case study which is important for building models. The principal contribution of this chapter is to highlight on the importance of the tools employed in making decision under risk and uncertainty. It draws on empirical evidence from the oil and gas companies in developing economy under the current oil prices. One can improve on national, global and institutional decision making under the risk and uncertainty, and use this information to minimize the effects of uncertainties regarding decision making in an organisation.

The rest of the chapter is organised as follows. A review of existing literature on decision making under risk and uncertainty is displayed in section two. The next section discusses the decision making models followed by the case of oil and gas industries. Finally, some practical lessons are highlighted and future lines of research are offered.

2. LITERATURE REVIEW

Decision Making Process

Historically scientists have emphasized two basic models of decision making: the rational model and the bounded rationality model (March, 2010).

The Rational Model

Decision making under this model is assumed to be *rational*. It represents the decision making under certainty. Under this model the alternatives, outcomes and the decision criteria are all known and have the ability to make the optimum choice and then to implement it (Towler, 2010). According to the rational model, the decision making process can be broken down into six steps (Schoenfeld, 2011). The relationship between information or data and the impact of the decision is used to improve or reinforce the learning process. Baker (2013) conducted a case study on rational decision making in a hybrid organization for a Southwestern Drug Court treatment program. Serrano González et al. (2013) successfully applied rational decision making to identify optimal structure of transmissions systems for offshore wind farms. Salem et. al. (2013) applied successfully rational multi-criteria decision making to choose an operational plan for bridge rehabilitation. A multi-criteria optimization is an optimization of problem with more than one objective (Steuer, 1986; Köksalan et al., 1995; Zionts & Wallenius, 1976).

One definition of rationality includes the concept of making an optimized decision. Practically this is not possible because of the limitation of the availability of information required to make such a decision and the limitation of the device to make sense of such incomplete decision (Simon, 1990). This is what is known as the theory of bounded rationality and was proposed by the Nobel Laureate Herbert Simon (Simon, 1957; Tisdell, 1996). The implication of this observation on many economic systems is quite substantial (Simon, 1991). It questions the truthfulness of the theory of the efficient market hypothesis especially given the fact that participants in the market are at best only rational within the bounds of limited information and limited model to make sense of the information. Lee (2013) built a model for analysing an economy using bounded rational agents. It was observed that rational agents amplify of the price bubble cooperation amongst rational agents. Gama (2013) successfully applied the concept of bounded rationality to investigate the behaviour of stream mining procedures and proposed ubiquitous stream mining and self-adaption models. Jiang et al. (2013) successfully applied bounded rationality in evolution game analysis of water saving and pollution prevention. Aviad and Roy (2012) applied the concept of bounded rationality to build a decision support technique and applied this to identify feature saliency in clustering problems. Bounded rationality was applied to deal with the problem of the availability of target attribute by using an S-shaped function as a saliency measure to characterize the end user's logic to identify attributes that describe each prospective group. Murata et al. (2012) applied the concept of bounded rationality to analyse the relationship between group heuristics and cooperative behaviour. They observed that group consciousness can assist to stimulate actively mutual cooperation.

The rational decision making model, characterizes the decision maker as completely rational. If a decision maker were completely rational, she would have perfect information: know all alternatives, determine every consequence, and establish a complete preference scale. Moreover, the steps in the decision-making process would consistently lead toward selecting the alternative that maximizes the solution to each decision problem. In contrast to complete rationality in decision making, bounded rationality implies the following (Simon, 2009):

1. Decisions will always be based on an incomplete and, to some degree, inadequate comprehension of the true nature of the problem being faced.
2. Decision makers will never succeed in generating all possible alternative solutions for consideration.
3. Alternatives are always evaluated incompletely because it is impossible to predict accurately all consequences associated with each alternative.
4. The ultimate decision regarding which alternative to choose must be based on some criterion other than maximization or optimization because it is impossible to ever determine which alternative is optimal.

The literature review studied above clearly indicates that the theory of bounded rationality is a powerful tool of analysis that has found usage in many diverse areas. This theory can be applied in Oil and Gas decision making. In the Oil and Gas industry, pipe failures can never be fully avoided; however, the overall risk of failure can be reduced to an acceptable level by opting efficient risk management strategies. The quantification of risk of Oil and Gas pipeline failure is a difficult task. Oil and Gas distribution systems comprise many (sometimes thousands) kilometers of pipes of different ages and various materials. Operational and environmental conditions are highly variable both temporally and spatially. Further, as pipes are mostly buried, limited data are available on their condition. Finally, some of the failure processes are not well understood and forensic investigation is very difficult because there is generally a time lag between the time of failure and the time at which the consequences are observed. Several studies dealt with different aspect related to risk assessment of pipelines (Jo & Ahn, 2002; Sklavounos & Rigas, 2006).

The term 'risk' is the cornerstone in decision making process. Risk of an undesired event is a function of a set of scenario, likelihood of occurrences and the consequences of events (AIChE, 2000; Kaplan & Garrick, 1981). Risk analysis is a systematic and scientific way to predict and prevent the occurrence of undesirable event(s) by gathering and integrating qualitative and quantitative information of potential causes, consequences, and likelihood of adverse events. Likelihood of an event refers to a quantitative measurement of occurrence, which is expressed either as frequency (i.e., rate of event occurs in per unit time) or probability (i.e., the chance of event to occur in defined conditions) of occurrences.

A number of qualitative and quantitative techniques, e.g. failure mode and effect analysis (FMEA), hazard and operability study (HAZOP), fault tree analysis (FTA), event tree analysis (ETA), have been used for the risk assessment (Khan & Abbasi, 2001). FTA and ETA are two well established techniques that individually assist the risk assessment by providing qualitative analysis of hazards identification and a detail quantitative assessment of likelihood for the undesired events (CMPT, 1999). 'Bow-tie' is a common platform which couples FTA and ETA by considering a common top-event named as critical event (Cockshott, 2005; Chevreau, Wybo, & Cauchois, 2006; Dianous & Fiévez, 2006; Duijm, 2009; Markowski, Mannan, & Bigoszewska, 2009). The traditional 'bow-tie' analysis requires the probability of input events as precise crisp data or defined probability density functions (PDFs) (Markowski *et al.*, 2009). The crisp data or PDFs are often 'hard' to come by and are subjected to a number of inherent uncertainties due to variant failure modes, design faults, poor understanding of failure mechanisms, as well as the vagueness of system phenomena (Sadiq, Saint-Martin, & Kleiner, 2008; Yuhua & Datao, 2005). Fuzzy Set Theory (FST) has been proven to be effective and efficient to handle epistemic uncertainty (due to impreciseness, vagueness, lack of knowledge or incompleteness) for expert's system applications (Agarwal, Renaud, Preston, & Padmanabhan, 2004; Ayyub & Klir, 2006; Bae, Grandhi, & Canfield, 2004; Cheng, 2000). Many attempts have been reported in literature to incorporate FST for risk analysis of different systems using FTA, ETA or 'bowtie' analysis (Ferdous et al., 2011; Huang, Chen, & Wang, 2001; Sadiq et al., 2008).

Previously, many optimization methods such as stochastic, fuzzy, and interval-parameter programming were developed for planning energy systems under uncertainty. Grosfeld-Nir and Tishler (1993) and Bunn and Paschentis (1996) used stochastic methods to optimize electricity generation processes. Nordhaus (1993), Manne et al. (1995), Peck and Teisberg (1995) introduced stochastic programming methods for supporting energy systems planning. These studies demonstrated that stochastic methods can deal with probabilistic uncertainties. However, the increased data requirements for specifying the parameter's probability distributions might affect their viability (Lv *et al.*, 2010; Sun & Huang, 2010). This was especially true for regional energy systems, where a large amount of modeling inputs may be required (Lin & Huang, 2009a; Lin et al., 2010a). In addition, probability distributions of many parameters might not be available (Lin et al., 2010b; Lin et al., 2009); for instance, it was hard to obtain stochastic information for the future prices of oil and natural gas. Mavrotas et al. (2003) developed a fuzzy linear programming (FLP) model to handle uncertainties regarding energy costs. Borges and Antunes (2003) investigated multi-objective optimization problems for energy systems planning. Sadeghi and Hosseini (2006) applied FLP to address uncertainties associated with energy supply planning.

The FLP methods were based on either possibilistic or flexible programming. The major problem of possibilistic FLP is the resulting sub-models are too complicated to be applicable to practical problems. In addition, the methods are indirect approaches containing intermediate control variables that can hardly be determined. In comparison, the flexible FLP methods do not greatly increase the modeling complexities. However, only stipulations can be represented as fuzzy sets in the flexible models, leading to difficulties in incorporating uncertainties into the coefficients of the objective function and constraints. The flexible methods are also indirect approaches in which intermediate control variables are used to generate optimal solutions. Thus, these methods are unable to communicate the uncertain inputs directly into the optimization process and resulting solutions. An interval-parameter programming method could incorporate uncertainties within its optimization process (Huang et al., 1992; Lin & Huang, 2008, 2009b, 2010a). Uncertainties in both model stipulations and coefficients were directly included in the model and communicated into the optimization processes, and thereby solutions reflecting the inherent uncertainties were generated (Lin & Huang, 2010b). The optimal interval solutions would be represented as lower and upper bounds, with the degree of uncertainty (DU) being defined as the interval divided by the mid-value between the two bounds (Huang et al., 1995a, 1995b). However, when the model stipulations are very uncertain, interval solutions with high DU will be generated. The higher the DU of the interval outputs, the lower their effectiveness and usefulness. When the DU is significantly high, the output results may be of no or little use to decision makers.

After a problem is identified, alternative solutions to the problem are generated. These are carefully evaluated, and the best alternative is chosen for implementation. The implemented alternative is then evaluated over time to assure its immediate and continued effectiveness. If difficulties arise at any stage in the process, recycling may be effected. Thus, decision making is a logical sequence of activities. That is, before alternatives are generated, the problem must be identified, and so on. The paragraphs below briefly elaborate on each of these steps and explain their interrelationships.

Identifying the Problem

Firms exist to achieve certain goals, such as production of hydrocarbons. Within the firm, each department or subunit has goals, such as increasing production, increasing accident prevention, and/or developing new approaches to drilling. Establishing these goals becomes the basis for identifying problem areas, deciding on courses of action, and evaluating the decision outcomes. A decision is said to be effective if it helps the firm to achieve a specific objective or set of goals for the organisation.

Effective decision makers are keenly aware of the importance of properly identifying the problem and understanding the problem situation. Kepner and Tregoe (2005) developed a method of problem analysis that suggests that the first step in decision making, identifying the problem, is the most important step. According to these authors, providing a good definition of the problem affects the quality of the decision. Their method suggests that it is often easier to define what the problem is not, rather than what it is. Also, the problem, and its solution, are prioritized with other problems, to clarify its relative importance.

Generating Alternatives

Once the problem has been identified, the second step in the decision-making process is to generate alternatives to the problem. In developing these alternative solutions, entities must first specify the goals that they hope to achieve through their decision. Are they trying to increase accident prevention, improve the quality of service, increase production, or new field explorations? Once the entities have determined their goals, they can search for alternative means of reaching them. Information must be collected regarding each of the alternatives and their likely consequences. More specifically, the managers must seek to learn as much as possible concerning the likelihood that each alternative will result in the achievement of various outcomes, and the extent to which those outcomes will contribute to the achievement of the goals and objectives being sought.

The extent of the search for alternatives is limited by the importance of the decision, the cost and value of additional information needed to evaluate alternatives, and the number of people affected by the decision (Zopounidis, 2011a, 2011b). The more important the decision, the more attention is directed to developing alternatives. The length and thoroughness of the search for alternatives depends on the cost of evaluating additional alternatives (Narayanan, 2005). Moreover, the greater the number of people affected by a problem, the more likely the organization will conduct a lengthy and thorough search for alternatives (Ehrgott, 2011).

Evaluating Alternatives

The third step in the decision-making process is *evaluating* each of the *alternatives* generated in step 2. In evaluating an alternative, managers must ask the following three questions:

1. Is the alternative, such as upstream profitability feasible?
2. Is it a satisfactory alternative?
3. What impact will it have on people? (Grant, 2011)

The first question, whether the alternative is feasible, simply means: Can it be done? For example, if one alternative requires a general layoff of workers but the firm has a collective bargaining agreement that prohibits such layoffs, that alternative is not feasible. Similarly, if a firm has limited capital, alternatives that require large capital outlays are not feasible, unless funds can be borrowed to meet the capital-outlay requirements. The second question concerns the extent to which the alternative is satisfactory — that is, the extent to which it addresses the problem. The third question addresses the impact of an alternative on firms' personnel. The alternative that is chosen must be acceptable to those who must live with the consequences of the decision. Failure to meet this condition is the single most likely reason for failure of the decision-making process to solve problems (Hastie, 2010). For this reason, questions of acceptability of a proposed alternative should be of great concern to the manager. On the one hand, even a mediocre solution to the problem may prove effective if it is implemented with enthusiasm and commitment. On the other hand, a technically correct alternative may fail to succeed if implementation is half-hearted.

Choosing an Alternative

Once the manager has evaluated all of the alternatives, he attempts to choose the best alternative. The evaluation phase will have eliminated some of the alternatives, but in most cases two or more will remain. How does a manager decide which alternative is the best? One approach is to select the alternative that is feasible, satisfactory, and acceptable to the work group (Gilboa, 2011). Because most situations do not lend themselves to sophisticated mathematical analysis, the manager uses this available information in combination with judgment and intuition to make the decision (Mendel, 2011). The basis of judgment should be how close the outcomes or consequences of the alternatives come to achieving the desired goals of the school.

Implementing the Decision

After choosing an alternative, the manager faces the challenge of *implementing the decision.* A sound decision can fail if implemented poorly. It is useful, therefore, to consider some suggestions for successful implementation (Ahmed, 2011).

1. Managers need to make sure that the alternative is clearly understood. This is accomplished by communicating the decision to all involved staff. Effective communication is necessary for effectively implementing decisions.
2. Managers need to encourage acceptance of the alternative as a necessary course of action. Committees can help managers achieve commitment. If the people who must carry out a decision participate in the process, they are more likely to endorse enthusiastically the outcome. Thus, the degree to which persons have or have not been involved in prior steps may substantially affect the success of the total decision-making process.
3. Managers need to provide enough resources to make the alternative succeed. Decision makers set up budgets and schedules for the actions they have decided to undertake. Specifically, the decision may require acquiring office space, hiring staff, procuring funds, and the like.
4. Managers need to establish workable timelines. The decision maker now faces a "how much" and "how soon" decision. As part of the process of implementation, he must ask himself whether to move forward step by step or whether to take the entire action at once.
5. Managers need to assign responsibilities clearly. In other words, what should be done by whom? Because the solution of most administrative problems requires the combined effort of many workers, each person should understand what role he or she is to play during each phase of the implementation process.

Evaluating Decision Effectiveness

The final step in the decision-making process is evaluating the effectiveness of the decision. When an implemented decision does not produce the desired results, there are probably a number of causes: incorrect definition of the problem, poor evaluation of alternatives, and/or improper implementation. Among these possible causes, the most common and serious error is an inadequate definition of the problem. When the problem is incorrectly defined, the alternative that is selected and implemented will not produce the desired result.

Evaluation is important because decision making is a continuous, never-ending process. Evaluation provides managers with information that can precipitate a new decision cycle. The decision alternative may fail, thus generating a new analysis of the problem, evaluation of alternatives, and selection of a new alternative. Some experts suggest that many large problems are solved by attempting several alternatives in sequence, each providing a modest improvement (Hicks, 2005). Evaluation is the part of the decision-making process that assesses whether a new decision needs to be made.

Types of Decisions

Routine and Non-Routine Decisions: Pringle et al. (2002) classify decisions on a continuum ranging from routine to non-routine, depending on the extent to which they are structured. The authors describe routine decisions as focusing on well-structured situations that recur frequently, involve standard decision procedures, and entail a minimum of uncertainty. Common examples include payroll processing, reordering standard inventory items, paying suppliers, and so on. The decision maker can usually rely on policies, rules, past precedents, standardized methods of processing, or computational techniques. Probably 90 percent of management decisions are largely routine (Pringle et al, 2002). Indeed, routine decisions usually can be delegated to lower levels to be made within established policy limits, and increasingly they can be programmed for computer "decision" if they can be structured simply enough.

Non-routine decisions, on the other hand, deal with unstructured situations of a novel, nonrecurring nature, often involving incomplete knowledge, high uncertainty, and the use of subjective judgment or even intuition, where no alternative can be proved to be the best possible solution to the particular problem. Such decisions become more and more common the higher one goes in management and the longer the future period influenced by the decision is. Unfortunately, almost the entire process of drilling by the engineer is based on the solution of highly structured problems for which there is a single "textbook solution." Engineers often find themselves unable to rise in management unless they can develop the "tolerance for ambiguity" that is needed to tackle unstructured problems.

Risk Analysis: Hydrocarbon Exploration

The historical origins of decision analysis can be partially traced to mathematical studies of probabilities in the 17th and 18th centuries by Pascal, Laplace, and Bernoulli. However, the applications of these concepts in business and general management appeared only after the Second World War (Covello & Mumpower, 1985; Bernstein, 1996). The problem involving decision-making when there are conditions of risk and uncertainty has been notorious since the beginnings of the oil industry. Early attempts to define risk were informal. The study by Allais (1956) on the economic feasibility of exploring the Algerian Sahara is a classic example because it is the first study in which the economics and risk of exploration were formally analyzed through the use of the probability theory and an explicit modeling of the sequential stages of exploration. Allais was a French economist who was awarded the Nobel Prize in Economics in 1988 for his development of principles to guide efficient pricing and resource allocation in large monopolistic enterprises. Allais' work was a useful means or preview to demonstrate Monte Carlo methods of computer simulation and how they might be used to perform complex probability analysis, instead of simplifications of risk estimation of large areas. During this period, there were several attempts to define resource level probabilities at various stages of exploration in a basin using resource distribution and risk analysis (Harris, 1984; Harbaugh, 1984; Harris, 1990). At that time governmental agencies (U.S. Geological Survey, Institut Français du Pétrole, etc.) were also beginning to employ risk analysis in periodic appraisals of oil and gas resources.

Risk Analysis: Field Appraisal and Development

During the hydrocarbon exploration phase, major uncertainties are related to volumes in place and economics. As the level of information increases, these uncertainties are mitigated and, consequently, the importance of the uncertainties related to technology and recovery factor increases. The situation is more critical in offshore fields and for heavy-oil reservoirs, where investments are higher and there is a lower operational flexibility (Pinto et al., 2001). In the preparation of development plans, field management decisions are complex issues because of

1. The number and type of decisions
2. The great effort required to predict production with the necessary accuracy
3. The dependency of production strategy definition on several types of uncertainty with significant impact on risk quantification

In order to avoid excessive computation effort, some simplifications are always necessary. The key point is to define the simplifications and assumptions that can be made to improve performance without significant precision loss. Simplifications are possible, for instance, in the modeling tool, treatment of attributes and in the way several types of uncertainties are integrated.

Decision Making Process, Value of Information and Flexibility

Making important decisions in the petroleum industry requires incorporation of major uncertainties, long time horizons, multiple alternatives, and complex value issues into the decision model. Decision analysis can be defined on different and embedded levels in petroleum exploration and production stages. Many complex Exploration and Production decision problems involve multiple conflicting objectives. Under these circumstances, managers have a growing need to employ improved and systematic decision processes that explicitly embody the firm's objectives, desired goals, and resource constraints. Over the last two decades, the advances in computer-aided decision making processes have provided a mechanism to improve the quality of decision making in the modern petroleum industry. Walls (1996) developed a decision support model that combines toolbox system components to provide a comprehensive approach to petroleum exploration planning from geological development through the capital allocation process.

An effective way to express uncertainty is to formulate a range of values, with confidence levels assigned to numbers comprising the range. Although geoscientists and engineers may be willing to make predictions about unknown Exploration and Production situations, there is a need to assess the level of uncertainty of the projects. So, it's necessary to define the value of information associated with important decisions such as deferring drilling of a geologic prospect or seismic survey. Information only has value in a decision problem if it results in a change in some action to be taken by a decision maker. Furthermore, this change must bring an expected benefit greater than the cost of information. The information is seldom perfectly reliable and generally it does not eliminate uncertainty, so the value of information depends on both the amount of uncertainty (or the prior knowledge available) and payoffs involved in

Exploration and Production projects. The value of information can be determined and compared to its actual cost and the natural path to evaluate the incorporation of this new data is by Bayesian analysis.

As the level of information increases, the decision making process becomes more complex because of the need for (1) more accurate prediction of field performance and (2) integration with production strategy. At this point, the concept of Value of Information (VoI) must be integrated with the Value of Flexibility (VoF) as shown by Hayashi et al. (2007). Therefore, risk may be mitigated by more information or flexibility in the production strategy definition. Reservoir development by stages and smart wells are good examples of investments in flexibility. The decision to invest in information or flexibility is becoming easier as more robust methodologies to quantify VoI and VoF are developed.

Information and Decision Making

Decision makers often face a severe lack of information. Probability assessment quantifies the information gap between what is known, and what needs to be known for an optimal decision. The probabilistic models are used for protection against adverse uncertainty, and exploitation of propitious uncertainty. Difficulty in probability assessment arises from information that is scarce, vague, inconsistent or incomplete.

It is a challenging task to compare several courses of action and then select one action to be implemented. At times, the task may prove too challenging. Difficulties in decision making arise through complexities in decision alternatives. The limited information processing capacity of a decision-maker can be strained when considering the consequences of only one course of action. Yet, choice requires that the implications of various courses of action be visualized and compared. In addition, unknown factors always intrude upon the problem situation and seldom are outcomes known with certainty. Almost always, an outcome depends upon the reactions of other people who may be undecided themselves. It is no wonder that decision makers sometimes postpone choices for as long as possible. Then, when they finally decide, they neglect to consider all the implications of their decision (van Gigch, 2002).

Business decision making is almost always accompanied by conditions of uncertainty. Clearly, the more information the decision maker has, the better the decision will be. Treating decisions as if they were gambles is the basis of decision theory. This means that one has to trade off the value of a certain outcome against its probability. To operate according to the canons of decision theory, one must compute the value of a certain outcome and its probabilities; hence, determining the consequences of our choices. The origin of decision theory is derived from economics by using the utility function of payoffs. It suggests that decisions be made by computing the utility and probability, the ranges of options, and also lays down strategies for good decisions (Ben-Haim, 2001).

Objectives are important both in identifying problems and in evaluating alternative solutions. Evaluating alternatives requires that a decision maker's objectives be expressed as criteria that reflect the attributes of the alternatives relevant to the choice. The systematic study of decision making provides a framework for choosing courses of action in a complex, uncertain or conflicting situation. The choices of possible actions, and the prediction of expected outcomes, derive from a logical analysis of the decision situation. A possible drawback in the decision analysis approach: You might have already noticed that the above criteria always result in selection of only one course of action. However, in many decision problems, the decision maker might wish to consider a combination of some actions. For example, in the investment problem, the investor might wish to distribute the assets among a mixture of the choices in such a way to optimize the portfolio's return (Ben-Haim, 2001).

Relevant information and knowledge used to solve a decision problem sharpens our flat probability. Useful information moves the location of a problem from the pure uncertain pole towards the deterministic pole. Probability assessment is nothing more than the quantification of uncertainty. In other words, quantification of uncertainty allows for the communication of uncertainty between persons. There can be uncertainties regarding events, states of the world, beliefs and so on. Probability is the tool for both communicating uncertainty and managing it. There are different types of decision models that help to analyse the different scenarios. Depending on the amount and degree of knowledge one has, the three most widely used types are decision making under pure uncertainty, decision making under risk and decision making by buying information (pushing the problem towards the deterministic pole)

Payoff Table

A payoff table is simply a table that gives the outcome of a decision under different conditions or states of nature. These states of nature may relate to possible demand for a product or they could be related to the national or global economy. For example, consider an Oil and Gas company whose premises is valued at $100,000, and has to decide whether to take out fire insurance at an annual cost of $300. The decision maker has an aim of minimising the costs and must choose the best alternative from insuring the premises, or do not insure the premises. Then an event happens, but the decision maker cannot control whether the premises burns down or the premises does not burn down. Each combination of choice and event has an outcome that can be shown in Table 1.

Obviously, the Oil and Gas company has simplified the problem, and in reality there is a choice of many insurance companies and policies, the premises may be damaged but not destroyed by fire, there may be cost of inconvenience, and so on. But the payoff matrix shows the underlying structure of the problem.

3. DECISION MAKING UNDER UNCERTAINTY

In decision making under pure uncertainty, the decision maker has absolutely no knowledge, not even about the likelihood of occurrence for any state of nature. In such situations, the decision maker's behaviour is purely based on his/her attitude toward the unknown. Some of these behaviours are optimistic, pessimistic and least regret, among others. Optimists are right; so are the pessimists. It is up to the decision maker to choose which one to be. The optimist sees opportunity in every problem; the pessimist sees problem in every opportunity. Both optimists and pessimists contribute to our society. The optimist invents the airplane and the pessimist the parachute. Whenever the decision maker has some knowledge regarding the states of nature, he/she may be able to assign subjective probability for the occurrence

Table 1. Payoff matrix

		Event	
		Premises Burns Down	**Premises Does Not Burn Down**
Alternatives	Insure the premises	$300	$300
	Do not insure the premises	$100,000	$0

of each state of nature. By doing so, the problem is then classified as decision making under risk. In many cases, the decision maker may need an expert's judgment to sharpen his/her uncertainties with respect to the likelihood of each state of nature. In such a case, the decision maker may buy the expert's relevant knowledge in order to make a better decision. The procedure used to incorporate the expert's advice with the decision maker's probabilities assessment is known as the Bayesian approach (Taha, 2007; Oakshott, 2006).

The domain of decision analysis models falls between two extreme cases. This depends upon the degree of knowledge one has about the outcome of an actions. One pole on this scale is deterministic. The opposite "pole" is pure uncertainty. Between these two extremes are problems under risk. The main idea here is that for any given problem, the degree of certainty varies among managers depending upon how much knowledge each one has about the same problem. This reflects the recommendation of a different solution by each person. Probability is an instrument used to measure the likelihood of occurrence for an event. When you use probability to express your uncertainty, the deterministic side has a probability of one (or zero), while the other end has a flat (all equally probable) probability. For example, if you are certain of the occurrence (or non-occurrence) of an event, you use the probability of one (or zero). If you are uncertain, and would use the expression "I really don't know," the event may or may not occur with a probability of 50 percent. This is the Bayesian notion that probability assessment is always subjective. That is, the probability always depends upon how much the decision maker knows. If someone knows all there is to know, then the probability will diverge either to one or zero. The decision situations with flat uncertainty have the largest risk. In decision making under pure uncertainty, the decision maker has no knowledge regarding any of the states of nature outcomes, and/or it is costly to obtain the needed information. In such cases, the decision making depends merely on the decision maker's personality type.

Personality Types and Decision Making

Personality type can have an influence on decision making. Assume Tullow Oil company wants to invest in either stock or bond or negotiable certificate of deposit under different states of the economy. To illustrate the personality types, the author uses the table below which represents the payoff matrix for the different alternative under different economic conditions (Table 2).

1. **Pessimism, or Conservative (Maximin):** It is a cautious decision rule based on maximising the minimum returns that can occur. This is the Wald decision criterion and it is the worst case scenario (Oakshott, 2006). Most organisations have limited resources and cannot afford to risk a big loss. The Wald decision assumes that decision makers are cautious and want to avoid big potential losses (Taha, 2007). The steps for Maximin Course of Action are:

Table 2. Payoff matrix

		State of Economy		
		Boom	**Steady**	**Recession**
Alternatives	Stock	10	4	(2)
	Deposit	7	6	2
	Bond	5	1	4

   a. Write the minimum number in each alternative row: Stock is -2 Deposit is 2 and Bond is 1.
   b. Choose maximum number and do that alternative: Maximum is 2 and the alternative is Deposit.
2. **Optimism, or Aggressive (Maximax):** This is an optimistic rule and maximises the maximum that can be gained (Taha, 2007). A manager in an Oil and Gas company says good things always happen to me. The steps for Maximax Course of Action are:
   a. Write the maximum number in each alternative row: Stock is 10, Deposit is 7 and Bond is 5.
   b. Choose maximum number and do that alternative: Maximum is 10 and the alternative is Stock.
3. **Coefficient of Optimism (Hurwicz's Index):** The Hurwicz criterion is a weighted average of the best and worst payoff of each alternative (Oaksshott, 2006). This may be considered more realistic than some of the earlier rules which are based solely on the extreme payoffs (Taha, 2007). The decision maker is neither too optimistic nor too pessimistic. It is calculated as follows:

Weighted payoff = α worst payoff + $(1 - \alpha)$ x best payoff

Alpha is a number between 0 and 1, sometimes called the pessimism-optimism index. The value of α chosen reflects the decision makers' attitude to the risk of poor payoff and the chance of good payoff. The option with the highest payoff is chosen. The following step are taken in Hurwicz rule.

a. Choose α between zero and one. One means optimistic and zero means pessimistic,
b. Choose largest and smallest numbers for each action,
c. Multiply largest payoff (row-wise) by α and the smallest by $(1-\alpha)$,
d. Pick an action with the largest sum.

For example, for $\alpha = 0.7$, we have the situation shown in Box 1.
Therefore, the Coefficient of Optimism course of action is

Stock: $(0.7*(2)) + (0.3*10) = 1.6$

Deposit: $(0.7*2) + (0.3*7) = 3.5$

Bond: $(0.7*1) + (0.3*5) = 2.2$

The decision maker selects the highest payoff which is 3.5. Therefore, the best alternative is to invest in Deposit. This method is a linear combination of all nature outcomes and can easily be extended for n outcomes and k nature states with their associate alternatives.

Box 1.

	Largest	**Smallest**
Stock	10	-2
Deposit	7	2
Bond	5	1

4. **Laplace:** As one cannot assign probabilities to the event, the Laplace criterion says that the events should be treated as equally likely (Taha, 2007). The procedure is as follows
   a. For each alternative find the mean value of outcome
   b. Choose the alternative with the best average outcome which is the lowest average cost or the highest average gain

The average outcomes are computed as shown below

Stock: (10 + 4 +(-2))/3 = 4

Deposit: (7 + 6 +2)/3 = 5

Bond: (5 + 1 + 4)/3 = 3.3

Choose the best average outcome. As these figures represent gain, the best is the highest which is to invest in deposit

5. **Minimax Regret: (Savag's Opportunity Loss):** The minimax regret rule minimises the maximum opportunity loss (Oakshott, 2007). The opportunity loss is the loss that occurs through not taking the best option. To work out the opportunity loss one has to subtract each payoff for a particular state of nature from the best that could be achieved given that state. Some production managers in Oil and Gas company think as follows: 'I hate regrets and therefore I have to minimize my regrets'. 'My decision should be made to increase oil production so that it is worth repeating'. 'I should only do those things that I feel I could happily repeat such as offering training on health and safety'. This reduces the chance that the outcome will make me feel regretful, or disappointed, or that it will be an unpleasant surprise. Regret is the payoff on what would have been the best decision in the circumstances minus the payoff for the actual decision in the circumstances. Therefore, the first step is to set up the regret table:
   a. Take the largest number in each state of nature column (boom economy).
   b. Subtract all the numbers in that state of nature column from it.
   c. Choose maximum number of each action.
   d. Choose minimum number from step (c) and take that action.

Stocks

The minimum number from the maximum is selected. Therefore, the alternative stock is selected. (See Table 3).

Table 3. The regret matrix

	State of Economy			
	Boom	**Steady**	**Recession**	**Maximum**
Stock	(10-10)	(6-4)	(4-2)	2
Deposit	(10-7)	(6-6)	(4-2)	3
Bond	(10-4)	(6-1)	(4-4)	6

Limitations of Decision Making Under Pure Uncertainty

Decision analysis in general assumes that the decision maker faces a decision problem where one has to choose at least and at most one option from a set of options. In some cases, this limitation can be overcome by formulating the decision making under uncertainty as a zero-sum two-person game. In decision making under pure uncertainty, the decision maker has no knowledge regarding which state of nature is most likely to happen. One is probabilistically ignorant concerning the state of nature; therefore, that person cannot be optimistic or pessimistic. In such a case, the decision maker invokes consideration of security. One can notice that any technique used in decision making under pure uncertainties is appropriate only for the private life decisions. Moreover, the public person (i.e., you, the manager) has to have some knowledge of the state of nature in order to predict the probabilities of the various states of nature. Otherwise, the decision maker is not capable of making a reasonable and defensible decision in this case.

4. DECISION MAKING UNDER RISK

With uncertainty one knows that there are a number of possible events, one of which will occur-but has no idea of the likelihood of each event. With decision making under risk one again has a number of events, but now can give each of them a probability. Probabilities must be assigned to all relevant events so that these probabilities add up to one. In decision making under risk one assumes that there exist a number of possible future states of nature (Taha, 2007). Each has a known (or assumed) probability of occurring, and there may not be one future state that results in the best outcome for all alternatives. Examples of future states and their probabilities are as follows:

- Alternative weather (weather) will affect the profitability of alternative construction schedules at the drilling site; here, the probabilities of rain and of good weather can be estimated from historical data.
- Alternative economic futures (boom or recession) determine the relative profitability of conservative versus high-risk investment strategy; here, the assumed probabilities of different economic futures might be based on the judgment of a panel of economists.

Risk implies a degree of uncertainty and an inability to fully control the outcomes or consequences of such an action. Risk or the elimination of risk is an effort that managers employ. However, in some instances the elimination of one risk may increase some other risks. Effective handling of a risk requires its assessment and its subsequent impact on the decision process. The decision process allows the decision-maker to evaluate alternative strategies prior to making any decision. The decision making under risk process is as follows:

1. The problem is defined and all feasible alternatives are considered. The possible outcomes for each alternative are evaluated.
2. Outcomes are discussed based on their monetary payoffs or net gain in reference to assets or time.
3. Various uncertainties are quantified in terms of probabilities.
4. Compute the expected payoff, also called the return (R), for each action. The quality of the optimal strategy depends upon the quality of the judgments.

The decision maker needs to identify and examine the sensitivity of the optimal strategy with respect to the crucial factors. Whenever the decision maker has some knowledge regarding the states of nature, one may be able to assign subjective probability estimates for the occurrence of each state. In such cases, the problem is classified as decision making under risk.

Expected Value

The usual way of solving problems with risk is to calculate the expected value of each alternative and choose the alternative with the best expected value. The expected value of each alternative is defined as the sum of the probabilities multiplied by the value of the outcomes. Given the future states of nature and their probabilities, the solution in decision making under risk is the alternative that provides the highest expected value. The expected value computation using the values from Table 2 is as follows.

Stock: 0.4(12) + 0.3(8) + 0.2(7) + 0.1(3) = 8.9

Deposit: 0.4(15) + 0.3(9) + 0.2(5) + 0.1(-2) = 9.5

Bond: 0.4(7) + 0.3(7) + 0.2(7) + 0.1(7) = 7

The decision maker now selects the option with the highest expected value which is to invest in deposit

Expected Opportunity Loss (EOL)

As a loss is the negative aspect of gain it is to be expected that opportunity loss and expected values are related (Taha, 2007). This is indeed so and the opportunity loss multiplied by the probabilities i.e. the expected opportunity loss can be used to arrive at the same ranking as that of expected value rule except that where the maximum expected value is chosen, the minimum expected opportunity loss is required. The steps of this method are as follows:

1. Set up a loss payoff matrix by taking largest number in each state of nature column, and subtract all numbers in that column from it,
2. For each action, multiply the probability and loss then add up for each action,
3. Choose the action with smallest EOL.

The Expected Opportunity Loss Matrix

Consider the opportunity loss table below based on the values from Table 2, and assume the probability of a boom economy is 0.4, steady and recession are 0.3 each; then expected opportunity loss is calculated as shown in Box 2.

Stock: 0.4(10-10) + 0.3(6-4) + 0.3(4-2) = 1.2

Deposit: 0.4(10 -7) + 0.3(6-6) + 0.3(4-2) = 1.8

Bond: 0.4(10-4) + 0.3(6-1) + 0.3(4-4) = 3.9

Box 2.

	State of Economy		
	Boom	**Steady**	**Recession**
Stock	(10-10)	(6-4)	(4-2)
Deposit	(10-7)	(6-6)	(4-2)
Bond	(10-4)	(6-1)	(4-4)

The action with the minimum EOL is stock, which is the most probable state of nature.

A Discussion on Expected Opportunity Loss (Expected Regret)

Comparing a decision outcome to its alternatives appears to be an important component of decision making. One important factor is the emotion of regret. This occurs when a decision outcome is compared to the outcome that would have taken place had a different decision been made. This is in contrast to disappointment, which results from comparing one outcome to another as a result of the same decision. Accordingly, large contrasts with counterfactual results have a disproportionate influence on decision making.

Regret results compare a decision outcome with what might have been. Therefore, it depends upon the feedback available to decision makers as to which outcome the alternative option would have yielded. Altering the potential for regret by manipulating uncertainty resolution reveals that the decision making behaviour that appears to be risk averse can actually be attributed to regret aversion. There is some indication that regret may be related to the distinction between acts and omissions. Some studies have found that regret is more intense following an action, than an omission. For example, in one study, participants concluded that a decision maker who switched stock funds from one company to another and lost money would feel more regret than another decision maker who decided against switching the stock funds but also lost money. People usually assigned a higher value to an inferior outcome when it resulted from an act rather than from an omission. Presumably, this is as a way of counteracting the regret that could have resulted from the act.

5. DECISION MAKING IN THE OIL AND GAS INDUSTRY

Oil and Gas has brought out both the best and worst of our civilisation for some time now. It has been both boon and burden. Energy is the basis of our industrial society. And of all energy sources – oil has loomed the largest and the most problematic because of its central role, its strategic character, its geographic distribution, the recurrent pattern of crisis in its supply – and the inevitable and irresistible temptation to grasp for its rewards ( ). The global industry is however changing. Four factors in particular are contributing to the uncertainty surrounding the industry's future.

1. **Field Size:** Globally many of the oil majors still generate much of their output – and profits – from giant fields discovered decades ago. Production from nearly all these giant fields is either near its peak or is already declining. New fields are rarely as large or as profitable as these earlier large

reservoirs. Recently few oilfields have been discovered in the African continent, they have not delivered the same economies of scale.

2. **Finite Resource:** Whilst virtually everyone is agreed that oil is a finite resource there is much disagreement in the industry about exactly when demand will irreversibly exceed supply.
3. **Demand:** World demand for oil and gas will depend on two contrary forces. Firstly, there is the possible reduction in demand by the countries in the Organisation for Economic Co-operation and Development (OECD) caused by structural changes, saturated markets, ageing populations and increasing efficiency. Such efficiency gains are driven by competition, concerns for energy security and environmental measures.
4. **Restructuring:** International oil prices are notoriously volatile. However, when, at the end of 2015, oil prices dropped to their lowest levels in real terms, the profit margins of even the largest companies will be squeezed and all companies will be forced to reduce costs. This will prove difficult and with the need to improve their return on capital employed, which has historically been lower than the cost of that capital. One way of arresting the situation is to make further savings was through big mergers, followed by ruthless restructuring.

Ghana's oil and gas industry is a recently emergent one. The nation joined the legion of oil producing countries in 2010 as it marked the year the nation started commercial production of hydrocarbon resources. Production of crude oil begun with 85,000 barrels of oil a day in the Jubilee Field off the coast of Ghana as was announced by Tullow Ghana Limited, one of the jubilee partners. There are three partners in the Jubilee Field, namely Kosmos Energy, EO group and Tullow Ghana Limited (GNPC, 2011). During the second half of 2012, Tullow Ghana and its partners discovered three other fields and therefore submitted a development plan to the government in those fields. The Jubilee field is a world-class oil field, substantially with estimated recoverable resources of about 1 billion barrels (Kastning, 2012). More development wells are being drilled by other licensed companies and the jubilee partners with some indicating gas reserves.

Since oil and gas industry is a risk venture, the author distributed questionnaire to 200 managers in the oil and gas industry in Ghana to ascertain how these managers make decision both under risk and uncertainty. 140 responded and were analysed. Table 4 shows a summary of the responses.

The managers were asked which decision criteria they used when faced with a problem involving uncertainty. 57 percent indicated Maximax followed by Minimax regret which was 29 percent. These figures, as shown in Table 5, indicate that majority of the managers are risk takers. None of the managers used Laplace or Maximin.

Table 4. Decision making under uncertainty

Decision Criteria	Total	Frequency	Percent
Maximax	140	79	57
Maximin	140	0	0
Hurwicz	140	20	14
Minimax Regret	140	41	29
Laplace	140	0	0
Total			100

Table 5. Decision making under risk

Decision Criteria	Total	Frequency	Percent
Expected Value	140	120	86
Expected Opportunity loss	140	20	14
Decision Tree	140	0	0
Total		140	100

Again the managers were asked which decision criteria they used when faced with a problem that involves risk. 86 percent used Expected Value followed by Expected Opportunity loss. These figures from Table 5 indicate that majority of the managers are long term planners as the expected value is a long run average. None of them opted for Decision Tree. Thirty of the managers are risk averse, thirty of them said they consider themselves neither one way nor the other, and finally the remaining stated that they like risk taking, however managers have to evaluate the alternatives before making any decision.

The oil and gas industry is characterized with a series of risky decision makings (Kastning, 2012). Even at the development and production stage, the engineering parameters embody a high level of uncertainties in relation to their critical variables (infrastructure, production schedule, quality of oil, operational costs, reservoir characteristics etc.). These uncertainties originated from geological models and coupled with economic and engineering models involve high-risk decision scenarios, with no guarantee of successfully discovering and developing hydrocarbons resources. Corporate managers continuously face important decisions regarding the allocation of scarce resources among investments that are characterized by substantial geological and financial risk. For instance, in the petroleum industry, managers are increasingly using decision analysis techniques to aid in making these decisions. In this sense, the petroleum industry is a classic case of uncertainty in decision-making; it provides an ideal setting for the investigation of corporate risk behaviour and its effects on the firm's performance. The wildcat drilling decision has long been a typical example of the application of decision analysis in classical textbooks.

Future trends in oil resource availability depend largely on the balance between the outcome of the cost-increasing effects of depletion and the cost-reducing effects of new technology. Based upon that scenario, new forms of reservoir exploitation and management will appear where the contributions of risk and decision models are one of the important ingredients. This trend can be seen in the last two decades. The new internationally focused hydrocarbon exploration and production strategies were driven in part by rapidly evolving new technologies. Technological advances allowed hydrocarbon exploration in well-established basins as well as in new frontier zones such as ultra-deep water. Those technology-driven international hydrocarbon exploration and production strategies combined with new and unique strategic elements where risk analysis and decision models represent important components of a series of investment decisions.

6. FUTURE RESEARCH

The result has shown an indication that there is the need to improve decision making under risk and uncertainty given the nature of the oil and gas industry. The findings of this research raise concerns on a number of important issues and may provide avenues for further research. For instance, several decision making criteria were discussed. One can undertake other research in the area of manufacturing industry under the current financial crisis. The impact of decision making on company's performance which will require more empirical data. A descriptive survey can also be employed to analyse company's policy regarding the decision making under uncertainty and risk.

7. CONCLUSION

The aim of this chapter was to review and investigate the decision making processes under risk and uncertainty of Oil and Gas companies. In achieving this aim existing literature was reviewed and the views of manager from eight oil and gas companies were solicited. Results revealed that during the hydrocarbon exploration phase, major uncertainties are related to volumes in place and economics. As the level of information increases, these uncertainties are mitigated and, the importance of the uncertainties related to technology and recovery factor increases. Many complex Exploration and Production decision problems involve multiple conflicting objectives. Although geoscientists and engineers may be willing to make predictions about unknown Exploration and Production situations, there is a need to assess the level of uncertainty of the projects. Probability assessment quantifies the information gap between what is known, and what needs to be known for an optimal decision. The probabilistic models are used for protection against adverse uncertainty, and exploitation of propitious uncertainty. In decision making under pure uncertainty, the decision maker has absolutely no knowledge about the state of nature. The decision maker's behaviour is purely based on his/her attitude toward the unknown. Some of these behaviours are optimistic, pessimistic and least regret, among others. With decision making under risk, probabilities must be assigned to all relevant events so that these probabilities add up to one

The oil and gas industry is characterized with a series of risky decision makings. Even at the development and production stage, the engineering parameters embody a high level of uncertainties in relation to their critical variables. Four factors contributing to the uncertainty surrounding the industry's future are field size, finite resource, demand and restructuring.

The study is not without limitations. Although decision making under risk and uncertainty in oil and gas industry is important the study sampled companies in Ghana and the results may not generalize markets or institutions due to marked institutional and organizational differences. The availability of data has affected the representativeness of the data. This undoubtedly will impact the generalizability of the findings to other oil and gas firms globally. Future research may examine other countries such as OPEC, to further deepen our understanding of decision making under risk and uncertainty in oil and gas industry.

REFERENCES

Agarwal, H., Renaud, E. J., Preston, L. E., & Padmanabhan, D. (2004). Uncertainty quantification using evidence theory in multidisciplinary design optimization. *Reliability Engineering & System Safety*, *85*(1-3), 281–294. doi:10.1016/j.ress.2004.03.017

Ahmed, P. K. (2011). *Innovative management: Context, strategies, systems, and processes*. Upper Saddle River, NJ: Prentice Hall.

Allais, M. (1956, January). Évaluation des perspectives économiques de la recherche minière sur de grands espaces - application au Sahara Algérien. Revue de l'Industrie Minérale, 329-383.

American Institute of Chemical Engineers (AIChE). (2000). Guidelines for chemical process quantitative risk analysis (2nd ed.). New York: AIChE.

Arsham, H. (1987). A Stochastic Model of Optimal Advertising Pulsing Policy. *Computers & Operations Research, 14*(3), 231–239. doi:10.1016/0305-0548(87)90026-8

Arsham, H. (1993). A Markovian Model of Consumer Buying Behavior and Optimal Advertising Pulsing Policy. *Computers & Operations Research, 20*(2), 35–48. doi:10.1016/0305-0548(93)90094-Y

Aviad, B., & Roy, G. A. (2012). Decision support method, based on bounded rationality concepts, to reveal feature saliency in clustering problems. *Decision Support Systems, 54*(1), 292–303. doi:10.1016/j.dss.2012.05.037

Ayyub, B., & Klir, J. G. (2006). *Uncertainty modeling and analysis in engineering and the sciences.* New York: Chapman & Hall. doi:10.1201/9781420011456

Bae, H., Grandhi, V. R., & Canfield, A. R. (2004). An approximation approach for uncertainty quantification using evidence theory. *Reliability Engineering & System Safety, 86*(3), 215–225. doi:10.1016/j.ress.2004.01.011

Baker, K. M. (2013). Decision Making in a Hybrid Organization: A Case Study of a Southwestern Drug Court Treatment Program. *Law & Social Inquiry, 38*(1), 27–54. doi:10.1111/j.1747-4469.2012.01295.x

Ben-Haim, Y. (2001). *Information-gap Decision Theory: Decisions under Severe Uncertainty*. San Diego, CA: Academic Press.

Bernstein, P. L. (1996). *Against the Gods: The remarkable story of risk*. New York: John Wiley & Sons.

Borges, A. R., & Antunes, C. H. (2003). A fuzzy multiple objective decision support model for energy-economy planning. *European Journal of Operational Research, 145*(2), 304–316. doi:10.1016/S0377-2217(02)00536-2

Bunn, D. W., & Paschentis, S. N. (1996). Development of a stochastic model for the economic despatch of electric power. *European Journal of Operational Research, 27*(2), 179–191. doi:10.1016/0377-2217(86)90059-7

Cheng, Y. (2000). Uncertainties in fault tree analysis. *Tamkang Journal of Science and Engineering, 3*(1), 23–29.

Chevreau, F. R., Wybo, J. L., & Cauchois, D. (2006). Organizing learning processes on risks by using the bow-tie representation. *Journal of Hazardous Materials, 130*(3), 276–283. doi:10.1016/j.jhazmat.2005.07.018 PMID:16125315

CMPT. (1999). *A guide to quantitative risk assessment for offshore installation.* The Centre of Marine and Petroleum Technology.

Cockshott, J. E. (2005). Probability bow-ties: A transparent risk management tool. *Process Safety and Environmental Protection, 83*(4B4), 307–316. doi:10.1205/psep.04380

Covello, V., & Mumpower, J. (1985). Risk Analysis and Risk Management: An Historical Perspective. *Risk Analysis*, *5*(2), 103–120. doi:10.1111/j.1539-6924.1985.tb00159.x

Dianous, V., & Fiévez, C. (2006). ARAMIS project: A more explicit demonstration of risk control through the use of bowetie diagrams and the evaluation of safety barrier performance. *Journal of Hazardous Materials*, *130*(3), 220–233. doi:10.1016/j.jhazmat.2005.07.010 PMID:16107301

Dismukes, D. E., & Christopher, P. P. (2011). *Diversifying energy industry risk in the GOM*. Retrieved from http://www.gom.gov.de/div/enrg.pdf

Duijm, N. J. (2009). Safety-barrier diagrams as a safety management tool. *Reliability Engineering & System Safety*, *94*(2), 332–341. doi:10.1016/j.ress.2008.03.031

Ehrgott, M. (2011). *Trends in multiple criteria decision analysis*. New York, NY: Springer.

Ferdous, R., Khan, F., Sadiq, R., Amyotte, P., & Veitch, B. (2011). Fault and event tree analyses for process systems risk analysis: Uncertainty handling formulations. *Journal of Risk Analysis*, *31*(1), 86–107. doi:10.1111/j.1539-6924.2010.01475.x PMID:20731791

Gilboa, I. (2011). *Rational choice*. Cambridge, MA: MIT Press.

GNPC. (2011). *Ghana National Petroleum Corporation Main Page*. Retrieved from http://www.gnpc-ghana.com/home/

Grant, R. (2011). *Contemporary strategy analysis*. New York, NY: Wiley.

Grosfeld-Nir, A., & Tishler, A. (1993). A stochastic model for the measurement of electricity outage costs. *The Energy Journal (Cambridge, Mass.)*, *14*(2), 157–174. doi:10.5547/ISSN0195-6574-EJ-Vol14-No2-8

Harbaugh, J. W. (1984). Quantitative estimation of petroleum prospect outcome probabilities: An overview of procedures. *Marine and Petroleum Geology*, *1*(November).

Harris, D. P. (1984). *Mineral Resources Appraisal: Mineral Endowment, Resources and Potential supply: Concepts, Methods and Cases*. Oxford, UK: Clarendon.

Harris, D. P. (1990). Mineral exploration decisions: A guide to economic analysis and modeling. New York: J. Wiley.

Hastie, R. (2010). *Rational choice in an uncertain world: The psychology of judgment and decision making*. Thousand Oaks, CA: Sage.

Hayashi, S. H. D., Ligero, E. L., & Schiozer, D. J. (2007). *Decision-making process in development of offshore petroleum fields*. SPE Latin American and Caribbean Petroleum Engineering Conference, SPE 107737, Buenos Aires, Argentina. doi:10.2118/107737-MS

Hicks, M. J. (2005). *Problem solving and decision making: Hard, soft, and creative approaches*. Belmont, CA: Cengage Learning.

Huang, D., Chen, T., & Wang, J. M. (2001). A fuzzy set approach for event tree analysis. *Fuzzy Sets and Systems*, *118*(1), 153–165. doi:10.1016/S0165-0114(98)00288-7

Huang, G. H., Baetz, B. W., & Patry, G. G. (1992). A grey linear programming approach for municipal solid waste management planning under uncertainty. *Civil Engineering Systems*, *9*(4), 319–335. doi:10.1080/02630259208970657

Huang, G. H., Baetz, B. W., & Patry, G. G. (1995a). Grey integer programming: An application to waste management planning under uncertainty. *European Journal of Operational Research*, *83*(3), 594–620. doi:10.1016/0377-2217(94)00093-R

Huang, G. H., Baetz, B. W., & Patry, G. G. (1995b). Grey fuzzy integer programming: An application to regional waste management planning under uncertainty. *Socio-Economic Planning Sciences*, *29*(1), 17–38. doi:10.1016/0038-0121(95)98604-T

Jarmon, G., & Anderson, P. (2007). *Crude Oil- Uncertainty about Future Oil Supply Makes It Important to Develop a Strategy for Addressing a Peak and Decline in Oil Production*. Government Accountability Office-07-283.

Jiang, R., Xie, J., Wang, N., & Li, J. (2013). Evolution game analysis of water saving and pollution prevention for city user groups based on bounded rationality. *Shuili Fadian Xuebao /Journal of Hydroelectric Engineering, 32*(1), 31-36.

Jo, Y. D., & Ahn, B. J. (2002). Analysis of hazard areas associated with high-pressure natural- gas pipelines. *Journal of Loss Prevention in the Process Industries*, *15*(3), 179–188. doi:10.1016/S0950-4230(02)00007-4

Kaplan, S., & Garrick, B. J. (1981). On the quantitative definition of risk. *Risk Analysis*, *1*(1), 11–27. doi:10.1111/j.1539-6924.1981.tb01350.x PMID:11798118

Kastning, T. (2012). *Basic Overview of Ghana's Emerging Oil Industry, Report for Friedrich Ebert Stiftung*. Retrieved from http://library.fes.de/pdf-files/bueros/ghana/10490.pdf

Kepner, C. H., & Tregoe, B. B. (2005). *The new rational manager* (rev. ed.). New York, NY: Kepner-Tregoe.

Khan, F. I., & Abbasi, S. A. (2001). Risk analysis of a typical chemical industry using ORA procedure. *Journal of Loss Prevention in the Process Industries*, *14*(1), 43–59. doi:10.1016/S0950-4230(00)00006-1

Köksalan, M. M., Sagala, P. N. S., & Sagala, P. N. S. (1995). Interactive Approaches for Discrete Alternative Multiple Criteria Decision Making with Monotone Utility Functions. *Management Science*, *41*(7), 1158–1171. doi:10.1287/mnsc.41.7.1158

Lee, I. H. (2013). Speculation under bounded rationality. *Journal of Economic Theory and Econometrics*, *24*(1), 37–53.

Lin, Q. G., & Huang, G. H. (2009a). A dynamic inexact energy systems planning model for supporting greenhouse-gas emission management and sustainable renewable energy development under uncertainty—A case study for the city of Waterloo, Canada. *Renewable & Sustainable Energy Reviews*, *13*(8), 1836–1853. doi:10.1016/j.rser.2009.01.021

Lin, Q. G., & Huang, G. H. (2010a). An inexact two-stage stochastic optimization model for managing greenhouse gas emission and sustainable energy systems development at a municipal level. *Energy*, *35*, 2270–2280. doi:10.1016/j.energy.2010.01.042

Lin, Q. G., Huang, G. H., Bass, B., Chen, B., Zhang, B. Y., & Zhang, X. D. (2009). CCEM: A city-cluster energy systems planning model. *Energy Sources Part A*, *31*(4), 273–286. doi:10.1080/15567030802592345

Lin, Q. G., Huang, G. H., Bass, B., Huang, Y. F., & Liu, L. (2010a). Optimization of energy systems under changing policies of greenhouse-gas emission control: A study for the province of Saskatchewan, Canada. *Energy Sources. Part A*, *32*, 1587–1602.

Lin, Q. G., Huang, G. H., Bass, B., Nie, X. H., Zhang, X. D., & Qin, X. S. (2010b). EMDSS: An optimization-based decision support system for energy systems management under changing climate conditions—An application to the Toronto-Niagara Region, Canada. *Expert Systems with Applications*, *37*(7), 5040–5051. doi:10.1016/j.eswa.2009.12.007

Lv, Y., Huang, G. H., Li, Y. P., Yang, Z. F., Liu, Y., & Cheng, G. H. (2010). Planning regional water resources system using an interval fuzzy bi-level programming method. *Journal of Environmental Informatics*, *16*, 43–56. doi:10.3808/jei.201000177

Manne, A., Mendelsohn, R., & Richels, R. (1995). MERGE, a model for evaluating regional and global effects of GHG reduction policies. *Energy Policy*, *23*(1), 17–34. doi:10.1016/0301-4215(95)90763-W

March, J. G. (2010). *Primer on decision making: How decisions happen*. New York, NY: Simon & Schuster.

Markowski, A. S., Mannan, M. S., & Bigoszewska, A. (2009). Fuzzy logic for process safety analysis. *Journal of Loss Prevention in the Process Industries*, *22*(6), 695–702. doi:10.1016/j.jlp.2008.11.011

Mavrotas, G., Demertzis, H., Meintani, A., & Diakoulaki, D. (2003). Energy planning in buildings under uncertainty in fuel costs: The case of a hotel unit in Greece. *Energy Conversion and Management*, *44*(8), 1303–1321. doi:10.1016/S0196-8904(02)00119-X

Mendel, J. (2011). *Perceptual computing: Aiding people in making subjective judgments*. New York, NY: Wiley.

Murata, A., Kubo, S., & Hata, N. (2012). Study on promotion of cooperative behaviour in social dilemma situation by introduction of bounded rationality - Effects of group heuristics on cooperative behaviours. *Proceedings of the SICE Annual Conference*.

Narayanan, M. P. (2005). *Finance for strategic decision making: What non-financial managers need to know*. New York, NY: Wiley.

Nordhaus, W. (1993). Rolling the DICE: An optimal transition path for controlling GHGs. *Resource and Energy Economics*, *15*(1), 27–50. doi:10.1016/0928-7655(93)90017-O

Oakshott, L. (2006). *Essential Quantitative Methods for Business Management and Finance* (3rd ed.). New York: Palgrave Macmillan.

Peck, S. C., & Teisberg, T. J. (1995). Optimal CO2 control policy with stochastic losses from temperature rise. *Climatic Change*, *31*(1), 19–34. doi:10.1007/BF01092979

Pinto, A. C. C., Guedes, S. S., Bruhn, C. H. L., Gomes, J. A. T., Sá, A. N., & Fagundes Neto, J. R. (2001). *Marlim Complex Development: A reservoir engineering overview*. SPE Latin American and Caribbean Petroleum Engineering Conference, SPE 69438, Buenos Aires, Argentina.

Sadeghi, M., & Hosseini, M. H. (2006). Energy supply planning in Iran by using fuzzy linear programming approach (regarding uncertainties of investment costs). *Energy Policy*, *34*(9), 993–1003. doi:10.1016/j.enpol.2004.09.005

Sadiq, R., Saint-Martin, E., & Kleiner, Y. (2008). Predicting risk of water quality failures in distribution networks under uncertainties using fault-tree analysis. *Urban Water Journal*, *5*(4), 287–304. doi:10.1080/15730620802213504

Salem, O. M., Miller, R. A., Deshpande, A. S., & Arurkar, T. P. (2010). Multi-criteria decision- making system for selecting an effective plan for bridge rehabilitation. *Structure and Infrastructure Engineering, 9*(8), 806-816.

Schoenfeld, A. H. (2011). *How we think: A theory of goal-oriented decision making and its educational applications*. New York, NY: Routledge.

Serrano-González, J., Burgos, P. M., & Riquelme, S. J. (2013). Optimum design of transmissions systems for offshore wind farms including decision making under risk. *Renewable Energy*, *59*, 115–127. doi:10.1016/j.renene.2013.03.024

Simon, H. (1957). A Behavioural Model of Rational Choice. In *Models of Man, Social and Rational: Mathematical Essays on Rational Human Behaviour in a Social Setting*. New York: Wiley.

Simon, H. (1990). A mechanism for social selection and successful altruism. *Science*, *250*(4988), 1665–1668. doi:10.1126/science.2270480 PMID:2270480

Simon, H. A. (2009). *Economics, bounded rationality, and the cognitive revolution*. Northampton, MA: Edward Elgar Publishing.

Sklavounos, S., & Rigas, F. (2006). Estimation of safety distances in the vicinity of fuel gas pipelines. *Journal of Loss Prevention in the Process Industries*, *19*(1), 24–31. doi:10.1016/j.jlp.2005.05.002

Sklavounos, S., & Rigas, F. (2006). Estimation of safety distances in the vicinity of fuel gas pipelines. *Journal of Loss Prevention in the Process Industries*, *19*(1), 24–31. doi:10.1016/j.jlp.2005.05.002

Steuer, R. E. (1986). *Multiple Criteria Optimization: Theory, Computation and Application*. New York: John Wiley.

Sun, W., & Huang, G. H. (2010). Inexact piecewise quadratic programming for waste flow allocation under uncertainty and nonlinearity. *Journal of Environmental Informatics*, *16*, 80–93. doi:10.3808/jei.201000180

Taha, H. A. (2007). *Operations Research, An introduction* (8th ed.). New York: Prentice Hall.

Tisdell, C. (1996). *Bounded Rationality and Economic Evolution: A Contribution to Decision Making*. Brookfield, UK: Economics, and Management. Cheltenham.

Towler, M. (2010). *Rational decision making: An introduction*. New York, NY: Wiley.

Walls, M. R., & Dyer, J. S. (1996). Risk propensity and firm performance: A study of the petroleum exploration industry. *Management Science*, *42*(7), 1004–1021. doi:10.1287/mnsc.42.7.1004

Yuhua, D., & Datao, Y. (2005). Estimation of failure probability of oil and gas transmission pipelines by fuzzy fault tree analysis. *Journal of Loss Prevention in the Process Industries*, *18*(2), 83–88. doi:10.1016/j.jlp.2004.12.003

Zionts, S., & Wallenius, J. (1976). An Interactive Programming Method for Solving the Multiple Criteria Problem. *Management Science*, *22*(6), 652–663. doi:10.1287/mnsc.22.6.652

Zopounidis, C. (2011a). *Multiple criteria decision aiding*. New York, NY: Nova Science Publishers.

Zopounidis, C. (2011b). *Handbook of multicriteria analysis*. New York, NY: Springer.

KEY TERMS AND DEFINITIONS

Decision Criteria: These are simple rule that recommend an alternative for decisions with uncertainty.

Maximax: The maximax rule involves selecting the alternative that maximises the maximum payoff available.

Maximin: The maximin rule involves selecting the alternative that maximises the minimum pay-off achievable.

Mineral Exploration: It is the process of finding commercially viable quantities of minerals to mine. The methods used for exploration vary at different stages of the process depending on the size of the area being explored, as well as the density and type of information sought.

Minimax Regret: The minimax regret strategy is the one that minimizes the maximum regret. It is useful for a risk-neutral decision maker. Essentially, this is the technique for a 'sore loser' who does not wish to make the wrong decision.

Probability: It is defined as the likelihood of an event occurring.

Regret: Regret in this context is defined as the opportunity loss through having made the wrong decision.

Chapter 10
Crisis Communication and Crisis Management during the Crisis:
Case Study of Croatia

Bilić Ivana
University of Split, Croatia

Franka Vrkić
University of Split, Croatia

ABSTRACT

Corporate managers are faced with one important role in managing company's overall communications, especially when one crisis event occurred. Since the whole business world was preoccupied with the crisis that has gripped the year 2008, it is interesting to explore the content and the level of development of crisis management teams and crisis communications guidelines in the biggest Croatian companies. The results of research showed that Croatian companies do not stay behind their peers in the rest of the business world in the terms of establishment and development crisis management and crisis communications. Deep business crisis did not stop Croatian companies to invest in their workforces and their communication skills in order to achieve competitiveness in the market. Even though the business environment was very turbulent during the observed period, and suffered from many cutoffs the research results showed even some improvements in 2014 compared to the research from 2011.

INTRODUCTION

Communication is an essential part of any relationship, particularly for a company in terms of a complex network of internal and external relationships with a large number of company's stakeholders. Corporate managers are faced with many important decisions in managing company's overall communications, especially when a crisis event occurs. The power of readiness of crisis communication, crisis management, crisis teams, and their potential in unexpected situation may turn crisis into a predictable chance, which

DOI: 10.4018/978-1-5225-0959-2.ch010

is highly connected with crisis team power and capability to make good decisions. Some prerequisites for that turnover are in the preparedness of the crisis management team and crisis communication. It is a part of corporate strategy and strategic decision of establishing corporate crisis management team as regular one. If the crisis management team is established in advance, and works as a proactive one, has defined roles assigned so as to act as a coherent group, with clearly defined duties, many of potential crisis could be alleviated or even prevented. Crisis communication can be a powerful company tool and a milestone in predicting, preventing, and overcoming a crisis situation. If a crisis event occurs, and good crisis management and crisis communication are developed at an appropriate level and coordinated with the overall corporate strategy, it will help a company survive the crisis, and, moreover, prevent the creation of rumors and destroying the reputation of the company.

Nevertheless, management teams in companies, the level of understanding the overall communication function, and a special connection between corporate communication strategy and corporate strategy are crucial in the decision-making process of communications function positioning in an organization, and decisions of protecting company's mission, vision, and values particularly during hard times.

Since the entire business world has been preoccupied with the crisis that started in 2008, it was interesting to explore the content and the level of development of crisis management teams and crisis communications guidelines in biggest Croatian companies which the authors surveyed in two iterations; first, at the beginning of the big global crisis and in the current moment (i.e. in 2014), while the crisis was still evident in Croatia. Throughout this chapter the authors explored companies' management and companies' communication teams for crisis management and communication in crisis, stressing that they all need to be analyzed and established in advance, as a strategic management decision, with the aim to protect company in crisis and enable it to survive in hard times. The aim of this research was to explore and compare the level of proactivity of companies for crisis event and crisis communication in Croatian in 2011 and in 2014. The main purpose was to explore the effects of crisis on crisis management and crisis communication over the period of long economic crisis, and find out whether the observed companies showed progress of declinations of its efforts in crisis management and crisis communication.

Literature review of previous research regarding the readiness of Croatian companies for a crisis is poor, particularly if it is observed over time. Google Scholar search confirmed author's assumption that there is a lack of surveys on crisis management in Croatian companies with zero result. Similar research results were found at EBSCOhost and Emerald Insight so authors realized that this research would broaden knowledge about critical decisions, made by Croatian top managers regarding companies' readiness to face crisis.

In order to investigate the above mentioned topic in Croatia, the reminder of the chapter is organized in five sections. The first section gives an overview of corporate crisis and previously explored causes of the crisis. In the second section, authors emphases the importance of strategic approach to crisis management. In the third section authors discuss the strategic approach to crisis communication. The fourth section is reserved for research methodology and methods, and present research findings. In the fifth section the concluding remarks and directions for future research are discussed.

CORPORATE CRISIS

Crises are becoming increasingly important social, political, economic, and environmental forces and arguably create more change more quickly than any other single phenomenon (Sellnow and Seeger,

2013). The history of corporate crisis is as long as it is history of corporations themselves. The first involvement of communication was in companies such as Pennsylvania Railroad Company, where Ivy L. Lee served as a communication professional, or Procter and Gamble with the Ivory Soap campaign and another famous father of modern public relations, Edward L. J. Bernays.

Crisis could be defined in many ways; it may be a corporate crisis, an environmental crisis, a health crisis or any other sort of crisis. Independently where they are coming from all of them possessed some mutual characteristics of a crisis (Argenti, 2009): (1) element of surprise, (2) insufficient information; and (3) the quick pace of the event.

Corporate crisis represents an unplanned process that damages primary goals of a company and implies ambivalent outcome (Osmanagić-Bedenik, 2003:12). Institute for Crisis Management (ICM, 2014) (hereinafter IMC) defined business crisis as any issue, problem or disruption which triggers negative stakeholder reactions that impact the organization's business and financial strength. In addition, ICM identifies four potential crisis types: Sudden, Perceptual, Smoldering, and Bizarre.

The results of Glamuzina and Lovrinčević's (2013) survey conducted on Presidents of Management Board of 200 Croatian companies in 2013 revealed there are two different sources of company's crisis, i.e. that crisis comes from inside or outside of the company. Research results revealed the following external causes which are as follows: (1) change in industry/market structure 71.8%; (2) loss of market customers 64.1%; (3) loss of major suppliers 5.1%; (4) loss of creditors-problems with ensuring 'fresh money'; and (5) changes in legislation 23.1%. From other perspectives some crisis is internally caused, so surveyed managers identified the following internal causes of crisis: (1) management mistakes 30.8%; (2) low responsiveness to the changes in business environment/opportunity losses 66.7%; (3) conflict between Management and Supervisory Board 0%; (4) bad credit loans (debt) decision 33.3%; and (5) inadequate control system 46.2%.

ICM report for 2014 revealed the following crisis categories as the top 10 crisis: mismanagement 33.47%; white-collar crime 13.86%; whistle blowers 6.52%; casualty accidents 6.39%; environmental damage 5.96%; executive dismissal 5.35%; consumer activism 4.32%; discrimination 4.11%; cyber-crime 3.96% and hostile takeover 3.67%. They also provided some interesting insights about the fact that the most crisis-prone industries in 2014 were: transportation, automobile manufacturing, banking and financial services, food, pharmaceutical, education, energy, retail, defense and aerospace, and health care, with one important observation that most of the crisis were smoldering (74.22%) and sudden (25.78%).

Whenever the crisis occurs it could be caused by controlled or uncontrolled reasons from the perspective of a company. It depends of the crisis type. Smoldering crisis is something what good crisis management may prevent, by doing its strategic contingency and a scenario planning in advance, as evidence about potential smoldering crisis is usually available before the crisis event occurs and has a huge potential to be resolved before the crisis event has even occurred. A good example of smoldering crisis could be the Volkswagen recent case of illegal software that masks emission (Neate, 2015), where company's top management had to be informed on the situation, and at least keep quiet intentionally, knowing that one day that the truth would be revealed. From other perspectives, sudden crisis happens without warning, no matter what the source of crisis is, i.e. whether the crisis is caused by internal of external factors. The sudden death of McDonald's CEO Jim Cantalupo (in his 60s), at company's convention in Orlando, (Bhatnagar, 2004) is the case of a sudden crisis, which a company could not predict, but at least needs to have it in its crisis manual.

It is very expensive for a company to experience a crisis; recent Burson-Marsteller research revealed that a crisis costs for small and medium-sized enterprises is from €10,000 to €49,999, and for enterprises from €500,000 to €999,999. The research also revealed that the average cost of a crisis is €549,000 (Burson-Marsteller, 2013).

STRATEGIC APPROACH TO CRISIS MANAGEMENT

Crisis management, by definition is the preparation and application of strategies and tactics that can prevent or modify the impact of major events on the company or organization (Stocker, 1997). Furthermore, crisis management incorporates all the decision, communications, and personal (crisis management team) necessary to prevent or deal with crisis. For a company in crisis it is essential that its management effectively recognizes signals of the crisis, creates a crisis plan, implements one or (usually) more strategies, maintains positive cash-flow, avoids longer blockades of companies account and prevents legal conditions for bankruptcy to occur (Kružić, Glamuzina and Lovrinčević, 2013).

A crisis, whatever the reason for it might be usually consists of these five phases (Fearn-Banks, 2011):

1. Detection
2. Prevention/preparation
3. Containment
4. Recovery
5. Learning

The first phase, i.e. the detection of the crisis may be very sensitive for the company. If it is the case of a smoldering crisis, then the company's top management is never ready for the crisis event. They would probably behave as if they expected that the crisis would never be revealed and the crisis is usually directed by affected stakeholders or media. Rarely may they expect that one day the truth will be revealed. In phase two, prevention/preparation, the power of crisis management and crisis communication is emphasized, independently of the crisis type in this particular moment. When the crisis is detected, a well-prepared crisis manual and effective crisis communication strategy may help company in a structured approach which will save human life, minimize the damage and finally save company's reputation. In phase three, it is highly important for a company to take control over the crisis. If it is not successful in that phase, the future of the company becomes uncertain. The most important advice for this phase is to show regret if the company caused the crisis. Considerable effort is needed by the company to resolve the situation with an accent put on future improvements that serve as a promise that something similar will never happen in the future. The fourth phase is recovery, returning back to the position before the crisis as much as possible. In all previous phases, it is very important for the company to keep in touch with its employees, i.e. to keep them informed. In a crisis, they are key ambassadors of company's stability. Last but not least, inevitable advice for any type of crisis is continuing with regular operations, whenever possible. Learning is the last phase of any crisis cycle, strongly connected with organization learning, starting by analyzing the experienced crisis, with the aim to help the company to be prepared for future challenges.

In hard times for the company, it is always good to remember the case of Johnson & Johnson's in Tylenol crisis, which occurred suddenly in 1982, when 7 people were killed after taking poisoned Tylenol capsules. Company's management was embarrassed by the events of sudden crisis. However, they took the offensive strategy, recalled all the products from the shelves which cost more than $100 million, they conducted intensive campaign and informed the public about the problem, tried to reduce the number of deaths, showed its human face and respected company's values and company's mission (Argenti and Forman, 2002). After all, the whole industry clearly saw the problem, and since then the protection of pills bottles has become more and more in the focus of the pharmaceutical industry, what may be seen as organizational learning, adopted in the whole industry.

Strategy as itself serves to lead company's management into a favorable and perspective future, with clear aims of what the company will be in recent or more distant future. In strategic planning, an important part of the plans is devoted to contingency and scenario plans with the purpose of protecting a company's future growth and development as its main goals. In a crisis situation, a company can choose different strategies, based on the market position, extent of the crisis, and type of the crisis and, finally, the goals which it plans to reach in a particular situation. Crisis strategies could be grouped into two main categories (Tipurić, Kružić, Lovrinčević, 2013 in Glamuzina and Lovrinčević, 2013):

1. Offensive crisis strategies – their main goal is turnaround
2. Defensive crisis strategies – their main goal is to leave the business

Two main crisis management strategies are further divided into subcategories which are more adjusted to the potential company's goal to survive or to leave the business (Figure 1). Offensive strategies, which

Figure 1. Crisis strategies
Source: Tipurić, Kružić, Lovrinčević, Strateški menadžment (Strategic Management), in Glamuzina and Lovrinčević (2013)

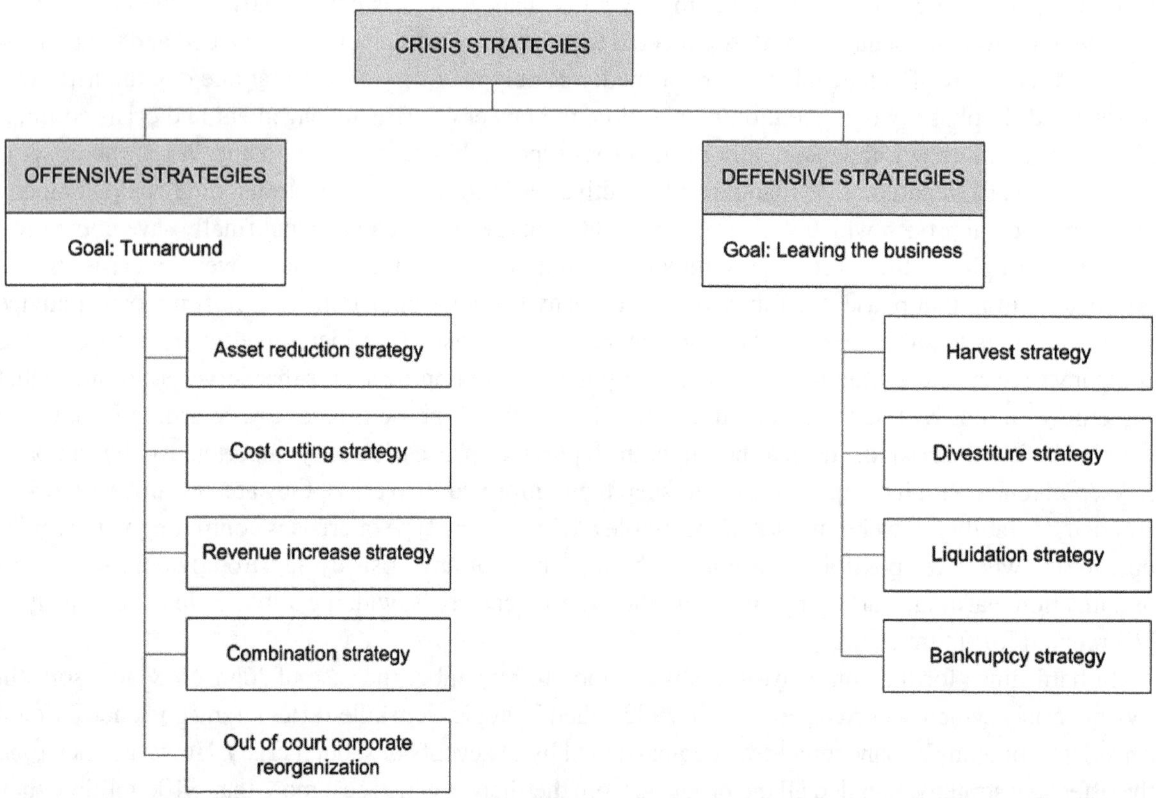

represent company's goal to survive changes and hard times, and recover core business are (Tipurić, Kružić, Lovrinčević, 2013 in Glamuzina and Lovrinčević, 2013)[1]:

- **Asset Reduction Strategies/Asset Retrenchment Strategy:** In this situation companies sell their assets which is not required or necessary for performing companies core business activities and they use that money to help company's effort for consolidation and turnaround in its core business.
- **Cost Cutting/Cost Reducing Strategy:** The basis of this strategy is cutting every possible cost, and is usually used when a company is near to its break-even point. This strategy begins with cost analytics and reduction followed by decreasing or cutting costs such as employees' salary, number of employees, marketing costs, eliminating non-profitable activities.
- **Revenue Increasing/Revenue Generation Strategies:** Is oriented towards creating increased sales volume with the purpose to increase company's revenue. Usually, companies use this option to achieve higher revenue with the aim to increase money flow in the short run: introducing new products, improving features of the existing products, special offers/sales without decreasing the price but offering additional offers to customers, decreasing the prices, additional services to customers and/or guarantees.
- **Combination Strategy:** Is usually used in time limited/urgent situations when the management (usually newly established crisis management team) needs to act fast because survival of the company is in an obvious danger. Time for action is limited. The more the situation is difficult for the company, the more probable is that the combination of previously listed strategies will be successful in terms of profit and loss account, decrease in assets, decrease in obligations and especially empowerment of company's cash flow.
- **Out of Court Corporate Reorganization:** Should ensure creditors and company in crisis to make an agreement based on both sides backing down with the purpose of financial, proprietary and operative restructuring and avoiding bankruptcy.

Sometimes, depending on the company's starting position, its problems, market position and perspectives for the successful recovery, the company's crisis management team may decide to employ some of the defensive strategies, with the purpose of generating maximum amount of money from leaving the business. In short, four defensive strategies according to Tipurić, Kružić and Lovrinčević (2013, in Glamuzina and Lovrinčević, 2013) are[2]:

- **Harvest Strategy:** Consists of controlled disinvestment from a company with the goal of improving cash flow in the period when the company is leaving the industry, accompanied by decreasing in investments, maintenance, marketing, research, distribution, product or assortment and reducing other investments or costs.
- **Divestiture Strategy:** Grounded on management's decision to sell a part or the entire company, is suitable for companies which do not possess a competitive advantage, and face significant changes in mission and vision; this strategy can also be caused by financial reasons.
- **Liquidation Strategy:** Is used when selling the company is the only option, and it means that the company will stop existing. It is the least preferred defensive strategy (along with the bankruptcy strategy), which results in the termination of the business.

- **Bankruptcy Strategy:** Is, in addition along with liquidation strategy, an end game exit strategy. Bankruptcy is a legal procedure led by court with the aim to satisfy company's creditors and lenders as much as possible by selling company's asset and debt collection.

Possessing a formal crisis plan is crucial for any organization, in terms of clearly defined team members and their duties. Although a formal crisis plan might show what should be done in a crisis situation, how a company actually performs is strongly and strictly connected with the chosen aforementioned crisis strategies, or a combination of them. A formal crisis plan, independent of the crisis type, should include some similar steps, across the countries and industries (adopted from Argenti, 2009):

1. A list of whom to notify in an emergency
2. An approach to media relations
3. A strategy for notifying employees
4. A location to serve as crisis headquarters
5. Written description of the plan

Whatever strategy is used, be it offensive or defensive, in crisis communication with all interested stakeholders it is critically vulnerable and sensitive period for the company, and many sensitive decisions, necessary for company's future need to be made. Along with choosing a crisis management strategy, in crisis management crisis communication strategy, that is the focus of the following sections, decisions about one need to be made in advance.

STRATEGIC APPROACH TO CRISIS COMMUNICATION

Corporate communications are a management function that offers a framework for effective coordination of all internal and external means of communications with the overall purpose of establishing and maintaining a favorable reputation with stakeholder groups upon which the organization is dependent (Cornelissen, 2008). A definition of crisis communication derives from the origins of corporate communication function. Fearn-Banks (2011) defined it as the dialog between the organization and its public(s) prior to, during and after the negative occurrence. Gruning (1992) highlighted the importance of strategic establishment and maintained communication with company's stakeholders' prior a crisis occurs.

The relationship between corporate strategy and corporate communications has been in the focus of many researches over time (Argenti, 2006, Argenti and Forman, 2005; Dembitz, 1987; Dolphin, 2003; 2004; Fombrun and Rindova, 1999; Goczol and Scoubeau, 2003; Goodman, 2001; Hackley, 1998; Lennon and Sheldon, 1992; Varey, 1997; Wright, 1997; Yalumba, 2008). Also, communication strategy where crisis communication represents an inevitable component is highly connected with the overall corporate strategy and corporate mission (Argenti, 2004). Many companies remember that they need a communication specialist only when a crisis occurs and they need somebody who will prepare or deliver press releases or organize a press conference. Communication function has been neglected over time and in different countries communication professionals struggling to prove importance of its strategic management position and recent survey has showed that the development of crisis communication is highly correlated with the strategic positioning of the corporate communication function (Bilić, 2011).

Furthermore, the same research proves that companies with higher positioning of crisis communication and crisis management function are those which make more profit.

Crisis communication should be integrated in communication plans, and communication professionals should be involved in crisis planning and crisis management, along with other managers and the senior management spokesperson who could serve as a spokesperson (Argenti, 2009; Stocker, 1997). However, both corporate communications and crisis communication are strategically positioned at top management level which shows the importance of communication in a company. Companies should also consider in advance, cooperation with external agency in case a crisis situation occurs. Independently of the performed crisis management strategy and crisis communication strategy, communication during the crisis should follow some recommended steps (Argenti, 2009):

1. Get control of the situation
2. Gather as much information as possible
3. Set up a centralized crisis management center
4. Communicate early and often
5. Understand the media's mission in a crisis
6. Communicate directly with affected constituents
7. Remember that business must continue
8. Make plans to avoid another crisis immediately

The key variable in situational crisis communication theory (hereinafter SCCT) is the degree to which stakeholders view the organization as (being) responsible for the crisis, and according to that SCCT provides companies with four potential response strategies to the crisis: (adopted from Sellnow and Seeger, 2013)

1. Denial strategies: Seek to remove any connection between the crisis and the organization.
2. Diminishment strategies: When the organization seeks to reduce attributions of organizational control over the crisis.
3. Rebuilding strategies: Which serve to improve organization's reputation.
4. Bolstering strategies: Seeking to build a positive connection between the organization and its stakeholders.

An overview and a short explanation of crisis communication strategies are presented in Figure 2.

Situational crisis communication theory provides 13 recommendations based on reputational threat for the crisis-affected companies, which are particularly useful if crisis management decides to adopt offensive crisis strategies, and decides to continue with companies' operations in the future. The recommendations are (adopted from Sellnow and Seeger, 2013):

1. Providing instructional information to all actual and potential victims on how to protect themselves from harm;
2. Provide adjusting information to victims by expressing concern for them and providing corrective action when (it is) possible;

Figure 2. Crisis communication strategies
Sources: Adopted from Cornelissen (2008)

Perception of low level of responsibility	
Nonexistence strategies	**Claim of denying crisis**
Denial	Denying existence of the crisis
Clarification	Explanation why there is no crisis
Attack and intimidation	Confronting with those who claims that a crisis exists
Distance strategies	**Claim of distancing organization from direct responsibility for the crisis**
Excuse	Denying intention or volition by scapegoating others for the crisis
Downplay	Convicting stakeholders and public that situation is not bad/using comparation to other crisis
Association strategies	**Claim of connecting the organization to things positively valued by stakeholders and public**
Bolstering	Reminding stakeholders and public about past positive aspects of organization/donations in order to offset the negatives
Transcendence	Associating the negatives with positive future effects, higher goals
Suffering strategy	**Claim that the organizaation saffer from the crisis**
Victimization	Presenting organization as a victim of the crisis
Perception of high level of responsibility	
Acceptance strategy	**Claim accepting responsibility or culpabilitiy for the crisis**
Full apology	Apologizing and accepting the blame
Remediation	Announcing some compensation or help for victims
Repentance	Apologizing and asking for forgiveness
Accommodative strategy	**Claim promising to prevent crisis from recurring again**
Rectification	Taking corrective action to prevent a recurrence of the crisis in the future

3. Use diminishment strategies for accidental crisis when there are no previous crisis or reputation issues; (4) use diminishment strategies for victim crisis when there are previous crisis or reputation issues;
4. Use rebuilding strategies for accident crisis when there are previous crisis or reputation issues;
5. Rebuilding strategy is recommended for any preventable crisis;
6. In the case of rumor crisis denial strategy is recommended;
7. In unwarranted challenges use denial strategies;
8. Corrective action is suitable for situations when other stakeholders behave in a supportive way;
9. Reinforcing strategies may serve as supplements to other response strategies;

10. The victimage response should be used only (in the case) when companies are within victim cluster (with other companies or individuals);
11. In order to be consistent, it is not recommended to mix denial strategy with diminishment and rebuilding strategies; and
12. Diminishment and rebuilding strategies can be combined.

READINES FOR CRISIS IN CROATIAN COMPANIES

A questionnaire[3] for this survey was developed by intensive desk research of academic papers and professional studies in the broader field of corporate communication and public relations, corporate strategy and crisis management, in other words wherever it was possible to find suggestions for successful crisis management and crisis communication. Along with this literature search, some questions seemed to be more important for crisis management and crisis communication success, and thus became part of this survey. The survey was carried out in two timely-distanced iterations, with a time lag of four years. In the development phases of the questionnaire, feedback and suggestions from practitioners and academics in the fields of management and communications were used, twofold from the perspective of content and once from the perspective of the survey questions clarity to an average respondent. Next step in designing of the questionnaire was psychologist and methodologist consultation, with the aim to improve the questionnaire and make it easier for the respondents to understand and fill, and avoid their potential tiredness.

Original questionnaire consisted of 63 closed questions on the strategic aspects of corporate communication, crisis communications, and basic demographic questions about respondents and surveyed companies. In the second phase, the questionnaire was reduced to 15 questions, related to the strategic positioning of corporate communications, crisis communication and crisis management. The majority of questions were rated on a 5-point Likert scale ranging from 1 - strongly disagree to 5 - strongly agree. These items, with closed choice questions required survey respondents to express their objective[4] attitudes about the development of corporate communications in their company.

The first round of the survey was conducted for the first time in Croatia from late November 2010 to February 2011 on 500 Croatian companies with the highest value added in the year 2009 (according to the Institute for Business Intelligence). Questionnaires were sent by regular mail, addressed on the corporate communications and public relations executives in the observed companies. The response rate was 14% (70 out of 500 companies) what is considered as representative in social surveys, considering previously conducted researches related to communication and management, conducted by other authors. Fombrun and Rindova reputation survey (1998) conducted on a sample of 1,000 American and British companies, with a response rate of 13.9% (139 out of 1,000 surveyed companies), which was accepted as relevant or Goodman's (2006) survey from March 2005 on a sample of the Fortune 1,000, addressed to the corporate communication executive, which in the second round was addressed to 300 holders of corporate communications, members of Arthur W. Page Society ended up with a return of 9.3%, which was considered acceptable, compared with other studies in social sciences, such as GAPIII Study in which the return rate was 3.7%.

The second round was conducted from June to November 2014, with the response rate of 44.29% (31 out of 70 companies)[5] from the 1st survey. In the second round, the questionnaire was delivered as on online

Table 1. Activities performed by corporative communications executives

Assess in which proportion you as corporate communication executive:	2011[6]	2011[7]	2014
Consult the Top management about crisis communication and its content	4.08	4.14	4.43
Inform the Board and Top Management about potential crisis	4.12	4.32	4.45
Consult the Top management on how to avoid crisis	3.77	3.96	4.10
Are familiar with external agencies, who have good background in crisis communication	3.48	4.00	3.77
Average grade for all activities performed by corporate communication executives	**3.86**	**4.11**	**4.19**

survey powered by Google survey, sent directly to e-mails of the respondents, corporate communication executives of the first survey, so the survey population was limited to 70 companies from the 1st survey.

The authors observed Croatian companies from twofold perspectives, activities performed by corporate communication executives and activities performed by company's management regarding crisis management and crisis communication (Table 1).

The satisfactory reliability of the scale in this study was confirmed by Cronbach's alpha coefficient of .787 in 2011 and .870 in 2014, which is more than the required level of .7.[8]

During the hard times, companies used to reduce costs, particularly on the communication function. However, research results showed improvement of the perception of communication function. Companies' management obviously realized the importance of crisis management and management function, and even started to cooperate with communication professionals and crisis management stronger, as can be seen from the answers on questions 1 to 3. The results showed the highest improvement in 'Consulting Top management about crisis communication and its content' during the time of crisis. Total scores for each activity performed by corporate communication executives in terms of crisis communication and crisis management were higher in 2014. When the results from two studies were compare, 2014 results showed higher average grades, compare with average grades in 2011 for all companies. The only differences that can be found is for companies that participated in both surveys (2011 and 2014), for the activities 'Are familiar with external agencies, who have good background in crisis communication', which showed lower average score in 2014. As it is clear to the authors of this paper, that the assessment of activities represents respondents' subjective perception of corporate communication executives those results could be explained in at least two ways: raising awareness of insufficient knowledge about that or more critical assessment about the agencies background in crisis communications.

When one observes the answers which represent companies' crisis management and crisis communication preparedness it is obvious that the time of global crisis has served as a good accelerator of those activities (Table 2). The average score of all the surveyed companies for all the observed activities is higher in 2014. Some results showed significant improvements, such as the activity 'Companies possess developed written manual for crisis situations'. Only one activity showed small decrease in 2014, i.e. 'Companies top management is educated for communication in crisis situations' what could be observed as result of experiencing the situation from corporative communication executives, and rising awareness about real situation, changes in management team, or small change in subjective assessment.

The satisfactory reliability of the scale in this study was confirmed by Cronbach's alpha coefficient of .933 in 2011 and .949 in 2014, which is more than the required level of .7.

Table 2. Activities performed by company's management regarding crisis management and crisis communication

Assessment of activities conducted by companies' management	2011[9]	2011[10]	2014
Existence of the basis of potential crisis situation	2.75	3.07	3.61
Crisis team or teams are defined for potential crisis	3.20	3.64	4.10
Spokespersons are defined for crisis situations	3.97	4.18	4.35
Media teams for crisis situations are prepared	3.08	3.48	3.80
Companies' top management is educated for communication in crisis situations	3.48	3.96	3.87
Crisis team is informed about duties and responsibilities in crisis situation	3.56	3.93	4.13
Companies possess developed written manual for crisis situations	2.62	2.79	3.87
Average grade for all activities performed by companies' management	3.24	3.58	3.96

Nevertheless, it is interesting to notice that companies who participated in both surveys were those with higher average assessment of any activities observed here than was the average score in the 1st survey. Also, all of them showed progress during the hard times which led researchers to next question which could be answered in this research, namely the link between corporate strategy and corporate communication strategy.

Research results showed an average level of the development of corporate communication strategy for 2011 at 3.61 and progress in 2014 up to 3.97. Coordination between corporate strategy and corporate communication strategy showed slightly smaller progress from 3.58 in 2011 to 3.90 in 2014.

Research results presented in Table 3 showed that the development of corporate communication function in Croatian companies is strongly correlated with activities which were observed in this survey, related to crisis communication and crisis management performed by companies' management and corporate communication executives. Furthermore, for the coordination between corporate strategy and corporate communication strategy for 2011, the observed activities that were performed by companies' management showed statistically significant correlation and progress in time, while the activities performed in 2011 by corporate communication executives were statistically insignificant, while in 2014 they improved, the relations became strong and statistically significant. Total company communication efforts related to crisis communication and crisis management showed relations became more developed and stronger in 2014.

The effect of organization learning happens when organizations acquire feedback and apply this knowledge to make meaningful changes in policy and procedures (Sellnow and Seeger, 2013) and use it to improve the organization. Furthermore, our research results showed (2014) that companies recognized the importance of the crisis management and crisis communication independently of the crisis. Levene's test of homogeneity of variance showed that the condition of homogeneity is met, therefore, enables testing the existence of differences in the development of certain elements of certain aspects of crisis communication. Tests on the differences in the average level of development of individual elements of crisis communication showed that the empirical significance of the test for all 13 variables was above 5% indicating the acceptance of the null hypothesis; i.e. it is concluded that there were differences in the development of certain aspects of crisis communication between companies due to the crisis.

The above presented results suggest that the level of application and the level of development of individual aspects of crisis communications does not show any differences between the companies that faced

Table 3. Correlation between strategic positioning of corporate communication function and crisis communication and crisis management activities performed in the observed companies

Correlation Between	Crisis Communication Performed by Companies' Management		Crisis Communication Activities Performed by Corporate Communications Executives		Total Companies Crisis Communication Efforts (Company and Communication Executives)	
	2011	2014	2011	2014	2011	2014
Development of corporate communication strategy	.790**	.762**	.526**	.677**	.498**	.769**
Coordination between corporate and communication strategy	.609**	.670**	.292	.666**	.297	.697**

**. Correlation is significant at the 0.01 level (2-tailed).

and survived the crisis during this turbulent recession times in Croatia. The lack of difference does not mean that the companies were not interested into developing crisis management and crisis communication. The best explanation may actually be that the observed companies represent those companies in which crisis management and crisis communication was more developed than it is the case in average companies in the 1st survey. Thus, the time of crisis, they slightly improved the already developed crisis management and crisis communication in the companies. The results indicated that the crisis communication was rather developed in the observed companies. Thus, the system is not significantly stronger in relation to the state before the crisis started. It is certainly true that the crisis teams hired more people in the times of the major impact of the crisis, but the whole system of crisis communications remained at the same level of development because it passes adequate professional standards and practices regardless of the crisis. This means that the companies are aware of the role of crisis management and crisis communication play and know they are an integral part of corporate strategy and corporate communication system, and do not represent the activation of casual collection mechanisms of communications in companies.

Another interesting question was answered in this survey. The authors were interested to find out to which extent the observed companies were used to involving external agencies in crisis communication, as more experienced and objective parts of crisis management teams. Research results showed that most of the observed companies, in 2014 performed their crisis communication in-house 73.45%, while only 15.07% were willing to involve external agencies in crisis communications.

CONCLUSION REMARKS AND DIRECTIONS FOR FUTURE RESEARCH

Communication represents an essential part of any for profit or nonprofit organization, particularly in the times of crisis. Research results presented in this chapter represent attitudes toward strategic position of the crisis management and the crisis communication in the best Croatian companies. Even though they showed an above average level of readiness for a crisis situation the weakest part of it is in the core of crisis survival such as: getting knowledge about potential crisis situations, readiness of top management to communicate in crisis situation, and last but the most important development of written crisis manual which should serve as a Bible if a crisis occurs.

The focus of this chapter was to research crisis management and crisis communication from the theoretical and practical point of view. However, the results presented in this chapter represent the phenomena solely from the perspective of one country, moreover, of the best companies in only one country. Therefore, the same research could be performed in different countries, at least in Eastern Europe, to broaden and reconfirm the research results, and help researchers and practitioners to make future decisions regarding crisis communication and crisis management. Also, the same survey fulfilled from the perspective of the top management or board of the directors about the development of crisis communication and crisis management may provide researchers with different insights about the crisis management and crisis communication, then this one, where corporative communication officers were respondents.

Corporate communication is highly connected with corporate strategy function, and it serves to implement corporate strategy in at least two ways, as a medium for collecting information from company's stakeholders and provides inputs for strategy development and as a medium to help company to communicate and performs strategies with all internal and external stakeholders. Previous research (Bilić, 2011) on Croatian companies revealed that higher development of overall corporate communication function is highly correlated with strategic positioning of corporate communication function, associated with companies' top management and development of crisis communication and crisis management component in the surveyed companies.

Crisis is the most sensitive part in a company's life cycle, and most Fortune 500 companies do not survive more than 40 years in a turbulent business environment. Recent study about expected life conducted by Ellen de Rooij of the Stratix Group in Amsterdam indicates that the average life expectancy of all firms, regardless of size, measured in Japan and much of Europe, is only 12.5 years, and the same can be expected for US companies (Bloomberg Businessweek, 2015). According to that fact it is more than obvious that companies that want to survive must anticipate changes in a turbulent environment, and continuously search ways how to survive in the best possible way. Management decisions and crisis management are essential parts of those efforts along with a developed and strategically positioned crisis communications.

The results of authors' comparative research led us to the conclusion that Croatian companies are not behind their peers in the rest of the business world in terms of establishment and development of crisis management and crisis communications, with or without a direct crisis event between this two surveys. A deep economic crisis, which Croatia has been facing, did not stop Croatian companies to invest in their workforce and their communication skills in order to achieve competitiveness in the market. Even though the business environment was very turbulent during the observed period, and suffered from many cutoffs, research results led authors to the conclusion that companies' crisis communication and crisis management showed some improvements in 2014 compared to the research from 2011.

REFERENCES

Argenti, P. (2004). It Pays to Talk Right: The Power and Influence o Corporate Communication. In J. Kurtzman, G. Rifkin, & V. Griffith (Eds.), *MBA in a box: practical ideas from the best brain in business*. New York: Crown Business.

Argenti, P. (2006). Communications and business value: Measuring the link. *The Journal of Business Strategy*, *27*(6), 29–40. doi:10.1108/02756660610710337

Argenti, P., & Formani, J. (2005). How Corporate Communication Influence Strategy Implementation, Reputation and the Corporate Brand: An Exploratory Qualitative Study. *Corporate Communication Review*, *8*(3), 245–264.

Argenti, P. A. (2009). *Corporate communication* (5th ed.). New York, NY: McGraw-Hill Irwin.

Bhatnagar, P. (2004). *Sad day at McDonald's.* Retrieved from CNN Money: http://money.cnn.com/2004/04/19/news/fortune500/mcdonalds_ceo/index.htm?iid=EL

Bilić, I. (2011). *Međuovisnost strateškog pozicioniranja korporativnog komunikaciranja, reputacije i organizacijskih performansi poduzeća*. (Unpublished doctoral dissertation). University of Split, Faculty of Economics, Split, Croatia.

Bloomberg Businessweek. (2015). *The Prologue - The Lifespan of a Company*. Retrieved September 21, 2015 from http://www.businessweek.com/chapter/degeus.htm

Burson-Marsteller. (2013). *Crisis Survey 2013.* Retrieved from http://www.burson-marsteller.com/wp-content/uploads/2014/07/2013-BM-EMEA-Crisis-survey-results.pdf

Dembitz, J. (1987). A specialist view of corporate communications. *Director (Cincinnati, Ohio)*, *41*(4), 129–130.

Dolphin, R. R. (2003). The corporate communication function: How well it is founded. *Corporate Communications: An International Journal*, *8*(1), 5–10. doi:10.1108/13563280310458867

Dolphin, R. R. (2004). Corporate reputation – a value creating strategy. *Corporate Governance*, *4*(3), 77–92. doi:10.1108/14720700410547521

Fearn-Banks, K. (2011). *Crisis Communications: a casebook approach* (4th ed.). New York, NY, U.S.: Routledge.

Fombrun, C. J., & Rindova, V. (1998). Reputation Management in Global 1000 Firms: A Benchmarking Study. *Corporate Reputation Review*, *1*(3), 205–212. doi:10.1057/palgrave.crr.1540044

George, D., & Mallery, P. (2003). *SPSS for Windows step by step: A simple guide and reference. 11.0 up date*. Boston: Allyn & Bacon.

Glamuzina, M., & Lovrinčević, M. (2013). Corporate crisis and crisis strategy implementation. *Montenegrin Journal of Economics*, *9*(2), 89–100.

Goczol, J., & Scoubeau, C. (2003). Corporate communication and strategy in the field of projects. *Corporate Communications: An International Journal*, *8*(1), 60–66. doi:10.1108/13563280310458920

Goodman, M. B. (2001). Current trends in corporate communication. *Corporate Communication: An International Journal*, *6*(3), 117–123. doi:10.1108/13563280110398956

Grunig, J. E. (Ed.). (1992). *Excellence in Public Relations and Communication Management*. New York, NY: Routledge.

Grunig, J. G., & Hunt, T. (1984). *Managing Public Relations*. Belmont, WA: Wadsworth/Tomson Learning.

Hackley, C. (1998). Mission statements as corporate communications: The consequences of social construction. *Corporate Communications: An International Journal*, *3*(3), 92–98. doi:10.1108/eb046557

Kružić, D., Glamuzina, M., & Lovrinčević, M. (2013). Top management effectiveness during crisis – Are traditional quantitative indicators of effectiveness enough? (pp.103-113). In *Proceedings of the 1st International OFEL Conference on Corporate Governance*.

Lennon, K., & Sheldon, K. A. (1992). *From Canada to California: New directions in corporate communication.* ABI/INFORM Global.

Neaete, R. (2015). *Volkswagen under investigation over illegal software that masks emissions*. Retrieved September 25, 2015 from the guardian: http://www.theguardian.com/business/2015/sep/18/epa-california-investigate-volkswagen-clean-air-violations

Sellnow, T. L., & Seeger, M. W. (2013). *Theorizing Crisis Communication*. West Sussex, UK: John Wiley & Sons Ltd.

Stocker, K. P. (1997). A Strategic Approach to Crisis Management. In The Handbook of Strategic Public Relations & Integrated Communications. New York: McGraw-Hill.

Tipurić, D., Kružić, D., & Lovrinčević, M. (2013). Strategije u kriznim uvjetima. Montenegrin Journal of Economics, 9(2), 89-100.

Varey, R. J. (1997). A picture of corporate communications management in UK. *Corporate Communications: An International Journal*, *2*(2), 59–69. doi:10.1108/eb046535

Wright, D. J. (1997). Perceptions of corporate communication as public relations. *Corporate Communications: An International Journal*, *2*(4), 143–154. doi:10.1108/eb046545

Yalumba, S. (2008). Communicating Yalumba's commitment to sustainable winemaking. *Corporate Communications: An International Journal*, *13*(1), 18–41. doi:10.1108/13563280810848175

KEY TERMS AND DEFINITIONS

Corporate Communications: Represents overall companies' efforts, strategically performed in two-way symmetric dialogue between corporate and its internal and external stakeholders.

Corporate Strategy: The net of companies' long- and short-term goals and the ways how to reach them in correlation with corporate mission and vision.

Crisis: Unpleasant and unplanned event, which affects individuals or organizations and brings them to a period of uncertainties. Even not welcomed, sometimes during the process of resolving it may bring or reveal extraordinary success.

Crisis Communications: Represents the way and the level companies communicate with all the interested stakeholders, and to which level of openness which is strongly connected with crisis management strategy.

Crisis Communications Strategies: Integrated the way how companies resolve the crisis, from a strategic approach and communicate it to all the affected and interested stakeholders.

Crisis Management: Management function, usually activated in the situation of crisis or change, consisted from in-house or external experts in change or issue management.

Crisis Management Strategy: The strategic management decision about the future of a company, and the network of goals and ways how to lead company to recovery or out of the business.

Crisis Manual: Written document, generated by company's authorities before a crisis occurred, with the aim to help and guide crisis management team in a future crisis.

Crisis Teams: A team constituted in advance or in the explicit crisis situation, consisting of company's top management, and experts needed in crisis moment. Members usually come from the top management team, communication, low, and core business representatives. External experts as a crisis management agencies or individuals may be brought in or consulted.

ENDNOTES

1 While reading the explanation of the potential crisis situation it should be noted that some specifics may not be derived from Croatian legislation such as: Bankruptcy Law and A Pre-Bankruptcy Settlement Law.

2 While reading the explanation of the potential crisis situation it should be noted that some specifics may not be derived from Croatian legislation such as: Bankruptcy Law and A Pre-Bankruptcy Settlement Law.

3 Original questionnaire was developed for the purpose of a bigger research conducted in 2011, after an extensive literature research review Bilić, I. (2011).

4 Some bias may be derived from the respondent's perception of the objectivity. However, that is something that the researchers could not prevent.

5 Which represents 6.2% respondents from the original sample.

6 This is an average score for all companies observed in 2011; 70 out of The best 500 companies according to the Value Added.

7 This averages score of companies from 2011 that participated in repeated survey in 2014.

8 Cronbach's alpha coefficient close to 1 showed greater internal consistency of the items in the scale. George and Mallery (2003) provide the following rule: "<0.9 is excellent, <0.8 is good, <0.7 is acceptable, <0.6 is questionable, <0.5 is poor, and <0.4 is unacceptable."

9 This is an average score for all the companies observed in 2011.

10 This is an averages score of all the companies from 2011 that participated in the repeated survey in 2014.

Chapter 11
Multi-Criteria Decision Making Approach for Choosing Business Process for the Improvement:
Upgrading of the Six Sigma Methodology

Marija Radosavljevic
University of Nis, Serbia

Aleksandra Andjelkovic
University of Nis, Serbia

ABSTRACT

Dynamic and global environment, does not offer a spot for managers that improvise and make business moves without relevant information. In order to gain relevant information, it is necessary to observe processes through which value is generated. This implies adoption of process orientation and, based on it, business process management, as a way of running a business. Useful concept for operationalization of business process management is the Six Sigma. One of very important managerial decisions under the Six Sigma concept implementation concerns choosing the process for the improvement. Very often managers must take into the account subjective data, based on their opinion and experience, as personal impression. However, subjective data may become objective when adequate tools and methods for the analysis are used. Quantification is necessary for making decisions and, also, for tracking the results of their implementation. Beside statistical, significant information may provide methods from multi-criteria decision making.

DOI: 10.4018/978-1-5225-0959-2.ch011

INTRODUCTION

Improving competitive posture involves increasing quality of products and services, quality of their design, faster production and delivery, adaptation to new or renewed requirements of customers or actions of competitors, while minimizing costs at the same time. Accomplishing all these will provide customers satisfaction and consequently their loyalty. This requires optimisation of business processes, bearing in mind, that at the same time, have to be taken into consideration issues concerning time, cost and quality.

This assumes that an enterprise has adopted process orientation and identified at least key business processes. Process orientation means that there are managers responsible for certain processes, who are supposed to continuously monitor those processes, from start to finish, through different organizational units or even through different enterprises, and constantly strive to manage them at all stages of the life cycle (Harmon, 2004). Process orientation can facilitate creating and maintaining a competitive advantage in many different ways. For example, it facilitates eliminating or decreasing delays and irrational spending of time through the elimination of those activities that do not create value, so process orientation enables reduction of time required to perform the tasks. Continual monitoring of processes represents the way for reducing the possibility for the occurrence of errors and inefficient use of resources.

Application of information technology creates numerous benefits in sense of facilitating the results' tracking, improving business processes and connecting functions and process-related partners, improving communication and information sharing, as well as collaboration of different departments and organizational levels, and faster and reliable decision-making. Process orientation enables sharing the best practices in managing business processes, which affect the quality of the process. Presence of process orientation enables increasing of profitability because it reduces unnecessary costs, investment and expenditure of time. Process orientation speeds up the process of development and commercialization of new products by encouraging continual innovation and improvement during the implementation of processes. Process orientation creates conditions for the growth (Delavari, Bandara, Marjanovic, Mathiesen, 2010) of enterprises through business expansion and possibilities to enter new markets, and easily overcomes recession in the economy because it makes it easier to reduce costs and better allocate resources and make better use of previously developed knowledge and competences.

In the enterprises with functional organization structure, often occurs a problem when it comes to the relations between functions or organizational units, because each of them concentrates only on realization of its own objectives. This leads to the creation of so-called sub-optimization effect, which indicates that some parts of the enterprise are successful, but due to a lack of cooperation and coordinated action, there is no optimization of the results at the enterprise level. Process orientation reduces the effects of sub-optimization, because it increases the level of cooperation and transparency of business processes, enabling different employees within the various functions to better understand how they contribute to creation of value for customers. This way of organizing business activities allows better understanding and meeting the needs of customers, on one hand, and increasing the participation of employees, not only during implementation, but also throughout the business process improvement, on the other hand.

Implementation of process orientation has facilitated achievement of expected business results (Harmon, 2003; Van Der Aalst, Ter Hofstede, Weske, 2003; Watson, 2004; Abdulmalek, Rajgopal, 2007; Trkman, 2010). Its systematic application, supported by adequate tools and techniques, as well as information technology, has led to the development of Business process management (BPM). Business process management is a systematic approach that helps enterprise to make significant changes in the way it does business, especially from quality standpoint, and to provide sustainable process improvement. It usually involves implementing, monitoring, measuring, analysing and continuously improving business processes, based on integration of process design and application of appropriate information technology.

The main problem during mentioned elements of business process management usually occurs when it comes to analysing and decision-making concerning ways of process improvement or segments of process that should be improved. It is known fact that decision making process is very important part of every manager's job. If the decision is bad, tangible and intangible resources used for its implementation will be wasted.

Generally, nowadays decision-making became very difficult since it assumes involving a lot of variables and parameters. Therefore, there are more and more decisions that cannot be made by pure observation of process or by implementing only management tools. In order to cope with complex problems, and include into the analysis as many variables as possible (for example, quality, time, cost, variability), managers must base their decisions on quantitative methods. In addition, very often, managers have access to different quantitative methods, which may be combined and used parallel, providing even more reliable results. In order to facilitate selection of process for the improvement and make correct decision, bearing in mind a lot of criteria and even more processes – candidates for the improvement, it seems appropriate to use multi-criteria decision analysis.

Business process improvement, as a part of Business process management has become a popular topic again at the beginning of the XXI century. It is very important from a practical point of view, but at the same time as a significant challenge for scientists and practitioners, primarily in the field of business management, but also in other social, technical and quantitative - mathematical disciplines, considering multidisciplinary nature of the phenomenon and necessity of quantification of decision-making process.

SIX SIGMA AS A SUPPORT FOR BUSINESS PROCESS MANAGEMENT

The roots of Business process management lie in measurement of process performances, which dates back from 1930s in Shewhart's (1931) control charts, indication tight connection between process management and quality management. Shewhart's ideas were further developed and popularized by Deming and Juran, whose ideas and methods represented the basis for Total Quality Management (TQM). One of the famous business concepts that arouse from TQM is the Six Sigma concept, which was, in its beginning, also focused only on incremental improvements. However, bearing in mind the fact that incremental changes may be sufficient to some extent or for some time, beside the methodology for incremental changes implementation, under the Six Sigma concept appeared another methodology, very similar to the ideas of Business process reengineering or BPR (De Feo & Bar-Ei, 2002). In that way, the Six Sigma concept became some kind of successor of TQM and BPR.

The two methodologies the Six Sigma is based on are DMAIC (define, measure, analyze, improve, control) and DMADV (define, measure, analyze, design, verify) methodology (Pande, Neuman, & Cavanagh, 2000; Brue, 2002; Gitlow & Levine, 2005). While, DMAIC methodology is used for improving the existing business process, DMADV methodology is used for creating or redesigning new processes in such a way that it results in a more predictable and defect free performance. Though they are implemented separately, these methodologies are very similar and they imply defining requirements of external, but also of internal customers, planning and identification of business processes needed for accomplishing these requirements, measuring performances of existing processes or designing new processes, analyzing results of measurement or optimization of designed processes, implementation of improvements, control of improved processes or verification of designed processes. Implementation of these methodologies implies basic knowledge about process and statistics measures and tools, some technical knowledge and project management skills.

By facilitating process management and especially improvement, Six Sigma represents significant support for BPM. If one takes into consideration the fact that Six Sigma assumes special training for process management, it is obvious that it actually promotes process orientation.

Six Sigma: Basic Ideas and Postulates

The Six Sigma DMAIC methodology was developed and first implemented in Motorola in the early 1980s. It appeared as American response to Japanese achievements in quality management, and in a way represents the successor of TQM. Therefore, the main objective of introducing such a methodology was to reduce the cost of quality, by reducing defects, primarily in manufacturing, then in the whole enterprise (Antony, 2002). The focus was on variations in quality of materials for production, in operations performed, production conditions and other factors that affect the variation in quality of the finished products (Brue, 2002). Over years, this methodology has outgrown into the concept and philosophy, which managers use to improve the business itself and not only individual processes.

The name of the concept originated from term *sigma*, which is used in statistics as a measure of variation in the processes, a set of data, or anything one can measure (Antony, 2002). Variations are the basis for defects or, in other words, defects appear as a consequence of variations. Unfortunately, variations may not cause defects sometimes. When variations exist, but they are accepted (in certain limits) they do not imply defects appearance. In the Six Sigma concept, defects yield is used to express quality of the processes. Defect yield represents number of defects in million opportunities and usually is marked as DMO (Pande, Neuman, Cavanagh, 2000). Instead of defect yield, for expressing quality of the processes one can use sigma numbers or sigma levels (George, 2005).

Today, Six Sigma is viewed as a philosophy of management, as a statistic, but as a process, too, since it represents accumulation of employees' intelligence and abilities, and their channeling to the priorities (George, 2005), and priorities are business processes that should be improved before some others. Six Sigma viewed as a process, involves a gradual, but continuous expansion of process orientation through an enterprise, and can be used as a guide for managers, in order to enable easier transition of an enterprise from lower to higher maturity level in quality management.

Basic idea of the Six Sigma concept is that high quality and low costs are not opposite goals, since they can be provided at the same time through appropriate process management. Four theses, which Six Sigma promotes, are:

- Slow processes are expensive processes.
- Slow processes are generally low-quality processes.
- Low-quality processes are expensive processes.
- Low-quality processes are slow processes.

In order to achieve high quality and low costs, at the same time, the Six Sigma concept suggests that managers should pay attention to its postulates, and they are (Pande, Neuman, & Cavanagh, 2000; Einset & Marzano, 2002; George, Rowlands, & Kastle, 2004):

- **Customers:** It is not unusual to hear that enterprises consider their customers as king; customers have to be the center of the universe for the enterprise, because they define quality and they except to receive it through products and services; their satisfaction and, further their loyalty will depend on successfulness of the enterprise to accomplish their requirements without gap between their expectations and perceptions when it is about quality, price (costs), time of delivery, specific needs (flexibility) and so on,
- **Process:** Considering the previously mentioned, processes should be observed from customers perspective; precisely, the information gathered from customers should be used as input for identification and improvement of business processes; bearing in mind that tangible and intangible resources are combined and used through processes, process approach is necessary for providing proper combination of those resources, such that will make customers satisfied in terms of quality, price (costs), time of delivery, specific needs (flexibility) and so on,
- **Employees:** Process orientation has made significant changes in traditional relationships between employees on different hierarchical levels; considering that people make results, it is necessary to motivate employees to develop and direct their knowledge, skills and abilities towards the satisfaction of customers; therefore quality must be assignment and responsibility of each and every employee in the enterprise, not only of the managers, and this assumes changing business culture parallel with introducing process orientation.

The Six Sigma concept promotes decision making based on relevant information, systematically problem solving, teamwork, process alignment with strategy and objectives. But, above all, the Six Sigma concept assumes usage of statistical tools for gaining information necessary for decision making. Statistical tools became integral part of the Six Sigma methodologies for process improvement. Even though it is not mentioned as a postulate of the Six Sigma concept, statistics plays a great role in its successful implementation.

Six Sigma Methodologies for Process Improvement

The Six Sigma concept incorporates a wide range of statistical process control tools and quality management tools. Those tools are systematized through methodologies that the Six Sigma concept is based on. The leading idea of using structured, methodological approach is in-depth observation of processes, avoidance of superficiality in resolution of problems, and focus on the causes of the problems. The Six Sigma concept supports business process improvement by providing managers significant database for decision making (Hammer, 2002). These data are gained and used under the Six Sigma methodologies, thus facilitating decision making on business process improvement.

Although they are similar to the famous PDCA cycle, the Six Sigma methodologies include very detailed procedure, with proposal of concrete measures, instruments and techniques. This is the approval for using the term methodology, and this is the important fact that distinguishes the Six Sigma concept positively from other quality improvement initiatives. The first of the two methodologies incorporated in the Six Sigma concept is intended for the introduction of incremental changes or for the incremental improvement of business processes. It is called DMAIC, and the acronym comes from the names of the phases of this methodology, which are (Smith, 2001):

- **Define:** Refers to identification of customers' requirements, in order to ensure fulfilment of the identified requirements, as well as the team that will be responsible for the improvement of these processes; this means that everything that happens in the enterprise has to be based on information provided by customers; identification of business processes makes process orientation prerequisite for successful implementation of the Six Sigma methodology,
- **Measure:** Assumes measuring performances of the processes, to determine the extent to which the enterprise is able to satisfy the requirements of customers and to which is capable to perform business processes consistently; it helps managers to identify the gap between the possibilities of the enterprise and customers' requirements; precisely because of the importance of this phase, an adequate system of key measures of process and product performances has to be established; this methodology uses different statistical measures and especially promotes sigma level, based on standard deviation,
- **Analyze:** Has a task to identify causes of problems, but also to decide whether to improve the process through minor changes or restructuring; this task is fulfilled by discovering relationships between inputs and process flow, on one hand, and the results of the process, on the other hand; base for decision-making through the analyze phase consists of the results of measuring; in this phase it is possible to use mathematical methods, as additional analysis for providing more reliable information for decision making,
- **Improve:** Includes a set of actions considering creation, selection and implementation of solutions for process improvement; in this phase changes are introduced, not only to eliminate the existing, but also to prevent the occurrence of potential problems,
- **Control:** Refers to measurement of the process and product performances; the aim of control is evaluation of the level of harmonization of product characteristics with customer requirements, but also the level of harmonization of product characteristics with the standards; in order to harmonize standards of product and process with customer requirements it is necessary to bear in mind the "voice of customers"; in order to harmonize product and process performances with the standards, it is necessary to bear in mind the "the voice of employees"; control assumes continual observation of business process in order to provide their sustainable stability.

Presented methodology was the first introduced under the Six Sigma concept. However, as it has been mentioned, when it has been realized that sometimes incremental changes are not sufficient, it became obvious that this methodology has to be further developed, to cover the other type of the changes, radical changes. For that reason, the second methodology has been developed, DMADV methodology. While, DMAIC methodology is used for existing business processes' improvement, DMADV methodology is used as a support for creating a new product or process designs in such a way that process results are more predictable and defect free. The core characteristics of both Six Sigma methodologies are represented in Table 1.

From the Table 1 it may be seen that the first three phases of those methodologies are very similar, with one very important difference and it is the fact that DMAIC methodology should be applied continually, on everyday basis, while DMADV methodology should be applied when incremental improvements are not sufficient to provide level of process quality, expected by users of its outputs. Also, DMADV methodology assumes involvement of employees from different departments and so-called competitive engineering. However, in both cases the key decision concerns choosing the process that is the best candidate for the improvement.

Table 1. DMAIC vs. DMADV methodology (Anđelković Pešić, 2006)

DMAIC Methodology	DMADV Methodology
Define customers' demands (voice of the customers), enterprises opportunities for fulfilling those demands and benchmarking demands and opportunities, in order to define core processes	Define the project goals and customers' (internal and external) needs, which have to be satisfied by new processes, that must be designed; check if an enterprise has appropriate resources and capabilities for satisfaction of these needs
Measure processes' performances, in terms of quality, time and costs in order to find out what must be improved; established measures have to be valid and reliable	Measure the existing processes' performance and identify specifications or limits of processes' performances
Analyze measurement results in order to find connection between inputs and outputs of the processes and to identify possibilities for improvement through analysis of get between *as-is state* and *should-be* state	Analyze the processes' options to meet the customers' needs, with accent on meeting the key customers' demands in the most efficient way, by using functional analysis, for example
Improve processes by implementation of chosen solution, but before that simulate effective solution in order to be sure that it will be efficient	Design processes to meet customers' needs and optimize designed process, based on so-called competitive engineering or design, involving multi-functional team
Control continually processes' variation in order to ensure that number of defects is decreasing, but also in order to prevent a new variations and defects	Verify the design of process and ability to meet customers' needs and to be stable and sustainable

Choosing Business Process for the Improvement

Managers usually do not have dilemma whether or not to implement Six Sigma, but how to implement it successfully or how to choose the right process for the improvement. According to some authors (Pande et al., 2000; Smith, 2001) this is probably the most difficult aspect of the Six Sigma concept. The wrong choice of process for the improvement may mean the lack of expected results. Therefore, choosing the right process for the improvement is considered as critical decision in business process management.

Since there are a lot of different criteria, including different measures and measurement units, managers usually decide to give priority to a criterion they believe is the most important for choosing a process for the improvement. Unfortunately, very often this kind of choice is misleading and, therefore, the expected results are lacking.

Selecting process for the improvement or choosing the Six Sigma project, whose implementation will provide process improvement, assumes usage of certain criteria and, usually, different approaches. This means that sometimes simple tools may be used, but sometimes it is more convenient or even necessary to use complex, quantitative methods. For example, for selecting process for the improvement managers may use project matrix in different shapes – assessment, ranking, selection (Banuelas, Tennant, Tuersley, & Tang, 2006), Pareto analysis (Larson, 2003), Cost-benefit analysis, Fishbone diagram, Design of experiments (DOE), Statistical process control (SPC), Brainstorming, Failure mode and effects analysis (FMEA), Quality function deployment (QFD) and so on (Pande, Neuman, & Cavanagh, 2000; Banuelas & Antony, 2002; Gitlow & Levine, 2005; Anđelković Pešić, 2009; Bošković, Janković Milić, & Anđelković Pešić, 2011).

In order to accomplish objective and find the most valuable process for the improvement, authors suggest different criteria. For example follows the list of 15 criteria (Meriyappa, 2015):

- Customer impact,
- Process stability,

- Defect definition,
- Data availability,
- Solution clarity,
- Benefits,
- Impact on service quality,
- Project sponsorship,
- Project alignment,
- Project timeline,
- Probability of implementation,
- Investment,
- Team availability,
- Controllability of inputs,
- Process redesign.

According to Antony (2004, p. 1011) the following criteria should be taken into consideration when making decision on process that should be improved:

- Impact on customer needs and expectations,
- Financial impact on the bottom-line,
- Duration of the projects considered,
- Resources required for projects under consideration,
- Expertise and skills required to carry out the projects,
- Probability of success of projects under consideration,
- Risk involved in projects.

According to the research of Pyzdek and Keller (2003, 191) as criteria availability of resources other than team, Scope in terms of Black Belt efforts, deliverable, time to complete, team membership, project charter, value of Six Sigma approach. However, these are only general criteria, which are further divided into huge number of individual, specific criteria.

Interesting set of criteria has been proposed by Bahri (2011), who believes that decision about process to be improved should be based on some precise criteria, such as project cost, project duration, probability of project success, customer satisfaction, rate of return, cost reduction information availability, sigma level, but he also includes certain hardly measured criteria, like top management commitment and team members motivation.

As it can be seen, according to previously shown authors' opinion about criteria that should be taken into account while making decision on process that should be improved, the list usually is long, and it could be even longer. In such a case it would be very hard to make a decision based on statistical tools and analysis. Precisely, in the area of information technology, due to such a complex context, managers need additional methods for decision making or, precisely.

As it may be noticed, Six Sigma methodologies are based on statistical measures and tools. However, in modern, dynamic business world this is not enough. It is necessary to borrow techniques from other disciplines and to provide better and easier decision making, bearing in mind complex context and variety of data.

Therefore, in the XXI century some authors suggest even greater quantification of quality, meaning that making proper decisions concerning quality and process management should be supported by some mathematical methods. For example, usually suggested methods are: Analytic Hierarchy Process (Banuelas & Antony, 2003; Pyzdek, 2003; Kumar, Crocker, Chitra, & Saranga, 2006), Data Envelopment Analysis (Kumar, Saranga, Ramírez-Márquez, & Nowicki, 2007), as well as Technique for Order Preference by Similarity to Ideal Solution (He, Tang, & Chang, 2010). Although those methods may be used separately, it is possible to use their combination, such as AHP-TOPSIS method (Ghosh, 2011; Maheshwarkar & Sohani, 2013; Nayeb, Jabari, & Attari, 2014).

QUANTIFICATION IN BUSINESS PROCESS MANAGEMENT THROUGH MULTI-CRITERIA DECISION MAKING

In order to improve and facilitate decision making process, almost on daily basis new concepts and methodologies appear. In most cases, they represent a kind of combination of the existing tools and techniques, only used in a different way or for a different purpose. This has been happening for years in the field of operations management, regarding business process improvement, and especially, during application of the Six Sigma methodologies. Very important issue concerning business process improvement, including the Six Sigma methodologies, involves multi-criteria decision analysis as a part of the improvement methodology. Usefulness of the multi-criteria decision analysis for process improvement has been the subject of research of many authors (Bañuelas & Antony, 2003; Kumar et al., 2006; Gurumurthy & Kodali, 2008; Hu et al., 2008). This part of the analysis represents an attempt to use few methods, under the multi-criteria decision analysis, in order to provide more reliable decisions focused on business process improvement.

Multi-criteria decision analysis refers to providing basis for making decisions in the presence of multiple, usually conflicting, criteria (Lai, Liu, & Hwang, 1994). The discipline that deals with multi-criteria decision analysis – decision making is relatively new, with a history of about 30 years.

The main steps of multi-criteria decision making include (Jahanshahloo, Lotfi, & Izadikhah, 2006, p. 1376):

- Establishing criteria that will be used for evaluation and that relate object of evaluation to goals.
- Developing alternatives for defined goals.
- Evaluating alternatives based on chosen criteria.
- Applying a normative multi-criteria analysis method.
- Accepting one alternative as optimal or preferred.
- If the final solution is not accepted, gathering additional information and repeat the mentioned iterations of multi-criteria optimization.

Techniques used for multi-criteria decision analysis can be described by decision matrix. For example, there are m alternatives to be assessed based on n attributes - criteria, a decision matrix is a $m \times n$ matrix, where each element Yij being the j-th attribute value of the i-th alternative. Among multi-criteria decision making methods there are AHP and TOPSIS methods. In this paper those two methods will be combined in order to provide objective decision making, as much as it is possible. In addition, prior to the mentioned methods, another method should be used, and it is Delphi method. This method is necessary for gaining initial data for identification of criteria critical for decision making. In this case the modified Delphi method is used. It consists of five steps (Chang, Wu, & Chen, 2008): (1) select the managers, which may be considered as experts; (2) conduct the first round of a survey and present them initial proposition of criteria; (3) conduct the second round of a questionnaire survey; (4) conduct the third round of a questionnaire survey; and (5) integrate a group of experts' opinions to reach a consensus. Steps (3) and (4) are typically repeated until a consensus is provided on a given topic.

Analytical Hierarchy Process (AHP)

The Analytical Hierarchy Process – AHP belongs to compensatory multi-criteria methods, which permit trade-offs between the observed attributes. It is developed to solve complex multi-criteria decision making problems, involving multiple qualitative and quantitative criteria (Perçin & Kahraman, 2010). This method calculates the scores for each alternative based on pair-wise comparisons. The AHP method assumes that criteria weights must be determined by experts who have a good understanding of evaluation criteria. As the name speaks for itself, AHP method is based on a hierarchy. At each level in the hierarchy, it is necessary to make pair-wise comparisons between decision alternatives and criteria using a ratio scale. In the following step AHP determines the relative ranks of the decision alternatives. The ranks of the decision alternatives are given by the elements of the normalized principal right-hand eigenvector of a preference matrix consisting of the pair-wise comparisons between alternatives (Paulson & Zahir, 1995).

AHP enables decision makers to take into the account subjective and objective evaluation measures, providing a useful mechanism for checking the consistency of the evaluation measures and alternatives suggested by managers - experts thus reducing the possibility for errors in decision making (Lai, Trueblood, & Wong, 1999). It was founded on three principles (Saaty, 1986):

- Creating hierarchical structure based on criteria, sub-criteria, and alternatives, where the number of levels determined by the problem characteristics.
- Comparative judgments of the criteria on single pair-wise comparisons of such criteria with respect to upper criteria.
- Linear-based synthesis of priorities where alternatives are evaluated in pairs with respect to the criteria on the next level of the hierarchy.

Pair-wise comparison of alternatives means answering the question which of the two observed attributes that characterize an alternative to the given criteria is better in terms of meeting the criteria and contribution to the certain objective. Strength of preference is expressed by the ratio scale with increments of 1-9 (Saaty & Vargas, 2012). The explanation of the scale is given in Table 2.

This scale can be very useful in helping a group of experts or an individual to make a decision. Based on pair wise comparison of alternatives, the reciprocal matrix can be formed (dimension $n \times n$ on the criteria level, or $m \times m$ on the alternatives level), where the elements $a_{ii} = 1$, while the elements a_{ji} are the reciprocal of the elements a_{ij}, i.e. $a_{ji} = 1/ a_{ij}$, $i \neq j$ and $i, j = 1, 2, ..., n$. After indentifying the evaluation criteria and making evaluations through pair-wise comparisons, weights for criteria and alternatives can be calculated, since the main purpose of AHP is to provide weights for each criterion and alternatives (Saaty, 1986).

Table 2. The Fundamental scale for pair-wise comparisons (Saaty, 1980)

Intensity of Importance	Definition	Explanation
1	Equal importance	Two elements contribute equally to the objective
3	Moderate importance	Experience and judgment slightly favoUr one element over another
5	Strong importance	Experience and judgment strongly favoUr one element over another
7	Very strong importance	One element is favoured very strongly over another; its dominance is demonstrated
9	Extreme importance	The evidence favouring one element over another is of the highest possible level

Intensities of 2, 4, 6 and 8 can be used to express intermediate values.

Therefore, it may be said that the AHP procedure consists of the following steps (Perçin, Kahraman, 2010, p. 613):

- Identifying evaluation criteria,
- Establishing a pair-wise comparison decision matrix,
- Normalizing the decision matrix and calculate the priorities of this matrix,
- Providing consistency check.

Very important is the last step and it is performed by evaluating the validity of the pair-wise comparison process obtained from decision makers' preferences. Therefore, after completing pair-wise comparisons, the consistency of the comparisons is assessed by using the Eigen value, λ, to calculate a consistency index (CI), where n is the size of the matrix (Ghosh, 2011, pp. 66):

$$CI = (\lambda\text{-}n)/(n\text{-}1) \quad (1)$$

Consistency check includes calculating the Consistency ratio (CR), by dividing the CI by a value obtained from a table of Random index or Random consistency index (RI). RI denotes the average index for randomly generated weights (Perçin & Kahraman, 2010, p. 613). To check for consistency, the table of random indexes of the matrices of order 1 to 10 can be used (Table 3).

Generally, if CR is less than 0.10, the comparisons are consistent and acceptable. If the CR is greater than 0.10, the judgment matrix should be considered inconsistent. To obtain a consistent matrix, the judgments should be reviewed and repeated (Maheshwarkar & Sohani, 2013).

Table 3. Average Random Consistency Index (Saaty, 1994)

Matrix Size	1	2	3	4	5	6	7	8	9	10
RI	0.00	0.00	0.58	0.90	1.12	1.24	1.32	1.41	1.45	1.49

Technique for Order Preference by Similarity to Ideal Solution (TOPSIS)

Another method that also belongs to compensatory multi-criteria methods is the Technique for Order Preference by Similarity to Ideal Solution – TOPSIS. TOPSIS method was first developed by Yoon and Hwang (1995). It is based on the idea that the ideal alternative has the best level for all attributes, whereas the negative ideal is the one with all of the worst attribute values (Maheshwarkar & Sohani, 2013). The performance ratings and the weights of the criteria used in under this method are given as exact values.

Application of the TOPSIS method includes the following steps (Opricovic & Tzeng, 2004):

- Calculating the normalized decision matrix,
- Calculating the weighted normalized decision matrix,
- Determining the positive ideal solution and negative ideal solution,
- Calculating the separation measures for each alternative from the positive and negative ideal solution,
- Calculating the relative closeness to the ideal solution for each alternative,
- Ranking the preference order.

This is so called compromising method, because it selects an alternative that is closest to the ideal solution. It can be used for identification of the solution from a finite set of alternatives. The main principle the TOPSIS method is based on refers to the selection of the alternative that has the shortest distance from the positive ideal solution – PIS and the farthest distance from the negative ideal solution – NIS (Jahanshahloo et al., 2006). The positive ideal solution maximizes the benefit criteria and minimizes the cost criteria, whereas the negative ideal solution maximizes the cost criteria and minimizes the benefit criteria (Lai et al., 1994). It has a number of applications in business practice, for example for comparing business performances, investments in the improvement of manufacturing system, financial ratios and so on (Ren, Zhang, Wang, & Sun, 2007).

Combined Approach

Mentioned methods may be used separately, but they can also be used together. Combination of the AHP and TOPSIS method has been confirmed, so far, as very productive and useful in decision making process, and therefore has been chosen for facilitating decision making under the Six Sigma concept (Table 4).

Table 4. Comparisons the characteristics of AHP and TOPSIS (Nayeb et al., 2014, pp. 355)

Characteristics	AHP	TOPSIS
Level	Numerical data MADM	Numerical data MADM
Main process	Paired comparisons	Distance from PIS and NIS
Index	Definite and clear	Definite and clear
Deduction of weight	Paired comparisons	Definite and clear
Compatibility checking	Yes	No
No of comparative indices	7±2	Very much
No of comparative options	7±2	Very much

TOPSIS method can meet the needs of paired comparisons and capacity constraints are not occurred, so it may be used for more comparisons than AHP (Rao & Davim, 2008). The application of AHP has restricted since it is accepted that maximum paired comparisons is 7±2. The reason for this lies in human limited capacity in information processing (Nayeb et al., 2014, pp. 355). On the other hand, the TOPSIS method does not offer an efficient procedure to determine the relative importance of criteria, which is precisely the great benefit from the AHP method.

Considering this, the intention of authors is to use the AHP method to calculate the weights of criteria and then to use the TOPSIS method for providing the final ranking results. In that way AHP-TOPSIS combined method will provide benefits arising from advantages of the both methods.

CASE STUDY: SELECTION OF PROCESS FOR THE IMPROVEMENT UNDER THE SIX SIGMA CONCEPT

The validity and usefulness of the suggested integrated method will be applied at the concrete case, in one small enterprise called ABC. The idea of application of the integrated method is to check the correctness of choices of the enterprise management, that were mostly based on the statistical analysis and the tools suggested by the Six Sigma, as business process management concept.

Modified Delphi Method

The enterprise belongs to the food industry, which makes even more important successfulness of the Six Sigma concept implementation, since quality is not an option, but the necessity for survival at the market. In this stage of the research, managers were asked to identify three processes that are most likely candidates for the improvement. At the same time, they were asked to define the list of the most important criteria for choosing process for the improvement. This has been performed under the modified Delphi method. Even though the facilitating was the fact that it is small enterprise with only four managers, in order to provide objectiveness and to ensure that the processes, candidates for the improvement, are the most important for strategy implementation, general manager was asked to make a proposal of those processes – candidates. Therefore, modified Delphi method was used only in part concerning choice of criteria for selection of processes – candidates. Managers were offered the list of possible criteria, involving some of already mentioned in this paper, but they were also allowed to propose some they found important for decision making. After three rounds, consensus was provided and six criteria were chosen. Here is the list of the criteria with the numbers in the brackets indicating their label in the following tables:

- Time of project implementation – time necessary for completing the improvement process (1),
- Availability of employees – existence of employees with skills and knowledge necessary for the improvement of the process (2),
- Alignment with strategy – the level of compliance of the process with the enterprise strategy (3),
- Investment – the sum needed for the improvement of the process (4),
- Decrease of variable costs – the savings that will be provided after the improvement of the process (5),
- Number of defects – calculated based on the Six Sigma popular measure called Defects per million opportunities or DMO (6).

AHP

Based on questionnaire survey and consensus that managers have made, paired comparison matrix was created. Through mutual comparison of the chosen criteria managers defined which are more important and to what extent, measured on scale 1 - 9, where 1 represents the equal importance of the criteria, 3 moderate importance, and so on, as shown in Table 2. Pair-wise comparison of the observed criteria is presented in Table 5.

In order to continue this procedure, it is necessary to normalise the values from the Table 5. Normalisation is performed based on the sum of the columns. Normalised or standardised values are shown in Table 6. The last column of this table indicates the weighted importance of each criterion in percentages (Wp). In this case, it may be said that the most important criteria for decision making (for choosing the process for the improvement) are fourth and fifth, precisely Investment and Decrease of variable cost.

The needed data from the AHP analysis are gained, but one more step is necessary for checking the validity of data. In order to avoid misleading with the data, it is necessary to perform consistency check (Table 7). The sum value in the last column represents so-called lambda (λ), which is used to calculate CI, as shown in the Equation (1).

Since the value for RI can be seen from Table 3, and is equal 1.24, CR can be easily calculated, as a ration of CI and RI, for the matrix size 6, since there are six criteria that have been analysed. From Table 8 it can be seen that CR is equal 0.093, which is less than 0.10, meaning that pair-wise comparisons shown in Table 5 are relatively consistent.

Table 5. Pair-wise comparison

	1	2	3	4	5	6
1	1	1	0.2	0.11	0.14	3
2	1	1	1	0.14	0.33	3
3	5	1	1	0.2	0.2	3
4	9	7	5	1	1	7
5	7	3	5	1	1	7
6	0.33	0.33	0.33	0.14	0.14	1
Sum	23.33	13.33	12.53	2.59	2.81	24

Table 6. Normalized matrix

	1	2	3	4	5	6	W	Wp
1	0.043	0.075	0.016	0.042	0.050	0.125	0.059	5.85%
2	0.043	0.075	0.080	0.054	0.117	0.125	0.082	8.24%
3	0.214	0.075	0.080	0.077	0.071	0.125	0.107	10.71%
4	0.386	0.525	0.399	0.386	0.356	0.292	0.391	39.06%
5	0.300	0.225	0.399	0.386	0.356	0.292	0.326	32.63%
6	0.014	0.025	0.026	0.054	0.050	0.042	0.035	3.51%
sum	1.000	1.000	1.000	1.000	1.000	1.000	1.000	

Table 7. Consistency check

	1	2	3	4	5	6	Ws
1	0.059	0.082	0.021	0.043	0.046	0.105	1.365
2	0.059	0.082	0.107	0.055	0.108	0.105	1.098
3	0.293	0.082	0.107	0.078	0.065	0.105	1.342
4	0.527	0.577	0.535	0.391	0.326	0.246	1.012
5	0.410	0.247	0.535	0.391	0.326	0.246	0.917
6	0.019	0.027	0.035	0.055	0.046	0.035	0.843
sum	1.365	1.098	1.342	1.012	0.917	0.843	**6.577**

Table 8. Consistency ratio

CI	0.11534827
RI (6)	1.24
CR	**0.0930228**

TOPSIS

After the calculation of weighted importance, shown in Table 6, in order to use TOPSIS method it is necessary to determine how the criteria will be expressed or what units will be used for further calculations. Table 9 includes the observed criteria, presented according to their weighted importance - W (from the most important till the least important), as well as the units they are expressed in.

In the Table 10 weighted importance from the Table 6 is used to provide weighted normalised matrix. To do so, beside the weighted importance, it is also necessary to have a real data about the criteria that are used, for each of the processes – candidates for the improvement, based on the data managers have at their disposal, which actually present decision variables.

The next step is to normalise the decision variables. The data obtained are shown in the first part of the Table 11. Since it is necessary to take into consideration the weighted importance, the second part of the Table 11 assumes multiplication of the decision variables by their respective weights to get a weighted normalized matrix.

Table 9. Selected criteria according to modified Delphi method

No.	Criteria	Expressed in
1	Time of project implementation	in days
2	Availability of employees	scale 1-9
3	Alignment with strategy	scale 1-9
4	Investment	in 000
5	Decrease of variable costs	in 000
6	Number of defects	DMO

Table 10. Weighted matrix

	1	2	3	4	5	6
W	0.059	0.082	0.107	0.391	0.326	0.035
Process 1	180	5	9	1200	285	12000
Process 2	300	9	5	1500	288	68000
Process 3	90	7	7	850	290	28000
	2100.595	74511.744	12.450	498.266	12.450	361.248

Table 11. Normalized and Weighed normalized matrix

	1	2	3	4	5	6
Normalised matrix						
Process 1	0.5713	0.1610	0.7229	0.5720	0.4016	0.4983
Process 2	0.7141	0.9126	0.4016	0.5780	0.7229	0.8305
Process 3	0.4046	0.3758	0.5623	0.5820	0.5623	0.2491
Weighed normalized matrix						
Process 1	0.0334	**0.0133**	**0.0774**	**0.2234**	**0.1310**	0.0175
Process 2	**0.0418**	**0.0752**	**0.0430**	0.2258	**0.2359**	**0.0292**
Process 3	**0.0237**	0.0310	0.0602	**0.2273**	0.1835	**0.0088**

The Table 12 shows the calculations needed to determine the separation between each alternative and the positive ideal solution / negative ideal solution. This actually means determining the shortest distance from the positive ideal solution and the farthest distance of the negative ideal solution. The last column contains total separation for each alternative, from positive, as well as, from negative ideal solution. From this table it can be seen that Process 2 is the closest one to the positive solution, and, at the same time, the farthest from the negative solution.

Table 12. Determining positive and negative ideal solution

	1	2	3	4	5	6	
Separation PIS							
Process 1	0.0001	0.0038	0.0000	0.0000	0.0110	0.0001	**0.1227**
Process 2	0.0003	0.0000	0.0012	0.0000	0.0000	0.0000	**0.0390**
Process 3	0.0000	0.0020	0.0003	0.0000	0.0027	0.0004	**0.0737**
Separation NIS							
Process 1	0.0001	0.0000	0.0012	0.0000	0.0000	0.0001	**0.0367**
Process 2	0.0000	0.0038	0.0000	0.0000	0.0110	0.0004	**0.1235**
Process 3	0.0003	0.0003	0.0003	0.0000	0.0027	0.0000	**0.0607**

Table 13. Final TOPSIS score

Processes	Scores
Process 1	0.2302
Process 2	**0.7602**
Process 3	0.4516

Final TOPSIS score is presented in the Table 13. As expected from the previous comment, Process 2 is ranked as the best candidate for the improvement under the Six Sigma concept.

Based on the results from the Table 13, graphical presentation has been made (Figure 1). This kind of visualisation is appropriate for presenting final results and justification for the decision that has been made, and which means that the first one that should be improved is the second process or Process 2.

Sensitivity Analysis

Although presented calculations and their results are valid and useful, due to the proven uncertainty of the market and environment, generally, it may be useful to conduct Sensitivity analysis. Sensitivity analysis means actually checking the sensitivity of the model or, precisely, seeing what will happen if certain scenario appears. If it is assumed that weighted importance will not change in the short term, then inside the TOPSIS method only, additional checking may be performed to see what will happen if some of the decision variables change. For example, it may be checked what will happen if additional investment is needed for certain alternative or what will happen if a new employee with needed skills

Figure 1. Graphical presentation of the final TOPSIS score

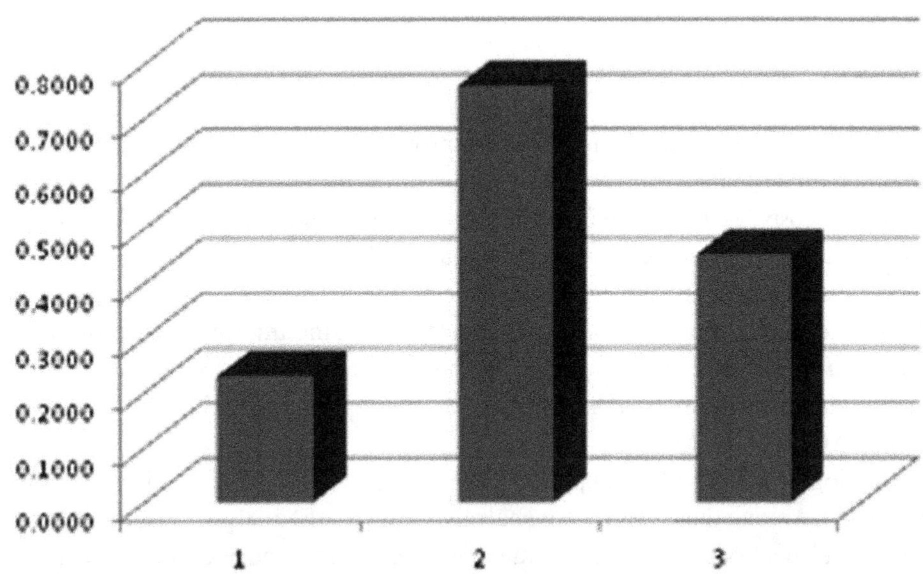

and knowledge for certain alternative is hired and so on. The Sensitivity analysis is very useful since it helps managers to be more flexible and more careful during decision making process.

Benchmarking

The analysis based on combined AHP–TOPSIS method has been conducted in order to check the accuracy of the decision which has been made by the managers, based on the statistical analysis, as the Six Sigma concept suggests. In this very case, they have used Statistical process control (in order to determine process stability and process capability) and Defects per million opportunities – DMO. These two criteria pointed to the Process 2. However, on the other side, two additional, also very important criteria concerning Time of project implementation and Investment have been indicating to the Process 3. So the situation has been conflicting, but since they wanted to provide results of the improvement faster, managers have chosen the Process 3. Comparing to the multi-criteria decision making process presented in this paper, their decision was not the best possible or the optimal solution.

Further Research

According to research results of many authors, some of them presented in this chapter, as well as based on the observations of the authors, it is obvious that all methods are imperfect and their usefulness usually depends on combination with some other method, which may neutralise its limitations. In this paper chosen combination included two multi-criteria decision making methods. However, as additional tool, prior to this combined method one can use Factor Analysis, as statistical tool for determining the most important factors, in this case the most important criteria. The results may be compared to the ones obtained and presented in this chapter. Also, for improving decision making process in performing Six Sigma selection task, some other multi-criteria decision making methods may be used, such as DEA or fuzzy form of already used AHP and TOPSIS method.

CONCLUSION

Six Sigma views process management and process improvement as daily responsibility of all employees, and above all operational managers and direct executives of business processes. This concept contributes that quality and costs, as well as their relationship, become an integral part of each employee's job, which represents the basic difference and the advantage of Six Sigma in comparison to the other concepts for process management and quality improvement. Important prerequisite for the implementation of the Six Sigma concept is process orientation, since Six Sigma improvement projects are intended for improvement of business processes. Additional advantage of the Six Sigma concept, compared to the other quality and process improvement initiatives, among them TQM, is assistance of structured methodologies, DMAIC and DMADV.

Both methodologies are based on application of statistical and managerial tools, which are used through their phases. Among them are: Pareto analysis, Cost-benefit analysis, Fishbone diagram, Design of experiments, Statistical process control, Brainstorming, Failure mode and effects analysis, Quality function deployment. However, in accordance with the Six Sigma concept philosophy that everything can be improved continually, the assumption has been that this concept may be improved itself, by involving methods useful for providing higher level of objectivity during decision making process. In this chapter proposed solution assumes combined AHP-TOPSIS method.

An application of case study, along with benchmarking and sensitivity analysis, which are used as auxiliary tools, provides final concluding on usefulness of the integrated AHP-TOPSIS method, and generally, multi-criteria decision making, for successful business process improvement. The case study indicates that, even though the Six Sigma concept is primarily statistically oriented, it may be and should be "open" for other tools and methods that provide quantification of qualitative data and make decisions more objective and more likely with positive results.

REFERENCES

Abdulmalek, F. A., & Rajgopal, J. (2007). Analyzing the benefits of lean manufacturing and value stream mapping via simulation: A process sector case study. *International Journal of Production Economics*, *107*(1), 223–236. doi:10.1016/j.ijpe.2006.09.009

Anđelković Pešić, M. (2006). Process and Project Management–Two Sides of Six Sigma Medal. *Economic Themes*, *44*(6), 111–120.

Anđelković Pešić, M. (2009). Quality Function Deployment as a Tool for The Improvement of Value Proposal in High Education. *Facta Universitatis. Series Economics and Organization*, *6*(2), 185–198.

Antony, J. (2002). Design for Six Sigma: A Breakthrough Business Improvement Strategy for Achieving Competitive Advantage. *Work Study*, *51*(1), 6–8. doi:10.1108/00438020210415460

Antony, J. (2004). Six Sigma in the UK service organisations: Results from a pilot survey. *Managerial Auditing Journal*, *19*(8), 1006–1013. doi:10.1108/02686900410557908

Bahri, M. (2011). *Six Sigma project selections by using a Multi-criteria Decision making approach: a Case study in PolyAcryl Corp*. Retrieved from: http://www.usc.edu/dept/ ise/caie/Checked%20Papers%20 %5Bruhi%2012th%20sept%5D/word%20format%20papers/REGISTRATION%20PAID%20PAPERS%20 FOR%20PROCEEDINGS/pdf/1554%23QJ3.PDF

Banuelas, R., & Antony, J. (2002). Critical success factors for the successful implementation of six sigma projects in organizations. *The TQM Magazine*, *14*(2), 92–99. doi:10.1108/09544780210416702

Banuelas, R., & Antony, J. (2003). Going from six sigma to design for six sigma: An exploratory study using analytic hierarchy process. *The TQM Magazine*, *15*(5), 334–344. doi:10.1108/09544780310487730

Banuelas, R., Tennant, C., Tuersley, I., & Tang, S. (2006). Selection of Six Sigma projects in the UK. *The TQM Magazine*, *18*(5), 514–527. doi:10.1108/09544780610685485

Bošković, G., Janković Milić, V., & Anđelković Pešić, M. (2011). Possibilities of Cusum Chart Implementation in Statistical Process Control. In *Proceedings from XI International conference Research and Development in Mechanical Industry (RaDMI 2011)*. Soko Banja, Serbia: SaTCIP.

Brue, G. (2002). *Six Sigma for Managers*. New York, NY: McGraw-Hill.

Chang, C. W., Wu, C. R., & Chen, H. C. (2008). Using expert technology to select unstable slicing machine to control wafer slicing quality via fuzzy AHP. *Expert Systems with Applications*, *34*(3), 2210–2220. doi:10.1016/j.eswa.2007.02.042

De Feo, J., & Bar-Ei, Z. (2002). Creating Strategic Change More Efficiently with a New Design for Six Sigma Process. *Journal of Change Management*, *3*(1), 60–81. doi:10.1080/714042521

Delavari, H., Bandara, W., Marjanovic, O., & Mathiesen, P. (2010). Business Process Management (BPM) education in Australia: A critical review based on content analysis. In *Proceedings of the 21st Australasian conference on information systems (ACIS2010)*. Brisbane, Australia: Queensland University of Technology.

Einset, E., & Marzano, J. (2002). Six Sigma Demystified. *Quality in Manufacturing*, *13*(12), 43–47.

George, M., Rowlands, D., & Kastle, B. (2004). *What is Lean Six Sigma?* New York, NY: McGraw Hill.

George, M. L. (2005). *The Lean Six Sigma Pocket Toolbook: A Quick Reference Guide to Nearly 100 Tools for Improving Process Quality, Speed, and Complexity*. New York, NY: McGraw Hill.

Ghosh, D. N. (2011). Analytic Hierarchy Process & TOPSIS Method to Evaluate Faculty Performance in Engineering Education. *Universal Journal of Computer Science and Technology*, *1*(2), 63–70.

Gitlow, H. S., & Levine, D. M. (2005). *Six Sigma for Green Belts and Champions: Foundations, DMAIC, Tools, Cases, and Certification*. New York, NY: Pearson Education, Prentice Hall.

Gurumurthy, A., & Kodali, R. (2008). A multi-criteria decision-making model for the justification of lean manufacturing systems. *International Journal of Management Science and Engineering Management*, *3*(2), 100–118.

Hammer, M. (2002). The future of Six Sigma. *MIT Sloan Management Review*. Retrieved from: http://venturepress.dk/wp-content/uploads/2014/08/Hammer-ProicessManagement-the-future-of-six-sigma.pdf

Harmon, P. (2003). *Business process change: a manager's guide to improving, redesigning, and automating processes*. San Francisco, CA: Morgan Kaufmann.

Harmon, P. (2004). Evaluating an organization's business process maturity. *Business Process Trends*, *2*(3), 1–11.

He, Y., Tang, X., & Chang, W. (2010). Technical decomposition approach of critical to quality characteristics for product design for six sigma. *Quality and Reliability Engineering International*, *26*(4), 325–339.

Hu, G., Wang, L., Fetch, S., & Bidanda, B. (2008). A multi-objective model for project portfolio selection to implement lean and Six Sigma concepts. *International Journal of Production Research*, *46*(23), 6611–6625. doi:10.1080/00207540802230363

Jahanshahloo, G. R., Lotfi, F. H., & Izadikhah, M. (2006). An algorithmic method to extend TOPSIS for decision-making problems with interval data. *Applied Mathematics and Computation*, *175*(2), 1375–1384. doi:10.1016/j.amc.2005.08.048

Kumar, U., Crocker, J., Chitra, T., & Saranga, H. (2006). *Reliability and Six Sigma*. Berlin: Springer.

Kumar, U., Saranga, H., Ramírez-Márquez, J. E., & Nowicki, D. (2007). Six sigma project selection using data envelopment analysis. *The TQM Magazine*, *19*(5), 419–441. doi:10.1108/09544780710817856

Lai, V. S., Trueblood, R. P., & Wong, B. K. (1999). Software selection: A case study of the application of the analytical hierarchical process to the selection of a multimedia authoring system. *Information & Management*, *36*(4), 221–232. doi:10.1016/S0378-7206(99)00021-X

Lai, Y. J., Liu, T. Y., & Hwang, C. L. (1994). Topsis for MODM. *European Journal of Operational Research*, *76*(3), 486–500. doi:10.1016/0377-2217(94)90282-8

Larson, A. (2003). *Demystifying Six Sigma*. New York, NY: American Management Association.

Maheshwarkar, M., & Sohani, N. (2013). Combined AHP-TOPSIS based approach for the evaluation of knowledge sharing capabilities of supply chain partners. *Management Science and Engineering*, *7*(3), 27–32.

Meriyappa, T. (2015). *15 Criteria for Selecting a Viable DMAIC Project*. Retrieved from: http://www.isixsigma.com/implementation/project-selection-tracking/15-criteriaselecting-viable-dmaic-project/

Nayeb, A., & Jabari, S., & Yousefi Nejad Attari, M. (2014). A combination of factor analysis and combined approach techniques (AHP-TOPSIS) for ranking criteria and evaluating the factors affecting brand. *Technical Journal of Engineering and Applied Sciences*, *4*(4), 349–358.

Opricovic, S., & Tzeng, G. H. (2004). Compromise solution by MCDM methods: A comparative analysis of VIKOR and TOPSIS. *European Journal of Operational Research*, *156*(2), 445–455. doi:10.1016/S0377-2217(03)00020-1

Pande, P., Neuman, R., & Cavanagh, R. (2000). *The Six Sigma Way*. New York, NY: McGraw-Hill.

Paulson, D., & Zahir, S. (1995). Consequences of uncertainty in the analytic hierarchy process: A simulation approach. *European Journal of Operational Research*, *87*(1), 45–56. doi:10.1016/0377-2217(94)00044-D

Perçin, S., & Kahraman, C. (2010). An integrated fuzzy multi-criteria decision-making approach for Six Sigma project. *International Journal of Computational Intelligence Systems*, *3*(5), 610–621. doi:10.1080/18756891.2010.9727727

Pyzdek, T. (2003). *The Six Sigma Project Planner*. New York, NY: McGraw-Hill.

Pyzdek, T., & Keller, P. A. (2003). *The six sigma handbook*. New York, NY: McGraw-Hill.

Rao, R. V., & Davim, J. P. (2008). A decision-making framework model for material selection using a combined multiple attribute decision-making method. *International Journal of Advanced Manufacturing Technology*, *35*(7-8), 751–760. doi:10.1007/s00170-006-0752-7

Ren, L., Zhang, Y., Wang, Y., & Sun, Z. (2007). Comparative analysis of a novel M-TOPSIS method and TOPSIS. *Applied Mathematics Research Express*. Retrieved from: http://citeseerx.ist.psu.edu/viewdoc/download?doi=10.1.1.99.4476&rep=rep1&type=pdf

Saaty, T. L. (1980). *The analytic hierarchy process: planning, priority setting, resources allocation*. New York, NY: McGraw-Hill.

Saaty, T. L. (1986). Axiomatic foundation of the analytic hierarchy process. *Management Science*, *32*(7), 841–855. doi:10.1287/mnsc.32.7.841

Saaty, T. L. (1994). Highlights and critical points in the theory and application of the analytic hierarchy process. *European Journal of Operational Research*, *74*(3), 426–447. doi:10.1016/0377-2217(94)90222-4

Saaty, T. L., & Vargas, L. G. (2012). *Models, methods, concepts & applications of the analytic hierarchy process*. New York, NY: Springer Science & Business Media. doi:10.1007/978-1-4614-3597-6

Shewhart, W. A. (1931). *Economic control of quality of manufactured product*. New York, NY: ASQ Quality Press.

Smith, L. (2001). Six Sigma and the Evolution of Quality in Product Development. *Six Sigma Forum Magazine*, *1*(1), 28–35.

Trkman, P. (2010). The critical success factors of business process management. *International Journal of Information Management*, *30*(2), 125–134. doi:10.1016/j.ijinfomgt.2009.07.003

Van Der Aalst, W. M., Ter Hofstede, A. H., & Weske, M. (2003). Business process management: A survey. In *Business process management*. Berlin: Springer. doi:10.1007/3-540-44895-0_1

Watson, G. H. (2004). Six Sigma: Controlling Business and Process. *Analysis Management*, *7*, 18–19.

Yoon, K. P., & Hwang, C. L. (1995). *Multiple attribute decision making: An introduction*. Thousand Oaks, CA: Sage Publications.

KEY TERMS AND DEFINITIONS

Analytical Hierarchical Process: A compensatory multi-criteria method, which calculates the scores for each alternative based on pair-wise comparisons and assumes that criteria weights must be determined by experts who understand evaluation criteria.

Business Process Management: A holistic management approach that focuses on identifying, monitoring, measuring, analysing and continuously improving business processes, based on integration of process design and application of appropriate information technology.

DMADV Methodology: The Six Sigma methodology, including phases define, measure, analyze, design, verify, used as a support for creating a new product or process designs in such a way that process results are more predictable and defect free.

DMAIC Methodology: The Six Sigma methodology, including phases define, measure, analyze, improve, control, used for the improvement of existing business processes.

Process Orientation: Running a business by adopting a process view, which assumes that at least key business processes are identified and their performances measured and improved.

Sensitivity Analysis: Sensitivity analysis means actually checking the sensitivity of the model or, precisely, seeing what will happen if certain scenario appears.

Six Sigma: A management philosophy that involves a gradual, but continuous expansion of process orientation through an enterprise, and can be used as a guide for managers, in order to enable easier transition of an enterprise from lower to higher maturity level in quality management.

TOPSIS: A compromising method, because it selects an alternative that is closest to the ideal solution, since its main principle on refers to the selection of the alternative that has the shortest distance from the positive ideal solution and the farthest distance from the negative ideal solution.

Total Quality Management: A comprehensive business management approach that promotes continual improvement of the quality of products and services, based on customers' feedback and statistical quality control tools.

Chapter 12
Rethinking Social Capital Measurement

Laurence Saglietto
Université Côte d'Azur, CNRS, GREDEG, France

Delphine David
University of Paris 13 Sorbonne Paris Cité, France

Cécile Cezanne
University of Paris 13 Sorbonne Paris Cité, France

ABSTRACT

Social capital is decisive to many of strategic objectives of organizations. Although it has been extensively defined in the literature, social capital continues to be discussed in particular concerning its measurement. What is the usability of the existing indicators of social capital? How do managers decide which one they would prefer? An overview of the literature reveals that there are very few measurements of social capital and those which have already developed are very complex. Direct measurements appear to provide a better understanding of the complexity of relationships than aggregated measurements. Yet, we show that they are of unsatisfactory quality. Using simple counter-examples, we advance that they give rise to contradictions. From this discussion and using Graph Theory, we propose two complementary indicators of social capital which we call "relational strength" and "relational potential". These operational indicators can be handled by any actors to position themselves within their social sphere.

INTRODUCTION

For several decades, sociologists and political scientists have written huge amounts of literature on sociability and social capital, first in the United States and then in Europe (for recent researches, see for example Häuberer, 2011; Tzanakis, 2013; Villalonga-Olives and Kawachia, 2015; Wincent et al., 2016). The ideas put forward have also attracted economists and managers. Is this just a trend or is there real interest in reading about the economic and managerial issues covered in these works? Could such a concept make a significant contribution to the comparative study of new theoretical approaches and the emergence of

DOI: 10.4018/978-1-5225-0959-2.ch012

a new measurement useful to researchers and managers alike? To what extent can social capital justify certain strategic objectives within a company? How much can an entity (group, company, alliance) rely on its members' social capital to create new momentum or remain prosperous? The authors see these as important questions which emphasise that the link between social capital and strategic behaviour is not incongruous. Nevertheless, it must be channelled if the authors want to move the debate forward and show the relationship's influence on performance. This is the topic covered herein.

The chapter has two aims: review current arguments over the notion of social capital and, more specifically, its measurement; and show that researchers and managers can be given an open-source operational tool that allows them to measure social capital more accurately. A kind of "actionable knowledge" as Argyris puts it (1995, p. 257): "knowledge that is both valid and can be put into action in everyday life".

The chapter is structured as follows. The authors first describe the issues surrounding social capital in the light of economic and managerial problems, and discuss available indicators while stressing their limitations. They then discuss existing ways of measuring social capital. On this basis, the authors propose an operational measure, articulated around two notions, which they call "relational strength" and "relational potential". This measurement system is helpful to analyse how actors position themselves within their social universe.

BACKGROUND: THE SCOPE OF SOCIAL CAPITAL

Elements of the Debate

According to Ponthieux (2004, p. 5), social capital has a multi-dimensional nature. It is a "mix of a structure's attributes, participants' perceptions and the benefits derived from the two". It is this distinctive trait that explains why it is so often used "as much in academic circles as in social management and intervention" (Lévesque and White, 1999) and why it is so hard to measure. A bibliometric search of different science databases (the main results of which are shown in table 1 below) for "social capital" and "social capital measure" sheds some interesting light on the scale of this research topic.

The plethora of scientific work on social capital has resulted in different theoretic starting points and ways of thinking, the reality of which varies greatly. However, there seems to be a consensus that social capital is a solution to numerous socio-economic, demographic and even geographic problems. It was against this backdrop that Coleman (1998) took a functional approach to social capital in 1988, defining it according to its function and referring to three forms: meeting obligations and expectations; the potential value of the information conveyed; standards and effective sanctions in communities (Levesque and White, 1999). Seeing the limits of this approach, a second group of researchers defined

Table 1. Bibliometric analysis

Database Keywords	Econlit	Science Direct	Wiley Blackwell	Business Source Complete
Social Capital	3449	14882	25517	5280
Social Capital Measure	388	325	263	427

Note: The search was carried out on 27/09/2015. In each of these databases we searched for the following terms: (i) "social capital" and (ii) "social capital measure".

social capital as a social resource (Lin, 1995) involved in social relations. The emphasis shifted from the functionality of social capital to its content, nature and ways of working. According to Lin (1995, p. 701), "social capital is an individual's investment in relations with others". It is composed of "resources that could be accessed by joining social networks" (Lévesque, 2000, p.25). Looking beyond individuals, if the authors concentrate on firms as independent entities, how can they determine whether social relations and their dynamics are an additional resource in achieving strategic objectives and therefore a major issue? Considering social capital from a social network perspective becomes a way of focusing on relationships and studying their direct or indirect impact on corporate performance. According to Arrègle et al. (2004, p. 18), "the individual social capital available to an entrepreneur to create or develop his business affects success in hitting targets". These authors go further, showing that "social capital is also an important aspect of a company in its mutual relations with stakeholders (clients, suppliers and employees) and can generate competitive advantages for firms" (Arrègle et al., 2004, p. 19).

However, research is less revealing on the measurement of social capital (from both qualitative and quantitative points of view) and its effects. This subject area is more complicated. As social capital is not a unique resource, the challenge is to discover a way of observing social capital and its operationalisation. Indeed, more and more writers use specific studies to show that researchers and managers have everything to gain by having a measurable idea of social capital.

Social Capital in Economics and Management: Outreach Through Social Networks

Academics in the fields of economics and management have often focused their research on social networks to remove any ambiguity from the definition of social capital (Huault, 2004). By concentrating on the structure and content of links, this approach makes it easier to compare disciplines and draw analogies. Viewing social capital as a "social resource" would appear to be more easily acceptable than taking other more functional approaches (Coleman, 1988). The advantage of looking at an actor's social capital (i.e. an individual's or an organisation's social capital) through relations with his social sphere is that any economic implications can be identified.

These result from a mutual benefit between social actor and network, involving an exchange of resources. After a lengthy debate on whether social capital is strictly proportionate to the number of relations, a consensus has emerged in sociologists' work: social capital is not just about the number of contacts as not all contacts have the same value; it mainly depends on the structural characteristics of relations. Social capital therefore results from the size of the personal network, volume of resources contained in this network (information, direct and indirect relational resources), opportunity to access these resources (Mercklé, 2004) and direct or potential relations. Variables introduced to gain a clearer idea of this concept all depend on the researcher's aims and context. For example, a structural analysis of social networks tries to understand how social capital arises, especially through strategies used to exercise a degree of power within a network. According to Lemieux (1999), the issue is therefore to break down individual behaviour into a complex system of social relations from which it takes meaning and to which it gives meaning. This leads Lévesque (2000, p. 52) "to the feeling that social capital could be a resource produced and driven in and by social networks, but which cannot be described as one". Sociologists' have therefore moved their attention towards the relations that social players maintain with each other, putting the features of these to one side. These analytical changes are considered to be signals, which have been received in other disciplines such as economics and management, extracting essential information on stakeholders' concerns. The authors now have a better understanding of why this sociological framework presents neighbouring disciplines with opportunities to revisit some old problems. As many authors have stressed (Lin, 2001; Lin et al., 2001), the notion of social capital and that of structural holes, the latter of which complements the former, shed new contextual and cultural light on the matter. Structural holes refer to the empty spaces between two members of a group; they are the absence of relations between two social actors, allowing a third party to come in as an intermediary and benefit from the situation. All in all, the current trend suggests that social networks have a very high capacity to solve problems that would otherwise persist. The illustration of business networks is just one example (explaining some sector concentrations, different types of alliances, etc.).

Social capital has undeniably become an economic and managerial concern given the weight and growth of intra- and inter-organisational networks. By its very nature, the structure of these networks' social capital is inclusive and systemic as it prioritises structural properties, companies' different positions in the structure, as well as their power and performance.

By limiting social networks to a simple relational structure underlying collective action in a social environment, the different theories apply as much to intra-organisational networks as inter-organisational ones. However, the most written-about topics, which focus on social capital and structural holes, concern intra-organisational networks and concentrate on interpersonal links, the interpretation of which can be supplemented with a psychological approach. They consider the influence and size of the organisation, the impact and spread of technology, the environment, group decision-making and even individual performances. In this regard, Bozionelos (2008, 2003) shows that the network's resources contribute to intra-organisational professional success and improve commitment to the organisation through the cumulative effects of interaction between the company's human resources and structural factors, albeit without accounting for individual differences in this success. Burt (1992), Davis (1991) and Haunschild (1993) remain key references for many authors working on the subject. For example, Burt (1992) explains that entrepreneurs who have a high proportion of structural holes in their network are more likely to generate high profits, while their margins are reduced if their suppliers or clients have numerous structural holes. Social capital therefore represents the benefit derived from having structural holes in a network. On this basis, Burt (1992; 1995) shows that the more isolated suppliers and clients are, the better the situation for entrepreneurs is. The benefits in terms of information and control are therefore cumulative and are increasing. Along with interplay, access to – and control of – various information sources are variables that help distinguish between a closed relational structure and an open structure. In a closed network, all firms have relations with each other. Interfirm flows of information leads to standards of cooperation and the collective building of a reputation. In an open network, in contrast, firms cannot rely on any social capital. If they are not fully connected, cooperative ties are harder to forge and information on relational behaviour spreads more slowly.

Studies on inter-organisational networks have focused on interlocking directorates (Carroll and Alexander, 1999; Frank and Yasumoto, 1998) and cooperation between firms (Dumoulin and Lecocq, 2001; Thorelli, 1986; Von Peter, 2007). These studies take into account industrial specificities and strategic considerations. They tend towards a global analysis (Walker et al., 1997) or a dyad approach (; Lorrain and White, 1971; Mizruchi and Marquis, 2006; Mizruchi, 1993). Common observations can be made from this research. Network formation is determined by two opposing forces. The first is the reproduction of the network structure as a general social resource for members; the second is an alternative to the network structure by members working for their own benefits (Walker et al., 1997). The network structure indicates both the frequency with which a firm establishes new relations and the location of social capital within the industry. It results in real opportunities for future entrepreneurial actions. It is neither uniformly dense, nor sparse. The network structure is unequal; it consists of "groups" having more or less strong relational densities, while firms' positions in the network are linked to these groups. The amount of social capital available to a business is thus determined by its position in the network structure. Well placed firms have more social capital than those with fewer relations. Corporate behaviour is not viewed as specific actions but similar actions (Mizruchi and Marquis, 2006; Walker et al., 1997). If firms have a role as informational mediators and are able to arbitrate, then partner selection rather than social capital will determine efficient cooperation (Walker et al., 1997). Each year, new interfirm relations affect the network structure as they are sensitive to change. When relations are established, the benefits of greater structural constraints are offset by reduced independence if the network is closed. If the network is open, however, firms have more leeway in their cooperation strategies. Ultimately, pursuing a new option becomes more attractive as firms believe that they can control the unknown through continued reliance on their network position and the benefits of the information that they can obtain (De Carolis and Saparito, 2006).

Limits of the Debate

Two points are worth mentioning about the different research on social capital and the intra- and inter-organisational networks that the authors have just described. Firstly, the link with a company's performance is not taken into account or is put to one side. Yet some studies show the relationship between performance and social capital. In this research, social capital plays an important (positive or negative) role in the search for existing and potential competitive advantages, whether through international growth of young tech companies (Maurer and Ebers, 2006; Prashantham, 2005), large manufacturers' innovation decisions (Landry et al., 2000) or even through cooperatives (Dasgupta, 2003). These studies show that there is a positive effect on performance when managers have relations outside their main industry. They emphasise the heuristic nature of social capital and the benefits that can be derived from participating in networks and deliberately constructing new networks in order to increase network capital. If social capital improves cooperation, firms will probably look for partners who are more restricted by the network structure than others. In other words, firms also try to increase their available social capital through new relations. Having numerous contacts is an advantage in business but quantity is not the overriding factor: the structure of contacts also plays a key role. Secondly, these studies provide only complex measurement tools that are hard to use. Indeed, suggested measures of social capital are as varied as the concept's definitions, being heavily dependent on context (nation, region or even community within a country) (Westlund and Adam, 2010). In the same way, Petersen (2002) shows that few academics, evaluators and practitioners agree on a definition of social capital and how it works. He questions the discovery of its key components and considers a possible operationalisation of social capital to measure it systematically, and in the community context that interests him. The situation has not changed much since. Very recent work by Kikuchi and Coleman (2012) confirms that links between concepts and measurements are not always clear, and that the operationalisation of social capital is by no means uniform in empirical studies. However, the authors note that social capital measurements require a static-dynamic dimension and a formal-informal dimension, which are often ignored. In their research on communications, they show that social relations depend on numerous variables such as neighbourhood, social support, contacts, sociability and network size, amongst others. More specifically, research carried out from a functionalist perspective looks at qualitative measures of social capital (Westlund and

Adam, 2010), applying the "dimensions" suggested by Coleman (1988) and Putnam (1995): meeting obligations and expectations; the potential value of the information conveyed; standards and effective sanctions in communities. These qualitative measures are deduced from local experience and observations and cannot be reproduced in identical situations. For example, Bouma et al. (2008) measure the link between social capital and community resource management in Indian villages and use different trust and voluntary involvement models as a social capital indicator to show the economic policies that should be taken into consideration in this type of management. This study follows on from those already conducted in South Africa and several Asian countries by other researchers (Carpenter and Seki, 2005; Carpenter et al., 2004; Carter and Castillo, 2002).

Research into social networks therefore assesses social capital with both qualitative (resources) and quantitative (links) measures. For example, work by Moore et al. (2011) proposes the sum of qualitative (trust, social participation in neighbourhood life, etc.) and quantitative (number of relations with the neighbourhood, etc.) variables as the measure of social capital. These examples help the authors see that the operationalisation of social capital is more complex than it appears. In the circumstances, the key question is whether it is possible to put forward a more operational tool so that a measure of social capital can be calculated and used by the general scientific and management communities? So the debate moves to existing measures of social capital. What are these measures? How accessible are they? The authors will show that, in the toolbox suggested, not all measures have the same degree of intelligibility in terms of understanding, applicability, suitable software or programming.

MAIN FOCUS OF THE CHAPTER: FORMALISATION OF NEW OPERATIONAL INDICATORS TO MEASURE SOCIAL CAPITAL

Issues: A New Debate

Mentioning an operational instrument implies that the definition of social capital can be converted into a mathematical formula. Several factors need to be taken into account. Firstly, only a minority of research on social capital proposes a measurement of this nature, one that is quite generic so that it can be applied to different contexts. Secondly, according to Bourdieu and Wacquant (1992, p. 119), "social capital is the sum of the resources, actual or virtual, that an individual or a group accrues by virtue of possessing a durable network of more or less institutionalized relationships of mutual acquaintance and recognition". It is hard to put forward a social capital indicator following this definition as there are too many unknowns. So the authors have to limit themselves to what is countable if they want an operational measurement tool. Several measurements of social capital have been described, becoming more sophisticated over time: direct measurements (Thurman, 1979; Lemieux, 1999) and aggregates of different variables in the form of a compound indicator (Burt, 1992; Casanueva and Gallego, 2010; Moore et al., 2011). For example, Moore et al., (2011) and Casanueva and Gallego (2010) measure social capital by aggregating several structural variables (such as different measures of the centrality of ego, number of ties). More specifically, the latter two authors assess these measures according to the nature and intensity of relations and resource access using indicators suggested by the Ucinet program (Borgatti et al., 2002).

According to the authors' opinion, work by Granovetter (1973), Thurman (1979), Burt (1992) and more recently Lemieux (1999) better illustrates this complexification of measuring social capital. Granovetter (1973) bases his indicator on low intensity relations and "betweenness". In other words, he builds it with infrequent connections between members of a network who are not particularly close, as well as their positions as intermediaries in the network. Works by Thurman (1979), Burt (1992), Lemieux (1999) and Casanueva and Gallego (2010) all use high intensity relations to represent social capital. However, their assessments of this capital differ. According to Thurman (1979), social capital is viewed as the "span" of each participant's ego's reticulums. This concept allows him to establish just how compact – or not – these networks are. "Span" is the number of direct links between ego and the other actors in ego's reticulums. It reports to the relative density of ego's contacts (i.e. the participant who is under study) and relations between them relative to the density of the network as a whole. Social capital is therefore the sum of ego's contacts plus the number of these contacts' contacts divided by the number of links in the whole network. In search of a direct measure, Lemieux (1999) defines social capital by distinguishing between contacts (direct connections between members) and sub-contacts (indirect connections between members, through an intermediary) as well as between possible and actual contacts and sub-contacts.

More specifically, he calls this social capital "connection capital" ("*capital connexionnel*") and measures it as "the number of a source's contacts, multiplied by two, over the number of possible contacts, plus the number of sub-contacts, over the possible number of these sub-contacts taking the contacts into account, all divided by three" (Lemieux, 1999, p. 96), i.e.:

$$\text{Connection capital} = \frac{2\frac{AC}{PC} + \frac{ASC}{PSC}}{3}$$

where *AC* is the number of Actual Contacts, *PC* the number of Possible Contacts, *ASC* the number of Actual Sub-Contacts and *PSC* the number of Possible Sub-Contacts taking the contacts into account.

Burt (1992) uses an aggregate measure as he is seeking an operational definition of social capital, going beyond basic definitions. In his endeavours, he manages to give analytical meaning to social capital by showing how the structure of a network offers competitive advantages to social actors. He therefore operationalises a certain measure of social capital's structural value by analysing social networks. To do this he introduces the structural properties of networks. The network constraint therefore measures social capital as a type of network structure. The constraint depends on the size of the network and the quality of ties (diversity of network member statuses, strength of relations between ego and network members and between network members), its density, and its hierarchy, measuring the concentration of direct and indirect relations. The network's aggregate constraint is an index of inequality, measuring the concentration of a network member's direct and indirect connections in a single contact:

$$C_i = \sum_j C_{ij} \text{ for individual } i,$$

where $C_{ij} = \left(P_{ij} + \sum_q P_{iq} P_{qj}\right)^2$, P_{ij} is the weighting allocated to the direct relationship between individual *i* and individual *j* (if one notes n_i the number of direct contacts of individual *i*, $P_{ij} = \frac{1}{n_i}$ for each contact *j*). Quantity $\sum_q P_{iq} P_{qj}$ represents the weighting allocated to the indirect relationship (i.e. going via individual q) between individual i and individual j. This weighting is calculated according to the different possible paths between two individuals.

According to Burt (1995), the aggregate constraint approaches zero in large networks of non-redundant contacts. The lower the constraint, the higher the social capital. The structural constraint approaches 1 in small, closely intertwined networks. The higher the constraint, the lower the social capital.

So as far as direct measures are concerned, with the Lemieux formula (1999) it is important to take into account direct contacts and potential and real direct sub-contacts. With Thurman's formula (1979), it is important to take into account relations between members of a network relative to the density of the network as a whole. Additional variables – network density and size – are used to build aggregate measures.

Controversies and Problems: A Criticism of the Main Existing Measures

The direct measures proposed by Burt (1992) and Lemieux (1999) seem to give a better understanding of the complexity of existing relations between members of a network. However, with the help of the counter-examples below, the authors show that they also lead to contradictions.

For illustrative purposes, the authors take the network of the eight individuals. A network of 3 core individuals is presented in Figure 1.

According to Lemieux (1999), the characteristics of individuals 1 and 2 are as presented in Table 2.

In this network, individual 1 therefore has less connection capital than individual 2. This is natural as individual 2 has one direct contact more than individual 1, their situations being otherwise equal.

Figure 1. Network of 3 core individuals

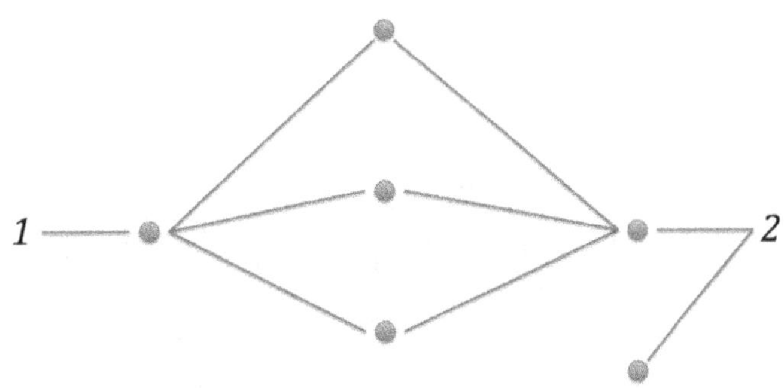

Table 2. Lemieux's connection capital in Figure 1

	Individual 1	Individual 2
AC	1	2
ASC	3	3
PC	7	7
PSC	6	12
Connection capital	0.2619	0.27

Let the authors now consider the following network, which is very similar to the last one but to which they have added a core individual. The network of 4 core individuals is presented in Figure 2.

The two individuals' characteristics now are as mentioned in Table 3.

Here, individual 1 has more connection capital than individual 2 and the higher the number of core individuals, the greater individual 1's connection capital will be relative to individual 2's. This results from the number of possible sub-contacts, which is determined according to the individual's number of actual contacts. The more contacts the individual has, the more potential sub-contacts he has and the more he may suffer as a result.

This contradiction is not present with Burt's constraint (1992). Table 4 identifies the Burt's constraint in Figures 1 and 2.

Individual 1's constraint is always greater than individual 2's; individual 2's social capital is therefore higher than individual 1's however many core individuals there are in the network.

Figure 2. Network of 4 core individuals

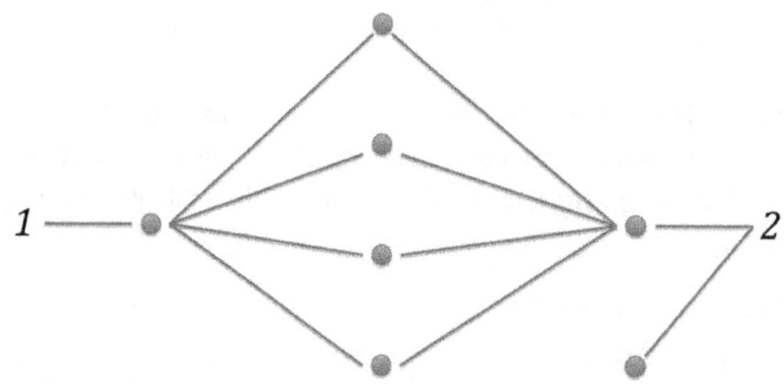

Table 3. Lemieux's connection capital in Figure 2

	Individual 1	Individual 2
AC	1	2
ASC	4	4
PC	8	8
PSC	7	14
Connection capital	0.2738	0.26

Table 4. Burt's constraint in Figures 1 and 2

	Constraint on Individual 1	Constraint on Individual 2
Figure 1	1.18	0.55
Figure 2	1.16	0.54

In his article, Burt writes that "the higher the constraint, the less social capital the person has" (Burt, 1992 p. 607). Based on Figure 3, the authors shall consider the example of a network for which this statement is incorrect.

The constraints on individuals 1 and 2 are as identified in Table 5.

As the constraint on individual 2 is higher, his social capital is lower. However, although both individuals have the same number of contacts, individual 2 has more sub-contacts than individual 1 so his social capital should be greater. Here the authors shall consider the formula used by Burt:

$$C_i = \sum_j C_{ij} \text{ for individual } i$$

where $C_{ij} = \left(P_{ij} + \sum_q P_{iq} P_{qj}\right)^2$. P_{ij} represents direct contacts and $\sum_q P_{iq} P_{qj}$ sub-contacts.

According to this formula, at constant contacts, an increase in the number of sub-contacts implies a higher constraint. Equally, at constant sub-contacts, an increase in the number of contacts implies a higher constraint. Social capital would be lower in both cases according to Burt (1992).

By way of comparison, the authors shall look at Lemieux's indicator (1999) for this example, what is presented in Table 6.

With Lemieux's indicator, individual 2's social capital is much higher than individual 1's.

Although each of the previous indicators is relevant to a specific situation, the counterexamples that the authors have just presented show that they are hard to apply across the board. The authors therefore need to create new, fairly simple, tools that can be used in any situation and will be comprehensive enough to provide relevant information.

Figure 3.

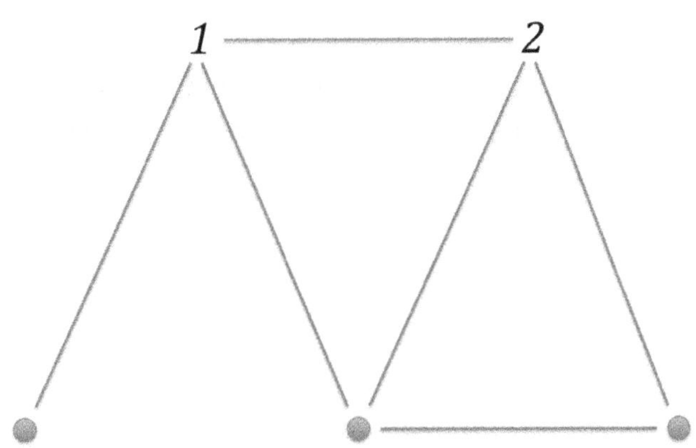

Table 5. Burt's constraint in Figure 3

Constraint on Individual 1	Constraint on Individual 2
0.5339	0.762

Table 6. Lemieux's connection capital in Figure 3

	Individual 1	Individual 2
AC	3	3
ASC	4	5
PC	4	4
PSC	9	9
Connection capital	0.648	0.685

SOLUTIONS AND RECOMMENDATIONS

Although consideration of actual and possible contacts and sub-contacts is essential to understanding a network properly, the examples in the previous section show that it is hard to create a single formula comprising all of these elements. In this part, the authors therefore present two complementary indicators, relational strength and relational potential, which allow individuals to find their place within a network. To make their proposed measure as applicable as possible to numerous situations, the authors have taken this simple example. A modestly sized group of firms (six) in a single sector, which establish formal relations (partnership agreements) to create an influential network in which each business adapts its status under the combined influence of the other firms: e.g. participating in a joint advertising campaign. In this situation, what is each business's relational strength within the network? How can it be measured simply? To give an example, consider Figure 4.

In Figure 4, the authors consider that relational strength (*RS*) in a finite network, for a firm or individual, is a "form" of social capital, which they suggest measuring in the following way:

$$\sum_q P_{iq} P_{qj}$$

where *AC* is the number of actual contacts, *ASC* the number of actual sub-contacts, *PC* the number of possible contacts (number of individuals in the network other than ego) and *PSC* the number of possible sub-contacts.

Figure 4.

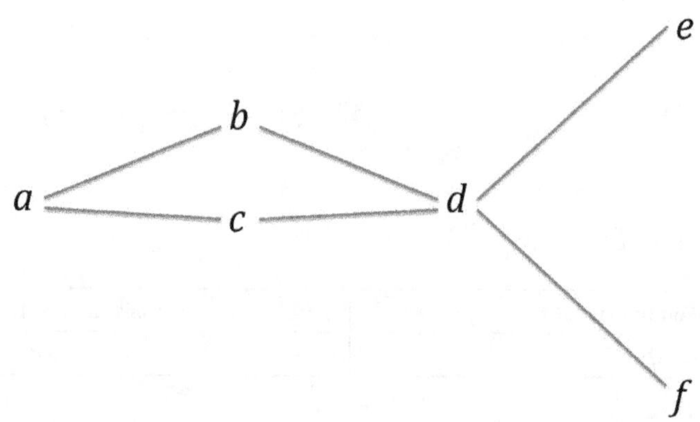

In this instance, the notion of possible sub-contacts is not the same as Lemieux's (1999) as the authors do not calculate them on the basis of the individual's actual contacts. Quantity $2 \times PC + PSC$ is therefore the same for each member of a given network and is used for consistency. However, the authors adapt the weighting already used by Lemieux (1999), which allows them to attach a heavier weighting to direct contacts than sub-contacts.

The data needed for this measurement is known to all managers and the calculation is straightforward. Let the authors specifically calculate the relational strength of individual d in the previous figure:

$$RS_d = \frac{2 \times AC_d + ASC_d}{2 \times PC + PSC} = \frac{2 \times 4 + 2}{2 \times 5 + 20} = 0.33$$

where:

$\sum_q P_{iq} P_{qj}$ number of actual contacts (number of direct contacts of *d*)

$AC_d = Card(\{b, c, e, f\}) = 4,$

$ASC_d =$ number of actual sub-contacts (number of neighbours (excluding d) of d's neighbours)

$ASC_d = Card(\{(b, a), (c, a)\}) = 2.$

Although individual *a* is the only sub-contact reached by *d*, he is counted twice as *a* is not only a contact of *b* but also a contact of *c*. With this calculation, the authors recognise the strength of the sub-contact (which is even greater as it is within reach of different contacts) and the compactness of the network.

$PC =$ number of possible contacts in the network (number of vertices excluding *d* (n-1))

$PC = Card(\{a, b, c, e, f\}) = 5,$

$PSC =$ number of possible sub-contacts in the network

$PSC = (n-1) \times (n-2) = 20.$

Of course, this relational strength can be formalised mathematically so that it can be generalised and programmed. Using graph theory, the authors deem a social network (or graph) to be a set of ties (individuals, firms) which are connected to each other by links (agreements, relations or edges). By definition, a graph comprises two series, *S* and *A*. *S* is all *s* vertices, and *A* all *a* edges (links between two vertices). It can be represented by a graph or matrix. A connection matrix is a square matrix where the lines and columns are ranked by vertex. The value 1 in position (*i,j*) means that there is an edge from the vertex i to the vertex j; the value 0 indicates that there isn't one. The table represents graph G such that $S=\{a,b,c,d,e,f\}$ and $A=\{\{a,b\},\{a,c\},\{b,d\},\{c,d\},\{d,e\},\{d,f\}\}$.

	a	b	c	d	e	f
a	0	1	1	0	0	0
b	1	0	0	1	0	0
c	1	0	0	1	0	0
d	0	1	1	0	1	1
e	0	0	0	1	0	0
f	0	0	0	1	0	0

From this table, the authors derive the following matrix:

$$M = \begin{pmatrix} 0 & 1 & 1 & 0 & 0 & 0 \\ 1 & 0 & 0 & 1 & 0 & 0 \\ 1 & 0 & 0 & 1 & 0 & 0 \\ 0 & 1 & 1 & 0 & 1 & 1 \\ 0 & 0 & 0 & 1 & 0 & 0 \\ 0 & 0 & 0 & 1 & 0 & 0 \end{pmatrix} = \left(a_{ij}\right), i = 1,\ldots,6, j = 1,\ldots,6.$$

For individual i,

$$AC_i = \sum_{j=1}^{6} a_{ij}.$$

To calculate ASC, the authors first consider the square matrix. This matrix gives them the number of sub-contacts between two individuals.

$$M^2 = \begin{pmatrix} 2 & 0 & 0 & 2 & 0 & 0 \\ 0 & 2 & 2 & 0 & 1 & 1 \\ 0 & 2 & 2 & 0 & 1 & 1 \\ 2 & 0 & 0 & 4 & 0 & 0 \\ 0 & 1 & 1 & 0 & 1 & 1 \\ 0 & 1 & 1 & 0 & 1 & 1 \end{pmatrix} = \left(b_{ij}\right), i = 1,\ldots,6, j = 1,\ldots,6.$$

The authors then calculate the value of individual i's ASC using this matrix:

$$ASC_i = \sum_{j \neq i, j=1}^{6} b_{ij}.$$

Using relational strength, the ranking between the members shown in Figure 4 is as identified in Table 7.

Considering the examples from the previous section, the results for the different figures can be summarised in Table 8.

The contradictions described previously do not appear with this indicator, which perfectly reflects the relative positions of each individual within his or her network.

An individual's or a firm's participation in a network largely depends on the relational strength of the contacts and sub-contacts. This is why the authors introduce a new indicator, "relational potential" (*RP*), to complete their study. This represents a weighted average of the relational strength of a person's contacts and sub-contacts. To clarify this point, the authors consider a new example of the network depicted in Figure 5.

The calculation of relational strength of individuals 1 and 2 determines that they are identical. Table 9 indicates the relational strength of individuals 1 and 2 in Figure 5.

However, individual 1 is clearly better connected to network members than individual 2 when contacts and sub-contacts are taken into account. To calculate the individuals' relational potential, the authors calculate the relational strength of all network members. Relational strength of all the network's members in Figure 5 is indicated in Table 10.

Table 7. Relational strength in Figure 4

Firm	Relational Strength
d	0.33
b and *c*	0.267
a	0.2
e and *f*	0.167

Table 8. Relational strength in Figures 1, 2 and 3

	RS of Individual 1	*RS* of Individual 2
Figure 1	0.089	0.125
Figure 2	0.08	0.11
Figure 3	0.5	0.55

Figure 5.

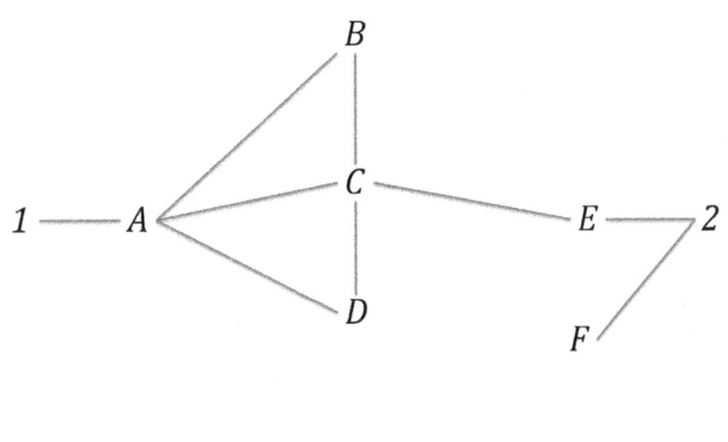

Table 9. Relational strength of individuals 1 and 2 in Figure 5

	Individual 1	Individual 2
AC	1	2
ASC	3	1
PC	7	7
PSC	42	42
Relational strength	0.089	0.089

Table 10. Relational strength of all the network's members in Figure 5

Individual	Relational Strength
C	0.25
A	0.23
B and *D*	0.178
E	0.1428
F	0.053

Individual 1's relational potential will therefore be:

$$RP_1 = \frac{2 \times RS_A + (RS_B + RS_C + RS_D)}{5} = 0.213$$

and individual 2's relational potential will be:

$$RP_2 = \frac{2 \times (RS_E + RS_F) + RS_C}{5} = 0.12.$$

Individual 1's relational potential is therefore greater than individual 2's: Individual 1's ties are better integrated in the network.

Although the relational potential formula is harder to write for general purposes, it is very easy to automate it with the help of a matrix tool.

The table associated with Figure 5 is as follows:

	1	A	B	C	D	E	F	2
1	0	1	0	0	0	0	0	0
A	1	0	1	1	1	0	0	0
B	0	1	0	1	0	0	0	0
C	0	1	1	0	1	1	0	0
D	0	1	0	1	0	0	0	0
E	0	0	0	1	0	0	0	1
F	0	0	0	0	0	0	0	1
2	0	0	0	0	0	1	1	0

The matrix associated with the figure is:

$$M = \begin{pmatrix} 0 & 1 & 0 & 0 & 0 & 0 & 0 & 0 \\ 1 & 0 & 1 & 1 & 1 & 0 & 0 & 0 \\ 0 & 1 & 0 & 1 & 0 & 0 & 0 & 0 \\ 0 & 1 & 1 & 0 & 1 & 1 & 0 & 0 \\ 0 & 1 & 0 & 1 & 0 & 0 & 0 & 0 \\ 0 & 0 & 0 & 1 & 0 & 0 & 0 & 1 \\ 0 & 0 & 0 & 0 & 0 & 0 & 0 & 1 \\ 0 & 0 & 0 & 0 & 0 & 1 & 1 & 0 \end{pmatrix} = \left(a_{ij}\right), i = 1,\ldots,8, j = 1,\ldots,8.$$

and therefore:

$$M^2 = \begin{pmatrix} 1 & 0 & 1 & 1 & 1 & 0 & 0 & 0 \\ 0 & 1 & 1 & 1 & 1 & 1 & 0 & 0 \\ 1 & 1 & 1 & 1 & 2 & 1 & 0 & 0 \\ 1 & 1 & 1 & 1 & 1 & 0 & 0 & 1 \\ 1 & 1 & 2 & 1 & 1 & 1 & 0 & 0 \\ 0 & 1 & 1 & 0 & 1 & 1 & 1 & 0 \\ 0 & 0 & 0 & 0 & 0 & 1 & 1 & 0 \\ 0 & 0 & 0 & 1 & 0 & 0 & 0 & 1 \end{pmatrix} = \left(b_{ij}\right), i = 1,\ldots,8, j = 1,\ldots,8.$$

Giving the following formula:

$$RP_i = \frac{2\sum_{j\neq i, j=1}^{8}\left(a_{ij} \times RS_j\right) + \sum_{j\neq i, j=1}^{8}\left(b_{ij} \times RS_j\right)}{2 \times AC_i + ASC_i}.$$

FUTURE RESEARCH AND DIRECTIONS

The authors' approach is interesting for a number of reasons. Firstly, it relies on a structural analysis in which the preferred unit of analysis is the tie itself, and the valuation of social capital can be interpreted and modelled.

The measures of relational strength and relational potential that the authors put forward carry several major advantages over other social capital measures. Firstly, even if prerequisite data is identical in some ways, the measure they propose is direct, unlike aggregate measures. Secondly, their calculation method is based on a matrix operation that is easy to apply in a basic spreadsheet; its source code is therefore free (open source) and follows current – especially French – recommendations on the development of free software for use by the authorities in particular (DISIC, 2012). Existing measures use software such as Ucinet (for different structural variables) and Pajeck (for Burt's constraint), or even software provided by consultants' firms, which have to be paid for and are closed source (it is impossible to access parts that would allow for correct use of the original mathematical formulas). Thirdly, it is more comprehensive as relational strength takes into account possible contacts and sub-contacts, whereas most other formulas only use actual contacts and sub-contacts, and relational potential introduces the relational characteristics of the contacts of the member in question. It is therefore a solid tool that, by correcting the other measures' faults, is more accessible.

And with the authors' proposal, relational strength, which assesses the scale of an actor's network (ego), can be fine-tuned. Indeed, it is entirely possible to use other structural indicators such as network size represented by the number of links (edges), network density or number of links relative to the maximum possible number (number of edges/maximum possible number of edges) and valuation of links. In this example, with point d as ego: size = 6, density = 0.4 and bridge = 1. The denser a network is, the narrower it will be and bridges will become essential. A "bridge" is an individual in an intermediate position between two different groups of participants. By measuring the tie between actors, relational strength gives an indication of close links and ultimately makes it possible to model them.

The authors' suggestion for direct measures of relational strength and relational potential should be attached to a corporate performance indicator that takes into account the firm's strategic choices. So by combining the proposed measures with variables such as profitability, sales growth and return on investment, it is possible to assess the firm's economic and/or financial health and answer the question about a possible link between social capital and business performance. However, there is a limitation: which performance indicator should be used? For this, it is obviously worth considering the firm's strategic goal. This is precisely what Westlund and Adam (2010) stress in a meta-analysis of 65 empirical studies on the link between social capital and economic performance published between 1993 and 2008. None of the 21 microeconomic articles use the same performance indicator. Some are qualitative (the firm's own opinion of its success in terms of competitiveness and performance, creating a new business, survival, innovation, etc.), others quantitative (growth in sales, profit margin, income per employee, value added, earnings, employment, market share, return on assets, market-to-book ratio, etc.). However, 18 of them reveal that social capital has a substantial positive impact on a corporate performance. So a positive correlation between the direct measure of relational strength presented in this article and any given variable of corporate performance can also be expected.

CONCLUSION

The aim of this chapter was to supplement existing work on the operationalisation of social capital. The authors have developed two additional measures, which they call relational strength and relational potential, taking into account not only the number of ties that an actor has but also the ties that could be had. This search for analytical meaning shows how the structure of a network offers competitive advantages to social actors. Indeed, understanding the creation and dynamics of networks is key to analysing the balance of strength in industry, which arises through a race for innovation. The economic applications of such work are numerous. They concern the innovation economy, shedding light on the spread of innovation in particular, as well as the industrial economy in exploring the very reasons for the formation of business-to-business relations. By way of illustration, as a proxy of social capital, trust is a way of cutting transaction costs by reducing the necessary amount of resources to prepare, execute and monitor contracts (Westlund and Adam, 2010). In this sense, it becomes a key notion for handling the boundaries of the firm, which are the subjects of fundamental research in industrial economics. Similarly, trust encourages informal news flows and knowledge sharing, facilitating the innovation process, especially in business networks. As innovation drives growth and competitiveness, confidence and cooperative behaviour contribute to business performance, which gives serious food for thought when considering the economics of innovation.

REFERENCES

Argyris, C. (2004). *Savoir pour agir.* Paris: Interéditions.

Arrègle, J. L., Durand, R. & Very, P. (2004). Origines du capital social et avantages concurrentiels des firmes familiales, *M@n@gement, 33*(1), 13-36.

Borgatti, S. P., Everett, M. G., & Freeman, L. C. (2002). *Ucinet 6 for windows. Software for social network analysis, user's guide.* Cambridge: Analytic Technologies.

Bouma, J., Bulte, E., & Van Soest, D. (2008). Trust and cooperation: Social capital and community resource management. *Journal of Environmental Economics and Management, 56*(2), 155–166. doi:10.1016/j.jeem.2008.03.004

Bourdieu, P., & Wacquant, L. (1992). *An invitation to reflexive sociology.* Chicago: University Of Chicago Press.

Bozionelos, N. (2003). Intra-organizational network resources: Relation to career success and personality. *The International Journal of Organizational Analysis, 11*(1), 41–66. doi:10.1108/eb028962

Bozionelos, N. (2008). Intra-organizational network resources: How they relate to career success and organizational commitment. *Personnel Review, 37*(3), 249–263. doi:10.1108/00483480810862251

Burt, R. S. (1992). *Structural holes: the social structure of competition.* Cambridge, MA: Harvard University Press.

Burt, R. S. (1995). Le capital social, les trous structuraux et lentrepreneur. *Revue Francaise de Sociologie, 36*(4), 599–628. doi:10.2307/3322448

Burt, R. S. (2005). *Brokerage and closure. An introduction to social capital.* New York: Oxford University Press.

Carpenter, J. P., Danière, A., & Takahashi, L. (2004). Cooperation, trust and social capital in Southeast Asian urban slums. *Journal of Economic Behavior & Organization, 55*(4), 533–551. doi:10.1016/j.jebo.2003.11.007

Carpenter, J. P., & Seki, E. (2005). *Do social preferences raise productivity? Field experimental evidence from fishermen in toyoma bay.* Iza Discussion Paper Series, 1697.

Carroll, W. K., & Alexander, M. (1999). Finance capital and capitalist class integration in the 1990s: Networks of interlocking directorships in Canada and Australia. *The Canadian Review of Sociology and Anthropology. La Revue Canadienne de Sociologie et d'Anthropologie*, *33*(3), 331–354.

Carter, M. R., & Castillo, M. (2002). *The altruism impact, trust and reciprocity: an experimental approach to social capital. Staff Paper 448.* Department Of Agricultural And Applied Economics, University Of Wisconsin-Madison.

Casanueva, C., & Gallego, A. (2010). Social capital and individual innovativeness in university research networks, *Innovation: Management. Policy & Practice*, *12*(1), 105–117. doi:10.5172/impp.12.1.105

Coleman, J. S. (1988). Social capital in the creation of human capital. *American Journal of Sociology*, *94*(Supplement), 95–120. doi:10.1086/228943

Dasgupta, P. (2003). Social capital and economic performance. In E. Ostrom & T.-K. Ahn (Eds.), *Critical writings in economic institutions: Foundations of social capital.* Cheltenham, UK: Edward Elgar.

Davis, G. F. (1991). Agents without principles? The spread of the poison pill through the incorporate network. *Administrative Science Quarterly*, *36*(4), 583–613. doi:10.2307/2393275

De Carolis, D. & Saparito, P. (2006, January). Social capital, cognition and entrepreneurial opportunities: a theoretical framework. *Entrepreneurship Theory and Practice*, 41-56.

Disic (Direction Interministérielle Des Systèmes d'information Et De Communication). (2012). *Usage Du Logiciel Libre Dans l'administration*. Author.

Dumoulin, R., & Lecocq, X. (2001). Du paradigme transactionnel a l'analyse multi-niveaux en sciences de gestion? Une application aux réseaux interorganisationnels. In *Perspectives en Management Stratégique*. Paris: Editions EMS.

Frank, K., & Yasumoto, J. (1998). Linking action to social structure within a system: Social capital within and between subgroups. *American Journal of Sociology*, *104*(3), 642–686. doi:10.1086/210083

Granovetter, M. S. (1973). The strength of weak ties. *American Journal of Sociology*, *78*(6), 1360–1380. doi:10.1086/225469

Häuberer, J. (2011). *Social capital theory*. Springer Fachmedien. doi:10.1007/978-3-531-92646-9

Haunschild, P. R. (1993). Interorganizational imitation: The impact of interlocks on corporate acquisition activity. *Administrative Science Quarterly*, *38*(4), 564–592. doi:10.2307/2393337

Huault, I. (2004). Une analyse des reseaux sociaux est-elle utile pour le management? Puissance et limites d'une theorie de l'encastrement structural. In Institutions Et Gestion.

Kikuchi, M., & Coleman, C. L. (2012). Explicating and measuring social relationships in social capital research. *Communication Theory*, *22*(2), 187–203. doi:10.1111/j.1468-2885.2012.01401.x

Landry, R., Amara, N., & Lamari, M. (2000). Does social capital determine innovation? To what extent? *4th International Conference On Technology Policy And Innovation*.

Lemieux, V. (1999). *Les réseaux d'acteurs sociaux*. Paris: PUF.

Lévesque, M. (2000). *Le capital social comme forme sociale de capital: reconstruction d'un quasi-concept et application à l'analyse de la sortie de l'aide sociale.* (PhD Thesis). Faculté des études supérieures, Université de Montréal.

Lévesque, M. & White, D. (1999). Le concept de capital social et ses usages. *Liens social et politiques, 41*, 23-33.

Lévesque, M., White, D., & Levesque, M. (2001). Capital social, capital humain et sortie de laide sociale pour les prestataires de longue durée. *Canadian Journal of Sociology, 26*(2), 167–192. doi:10.2307/3341677

Lin, N. (1995). Les ressources sociales: Une théorie du capital social. *Revue Francaise de Sociologie, 36*(4), 685–704. doi:10.2307/3322451

Lin, N. (2001). *Social capital: a theory of social structure and action.* New York: Cambridge University Press. doi:10.1017/CBO9780511815447

Lin, N., Cook, K., & Burt, R. (2001). *Social capital: Theory and research.* Transactions Publishers. doi:10.1017/CBO9780511815447

Lorrain, F., & White, H. (1971). Structural equivalence of individuals in social networks. *The Journal of Mathematical Sociology, 1*(1), 49–80. doi:10.1080/0022250X.1971.9989788

Maurer, I., & Ebers, M. (2006). Dynamics of social capital and their performance implications: Lessons from biotechnology start-ups. *Administrative Science Quarterly, 51*(2), 262–292. doi:10.2189/asqu.51.2.262

Mercklé, M. (2004). *Sociologie des réseaux sociaux.* Paris: La Découverte.

Mizruchi, M. (1993). Cohesion, equivalence, and similarity of behaviour: A theoretical and empirical assessment. *Social Networks, 15*(3), 275–307. doi:10.1016/0378-8733(93)90009-A

Mizruchi, M., & Marquis, C. (2006). Egocentric, sociocentric or dyadic? Identifying the appropriate level of analysis in the study of organizational networks. *Social Networks, 28*(3), 187–208. doi:10.1016/j.socnet.2005.06.002

Moore, S., Bockenholt, U., Daniel, M., Frohlich, K., Kestens, Y., & Richard, L. (2011). Social capital and core network ties: A validation study of individual-level social capital measures and their association with extra and intra-neighborhood ties and self-rated health. *Health & Place, 17*(2), 536–544. doi:10.1016/j.healthplace.2010.12.010 PMID:21208822

Petersen, D. (2002). The potential of social capital measures in the evaluation of comprehensive community-based health initiatives. *The American Journal of Evaluation, 23*(1), 55–64. doi:10.1177/109821400202300106

Ponthieux, S. (2004). *Le concept de capital social, Analyse critique.* 10th ACN Conference, Paris, France.

Prashantham, S. (2005). *Social capital and the international growth of young firms: A temporal perspective.* Working Paper. University of Strathclyde.

Putnam, R. (1995). Bowling alone: Americas declining social capital. *Journal of Democracy, 6*(1), 65–78. doi:10.1353/jod.1995.0002

Thorelli, H. (1986). Networks, between markets and hierarchies. *Strategic Management Journal*, *7*(1), 37–51. doi:10.1002/smj.4250070105

Thurman, B. (1979). In the office: Networks and coalitions. *Social Networks*, *2*(1), 47–63. doi:10.1016/0378-8733(79)90010-8

Tzanakis, M. (2013). Social capital in Bourdieu's, Coleman's and Putnam's theory: Empirical evidence and emergent measurement issues. *Educate*, *13*(2), 2–23.

Villalonga-Olives, E., & Kawachi, I. (2015). The measurement of bridging social capital in population health research. *Health & Place*, *36*, 47–56. doi:10.1016/j.healthplace.2015.09.002 PMID:26409896

Von Peter, G. (2007, December). International banking centres: A network perspective. *BIS Quarterly Review*, 33-45.

Walker, G., Kogut, B., & Shan, W. (1997). Social capital, structural holes and the formation of an industry network. *Organization Science*, *8*(2), 109–125. doi:10.1287/orsc.8.2.109

Westlund, H., & Adam, F. (2010). Social capital and economic performance: A meta- analysis of 65 studies. *European Planning Studies*, *18*(6), 893–919. doi:10.1080/09654311003701431

Wincent, J., Thorgren, S., & Anokhin, S. (2016). Costly ties: Social capital as a retardant of network-level entrepreneurial orientation. *Journal of Small Business Management*, *54*(1), 229–243. doi:10.1111/jsbm.12140

Compilation of References

Abdulmalek, F. A., & Rajgopal, J. (2007). Analyzing the benefits of lean manufacturing and value stream mapping via simulation: A process sector case study. *International Journal of Production Economics*, *107*(1), 223–236. doi:10.1016/j.ijpe.2006.09.009

Abraham, K. G., & Katz, L. F. (1984). *Cyclical Unemployment: Sectoral Shifts or Agregate Disturbances?* National Bureau of Economic Research Cambridge, Working Paper No. 1410.

Acemoglu, D., Johnson, S., & Robinson, J. (2001). The Colonial Origins of Comparative Development: An Empirical Investigation. *The American Economic Review*, *91*(5), 1369–1401. doi:10.1257/aer.91.5.1369

Agarwal, H., Renaud, E. J., Preston, L. E., & Padmanabhan, D. (2004). Uncertainty quantification using evidence theory in multidisciplinary design optimization. *Reliability Engineering & System Safety*, *85*(1-3), 281–294. doi:10.1016/j.ress.2004.03.017

Agenor, P., & da Silva, L. (2011). *Macroprudential Regulation and the Monetary Transmission Mechanism.* Working Papers Series 254. Central Bank of Brazil, Research Department.

Ahmed, P. K. (2011). *Innovative management: Context, strategies, systems, and processes.* Upper Saddle River, NJ: Prentice Hall.

Akbar, M., & Naqvi, Z. (2000). Export diversification and the structural dynamics in the growth process: The case of Pakistan. *Pakistan Development Review*, *39*(4), 573–589.

Akincilar, A., Temiz, I., & Sahin, E. (2011). An application of exchange rate forecasting in Turkey. *Gazi University Journal of Science*, *24*(4), 817–828.

Alesina, A. (1998). The Political Economy of High and Low Growth.*Annual World Bank Conference on Development Economics 1997.* Washington DC: World Bank.

Allais, M. (1956, January). Évaluation des perspectives économiques de la recherche minière sur de grands espaces - application au Sahara Algérien. Revue de l'Industrie Minérale, 329-383.

Allen, F., Carletti, E., & Gale, D. (2009). Interbank market liquidity and central bank intervention. *Journal of Monetary Economics*, *56*(5), 639–652. doi:10.1016/j.jmoneco.2009.04.003

American Institute of Chemical Engineers (AIChE). (2000). Guidelines for chemical process quantitative risk analysis (2nd ed.). New York: AIChE.

Amihud, Y., & Mendelson, H. (1980). Dealership market. *Journal of Financial Economics*, *8*(1), 31–35. doi:10.1016/0304-405X(80)90020-3

Amihud, Y., & Mendelson, H. (1986). Asset pricing and the bid-ask spread. *Journal of Financial Economics*, *17*(2), 223–249. doi:10.1016/0304-405X(86)90065-6

Amihud, Y., & Mendelson, H. (1991). Liquidity, maturity and the yields on US government securities. *The Journal of Finance*, *46*(4), 1411–1426. doi:10.1111/j.1540-6261.1991.tb04623.x

Amihud, Y., & Mendelson, H. (2003). The liquidity route to a lower cost of capital. In J. M. Stern & D. H. Chew Jr., (Eds.), *The revolution in corporate finance* (pp. 70–88). Blackwell Publishing.

Amiri, A., & Gerdtham, G. (2011). *Relationship between exports, imports and economic growth in France: evidence from cointegration analysis and Granger causality with using geostatistical models. MPRA Paper nº 34190*. University Library of Munich.

Anđelković Pešić, M. (2006). Process and Project Management–Two Sides of Six Sigma Medal. *Economic Themes*, *44*(6), 111–120.

Anđelković Pešić, M. (2009). Quality Function Deployment as a Tool for The Improvement of Value Proposal in High Education. *Facta Universitatis. Series Economics and Organization*, *6*(2), 185–198.

Anderson, J. H. (2009). *A Review of Governance and Anticorruption Indicators in East Asia and Pacific*. World Bank.

Andrade, J. S., Duarte, A., & Simões, M. (2014). A Quantile Regression Analysis of Growth and Convergence in the EU: Potential Implications for Portugal. *Notas Económicas*, *39*(39), 48–70. doi:10.14195/2183-203X_39_3

Angelidis, P. (2007). Shellfish culture in estuary zones and the sanitary restrictions. *Scientific Annals of the Danube Delta Institute*, *13*, 161–174.

Angkinand, A., & Wihlborg, C. (2005). *Deposit insurance coverage, credibility of non-insurance and banking crisis*. Center for Law, Economics and Financial Institutions at CBS (LEFIC), Copenhagen Business School, Working Paper, (2005-010).

Antony, J. (2002). Design for Six Sigma: A Breakthrough Business Improvement Strategy for Achieving Competitive Advantage. *Work Study*, *51*(1), 6–8. doi:10.1108/00438020210415460

Antony, J. (2004). Six Sigma in the UK service organisations: Results from a pilot survey. *Managerial Auditing Journal*, *19*(8), 1006–1013. doi:10.1108/02686900410557908

Argenti, P. (2004). It Pays to Talk Right: The Power and Influence o Corporate Communication. In J. Kurtzman, G. Rifkin, & V. Griffith (Eds.), *MBA in a box: practical ideas from the best brain in business*. New York: Crown Business.

Argenti, P. (2006). Communications and business value: Measuring the link. *The Journal of Business Strategy*, *27*(6), 29–40. doi:10.1108/02756660610710337

Argenti, P. A. (2009). *Corporate communication* (5th ed.). New York, NY: McGraw-Hill Irwin.

Argenti, P., & Formani, J. (2005). How Corporate Communication Influence Strategy Implementation, Reputation and the Corporate Brand: An Exploratory Qualitative Study. *Corporate Communication Review*, *8*(3), 245–264.

Argyris, C. (2004). *Savoir pour agir*. Paris: Interéditions.

Arndt, C. & Oman, C. (2006). *Uses and Abuses of Governance Indicators*. OECD Development Center Study.

Arnold, J. (2015). *Boosting export performance in Portugal*. OECD Economics Department Working Papers, No. 1257. OECD Publishing.

Arrègle, J. L., Durand, R. & Very, P. (2004). Origines du capital social et avantages concurrentiels des firmes familiales, *M@n@gement, 33*(1), 13-36.

Arsham, H. (1987). A Stochastic Model of Optimal Advertising Pulsing Policy. *Computers & Operations Research, 14*(3), 231–239. doi:10.1016/0305-0548(87)90026-8

Arsham, H. (1993). A Markovian Model of Consumer Buying Behavior and Optimal Advertising Pulsing Policy. *Computers & Operations Research, 20*(2), 35–48. doi:10.1016/0305-0548(93)90094-Y

Asness, S. C. (1995). *The power of past stock returns to explain future stock returns.* Working paper. Goldman Sachs Asset Management.

Aviad, B., & Roy, G. A. (2012). Decision support method, based on bounded rationality concepts, to reveal feature saliency in clustering problems. *Decision Support Systems, 54*(1), 292–303. doi:10.1016/j.dss.2012.05.037

Ayyub, B., & Klir, J. G. (2006). *Uncertainty modeling and analysis in engineering and the sciences.* New York: Chapman & Hall. doi:10.1201/9781420011456

Bae, H., Grandhi, V. R., & Canfield, A. R. (2004). An approximation approach for uncertainty quantification using evidence theory. *Reliability Engineering & System Safety, 86*(3), 215–225. doi:10.1016/j.ress.2004.01.011

Bahri, M. (2011). *Six Sigma project selections by using a Multi-criteria Decision making approach: a Case study in Poly Acryl Corp.* Retrieved from: http://www.usc.edu/dept/ ise/caie/Checked%20Papers%20%5Bruhi%2012th%20sept%5D/word%20format%20papers/REGISTRATION%20PAID%20PAPERS%20FOR%20PROCEEDINGS/pdf/1554%23QJ3.PDF

Baillie, R. T., Bollerslev, T., & Mikkelsen, H. O. (1996). Fractionally integrated generalized autoregressive conditional heteroskedasticity. *Journal of Econometrics, 74*(1), 3–30. doi:10.1016/S0304-4076(95)01749-6

Baker, K. M. (2013). Decision Making in a Hybrid Organization: A Case Study of a Southwestern Drug Court Treatment Program. *Law & Social Inquiry, 38*(1), 27–54. doi:10.1111/j.1747-4469.2012.01295.x

Balassa, B. (1978). Exports and Economic Growth: Further Evidence. *Journal of Development Economics, 5*(2), 181–189. doi:10.1016/0304-3878(78)90006-8

Banuelas, R., & Antony, J. (2002). Critical success factors for the successful implementation of six sigma projects in organizations. *The TQM Magazine, 14*(2), 92–99. doi:10.1108/09544780210416702

Banuelas, R., & Antony, J. (2003). Going from six sigma to design for six sigma: An exploratory study using analytic hierarchy process. *The TQM Magazine, 15*(5), 334–344. doi:10.1108/09544780310487730

Banuelas, R., Tennant, C., Tuersley, I., & Tang, S. (2006). Selection of Six Sigma projects in the UK. *The TQM Magazine, 18*(5), 514–527. doi:10.1108/09544780610685485

Barnett, K., & Harder, S. (2014). *Remedies in Australian Private Law.* Cambridge University Press.

Barnichon, R., Elsby, M., Hobijn, B., & Sahin, A. (2011). *Which Industries are Shifting the Beveridge Curve.* Federal Reserve Bank of San Francisco, Working Paper No. 2010-32.

Bassett, W. F., Lee, S. J., & Spiller, T. W. (2012). *Estimating changes in supervisory standards and their economic effects.* Federal Reserve Board, Finance and Economics Discussion Series (FEDS).

Baxter, N. D. (1967). Leverage, risk of ruin and the cost of capital. *The Journal of Finance, 22*(3), 395–403.

Ben-Haim, Y. (2001). *Information-gap Decision Theory: Decisions under Severe Uncertainty*. San Diego, CA: Academic Press.

Benigno, G., Chen, H., Otrok, C., Rebucci, A., & Young, E. (2012). Financial crises and macro-prudential policies. *Journal of International Economics*, *89*(2), 453–470. doi:10.1016/j.jinteco.2012.06.002

Bernstein, P. L. (1996). *Against the Gods: The remarkable story of risk*. New York: John Wiley & Sons.

Bhatnagar, P. (2004). *Sad day at McDonald's*. Retrieved from CNN Money: http://money.cnn.com/2004/04/19/news/fortune500/mcdonalds_ceo/index.htm?iid=EL

Bilić, I. (2011). *Međuovisnost strateškog pozicioniranja korporativnog komunikaciranja, reputacije i organizacijskih performansi poduzeća*. (Unpublished doctoral dissertation). University of Split, Faculty of Economics, Split, Croatia.

Black, F., Jensen, M., & Scholes, M. (1792). *The Capital Asset Pricing Model: Some Empirical Tests*. Praeger Publishers: Studies in The Theory of Capital Markets. Retrieved June 2, 2014, from http://ssrn.com/abstract=908569

Black, F. (1972). Capital market equilibrium with restricted borrowing. *The Journal of Business*, *45*(3), 444–455. doi:10.1086/295472

Black, F., & Scholes, M. (1973, May - June). The pricing of options and corporate liabilities. *Journal of Political Economy*, *81*(3), 637–654. doi:10.1086/260062

Blair, A. R., Nachtmann, R., Olson, J. E., & Saaty, T. L. (1987). Forecasting foreign exchange rates: An expert judgment approach. *Socio-Economic Planning Sciences*, *21*(6), 363–369. doi:10.1016/0038-0121(87)90010-3

Blair, A. R., Nachtmann, R., Saaty, T. L., & Whitaker, R. (2002). Forecasting the resurgence of the US economy in 2001: An expert judgment approach. *Socio-Economic Planning Sciences*, *44*(3), 114–121. doi:10.1016/j.seps.2010.03.002

Blanchard, O. J., Diamond, P., Hall, R. E., & Murphy, K. (1990). The Cyclical Behavior of the Gross Flows of U.S. Workers. *Brookings Papers on Economic Activity*, *1990*(2), 85–143. doi:10.2307/2534505

Bloomberg Businessweek. (2015). *The Prologue - The Lifespan of a Company*. Retrieved September 21, 2015 from http://www.businessweek.com/chapter/degeus.htm

Bollerslev, T. (1986). Generalized autoregressive conditional heteroskedasticity. *Journal of Econometrics*, *31*(3), 307–327. doi:10.1016/0304-4076(86)90063-1

Bollerslev, T., & Wright, J. H. (2001). High-frequency data, frequency domain inference, and volatility forecasting. *The Review of Economics and Statistics*, *83*(4), 596–602. doi:10.1162/003465301753237687

Booth, J. R. (1992). Contract costs, bank loans, and the cross-monitoring hypothesis. *Journal of Financial Economics*, *31*(1), 25–41. doi:10.1016/0304-405X(92)90010-U

Borgatti, S. P., Everett, M. G., & Freeman, L. C. (2002). *Ucinet 6 for windows. Software for social network analysis, user's guide*. Cambridge: Analytic Technologies.

Borges, A. R., & Antunes, C. H. (2003). A fuzzy multiple objective decision support model for energy-economy planning. *European Journal of Operational Research*, *145*(2), 304–316. doi:10.1016/S0377-2217(02)00536-2

Bošković, G., Janković Milić, V., & Anđelković Pešić, M. (2011). Possibilities of Cusum Chart Implementation in Statistical Process Control. In *Proceedings from XI International conference Research and Development in Mechanical Industry (RaDMI 2011)*. Soko Banja, Serbia: SaTCIP.

Bouma, J., Bulte, E., & Van Soest, D. (2008). Trust and cooperation: Social capital and community resource management. *Journal of Environmental Economics and Management*, *56*(2), 155–166. doi:10.1016/j.jeem.2008.03.004

Bourdieu, P., & Wacquant, L. (1992). *An invitation to reflexive sociology*. Chicago: University Of Chicago Press.

Box, G. E. P., & Jenkins, G. M. (1976). *Time Series Analysis: Forecasting and Control*. San Francisco: Holden Day.

Bozionelos, N. (2003). Intra-organizational network resources: Relation to career success and personality. *The International Journal of Organizational Analysis*, *11*(1), 41–66. doi:10.1108/eb028962

Bozionelos, N. (2008). Intra-organizational network resources: How they relate to career success and organizational commitment. *Personnel Review*, *37*(3), 249–263. doi:10.1108/00483480810862251

Brainard, L. S., & Cutler, D. M. (1990). *Sectoral Shifts and Cyclical Unemployment Reconsider.* National Bureau of Economic Research Cambridge Working Paper No. 3491.

Brandl, B., Keber, C., & Schuster, M. G. (2006). An automated econometric decision support system: Forecasts for foreign exchange trades. *Central European Journal of Operations Research*, *14*(4), 401–415. doi:10.1007/s10100-006-0013-8

Braun, H., De Bock, R., & DiCecio, R. (2006). *Aggregate Shocks and Labor Market Fluctuations*. Federal Reserve Bank of St. Louis Working Paper No. 2006-004A.

Braun, H., De Bock, R., & DiCecio, R. (2007). *Supply Shocks, Demand Shocks, and Labor Market Fluctuations*. Federal Reserve Bank of St. Louis Working Paper No. 2007-015A.

Breeden, T. D. (1979). An intertemporal asset pricing model with stochastic consumption and investment opportunities. *Journal of Financial Economics*, *7*(3), 265–296. doi:10.1016/0304-405X(79)90016-3

Brennan, M. J. (1970). Taxes, Market Valuation and Corporation Financial Policy. *National Tax Journal*, *23*(4). Retrieved from http://www.albany.edu/faculty/faugere/PhDcourse/BrennanCAPM.pdf

Brown, R. G. (1963). *Smoothing, forecasting and prediction of discrete time series*. Englewood Cliffs: Prentice-Hall.

Brue, G. (2002). *Six Sigma for Managers*. New York, NY: McGraw-Hill.

Bunn, D. W., & Paschentis, S. N. (1996). Development of a stochastic model for the economic despatch of electric power. *European Journal of Operational Research*, *27*(2), 179–191. doi:10.1016/0377-2217(86)90059-7

Burson-Marsteller. (2013). *Crisis Survey 2013*. Retrieved from http://www.burson-marsteller.com/wp-content/uploads/2014/07/2013-BM-EMEA-Crisis-survey-results.pdf

Burt, R. S. (1992). *Structural holes: the social structure of competition*. Cambridge, MA: Harvard University Press.

Burt, R. S. (1995). Le capital social, les trous structuraux et l'entrepreneur. *Revue Francaise de Sociologie*, *36*(4), 599–628. doi:10.2307/3322448

Burt, R. S. (2005). *Brokerage and closure. An introduction to social capital*. New York: Oxford University Press.

Calderón, C., & Chong, A. (2000). Causality and Feedback between Institutional Measures and Economic Growth. *Economics and Politics*, *12*(1), 69–81. doi:10.1111/1468-0343.00069

Campbell, Y. J. (1993). Intertemporal asset pricing without consumption data. *The American Economic Review*, *83*(3), 487–512.

Čámský, F. (2007). *Určení optimálního portfolia*. Retrieved May 5, 2014, from www.derivat.sk/files/2007%20jan-jun/HotJan2007Camsky2.doc

Cardoso, F., Esteves, P. S., & Rua, A. (2013, Autumn). The import content of global demand in Portugal. *Banco de Portugal Economic Bulletin*, 107-121

Carpenter, J. P., & Seki, E. (2005). *Do social preferences raise productivity? Field experimental evidence from fishermen in toyoma bay.* Iza Discussion Paper Series, 1697.

Carpenter, J. P., Danière, A., & Takahashi, L. (2004). Cooperation, trust and social capital in Southeast Asian urban slums. *Journal of Economic Behavior & Organization*, *55*(4), 533–551. doi:10.1016/j.jebo.2003.11.007

Carroll, W. K., & Alexander, M. (1999). Finance capital and capitalist class integration in the 1990s: Networks of interlocking directorships in canada and australia. *The Canadian Review of Sociology and Anthropology. La Revue Canadienne de Sociologie et d'Anthropologie*, *33*(3), 331–354.

Carter, M. R., & Castillo, M. (2002). *The altruism impact, trust and reciprocity: an experimental approach to social capital. Staff Paper 448.* Department Of Agricultural And Applied Economics, University Of Wisconsin-Madison.

Casanueva, C., & Gallego, A. (2010). Social capital and individual innovativeness in university research networks, *Innovation: Management,Policy & Practice*, *12*(1), 105–117. doi:10.5172/impp.12.1.105

Cashin, P. A., & Duttagupta, R. (2008). *The anatomy of banking crises.* IMF Working Papers.

Chang, C. W., Wu, C. R., & Chen, H. C. (2008). Using expert technology to select unstable slicing machine to control wafer slicing quality via fuzzy AHP. *Expert Systems with Applications*, *34*(3), 2210–2220. doi:10.1016/j.eswa.2007.02.042

Cheng, Y. (2000). Uncertainties in fault tree analysis. *Tamkang Journal of Science and Engineering*, *3*(1), 23–29.

Chen, Z., Chen, W., Chen, Q., & Chen, M. (2006). Trend Relational Analysis and Grey-Fuzzy Clustering Method. *Proceedings of the 2006 SIAM International Conference on Data Mining*, (pp. 234-245). doi:10.1137/1.9781611972764.21

Chevreau, F. R., Wybo, J. L., & Cauchois, D. (2006). Organizing learning processes on risks by using the bow-tie representation. *Journal of Hazardous Materials*, *130*(3), 276–283. doi:10.1016/j.jhazmat.2005.07.018 PMID:16125315

Chordia, T., Roll, R., & Subrahmanyam, A. (2000). Commonality in liquidity. *Journal of Financial Economics*, *56*(1), 3–28. doi:10.1016/S0304-405X(99)00057-4

Christiano, L. J., Eichenbaum, M. S., & Trabandt, M. (2013). *Unemployment and Business Cycles.* National Bureau of Economic Research Cambridge Working Paper No. 19265.

Christiano, L. J., Eichenbaum, M. S., & Trabandt, M. (2014). *Understanding the Great Recession.* National Bureau of Economic Research Cambridge Working Paper No. 20040.

Christiano, L. J., Trabandt, M., & Walentin, K. (2010). *Involuntary Unemployment and the Business Cycle.* National Bureau of Economic Research Cambridge Working Paper No. 15901.

Chuang, Y. (1998). Learning by doing, the technology gap, and growth. *International Economic Review*, *39*(3), 697–721. doi:10.2307/2527396

Chu, F. L. (2009). Forecasting tourism demand with ARMA-based methods. *Tourism Management*, *30*(5), 740–751. doi:10.1016/j.tourman.2008.10.016

CMPT. (1999). *A guide to quantitative risk assessment for offshore installation.* The Centre of Marine and Petroleum Technology.

Coase, R. H. (1960). The problem of social cost. *The Journal of Law & Economics*, *3*, 1–43. doi:10.1086/466560

Cockshott, J. E. (2005). Probability bow-ties: A transparent risk management tool. *Process Safety and Environmental Protection*, *83*(4B4), 307–316. doi:10.1205/psep.04380

Cohen, K., & Pogue, J. (1968). *Some Comments Concerning Mutual Fund Vs. Random Portfolio Performance.* Sloan School of Management. Retrieved May 15, 2014, from http://dspace.mit.edu/bitstream/handle/1721.1/49022/somecommentsconc00cohe.pdf

Cohen, K., Maier, S., Schwartz, R., & Whitcomb, D. (1981). Transaction costs, order placement strategy, and existance of the bid–ask spread. *Journal of Political Economy*, *89*(2), 287–305. doi:10.1086/260966

Coleman, J. S. (1988). Social capital in the creation of human capital. *American Journal of Sociology*, *94*(Supplement), 95–120. doi:10.1086/228943

Copeland, T., & Galai, D. (1983). Information effects on the bid–ask spread. *The Journal of Finance*, *38*(5), 1457–1469. doi:10.1111/j.1540-6261.1983.tb03834.x

Corvers, F., & Dupuy, A. (2009). *Estimating Employment Dynamics across Occupations and Sectors of Industry.* IZA Bonn Discussion Paper Series No. 4428.

Covello, V., & Mumpower, J. (1985). Risk Analysis and Risk Management: An Historical Perspective. *Risk Analysis*, *5*(2), 103–120. doi:10.1111/j.1539-6924.1985.tb00159.x

Cuaresma, C. J., & Worz, J. (2005). On Export Composition and Growth. *Review of World Economics. Weltwirtschaftliches Archiv*, *141*(1), 33–49. doi:10.1007/s10290-005-0014-z

Cui, J., Dang, Y., & Liu, S. (2009). Study on Novel Property of Some Grey Relational Analysis Models. *Journal of Grey System*, *12*(2), 83–88.

Damodaran, A. (2011). *The Little Book of Valuation: How to Value a Company, Pick a Stock and Profit.* John Wiley & Sons.

Dasgupta, P. (2003). Social capital and economic performance. In E. Ostrom & T.-K. Ahn (Eds.), *Critical writings in economic institutions: Foundations of social capital*. Cheltenham, UK: Edward Elgar.

Davidson, P. (2002). *Financial markets, money, and the real world.* Cheltenham, UK: Edward Elgar Publishing. doi:10.4337/9781843765585

Davis, S. J., Faberman, J. R., & Haltiwanger, J. (2006). *The Flow Approach to Labor Markets: New Data Sources and Micro-Macro Links*. National Bureau of Economic Research Cambridge Working Paper No. 12167.

Davis, S. J., Faberman, J., & Haltiwanger, J. C. (2011). *Labor Market Flows in the Cross Section and Over Time*. National Bureau of Economic Research Cambridge Working Paper No. 17294.

Davis, G. F. (1991). Agents without principles? The spread of the poison pill through the incorporate network. *Administrative Science Quarterly*, *36*(4), 583–613. doi:10.2307/2393275

De Carolis, D. & Saparito, P. (2006, January). Social capital, cognition and entrepreneurial opportunities: a theoretical framework. *Entrepreneurship Theory and Practice*, 41-56.

De Feo, J., & Bar-Ei, Z. (2002). Creating Strategic Change More Efficiently with a New Design for Six Sigma Process. *Journal of Change Management*, *3*(1), 60–81. doi:10.1080/714042521

de Walque, G., Pierrard, O., & Rouabah, A. (2010). Financial (In)Stability, Supervision and Liquidity Injections: A Dynamic General Equilibrium Approach. *Revue Economique et Sociale*, *120*(549), 1234–1261.

DeBondt, F. M. W., & Thaler, R. (1985). Does the stock market overreact. *The Journal of Finance*, *40*(3), 793–805. doi:10.1111/j.1540-6261.1985.tb05004.x

Delavari, H., Bandara, W., Marjanovic, O., & Mathiesen, P. (2010). Business Process Management (BPM) education in Australia: A critical review based on content analysis. In *Proceedings of the 21st Australasian conference on information systems (ACIS2010)*. Brisbane, Australia: Queensland University of Technology.

Delis, M. D., & Staikouras, P. K. (2011). Supervisory Effectiveness and Bank Risk. *Review of Finance*, *15*(3), 511–543. doi:10.1093/rof/rfq035

Deloitte. (2014). *2014 global survey on reputation risk*. Deloitte Touche Tohmatsu.

Dembitz, J. (1987). A specialist view of corporate communications. *Director (Cincinnati, Ohio)*, *41*(4), 129–130.

Diamond, D. W. (1984). Financial intermediation and delegated monitoring. *The Review of Economic Studies*, *51*(3), 393–414. doi:10.2307/2297430

Dianous, V., & Fiévez, C. (2006). ARAMIS project: A more explicit demonstration of risk control through the use of bowetie diagrams and the evaluation of safety barrier performance. *Journal of Hazardous Materials*, *130*(3), 220–233. doi:10.1016/j.jhazmat.2005.07.010 PMID:16107301

Dickey, D., & Fuller, W. (1979). Distribution of the Estimators for Time Series Regressions with a Unit Root. *Journal of the American Statistical Association*, *74*(366), 427–431. doi:10.2307/2286348

Dickson, J., & Einstein, A. (2010). On measures for illustrating credit risk assessments: The case of heat maps, risk matrices and cubes. *IFC Bulletin*, *25*, 365.

Disic (Direction Interministérielle Des Systèmes d'information Et De Communication). (2012). *Usage Du Logiciel Libre Dans l'administration*. Author.

Dismukes, D. E., & Christopher, P. P. (2011). *Diversifying energy industry risk in the GOM*. Retrieved from http://www.gom.gov.de/div/enrg.pdf

Doan, T., Litterman, R., & Sims, C. (1984). Forecasting and Conditional Projection Using Realistic Prior Distributions. *Econometric Reviews*, *3*(1), 1–100. doi:10.1080/07474938408800053

Dolphin, R. R. (2003). The corporate communication function: How well it is founded. *Corporate Communications: An International Journal*, *8*(1), 5–10. doi:10.1108/13563280310458867

Dolphin, R. R. (2004). Corporate reputation – a value creating strategy. *Corporate Governance*, *4*(3), 77–92. doi:10.1108/14720700410547521

Duijm, N. J. (2009). Safety-barrier diagrams as a safety management tool. *Reliability Engineering & System Safety*, *94*(2), 332–341. doi:10.1016/j.ress.2008.03.031

Dumoulin, R., & Lecocq, X. (2001). Du paradigme transactionnel a l'analyse multi-niveaux en sciences de gestion? Une application aux réseaux interorganisationnels. In *Perspectives en Management Stratégique*. Paris: Editions EMS.

Dutt, S. D., & Ghosh, D. (1994). An Empirical Investigation of the Export Growth – Economic Growth Relationship. *Applied Economics Letters*, *1*(3), 44–48. doi:10.1080/135048594358285

Easley, D., & O'Hara, M. (1992). Adverse selection and large trade volume: The implications for market efficiency. *Journal of Financial and Quantitative Analysis*, *27*(2), 185–208. doi:10.2307/2331367

Economou, V., Papadopoulou, C., Brett, M., Kansouzidou, A., Charalabopoulos, K., Filioussis, G., & Seferiadis, K. (2007). Diarrheic shellfish poisoning due to toxic mussel consumption: The first recorded outbreak in Greece. *Food Additives and Contaminants*, *24*(3), 297–305. doi:10.1080/02652030601053139 PMID:17364933

Ehrgott, M. (2011). *Trends in multiple criteria decision analysis*. New York, NY: Springer.

Einset, E., & Marzano, J. (2002). Six Sigma Demystified. *Quality in Manufacturing*, *13*(12), 43–47.

El Shazy, M. R., & El Shazy, H. E. (1997). Comparing the forecasting performance of neural networks and forward exchange rates. *Journal of Multinational Financial Management*, *7*(4), 345–356. doi:10.1016/S1042-444X(97)00018-2

Elsby, M. W., Hobijn, B., & Sahin, A. (2013). *On the Importance of the Participation Margin for Market Fluctuations*. Federal Reserve Bank of San Francisco Working Paper No. 2013-05.

Elsby, M. W., Hobijn, B., Sahin, A., & Valletta, R. G. (2011). *The Labor Market in the Great Recession: an Update*. Federal Reserve Bank of San Francisco Working Paper Series No. 2011-29.

Elsby, M., Hobijn, B., & Sahin, A. (2008). *Unemployment Dynamics in the OECD*. National Bureau of Economic Research Cambridge Working Paper No. 14617.

Elsby, M. W., Michaels, R., & Solon, G. (2009). The Ins and Outs of Cyclical Unemployment. *American Economic Journal. Macroeconomics*, *1*(1), 84–110. doi:10.1257/mac.1.1.84

Emery, R. F. (1967). The Relation of Exports and Growth. *Kyklos*, *20*(4), 470–486. doi:10.1111/j.1467-6435.1967.tb00859.x

Engle, R. F. (1982). Autoregressive conditional heteroscedasticity with estimates of the variance of the United Kingdom inflation. *Econometrica*, *50*(4), 987–1008. doi:10.2307/1912773

Ericsson, J., Jacobs, K., & Oviedo, R. (2009). The determinants of credit default swap premia. *Journal of Financial and Quantitative Analysis*, *44*(01), 109–132. doi:10.1017/S0022109009090061

Estrada, J. (2002). Systemic Risk In Emerging Markets: The D-CAPM. *Emerging Market Review*, *3*(4). Retrieved February 10, 2014, from http://www.sciencedirect.com/science/article/pii/S1566014102000420

European Commission. (2014). *Facts and figures on the Common Fisheries Policy, basic statistical data*. Publications Office of the European Union.

Evans, P., & Rauch, J. E. (1999). Bureaucracy and Growth: A Cross- National Analysis of the Effects of 'Weberian' State Structures on Economic Growth. *American Sociological Review*, *64*(5), 748–765. doi:10.2307/2657374

Ewing, J. (2015, March). A Fragile Recovery. As Cyprus Recovers From Banking Crisis, Deep Scars Remain. *New York Times*, pp. B2, B7.

Experian. (2014). Credit Risk Management For Small Businesses. *Business Credit Risk*.

Fallick, B., & Fleischmann, C. A. (2004). *Employer-to-Employer Flows in the U.S. Labor Market: The Complete Picture of Gross Worker Flows*. Finance and Economic Discussion Series Washington Working Paper No. 2004-34.

Fama, F. E., & French, K. R. (2013). *A five-factor asset pricing model*. SSRN Working Paper No. 2287202.

Fama, E. (1965). Random Walks in Stock Market Prices. *The Journal of Business*, *38*(1), 34. doi:10.1086/294743

Fama, E., & French, K. R. (2004). The Capital Asset Pricing Model: Theory and Evidence. *The Journal of Economic Perspectives*, *18*(5). Retrieved from http://www1.american.edu/academic.depts/ksb/finance_realestate/mrobe/Library/capm_Fama_French_JEP04.pdf

Fama, F. E., & French, K. R. (1992). The cross-section of expected returns. *The Journal of Finance*, *47*(2), 427–465. doi:10.1111/j.1540-6261.1992.tb04398.x

Fama, F. E., & French, K. R. (1993). Common risk factors in the returns on stock and bonds. *Journal of Financial Economics*, *33*(1), 3–56. doi:10.1016/0304-405X(93)90023-5

Fama, F. E., & French, K. R. (1996). Multifactor explanations of asset pricing anomalies. *The Journal of Finance*, *51*(1), 55–84. doi:10.1111/j.1540-6261.1996.tb05202.x

FAO. (2015). *FAO Global Aquaculture Production database updated to 2013*. FAO.

Fearn-Banks, K. (2011). *Crisis Communications: a casebook approach* (4th ed.). New York, NY, U.S.: Routledge.

Ferdous, R., Khan, F., Sadiq, R., Amyotte, P., & Veitch, B. (2011). Fault and event tree analyses for process systems risk analysis: Uncertainty handling formulations. *Journal of Risk Analysis*, *31*(1), 86–107. doi:10.1111/j.1539-6924.2010.01475.x PMID:20731791

Fildes, R., & Goodwin, P. (2013). What we know, what we need to know. *International Journal of Forecasting*, *29*(2), 290–294. doi:10.1016/j.ijforecast.2013.01.001

Fombrun, C. J., & Rindova, V. (1998). Reputation Management in Global 1000 Firms: A Benchmarking Study. *Corporate Reputation Review*, *1*(3), 205–212. doi:10.1057/palgrave.crr.1540044

Foster, N., & Poschl, J. (2009). *The Importance of Labour Mobility for Spillovers across Industries*. The Vienna Institute for International Economic Studies Working Paper No. 58.

Frank, K., & Yasumoto, J. (1998). Linking action to social structure within a system: Social capital within and between subgroups. *American Journal of Sociology*, *104*(3), 642–686. doi:10.1086/210083

Frank, M. W. (2009). Income inequality, human capital, and income growth: Evidence from a state level VAR analysis. *Atlantic Economic Journal*, *37*(2), 173–185. doi:10.1007/s11293-009-9172-z

Fred. (2014). *Federal reserve economic data – FRED – St. Louis Fed.* Federal Reserve Bank of St. Louis. Retrieved June 3, 2014, from http://research.stlouisfed.org/

Freixas, X., Martin, A., & Skeie, D. (2011). Bank liquidity, interbank markets, and monetary policy. *Review of Financial Studies*, *24*(8), 2656–2692. doi:10.1093/rfs/hhr018

Fujita, S., & Ramey, G. (2006). *The Cyclicality of Job Loss and Hiring*. Federal Reserve Bank of Philadelphia Working Paper No. 06-17.

Fujita, S., & Ramey, G. (2008). *The Cyclicality of Separation and Job Finding Rates*. Federal Reserve Bank of Philadelphia Working Paper No. 07-19/R.

Fujita, S., Nekarda, C. J., & Ramey, G. (2007). *The Cyclicality of Worker Flows: New Evidence from the SIPP*. Federal Reserve Bank of Philadelphia Working Paper No. 07-5.

Fujita, S., & Ramey, G. (2009). The Cyclicality of Separation and Job Finding Rates. *International Economic Review*, *50*(2), 415–430. doi:10.1111/j.1468-2354.2009.00535.x

Fukuyama, F. (2013). *What Is Governance?* Center for Global Development Working Paper 314.

Fuller, R. J., & Wong, G. W. (1988). Traditional versus Theoretical Risk Measures. *Financial Analyst Journal, 44*(2). Retrieved May 8, 2014, from http://www.jstor.org/stable/4479102

Gali, J., & Blanchard, O. (2008). *Labor Markets and Monetary Policy: A New-Keynesian Model with Unemployment*. National Bureau of Economic Research Cambridge Working Paper No. 13897.

Galinou-Mitsoudi, S., Savvidis, Y., & Dimitriadis, X. (2006). Interaction between mussel culture and hydrodynamics: A preliminary study in the gulfs of Thessaloniki and Thermaikos, Greece. *Journal of Biological Research*, *6*, 139–145.

Garman, M. (1976). Market microstructure. *Journal of Financial Economics*, *3*(3), 257–275. doi:10.1016/0304-405X(76)90006-4

Gencay, R. (1999). Linear, non-linear and essential foreign exchange rate prediction with simple technical trading rules. *Journal of International Economics*, *47*(1), 91–107. doi:10.1016/S0022-1996(98)00017-8

George, D., & Mallery, P. (2003). *SPSS for Windows step by step: A simple guide and reference. 11.0 up date*. Boston: Allyn & Bacon.

George, M. L. (2005). *The Lean Six Sigma Pocket Toolbook: A Quick Reference Guide to Nearly 100 Tools for Improving Process Quality, Speed, and Complexity*. New York, NY: McGraw Hill.

George, M., Rowlands, D., & Kastle, B. (2004). *What is Lean Six Sigma?* New York, NY: McGraw Hill.

Gertler, M., & Kiyotaki, N. (2010). *Financial Crises, Bank Risk Exposure and Government Financial Policy*. Princeton University Press.

Gertler, M., & Trigari, A. (2009). Unemployment Fluctuations with Staggered Nash Wage Bargaining. *Journal of Political Economy*, *117*(1), 38–86. doi:10.1086/597302

Ghatak, S., Milner, C., & Uktulu, U. (1997). Exports, export composition and growth: Cointegration and causality evidence for Malaysia. *Applied Economics*, *29*(2), 213–223. doi:10.1080/000368497327272

Ghosh, D. N. (2011). Analytic Hierarchy Process & TOPSIS Method to Evaluate Faculty Performance in Engineering Education. *Universal Journal of Computer Science and Technology*, *1*(2), 63–70.

Gilboa, I. (2011). *Rational choice*. Cambridge, MA: MIT Press.

Giles, J., & Williams, C. (2001a). Export-led growth: A survey of the empirical literature and some non-causality results. Part 1. *The Journal of International Trade & Economic Development*, *9*(3), 261–337. doi:10.1080/09638190050086177

Giles, J., & Williams, C. (2001b). Export-led growth: A survey of the empirical literature and some non-causality results. Part 2. *The Journal of International Trade & Economic Development*, *9*(4), 445–470. doi:10.1080/096381900750056867

Gillespie, B., Hackwood, J., & Mihos, C. (2010). *Managing credit risk for global commodity producers*. PricewaterhouseCoopers.

Gitlow, H. S., & Levine, D. M. (2005). *Six Sigma for Green Belts and Champions: Foundations, DMAIC, Tools, Cases, and Certification*. New York, NY: Pearson Education, Prentice Hall.

Gkagka, A., & Zarotiadis, G. (2011). Growth and EU Trade Relations: A case study. *South-Eastern Europe Journal of Economics*, *1*, 1–11.

Glamuzina, M., & Lovrinčević, M. (2013). Corporate crisis and crisis strategy implementation. *Montenegrin Journal of Economics*, *9*(2), 89–100.

Glosten, L., & Milgrom, P. (1985). Bid, ask, and transaction prices in a specialist market with heterogeneously informed traders. *Journal of Financial Economics*, *14*(1), 71–100. doi:10.1016/0304-405X(85)90044-3

GNPC. (2011). *Ghana National Petroleum Corporation Main Page*. Retrieved from http://www.gnpcghana.com/home/

Gobbin, N., & Rayp, G. (2008). Different ways of looking at old issues: A time-series approach to inequality and growth. *Applied Economics*, *40*(7), 885–895. doi:10.1080/00036840600771106

Goczol, J., & Scoubeau, C. (2003). Corporate communication and strategy in the field of projects. *Corporate Communications: An International Journal*, *8*(1), 60–66. doi:10.1108/13563280310458920

Gonul, M. S., Onkal, D., & Goodwin, P. (2012). Why should I trust your forecasts? *Foresight: The International Journal of Applied Forecasting*, *27*, 5–9.

Gonul, S., Onkal, D., & Goodwin, P. (2009). Expectations, use and judgmental adjustment of external financial and economic forecasts: An empirical investigation. *Journal of Forecasting*, *28*(1), 19–37. doi:10.1002/for.1082

Goodman, M. B. (2001). Current trends in corporate communication. *Corporate Communication: An International Journal*, *6*(3), 117–123. doi:10.1108/13563280110398956

Goodwin, P., Onkal, D., & Lawrence, M. (2011). Improving the role of judgment in economic forecasting. In M. P. Clements & D. F. Hendry (Eds.), *The Oxford Handbook of Economic Forecasting* (pp. 163–189). Oxford University Press. doi:10.1093/oxfordhb/9780195398649.013.0007

Goodwin, T., & Pierola, M. (2015). *Export competitiveness: Why Domestic Market Competition Matters. Public Policy for the Private Sector NoteNo. 348, Trade & Competition, World Bank.* GTCDR.

Gopalan, R., Nanda, V., & Yerramilli, V. (2011). Does poor performance damage the reputation of financial intermediaries? Evidence from the loan syndication market. *The Journal of Finance*, *66*(6), 2083–2120. doi:10.1111/j.1540-6261.2011.01692.x

Gorton, G., & Pennacchi, G. (1990). Financial intermediation and liquidity creation. *The Journal of Finance*, *45*(1), 49–71. doi:10.1111/j.1540-6261.1990.tb05080.x

Graham, B., & Dodd, D. L. (2008). Security Analysis (6th ed.). McGraw-Hill.

Graham, J., Amos, B., & Plumptre, T. (2003). *Principles for Good Governance in the 21st Century. Policy Brief no 15.* Ontario, Canada: Institute on Governance.

Granovetter, M. S. (1973). The strength of weak ties. *American Journal of Sociology*, *78*(6), 1360–1380. doi:10.1086/225469

Grant, R. (2011). *Contemporary strategy analysis.* New York, NY: Wiley.

Grauer, R. R. (1978). Generalized two parameter asset pricing models: Some empirical evidence. *Journal of Financial Economics*, *6*(1), 11–32. doi:10.1016/0304-405X(78)90018-1

Grosfeld-Nir, A., & Tishler, A. (1993). A stochastic model for the measurement of electricity outage costs. *The Energy Journal (Cambridge, Mass.)*, *14*(2), 157–174. doi:10.5547/ISSN0195-6574-EJ-Vol14-No2-8

Grossman, G. M., & Helpman, E. (1991). Trade, Knowledge Spillovers, and Growth. *European Economic Review*, *35*(3), 517–526. doi:10.1016/0014-2921(91)90153-A

Grossman, J. S., & Miller, H. M. (1988). Liquidity and market structure. *The Journal of Finance*, *43*(3), 617–633. doi:10.1111/j.1540-6261.1988.tb04594.x

Grunig, J. E. (Ed.). (1992). *Excellence in Public Relations and Communication Management.* New York, NY: Routledge.

Grunig, J. G., & Hunt, T. (1984). *Managing Public Relations.* Belmont, WA: Wadsworth/Tomson Learning.

Gumbel, P. (2013, March 25). Cyprus Rescue: The Destruction of a Tax Haven. *Time.*

Gurumurthy, A., & Kodali, R. (2008). A multi-criteria decision-making model for the justification of lean manufacturing systems. *International Journal of Management Science and Engineering Management*, *3*(2), 100–118.

Hackley, C. (1998). Mission statements as corporate communications: The consequences of social construction. *Corporate Communications: An International Journal*, *3*(3), 92–98. doi:10.1108/eb046557

Hall, R. E. (2005). *Job Loss, Job Finding, and Unemployment in the U.S. Economy over the Past Fifty Years*. National Bureau of Economic Research Cambridge Working Paper No. 11678.

Hall, R. E. (2005). Employment Efficiency and Sticky Wages: Evidence from Flows in the Labor Market. *The Review of Economics and Statistics*, *297*(3), 397–407. doi:10.1162/0034653054638346

Hall, R. E., & Jones, C. I. (1999). Why Do Some Countries Produce so Much More Output per Worker than Others? *The Quarterly Journal of Economics*, *114*(1), 83–116. doi:10.1162/003355399555954

Hammer, M. (2002). The future of Six Sigma. *MIT Sloan Management Review*. Retrieved from: http://venturepress.dk/wp-content/uploads/2014/08/Hammer-ProicessManagement-the-future-of-six-sigma.pdf

Harbaugh, J. W. (1984). Quantitative estimation of petroleum prospect outcome probabilities: An overview of procedures. *Marine and Petroleum Geology*, *1*(November).

Hardy, D. C., & Nieto, M. J. (2008). *Cross-Border Coordination of Prudential Supervision and Deposit Guarantees*. IMF Working Paper WP/08/283.

Harmon, P. (2003). *Business process change: a manager's guide to improving, redesigning, and automating processes*. San Francisco, CA: Morgan Kaufmann.

Harmon, P. (2004). Evaluating an organization's business process maturity. *Business Process Trends*, *2*(3), 1–11.

Harris, D. P. (1990). Mineral exploration decisions: A guide to economic analysis and modeling. New York: J. Wiley.

Harris, D. P. (1984). *Mineral Resources Appraisal: Mineral Endowment, Resources and Potential supply: Concepts, Methods and Cases*. Oxford, UK: Clarendon.

Harris, L. (2003). *Trading and exchange: market microstructure for practitioners*. New York: Oxford University Press.

Hasni, H., Tabatabaei, A., & Amiri, G. (2012). Grey Relational Analysis to Determine the Optimum Process Parameters for Open-End Spinning Yarns. *Yournal of Engineered Fibers and Fabrics*, *7*(2), 81–86.

Hastie, R. (2010). *Rational choice in an uncertain world: The psychology of judgment and decision making*. Thousand Oaks, CA: Sage.

Häuberer, J. (2011). *Social capital theory*. Springer Fachmedien. doi:10.1007/978-3-531-92646-9

Haugen, R. A. (1999). The New Finance: The Case Against Efficient Markets (2nd ed.). Prentice Hall.

Haunschild, P. R. (1993). Interorganizational imitation: The impact of interlocks on corporate acquisition activity. *Administrative Science Quarterly*, *38*(4), 564–592. doi:10.2307/2393337

Hausmann, R., Hwang, J., & Rodrik, D. (2007). What you export matters. *Journal of Economic Growth*, *12*(1), 1–25. doi:10.1007/s10887-006-9009-4

Hayashi, S. H. D., Ligero, E. L., & Schiozer, D. J. (2007). *Decision-making process in development of offshore petroleum fields*. SPE Latin American and Caribbean Petroleum Engineering Conference, SPE 107737, Buenos Aires, Argentina. doi:10.2118/107737-MS

Herzer, D., Nowark-Lehmann, F. D., & Siliverstors, B. (2004). *Export-Led Growth in Chile: Assessing the Role of Exports.* Ibero-America Institute For Economic Research. Discussion Paper No.103.

He, Y., Tang, X., & Chang, W. (2010). Technical decomposition approach of critical to quality characteristics for product design for six sigma. *Quality and Reliability Engineering International*, *26*(4), 325–339.

Hicks, M. J. (2005). *Problem solving and decision making: Hard, soft, and creative approaches*. Belmont, CA: Cengage Learning.

Holmström, B., & Tirole, J. (1996). Modeling aggregate liquidity. *The American Economic Review*, *86*(2), 187–191.

Holmström, B., & Tirole, J. (1998). Private and public supply of liquidity. *Journal of Political Economy*, *106*(1), 1–40. doi:10.1086/250001

Holmström, B., & Tirole, J. (2001). LAPM: A liquidity-based asset pricing model. *The Journal of Finance*, *56*(5), 1837–1867. doi:10.1111/0022-1082.00391

Holt, C. C. (2004). Forecasting seasonals and trends by exponentially weighted moving averages. *International Journal of Forecasting*, *20*(1), 5–13. doi:10.1016/j.ijforecast.2003.09.015

Ho, T., & Stoll, H. (1981). Optimal dealer pricing under transactions and return uncertainty. *Journal of Financial Economics*, *9*(1), 47–73. doi:10.1016/0304-405X(81)90020-9

Huang, D., Chen, T., & Wang, J. M. (2001). A fuzzy set approach for event tree analysis. *Fuzzy Sets and Systems*, *118*(1), 153–165. doi:10.1016/S0165-0114(98)00288-7

Huang, G. H., Baetz, B. W., & Patry, G. G. (1992). A grey linear programming approach for municipal solid waste management planning under uncertainty. *Civil Engineering Systems*, *9*(4), 319–335. doi:10.1080/02630259208970657

Huang, G. H., Baetz, B. W., & Patry, G. G. (1995a). Grey integer programming: An application to waste management planning under uncertainty. *European Journal of Operational Research*, *83*(3), 594–620. doi:10.1016/0377-2217(94)00093-R

Huang, G. H., Baetz, B. W., & Patry, G. G. (1995b). Grey fuzzy integer programming: An application to regional waste management planning under uncertainty. *Socio-Economic Planning Sciences*, *29*(1), 17–38. doi:10.1016/0038-0121(95)98604-T

Huang, Y., & Lin, C. (2009). Constructing grea relational analysis model evaluation of tourism. *Journal of Information and Optimization Sciences*, *30*(6), 1129–1138. doi:10.1080/02522667.2009.10699931

Huault, I. (2004). Une analyse des reseaux sociaux est-elle utile pour le management? Puissance et limites d'une theorie de l'encastrement structural. In Institutions Et Gestion.

Hu, G., Wang, L., Fetch, S., & Bidanda, B. (2008). A multi-objective model for project portfolio selection to implement lean and Six Sigma concepts. *International Journal of Production Research*, *46*(23), 6611–6625. doi:10.1080/00207540802230363

ILO. (2014). *Key Indicators of the Labour Market (KILM)* (8th ed.). Retrieved July 2, 2014 from Key Indicators of the Labour Market (KILM): http://www.ilo.org/empelm/what/WCMS_114240/lang--en/index.htm

Ince, H., & Trafalis, T. B. (2006). A hybrid model for exchange rate prediction. *Decision Support Systems*, *42*(2), 1054–1062. doi:10.1016/j.dss.2005.09.001

Infosys. (2012). *Needed, A Holistic Approach to Reputation Risk Management in Banks*. Building Tomorrow's Enterprise.

Jagannathan, R., & Wang, Z. (1995). The conditional CAPM and the cross-section of expected returns. *The Journal of Finance*, *51*(1), 3–53. doi:10.1111/j.1540-6261.1996.tb05201.x

Jahanshahloo, G. R., Lotfi, F. H., & Izadikhah, M. (2006). An algorithmic method to extend TOPSIS for decision-making problems with interval data. *Applied Mathematics and Computation*, *175*(2), 1375–1384. doi:10.1016/j.amc.2005.08.048

Jankovic-Milic, V., & Jovanovic, S. (2014). Application of Grey relational analysis in considering competitiveness of the South Eastern Europe countries. In B. Krstic (Ed.), *Determinants of improving the competitiveness of national economies and enterprises* (pp. 45–65). Nis: Faculty of Economics.

Jarmon, G., & Anderson, P. (2007). *Crude Oil- Uncertainty about Future Oil Supply Makes It Important to Develop a Strategy for Addressing a Peak and Decline in Oil Production*. Government Accountability Office-07-283.

Jegadeesh, N., & Titman, S. (1993). Returns to buying winners and selling losers: Implications for stock market efficiency. *The Journal of Finance*, *48*(1), 65–91. doi:10.1111/j.1540-6261.1993.tb04702.x

Jiang, R., Xie, J., Wang, N., & Li, J. (2013). Evolution game analysis of water saving and pollution prevention for city user groups based on bounded rationality. *Shuili Fadian Xuebao /Journal of Hydroelectric Engineering, 32*(1), 31-36.

Johansen, S. (1995). *Likelihood - Based Inference in Cointegrated Vector Autoregressive Models. Advanced Texts in Econometrics*. Oxford, UK: Oxford University Press. doi:10.1093/0198774508.001.0001

Jordaan, A. C., & Eita, J. H. (2007). Export and Economic Growth in Namibia: A Granger Causality Analysis. *The South African Journal of Economics*, *75*(3), 540–547. doi:10.1111/j.1813-6982.2007.00132.x

Jo, Y. D., & Ahn, B. J. (2002). Analysis of hazard areas associated with high-pressure natural- gas pipelines. *Journal of Loss Prevention in the Process Industries*, *15*(3), 179–188. doi:10.1016/S0950-4230(02)00007-4

Jung, W. S., & Marshall, P. J. (1985). Exports, Growth and Causality in Developing Countries. *Journal of Development Economics*, *18*(2), 1–12. doi:10.1016/0304-3878(85)90002-1

Kandel, S., & Stambaugh, R. (1995). Portfolio inefficiency and the cross-section of expected returns. *The Journal of Finance*, *50*(1), 157–184. doi:10.1111/j.1540-6261.1995.tb05170.x

Kane, S. (1999). What happened to the utility functions? Imprecise expectations of security prices. *International Review of Financial Analysis*, *8*(2), 165–175. doi:10.1016/S1057-5219(99)00014-9

Kaplan, S., & Garrick, B. J. (1981). On the quantitative definition of risk. *Risk Analysis*, *1*(1), 11–27. doi:10.1111/j.1539-6924.1981.tb01350.x PMID:11798118

Karagiannis, D., Vatsos, I., Theodoridis, A., & Angelidis, P. (2013). Effect of culture system on the prevalence of parasites of the Mediterranean mussel *Mytilus galloprovincialis* (Lamark, 1819). *Journal of Hellenic Veterinary Medical Society*, *64*, 113–122.

Kastning, T. (2012). *Basic Overview of Ghana's Emerging Oil Industry, Report for Friedrich Ebert Stiftung*. Retrieved from http://library.fes.de/pdf-files/bueros/ghana/10490.pdf

Kaufmann, D., Kraay, A., & Mastruzzi, M. (2005). *Governance Matters IV: Governance Indicators for 1996-2004*. Policy Research Working Paper No. 3630. Washington, DC: World Bank.

Kaufmann, D., Kraay, A., & Mastruzzi, M. (2009). *Governance Matters VIII: Aggregate and Individual Governance Indicators for 1996-2008*. World Bank Policy Research Working Paper No. 4978. Washington, DC: World Bank.

Kaufmann, D., Kraay, A., & Mastruzzi, M. (2010). *The Worldwide Governance Indicators: Methodology and Analytical Issues*. Policy Research Working Paper Series 5430. The World Bank.

Kaufmann, D., & Kraay, A. (2008). Governance Indicators: Where Are We, Where Should We Be Going? *World Bank Research Observer*, *23*(1), 1–30. doi:10.1093/wbro/lkm012

Kayacan, E., Ulutas, B., & Kaynak, O. (2010). Grey system theory-based models in time series prediction. *Expert Systems with Applications*, *37*(2), 1784–1789. doi:10.1016/j.eswa.2009.07.064

Keefer, P. (2004). *A Review of the Political Economy of Governance: From Property Rights to Voice*. World Bank Policy Research Working Paper No. 3315. Washington DC: World Bank.

Keefer, P., & Knack, S. (2002). Polarization, Politics and Property Rights: Links between Inequality and Growth. *Public Choice*, *111*(1-2), 127–154. doi:10.1023/A:1015168000336

Kepner, C. H., & Tregoe, B. B. (2005). *The new rational manager* (rev. ed.). New York, NY: Kepner-Tregoe.

Keynes, J. M. (1936). *The general theory of employment, interest and money*. Harcourt.

Keynes, J. M. (1936). *The general theory of employment interest and money. The collected writings of John Maynard Keynes* (Vol. 7). London, UK: The Royal Economic Society.

Khalafalla, K. Y., & Webb, A. J. (2001). Export-Led Growth and Structural Change: Evidence from Malaysia. *Applied Economics*, *33*(13), 1703–1715. doi:10.1080/00036840010015066

Khan, F. I., & Abbasi, S. A. (2001). Risk analysis of a typical chemical industry using ORA procedure. *Journal of Loss Prevention in the Process Industries*, *14*(1), 43–59. doi:10.1016/S0950-4230(00)00006-1

Kikuchi, M., & Coleman, C. L. (2012). Explicating and measuring social relationships in social capital research. *Communication Theory*, *22*(2), 187–203. doi:10.1111/j.1468-2885.2012.01401.x

King, T. B. (2011). *Variable Participation and Cyclical Unemployment*. Division of Monetary Affairs, Federal Reserve Board Washington.

Knack, S., & Keefer, P. (1995). Institutions and Economic Performance: Cross Country Tests Using Alternative Institutional Measures. *Economics and Politics*, *7*(3), 207–227. doi:10.1111/j.1468-0343.1995.tb00111.x

Knight, F. (1921). *Risk, uncertainty and profit*. Cambridge, MA: Houghton Mifflin Company, The Riverside Press.

Kohout, P. (2008). Investiční strategie pro třetí tisíciletí (5th ed.). Praha: Grada Publishing.

Köksalan, M. M., Sagala, P. N. S., & Sagala, P. N. S. (1995). Interactive Approaches for Discrete Alternative Multiple Criteria Decision Making with Monotone Utility Functions. *Management Science*, *41*(7), 1158–1171. doi:10.1287/mnsc.41.7.1158

Kónya, L. (2004). Export Led Growth, Growth Driven Exports, Both or None? Granger Causality Analysis On OECD Countries. *Applied Econometrics and International Development*, *4*(1), 73–94.

Kónya, L. (2006). Exports and growth: Granger causality analysis on OECD countries with a panel data approach. *Economic Modelling*, *23*(6), 978–992. doi:10.1016/j.econmod.2006.04.008

Kostolany, A. (1989). Und was macht der Dollar? Im Irrgarten d. Währungsspekulationen. Aktualisierte Taschenbuchausg. München: Heyne.

Kravis, I. B. (1970). Trade as a Handmaiden of Growth. *The Economic Journal*, *80*(323), 850–870. doi:10.2307/2229902

Krusell, P., Mukoyama, T., Rogerson, R., & Sahin, A. (2012). *Is Labor Supply Important for Business Cycles*. National Bureau of Economic Research Cambridge Working Paper No. 17779.

Kružić, D., Glamuzina, M., & Lovrinčević, M. (2013). Top management effectiveness during crisis – Are traditional quantitative indicators of effectiveness enough? (pp.103-113). In *Proceedings of the 1st International OFEL Conference on Corporate Governance*.

Kumar, U., Crocker, J., Chitra, T., & Saranga, H. (2006). *Reliability and Six Sigma*. Berlin: Springer.

Kumar, U., Saranga, H., Ramírez-Márquez, J. E., & Nowicki, D. (2007). Six sigma project selection using data envelopment analysis. *The TQM Magazine*, *19*(5), 419–441. doi:10.1108/09544780710817856

Kurtz, M. J., & Schrank, A. (2007). Growth and Governance: Models, Measures and Mechanisms. *The Journal of Politics*, *69*(2), 538–554. doi:10.1111/j.1468-2508.2007.00549.x

Kwiatkoswaski, D., Phillips, P., Schmidt, P., & Shin, Y.-J. (1992). Testing the Null Hypothes is of Stationary Against the Alternative of a Unit Root: How Sure Are We That Economic Time Series Have a Unit Root? *Journal of Econometrics*, *54*, 159–178. doi:10.1016/0304-4076(92)90104-Y

Kyle, A. (1985). Continuous auction and insider trading. *Econometrica*, *53*(6), 1315–1335. doi:10.2307/1913210

Lai, V. S., Trueblood, R. P., & Wong, B. K. (1999). Software selection: A case study of the application of the analytical hierarchical process to the selection of a multimedia authoring system. *Information & Management*, *36*(4), 221–232. doi:10.1016/S0378-7206(99)00021-X

Lai, Y. J., Liu, T. Y., & Hwang, C. L. (1994). Topsis for MODM. *European Journal of Operational Research*, *76*(3), 486–500. doi:10.1016/0377-2217(94)90282-8

Landry, R., Amara, N., & Lamari, M. (2000). Does social capital determine innovation? To what extent? *4th International Conference On Technology Policy And Innovation.*

Langbein, L., & Knack, S. (2008). *The Worldwide Governance Indicators and Tautology: Causally Related Separable Concepts, Indicators of a Common Cause, or Both?* World Bank Policy Research Working Paper 4669. Washington, DC: World Bank.

Larson, A. (2003). *Demystifying Six Sigma*. New York, NY: American Management Association.

Lawrence, M., Goodwin, P., O'Connor, M., & Onkal, D. (2006). Judgmental forecasting: A review of progress over the last 25 years. *International Journal of Forecasting*, *22*(3), 493–518. doi:10.1016/j.ijforecast.2006.03.007

Lee, I. H. (2013). Speculation under bounded rationality. *Journal of Economic Theory and Econometrics*, *24*(1), 37–53.

Leitner, J., & Leopold-Wildburger, U. (2011). Experiments on forecasting behaviour with several sources of information – a review of the literature. *European Journal of Operational Research*, *213*(3), 459–469. doi:10.1016/j.ejor.2011.01.006

Leitner, J., & Schmidt, R. (2006). A systematic comparison of professional exchange rate forecasts with the judgemental forecasts of novices. *Central European Journal of Operations Research*, *14*(1), 87–102. doi:10.1007/s10100-006-0161-x

Lemieux, V. (1999). *Les réseaux d'acteurs sociaux*. Paris: PUF.

Lennon, K., & Sheldon, K. A. (1992). *From Canada to California: New directions in corporate communication.* ABI/INFORM Global.

Leshno, M., & Levy, H. (2002). Preferred by "all" and preferred by "most" decision makers: Almost stochastic dominance. *Management Science*, *48*(8), 1074–1085. doi:10.1287/mnsc.48.8.1074.169

Lesmond, A. D. (2005). Liquidity of emerging markets. *Journal of Financial Economics*, *77*(2), 411–452. doi:10.1016/j.jfineco.2004.01.005

Leu, Y., Lee, C. P., & Jou, Y. Z. (2009). A distance-based fuzzy time series model for exchange rates forecasting. *Expert Systems with Applications*, *36*(4), 8107–8114. doi:10.1016/j.eswa.2008.10.034

Lévesque, M. & White, D. (1999). Le concept de capital social et ses usages. *Liens social et politiques*, *41*, 23-33.

Lévesque, M. (2000). *Le capital social comme forme sociale de capital: reconstruction d'un quasi-concept et application à l'analyse de la sortie de l'aide sociale.* (PhD Thesis). Faculté des études supérieures, Université de Montréal.

Lévesque, M., White, D., & Levesque, M. (2001). Capital social, capital humain et sortie de l'aide sociale pour les prestataires de longue durée. *Canadian Journal of Sociology, 26*(2), 167–192. doi:10.2307/3341677

Levy, H. (1983). The capital asset pricing model: Theory and empiricism. *The Economic Journal, 93*(369), 145–165. doi:10.2307/2232170

Levy, H. (2010). The CAPM is alive and well: A review and synthesis. *European Financial Management, 16*(1), 43–71. doi:10.1111/j.1468-036X.2009.00530.x

Levy, M., & Roll, R. (2010). The market portfolio may be mean-variance efficient after all. *Review of Financial Studies, 23*(6), 2464–2491. doi:10.1093/rfs/hhp119

Lin, H. & Paravisini, D. (2011). *What's bank reputation worth? The effect of fraud on financial contracts and investment.* The Effect of Fraud on Financial Contracts and Investment.

Lin, N. (1995). Les ressources sociales: Une théorie du capital social. *Revue Francaise de Sociologie, 36*(4), 685–704. doi:10.2307/3322451

Lin, N. (2001). *Social capital: a theory of social structure and action.* New York: Cambridge University Press. doi:10.1017/CBO9780511815447

Lin, Q. G., & Huang, G. H. (2009a). A dynamic inexact energy systems planning model for supporting greenhouse-gas emission management and sustainable renewable energy development under uncertainty—A case study for the city of Waterloo, Canada. *Renewable & Sustainable Energy Reviews, 13*(8), 1836–1853. doi:10.1016/j.rser.2009.01.021

Lin, Q. G., & Huang, G. H. (2010a). An inexact two-stage stochastic optimization model for managing greenhouse gas emission and sustainable energy systems development at a municipal level. *Energy, 35*, 2270–2280. doi:10.1016/j.energy.2010.01.042

Lin, Q. G., Huang, G. H., Bass, B., Chen, B., Zhang, B. Y., & Zhang, X. D. (2009). CCEM: A city-cluster energy systems planning model. *Energy Sources Part A, 31*(4), 273–286. doi:10.1080/15567030802592345

Lin, Q. G., Huang, G. H., Bass, B., Huang, Y. F., & Liu, L. (2010a). Optimization of energy systems under changing policies of greenhouse-gas emission control: A study for the province of Saskatchewan, Canada. *Energy Sources. Part A, 32*, 1587–1602.

Lin, Q. G., Huang, G. H., Bass, B., Nie, X. H., Zhang, X. D., & Qin, X. S. (2010b). EMDSS: An optimization-based decision support system for energy systems management under changing climate conditions—An application to the Toronto-Niagara Region, Canada. *Expert Systems with Applications, 37*(7), 5040–5051. doi:10.1016/j.eswa.2009.12.007

Lintner, J. (1965). The valuation of risk assets and selection of risky investments in stock portfolios and capital budgets. *The Review of Economics and Statistics, 47*(1), 13–37. doi:10.2307/1924119

Lin, V. S., Goodwin, P., & Song, H. (2014). Accuracy and bias of experts' adjusted forecasts. *Annals of Tourism Research, 48*, 156–174. doi:10.1016/j.annals.2014.06.005

Liška, V., & Gazda, J. (2004). *Kapitálové trhy a kolektivní investování.* Praha: Professional Publishing.

Lo, A. W., & MacKinlay, A. C. (2002). *A Non-Random Walk Down Wall Street.* Princeton, NJ: Princeton University Press.

Lorrain, F., & White, H. (1971). Structural equivalence of individuals in social networks. *The Journal of Mathematical Sociology, 1*(1), 49–80. doi:10.1080/0022250X.1971.9989788

Lv, Y., Huang, G. H., Li, Y. P., Yang, Z. F., Liu, Y., & Cheng, G. H. (2010). Planning regional water resources system using an interval fuzzy bi-level programming method. *Journal of Environmental Informatics*, *16*, 43–56. doi:10.3808/jei.201000177

Maddaloni, A., & Peydro, J. (2013). *Monetary Policy, Macroprudential Policy and Banking Stability: Evidence from the Euro Area*. ECB Working Paper Series No. 1560.

Madhavan, A. (2000). Market microstructure: A survey. *Journal of Financial Markets*, *3*(3), 205–258. doi:10.1016/S1386-4181(00)00007-0

Maheshwarkar, M., & Sohani, N. (2013). Combined AHP-TOPSIS based approach for the evaluation of knowledge sharing capabilities of supply chain partners. *Management Science and Engineering*, *7*(3), 27–32.

Ma, J., Fan, Z., & Huang, L. (1999). A Subjective and Objective Integrated Approach to Determine Attribute Weights. *European Journal of Operational Research*, *112*(2), 397–404. doi:10.1016/S0377-2217(98)00141-6

Malkiel, B. G. (2012). *Náhodná procházka po Wall Street* (10th ed.). Praha: Pragma.

Manne, A., Mendelsohn, R., & Richels, R. (1995). MERGE, a model for evaluating regional and global effects of GHG reduction policies. *Energy Policy*, *23*(1), 17–34. doi:10.1016/0301-4215(95)90763-W

March, J. G. (2010). *Primer on decision making: How decisions happen*. New York, NY: Simon & Schuster.

Marinkovic, S. (2014). Non-parametric sign test and paired samples test of effectiveness of official fx intervention. *Economic Annals*, *59*(202), 107–130. doi:10.2298/EKA1402107M

Markowitz, H. (1952). Portfolio selection. *The Journal of Finance*, *7*(1), 77–91.

Markowski, A. S., Mannan, M. S., & Bigoszewska, A. (2009). Fuzzy logic for process safety analysis. *Journal of Loss Prevention in the Process Industries*, *22*(6), 695–702. doi:10.1016/j.jlp.2008.11.011

Maurer, I., & Ebers, M. (2006). Dynamics of social capital and their performance implications: Lessons from biotechnology start-ups. *Administrative Science Quarterly*, *51*(2), 262–292. doi:10.2189/asqu.51.2.262

Mauro, P. (1995). Corruption and Growth. *The Quarterly Journal of Economics*, *110*(3), 681–712. doi:10.2307/2946696

Mavrotas, G., Demertzis, H., Meintani, A., & Diakoulaki, D. (2003). Energy planning in buildings under uncertainty in fuel costs: The case of a hotel unit in Greece. *Energy Conversion and Management*, *44*(8), 1303–1321. doi:10.1016/S0196-8904(02)00119-X

Mehrez, A., Regev, U., & Spivak, A. (1984). An analysis of risky financial decisions. *Managerial and Decision Economics*, *5*(1), 19–24. doi:10.1002/mde.4090050105

Mendel, J. (2011). *Perceptual computing: Aiding people in making subjective judgments*. New York, NY: Wiley.

Mercklé, M. (2004). *Sociologie des réseaux sociaux*. Paris: La Découverte.

Meriyappa, T. (2015). *15 Criteria for Selecting a Viable DMAIC Project*. Retrieved from: http://www.isixsigma.com/implementation/project-selection-tracking/15-criteriaselecting-viable-dmaic-project/

Merton, C. R. (1973). An Intertemporal capital asset pricing model. *Econometrica*, *41*(5), 867–887. doi:10.2307/1913811

Merton, R. C. (1974). On the pricing of corporate debt: The risk structure of interest rates. *The Journal of Finance*, *29*(2), 449–470.

Michaely, M. (1977). Exports and economic growth: An empirical investigation. *Journal of Development Economics*, *4*(1), 49–53. doi:10.1016/0304-3878(77)90006-2

Milgrom, P., & Stokey, N. (1982). Information, trade, and common knowledge. *Journal of Economic Theory*, *26*(1), 17–27. doi:10.1016/0022-0531(82)90046-1

Minsky, H. (1995). Financial factors in the economics of capitalism. *Journal of Financial Services Research*, *9*(3-4), 197–208. doi:10.1007/BF01051746

Mishra, P. K. (2011). The Dynamics of Relationship between exports and economic growth in India. *International Journal of Economic Sciences and Applied Research*, *4*(2), 53–70.

Mizruchi, M. (1993). Cohesion, equivalence, and similarity of behaviour: A theoretical and empirical assessment. *Social Networks*, *15*(3), 275–307. doi:10.1016/0378-8733(93)90009-A

Mizruchi, M., & Marquis, C. (2006). Egocentric, sociocentric or dyadic? Identifying the appropriate level of analysis in the study of organizational networks. *Social Networks*, *28*(3), 187–208. doi:10.1016/j.socnet.2005.06.002

Moore, S., Bockenholt, U., Daniel, M., Frohlich, K., Kestens, Y., & Richard, L. (2011). Social capital and core network ties: A validation study of individual-level social capital measures and their association with extra and intra-neighborhood ties and self-rated health. *Health & Place*, *17*(2), 536–544. doi:10.1016/j.healthplace.2010.12.010 PMID:21208822

Morkowitz, H. (1952). Portfolio Selection. *The Journal of Finance*, *7*(1). Retrieved from http://onlinelibrary.wiley.com/doi/10.1111/j.1540-6261.1952.tb01525.x/pdf

Moskowitz, J. T., & Grinblatt, M. (1999). Do industries explain momentum? *The Journal of Finance*, *54*(4), 1249–1290. doi:10.1111/0022-1082.00146

Mossin, J. (1966). Equilibrium in a Capital Asset Market. *Econometrica*, *34*(4), 768. doi:10.2307/1910098

Mueller, A. I. (2012). *Separations, Sorting and Cyclical Unemployment*. IZA Bonn Discussion Paper No. 6849.

Mukoyama, T. (2013). *The Cyclicality of Job-to-Job Transitions and Its Implications for Aggregate Productivity*. Board of Governors of the Federal Reserve System Washington, International Finance Discussion Papers No. 1074.

Muranaga, J., & Shimizu, T. (2000). *Expectations and market microstructure when liquidity is lost*. Bank of Japan.

Murata, A., Kubo, S., & Hata, N. (2012). Study on promotion of cooperative behaviour in social dilemma situation by introduction of bounded rationality - Effects of group heuristics on cooperative behaviours. *Proceedings of the SICE Annual Conference*.

Musílek, P. (2011). *Trhy cenných papírů* (2nd ed.). Praha: Ekopress.

Narayanan, M. P. (2005). *Finance for strategic decision making: What non-financial managers need to know*. New York, NY: Wiley.

Nasdaq - Revenue and EPS Summary. (2014). *NASDAQ Stock Market*. Retrieved May 6, 2014, from http://www.nasdaq.com/quotes/revenue-eps.aspx

Nayeb, A., & Jabari, S., & Yousefi Nejad Attari, M. (2014). A combination of factor analysis and combined approach techniques (AHP-TOPSIS) for ranking criteria and evaluating the factors affecting brand. *Technical Journal of Engineering and Applied Sciences*, *4*(4), 349–358.

Neaete, R. (2015). *Volkswagen under investigation over illegal software that masks emissions.* Retrieved September 25, 2015 from the guardian: http://www.theguardian.com/business/2015/sep/18/epa-california-investigate-volkswagen-clean-air-violations

Ngumi, P., Wambugu, A., Kimuyu, P., & Gakure, R. (2013). Exports and Economic Growth. The case of Kenya. *Prime Journal of Business Administration and Management, 3*(4), 950–959.

Nordhaus, W. (1993). Rolling the DICE: An optimal transition path for controlling GHGs. *Resource and Energy Economics, 15*(1), 27–50. doi:10.1016/0928-7655(93)90017-O

Northcott, C. A. (2004). *Competition in banking: A review of the literature*. Working Paper. Bank of Canada.

North, D. (1981). *Structure and Change in Economic History*. New York: W.W. Norton.

North, D. (1990). *Institutions, Institutional Change and Economic Performance*. Cambridge, UK: Cambridge University Press. doi:10.1017/CBO9780511808678

Nurošis, M. J. (2012). *IBM SPSS Statistics 19 Statistical Procedures Companion*. Prentice Hall Inc.

O'Hara, M. (2004). *Market microstructure theory*. Cambridge, MA: Blackwell Publishers.

Oakshott, L. (2006). *Essential Quantitative Methods for Business Management and Finance* (3rd ed.). New York: Palgrave Macmillan.

OECD. (2014). *OECD Economic Surveys - PORTUGAL overview*. Paris: OECD Publishing.

OECD. (2014). *Portugal: Deepening structural reform to support growth and competitiveness.* Better Policies Series. OECD.

Olson, M. Jr. (1996). Big Bills Left on the Sidewalk: Why Some Nations are Rich and Others Poor. *The Journal of Economic Perspectives, 10*(2), 3–24. doi:10.1257/jep.10.2.3

Oman, C. (2000). Policy Competition for Foreign Direct Investment: A Study of Competition Among Governments to Attract FDI. OECD Development Centre.

Oman, C. P., & Arndt, C. (2010). *Measuring Governance*. Policy Brief no 39. OECD Development Centre, OECD. doi:10.1787/9789264181083-en

Onkal, D., Yates, J. F., Simga-Mugan, C., & Oztin, S. (2003). Professional vs. amateur judgment accuracy: The case of foreign exchange rates. *Organizational Behavior and Human Decision Processes, 91*(2), 169–185. doi:10.1016/S0749-5978(03)00058-X

Opricovic, S., & Tzeng, G. H. (2004). Compromise solution by MCDM methods: A comparative analysis of VIKOR and TOPSIS. *European Journal of Operational Research, 156*(2), 445–455. doi:10.1016/S0377-2217(03)00020-1

Oxley, L. (1993). Cointegration, Causality and Export-led Growth in Portugal, 1865-1985. *Economics Letters, 43*(2), 163–166. doi:10.1016/0165-1765(93)90030-G

Palley, T. I. (2011). *The Rise and fall of Export-Led Growth.* Levy Economics Institute of Bard College Working Paper No. 675.

Panda, C., & Narasimhan, V. (2007). Forecasting exchange rate better with artificial neural network. *Journal of Policy Modeling, 29*(2), 227–236. doi:10.1016/j.jpolmod.2006.01.005

Pande, P., Neuman, R., & Cavanagh, R. (2000). *The Six Sigma Way*. New York, NY: McGraw-Hill.

Pástor, Ľ., & Veronesi, P. (1999). Technological Revolutions and Stock. *The American Economic Review*, *99*(4). Retrieved from http://www.jstor.org/stable/25592515

Paulson, D., & Zahir, S. (1995). Consequences of uncertainty in the analytic hierarchy process: A simulation approach. *European Journal of Operational Research*, *87*(1), 45–56. doi:10.1016/0377-2217(94)00044-D

Peck, S. C., & Teisberg, T. J. (1995). Optimal CO2 control policy with stochastic losses from temperature rise. *Climatic Change*, *31*(1), 19–34. doi:10.1007/BF01092979

Perçin, S., & Kahraman, C. (2010). An integrated fuzzy multi-criteria decision-making approach for Six Sigma project. *International Journal of Computational Intelligence Systems*, *3*(5), 610–621. doi:10.1080/18756891.2010.9727727

Petersen, D. (2002). The potential of social capital measures in the evaluation of comprehensive community-based health initiatives. *The American Journal of Evaluation*, *23*(1), 55–64. doi:10.1177/109821400202300106

Petroff, A. (2013, June 27). Europe bank rescue plan would hit investors.CNN Money.

Petrongolo, B., & Pissarides, C. A. (2008). The Ins and Outs of European Unemployment. *The American Economic Review*, *98*(2), 256–262. doi:10.1257/aer.98.2.256

Pettengill, N. G., Sridhar, S., & Mathur, I. (1995). The conditional relation between beta and returns. *Journal of Financial and Quantitative Analysis*, *30*(1), 101–116. doi:10.2307/2331255

Pinto, A. C. C., Guedes, S. S., Bruhn, C. H. L., Gomes, J. A. T., Sá, A. N., & Fagundes Neto, J. R. (2001). *Marlim Complex Development: A reservoir engineering overview*. SPE Latin American and Caribbean Petroleum Engineering Conference, SPE 69438, Buenos Aires, Argentina.

Pioneer Ibbotson Asset Allocation Series. (2013). *Pioneer Investments Global Asset Management.* Retrieved May 11, 2014, from http://us.pioneerinvestments.com/misc/pdfs/brochures/pio_ibb.pdf

Pistikos, K., & Zarotiadis, G. (2014). Tie or Try: Intra-Eu Trade in Times of Economic Crisis. *Journal of Sociological Research*, *5*(1), 126–137.

Ponthieux, S. (2004). *Le concept de capital social, Analyse critique*. 10th ACN Conference, Paris, France.

Prashantham, S. (2005). *Social capital and the international growth of young firms: A temporal perspective.* Working Paper. University of Strathclyde.

Pullock, A. C., Macaulay, A., Thomson, M. E., & Onkal, D. (2005). Performance evaluation of judgemental directional exchange rate predictions. *International Journal of Forecasting*, *21*(3), 473–489. doi:10.1016/j.ijforecast.2004.12.006

Putnam, R. (1995). Bowling alone: America's declining social capital. *Journal of Democracy*, *6*(1), 65–78. doi:10.1353/jod.1995.0002

Pyzdek, T. (2003). *The Six Sigma Project Planner*. New York, NY: McGraw-Hill.

Pyzdek, T., & Keller, P. A. (2003). *The six sigma handbook*. New York, NY: McGraw-Hill.

Ram, R. (1987). Exports and Economic Growth in Developing countries: Evidence from Time Series and Cross Section Data. *Economic Development and Cultural Change*, *36*(1), 51–72. doi:10.1086/451636

Randjelovic, D., Stankovic, J., Jankovic-Milic, V., & Stanković, J. (2013). Weight Coefficents Determination Based on Parameters in Factor Analysis. *Metalurgia International*, *18*(3), 128–132.

Rao, R. V., & Davim, J. P. (2008). A decision-making framework model for material selection using a combined multiple attribute decision-making method. *International Journal of Advanced Manufacturing Technology*, *35*(7-8), 751–760. doi:10.1007/s00170-006-0752-7

Ratnovski, L. (2013). Liquidity and transparency in bank risk management. *Journal of Financial Intermediation*, *22*(3), 422-439.

Reilly, F. K., & Brown, K. C. (2012). Investment Analysis & Portfolio Management (10th ed.). Mason, OH: Cengage Learning.

Ren, L., Zhang, Y., Wang, Y., & Sun, Z. (2007). Comparative analysis of a novel M-TOPSIS method and TOPSIS. *Applied Mathematics Research Express*. Retrieved from: http://citeseerx.ist.psu.edu/viewdoc/download?doi=10.1.1.99.4476&rep=rep1&type=pdf

Robert, S. (2005). The Cyclical Behavior of Equilibrium Unemployment and Vacancies. *The American Economic Review*, *95*(1), 25–49. doi:10.1257/0002828053828572

Rodriguez, F., & Rodrik, D. (2001). Trade Policy and Economic Growth: A Skeptic's Guide to the Cross-National Evidence. In B. Bernanke & K. S. Rogoff (Eds.), *NBER macroeconomics annual* (pp. 261–338). Cambridge, MA: MIT Press.

Rodrik, D., Subramanian, A., & Trebbi, F. (2004). Institutions Rule: The Primacy of Institutions over Geography and Integration in Economic Development. *Journal of Economic Growth*, *9*(2), 131–165. doi:10.1023/B:JOEG.0000031425.72248.85

Roll, R. (1977). A critique of the asset pricing theory's tests. *Journal of Financial Economics*, *4*(2), 129–176. doi:10.1016/0304-405X(77)90009-5

Rose-Ackerman, S., & Kornai, J. (Eds.). (2004). *Building a Trustworthy State in Post-Socialist Transition*. New York: Palgrave/Macmillan.

Ross, A. S. (1976). The arbitrage theory of capital asset pricing. *Journal of Economic Theory*, *13*(3), 341–360. doi:10.1016/0022-0531(76)90046-6

Rothstein, B. (2005). *Social Traps and the Problem of Trust*. Cambridge, UK: Cambridge University Press. doi:10.1017/CBO9780511490323

Rothstein, B., & Teorell, J. (2008). What Is Quality of Government? A Theory of Impartial Government Institutions. *Governance: An International Journal of Policy, Administration and Institutions*, *21*(2), 165–190. doi:10.1111/j.1468-0491.2008.00391.x

Rouwenhorst, K. G. (1998). International momentum strategies. *The Journal of Finance*, *53*(1), 267–284. doi:10.1111/0022-1082.95722

Saaty, T. L. (1980). *The analytic hierarchy process: planning, priority setting, resources allocation*. New York, NY: McGraw-Hill.

Saaty, T. L. (1986). Axiomatic foundation of the analytic hierarchy process. *Management Science*, *32*(7), 841–855. doi:10.1287/mnsc.32.7.841

Saaty, T. L. (1994). Highlights and critical points in the theory and application of the analytic hierarchy process. *European Journal of Operational Research*, *74*(3), 426–447. doi:10.1016/0377-2217(94)90222-4

Saaty, T. L. (2001). *The Analytic Network Process*. Pittsburgh, PA: RWS Publications. doi:10.1007/1-4020-0611-X_32

Saaty, T. L., & Vargas, L. G. (2012). *Models, methods, concepts & applications of the analytic hierarchy process*. New York, NY: Springer Science & Business Media. doi:10.1007/978-1-4614-3597-6

Sadeghi, M., & Hosseini, M. H. (2006). Energy supply planning in Iran by using fuzzy linear programming approach (regarding uncertainties of investment costs). *Energy Policy*, *34*(9), 993–1003. doi:10.1016/j.enpol.2004.09.005

Sadiq, R., Saint-Martin, E., & Kleiner, Y. (2008). Predicting risk of water quality failures in distribution networks under uncertainties using fault-tree analysis. *Urban Water Journal*, *5*(4), 287–304. doi:10.1080/15730620802213504

Salem, O. M., Miller, R. A., Deshpande, A. S., & Arurkar, T. P. (2010). Multi-criteria decision- making system for selecting an effective plan for bridge rehabilitation. *Structure and Infrastructure Engineering*, *9*(8), 806-816.

Samuelson, P. (1963). Risk and uncertainty: A fallacy of large numbers. *Scientia*, *98*, 108–113.

Santos, P. (2012). *Destination and product structure of exports: Impact on the economic growth of Europe*. Faculdade de Economia da Universidade do Porto.

Santos, P., Ribeiro, A., & Carvalho, V. (2013). *Export-Led Growth in Europe: Where and What to Export?* FEP Working papersNo. 479.

Schoenfeld, A. H. (2011). *How we think: A theory of goal-oriented decision making and its educational applications*. New York, NY: Routledge.

Schoenmaker, D. (2011). Financial Supervision in the EU. Forthcoming. In G. Caprio (Ed.), *Encyclopedia of Financial Globalization*. Elsevier Amsterdam.

Sellnow, T. L., & Seeger, M. W. (2013). *Theorizing Crisis Communication*. West Sussex, UK: John Wiley & Sons Ltd.

Serrano-González, J., Burgos, P. M., & Riquelme, S. J. (2013). Optimum design of transmissions systems for offshore wind farms including decision making under risk. *Renewable Energy*, *59*, 115–127. doi:10.1016/j.renene.2013.03.024

Ševčíková, B. (2008). *Metody výpočtu vah (podílů) cenných papírů v portfoliu*. Brno: Přírodovědecká fakulta Masarykovy univerzity.

Sharpe, W. F. (1964). Capital Asset Prices: A Theory of Market Equilibrium under Conditions of Risk. *The Journal of Finance*, *19*(3). Retrieved June 1, 2014, from http://www.jstor.org/stable/2977928

Sharpe, F. W. (1964). Capital asset prices: A theory of market equilibrium under condition of risks. *The Journal of Finance*, *19*(3), 425–442.

Sharpe, F. W. (1991). Capital asset prices with and without negative holdings. *The Journal of Finance*, *46*(2), 489–509. doi:10.1111/j.1540-6261.1991.tb02671.x

Sharpe, W. F. (2000). *Portfolio Theory and Capital Markets* (1st ed.). New York: McGraw-Hill.

Shen, P., & Starr, R. (1998). Liquidity of the treasury bill market and the term structure of interest rates. *Journal of Economics and Business*, *50*(5), 401–417. doi:10.1016/S0148-6195(98)00012-5

Shewhart, W. A. (1931). *Economic control of quality of manufactured product*. New York, NY: ASQ Quality Press.

Shimer, R. (2007). *Reassessing the Ins and Outs of Unemployment*. National Bureau of Economic Research Cambridge Working paper series No 13421.

Shimer, R. (2012). Reassessing the Ins and Outs of Unemployment. *Review of Economic Dynamics*, *15*(2), 127–148. doi:10.1016/j.red.2012.02.001

Siegel, J. (2011). *Investice do akcií: Běh na dlouhou trať*. Praha: Grada Publishing.

Simon, H. (1957). A Behavioural Model of Rational Choice. In *Models of Man, Social and Rational: Mathematical Essays on Rational Human Behaviour in a Social Setting*. New York: Wiley.

Simon, H. (1990). A mechanism for social selection and successful altruism. *Science*, *250*(4988), 1665–1668. doi:10.1126/science.2270480 PMID:2270480

Simon, H. A. (2009). *Economics, bounded rationality, and the cognitive revolution*. Northampton, MA: Edward Elgar Publishing.

Širůček, M. (2013a). *Působení peněžní nabídky na akciové trhy*. Brno: Provozně ekonomická fakulta Mendelovy univerzity v Brně.

Širůček, M. (2013b). *Impact of Money Supply on Stock bubbles*. Brno: Acta Universitatis Agriculturae et Silviculturae Mendelianae Brunensis.

Širůček, M., Šoba, O., & Něměček, J. (2014). CAPM Validity on the US Stock Market. *Trends Economics and Management, 8*(18), 87-100.

Sklavounos, S., & Rigas, F. (2006). Estimation of safety distances in the vicinity of fuel gas pipelines. *Journal of Loss Prevention in the Process Industries*, *19*(1), 24–31. doi:10.1016/j.jlp.2005.05.002

Smith, J. C. (2010). *The Ins and Outs of UK Unemployment*. The University of Warwick, Department of Economics, Warwick Economic Research Papers No. 944.

Smith, L. (2001). Six Sigma and the Evolution of Quality in Product Development. *Six Sigma Forum Magazine*, *1*(1), 28–35.

Snyder, M. (2013, September). Cyprus-Style Wealth Confiscation Is Now Starting To Happen All Over The Globe. *Global Research*.

Solnik, H. B. (1974). An equilibrium model of the international capital market. *Journal of Economic Theory*, *8*(4), 500–524. doi:10.1016/0022-0531(74)90024-6

Solnik, H. B. (1983). International arbitrage pricing theory. *The Journal of Finance*, *38*(2), 449–457. doi:10.1111/j.1540-6261.1983.tb02251.x

Song, H., & Li, G. (2008). Tourism demand modelling and forecasting-A review of recent research. *Tourism Management*, *29*(2), 203–220. doi:10.1016/j.tourman.2007.07.016

SPSS. (2002). *SPSS Categories 11.5. A Software Package, Version 11.0*. Chicago: SPSS Inc.

Stanley, D. T., & Girth, M. (1971). *Bankruptcy: Problem, process, reform*. Brookings Institution Press.

Steuer, R. E. (1986). *Multiple Criteria Optimization: Theory, Computation and Application*. New York: John Wiley.

Stocker, K. P. (1997). A Strategic Approach to Crisis Management. In The Handbook of Strategic Public Relations & Integrated Communications. New York: McGraw-Hill.

Stoll, H. (1978). The supply of dealer services in securities markets. *The Journal of Finance*, *33*(4), 1133–1151. doi:10.1111/j.1540-6261.1978.tb02053.x

Stulz, M. R. (1981). A model of international asset pricing. *Journal of Financial Economics*, *9*(4), 383–406. doi:10.1016/0304-405X(81)90005-2

Sun, W., & Huang, G. H. (2010). Inexact piecewise quadratic programming for waste flow allocation under uncertainty and nonlinearity. *Journal of Environmental Informatics*, *16*, 80–93. doi:10.3808/jei.201000180

Svensson, J. (1998). Investment, Property Rights and Political Instability: Theory and Evidence. *European Economic Review*, *42*(7), 1317–1341. doi:10.1016/S0014-2921(97)00081-0

Taha, H. A. (2007). *Operations Research, An introduction* (8th ed.). New York: Prentice Hall.

Tang, C.F., & Lai, Y.W. (2011). *The stability of export led growth hypothesis: Evidence from Asia's four little Dragons.* Munich personal Re PEc Archive paper No. 27962.

Technologies, C. A. (2014). *Project Risk Score Calculation*. CA Clarity PPM Cookbook.

Theodorou, A., Viaene, J., Sorgeloos, P., & Tzovenis, I. (2011). Production and marketing trends of the cultured mediterranean mussel Mytilus galloprovincialis Lamarck 1819, in Greece. *Journal of Shellfish Research*, *30*(3), 859–874. doi:10.2983/035.030.0327

Theodorou, J., Sorgeloos, P., Adams, C., Viaene, J., & Tzovenis, I. (2010). Optimal farm size for the production of the Mediterranean mussel (Mytilus galloprovincialis) in Greece.*Proceedings of the 15th Biennial Conference of the International Institute of Fisheries Economics and Trade Conference (IIFET 2010).*

Thomson, M. E., Pollock, A. C., Gonul, M. S., & Onkal, D. (2013). Effects of trend strength and direction on performance and consistency in judgmental exchange rate forecasting. *International Journal of Forecasting*, *29*(2), 337–353. doi:10.1016/j.ijforecast.2012.03.004

Thorelli, H. (1986). Networks, between markets and hierarchies. *Strategic Management Journal*, *7*(1), 37–51. doi:10.1002/smj.4250070105

Thurman, B. (1979). In the office: Networks and coalitions. *Social Networks*, *2*(1), 47–63. doi:10.1016/0378-8733(79)90010-8

Tipurić, D., Kružić, D., & Lovrinčević, M. (2013). Strategije u kriznim uvjetima. Montenegrin Journal of Economics, 9(2), 89-100.

Tisdell, C. (1996). *Bounded Rationality and Economic Evolution: A Contribution to Decision Making*. Brookfield, UK: Economics, and Management. Cheltenham.

Tobin, J. (1958). Liquidity preference as behavior towards risk. *The Review of Economic Studies*, *25*(2), 65–86. doi:10.2307/2296205

Towler, M. (2010). *Rational decision making: An introduction*. New York, NY: Wiley.

Treynor, J. L. (1962). *Towards a Theory of Market Value of Risky Assets*. Unpublished Manuscript.

Trkman, P. (2010). The critical success factors of business process management. *International Journal of Information Management*, *30*(2), 125–134. doi:10.1016/j.ijinfomgt.2009.07.003

Tyler, W. G. (1981). Growth and expansion in developing countries some empirical evidence. *Journal of Development Economics*, *9*(1), 121–130. doi:10.1016/0304-3878(81)90007-9

Tzanakis, M. (2013). Social capital in Bourdieu's, Coleman's and Putnam's theory: Empirical evidence and emergent measurement issues. *Educate*, *13*(2), 2–23.

Ulengin, F., & Ulengin, B. (1994). Forecasting foreign exchange rates: A comparative evaluation of AHP. *Omega*, *22*(5), 505–519. doi:10.1016/0305-0483(94)90031-0

United Nations Development Programme. (1997) Governance for sustainable human development. UNDP Policy Document.

Van Der Aalst, W. M., Ter Hofstede, A. H., & Weske, M. (2003). Business process management: A survey. In *Business process management*. Berlin: Springer. doi:10.1007/3-540-44895-0_1

Van Horne, J. (1974). *Fundamentals of Financial Management*. Prentice Hall.

Vanston, N. (2012). *Trust and reputation in financial services. Driver Review DR30. Foresight*. Government Office for Science.

Varey, R. J. (1997). A picture of corporate communications management in UK. *Corporate Communications: An International Journal*, *2*(2), 59–69. doi:10.1108/eb046535

Veselá, J. (2007). *Investování na kapitálových trzích*. Praha: Aspi.

Villalonga-Olives, E., & Kawachi, I. (2015). The measurement of bridging social capital in population health research. *Health & Place*, *36*, 47–56. doi:10.1016/j.healthplace.2015.09.002 PMID:26409896

Von Peter, G. (2007, December). International banking centres: A network perspective. *BIS Quarterly Review*, 33-45.

Walker, G., Kogut, B., & Shan, W. (1997). Social capital, structural holes and the formation of an industry network. *Organization Science*, *8*(2), 109–125. doi:10.1287/orsc.8.2.109

Wall Street Journal. (2004, October 18). As Two Economists Debate Markets, The Tide Shifts: Belief in Efficient Valuation Yields Ground to Role Of Irrational Investors. *Wall Street Journal*. Retrieved June 1, 2014, from http://www.wsj.com/articles/SB109804865418747444

Walls, M. R., & Dyer, J. S. (1996). Risk propensity and firm performance: A study of the petroleum exploration industry. *Management Science*, *42*(7), 1004–1021. doi:10.1287/mnsc.42.7.1004

Watson, G. H. (2004). Six Sigma: Controlling Business and Process. *Analysis Management*, *7*, 18–19.

Westlund, H., & Adam, F. (2010). Social capital and economic performance: A meta- analysis of 65 studies. *European Planning Studies*, *18*(6), 893–919. doi:10.1080/09654311003701431

Williams, J. B. (1938). *The Theory of Investment Value*. Cambridge, UK: Harvard University Press.

Wincent, J., Thorgren, S., & Anokhin, S. (2016). Costly ties: Social capital as a retardant of network-level entrepreneurial orientation. *Journal of Small Business Management*, *54*(1), 229–243. doi:10.1111/jsbm.12140

Witt, S. F., & Witt, C. A. (1991). Tourism forecasting: Error magnitude, direction of change of error and trend error. *Journal of Travel Research*, *30*(2), 26–33. doi:10.1177/004728759103000205

Woodward, S. (1983). The liquidity premium and solidity premium. *The American Economic Review*, *73*(3), 348–361.

World Bank. (1992). *Governance and development*. Washington, DC: The World Bank.

World Bank. (1997). *The State in a Changing World—World Development Report 1997*. New York: Oxford University Press.

World Bank. (2002). *Building Institutions for Markets*. Washington, DC: Oxford University Press.

World Bank. (2007a). *Main Report*. Washington, DC: World Bank Group.

World Bank. (2007b). *Strengthening World Bank Group Engagement On Governance And Anticorruption*. Washington, DC: World Bank Group.

Wright, D. J. (1997). Perceptions of corporate communication as public relations. *Corporate Communications: An International Journal*, *2*(4), 143–154. doi:10.1108/eb046545

Yahoo Finance – Stock Center. (2014). *Yahoo Finance*. Retrieved May 6, 2014, from http://finance.yahoo.com/stock-center/

Yalumba, S. (2008). Communicating Yalumba's commitment to sustainable winemaking. *Corporate Communications: An International Journal*, *13*(1), 18–41. doi:10.1108/13563280810848175

Yoon, K. P., & Hwang, C. L. (1995). *Multiple attribute decision making: An introduction*. Thousand Oaks, CA: Sage Publications.

Yuhua, D., & Datao, Y. (2005). Estimation of failure probability of oil and gas transmission pipelines by fuzzy fault tree analysis. *Journal of Loss Prevention in the Process Industries*, *18*(2), 83–88. doi:10.1016/j.jlp.2004.12.003

Zionts, S., & Wallenius, J. (1976). An Interactive Programming Method for Solving the Multiple Criteria Problem. *Management Science*, *22*(6), 652–663. doi:10.1287/mnsc.22.6.652

Zopounidis, C. (2011a). *Multiple criteria decision aiding*. New York, NY: Nova Science Publishers.

Zopounidis, C. (2011b). *Handbook of multicriteria analysis*. New York, NY: Springer.

About the Contributors

Srđan Marinković is a professor of banking and finance at the University of Niš, Faculty of Economics (Serbia). He holds Ph.D. and BSc. in Economics from the University of Niš, Faculty of Economics, and MSc. in Economics from Belgrade University, Faculty of Economics. Prof. Marinković has successfully accomplished several courses within doctoral studies at Aarhus School of Business and Universitetet i Oslo, as well as postdoctoral research at London School of Economics and Political Science. He was visiting fellow of a number of foreign academic institutions, i.e. Norwegian School of Economics (Norges Hadleshøyskole), London School of Economics and Political Science, and Univerza v Ljubljani. At the moment, he serves as a member of Presidency of the National Scientific Society of Economists. He was formerly the Editor-in-Chief of the academic journal Economic Themes (De Gruyter, Germany). He has published with Springer, and co-edited volumes of Springer and Elsevier. His research has been published in Managerial Finance (Emerald), and many ISI indexed journals, i.e. Economic Research (Routledge; Taylor & Francis Group), Proceedings of Rijeka Faculty of Economics: Journal of Economics and Business, etc.

***

Aykan Akincilar is a PhD candidate in the department of industrial engineering, institute of natural and applied sciences, Gazi University, Turkey. Also he has been employed as a research assistant in the department of industrial engineering, faculty of engineering, Celal Bayar University. His interest area includes robust optimization, multi-criteria decision making, forecasting.

Aleksandra Andjelkovic is a Teaching Assistant at the Faculty of Economics, University of Nis, for narrow scientific field Business Management. Doctoral dissertation "Supply chain risk management for the purpose of increasing its resilience" she defended at the Faculty of Economics in Nis in 2015. Aleksandra Andjelkovic was a trainer of employees in municipalities of Svrljig and Merošina, on the subject of Instruments of economic development and available funds for investment attraction in 2010. As a scholar of Austrian Exchange Service (OeAD-GmbH) in 2013 she was visiting researcher at the Department of Production and Logistics (Faculty of Business, Economics and Statistics, University of Vienna). Her key interest areas are: strategic management of logistics, international logistics, supply chains, international marketing, and marketing channels. So far, she has published more than 40 papers in journals and proceedings from the conferences (national and international).

Ivana Bilic received her PhD in Business from the University of Split in 2011 and currently she is an Assistant Professor at the Department of Management of Faculty of Economics, University of Split. She is an alumna of JFDP exchange program financed by U.S. Department of State. Her main scientific interests are public relations, corporate communications, community management, crisis management, entrepreneurship, and reputation management. Dr. Bilić is a member of national public relations associations and currently serves as the President of the U.S. Alumni Community of Croatia, and 3psplit.org. In scientific area she has published two book chapters and more than 20 articles in international peer-reviewed journals or international scientific conference.

Christopher Boachie is a lecturer of Central Business School, Central University in Ghana, an academic and a practising Chartered Accountant (FCCA-UK) with specialization in corporate finance, international trade, auditing, financial statement fraud and financial risk management. He was educated in Kwame Nkrumah University of Science and Technology in Kumasi Ghana, Technical University of Freiberg in Germany and the London School of Accountancy (UK). He is currently reading his PhD at Open University of Malaysia. He has considerable, teaching, consulting and practise experience in the application of accountancy and finance theory and risk management.

Gonçalo Carvalho is a student at the Faculty of Economics, University of Coimbra.

Cécile Cezanne is a lecturer accredited to supervise research in Economics at the University of Paris 13 Sorbonne Paris Cité, France. She is a permanent researcher at the Economics Laboratory of Paris Nord (CEPN) and a research fellow at the Research Group in Economics, Law and Management (GREDEG), Cote d'Azur University (France). She is specialised in Industrial Economics and more precisely her research is focused on the theory of the firm and corporate governance. These areas of expertise have led her to collaborate and compare viewpoints notably with researchers in Management on major subjects like intra- and inter-enterprises cooperation and the boundaries of organizations within networks.

Delphine David is an Assistant Professor in Applied Mathematics.

António Portugal Duarte is a Senior Lecturer at the University of Coimbra, Faculty of Economics and a researcher affiliated with GEMF and CeBER.

Marija Džunić is currently employed as associate professor at Faculty of Economics, University of Nis, Serbia, Department for General Economic Theory. She teaches two graduate courses (Introduction to Economics and Political Economy). At postgraduate studies she teaches Social Economics and Economics of Public Choice. Her research is focused on social capital, political institutions and economic growth, with broad research interests aimed at understanding how social and political factors shape economic outcomes. She obtained her Ph.D. in Economics at Faculty of Economics, University of Belgrade, in 2010, defending the dissertation "A Study of the Effects of Social Capital in Post-socialist Economies".

Julio Blanco Fernández studied Industrial Engineering and PhD studies in the University of the Basque Country (Spain). Currently he works in the Mechanical Engineering Department (Director of the grade on Mechanical Engineering). He has published more than 150 works (39 JCR works), 45 patents, has participated in more than 35 research projects and has been Director of Chair of Innovation, Technology and Knowledge Management of the La Rioja.

Jorge Luis García-Alcaraz is a full time researcher of the Department of Industrial Engineering at the Autonomous University of Ciudad Juarez. He received a MSc in Industrial Engineering from the Colima Technology Institute (Mexico), a PhD in Industrial Engineering from Ciudad Juarez Technology Institute (Mexico) and a Postdoc from University of La Rioja (Spain). His main research areas are related to Multicriteria decision making applied to manufacturing, production process modeling and statistical inference. He is founding member of the Mexican Society of Operation Research and active member in the Mexican Academy of Industrial Engineering. Currently, Dr. Garcia is a National Researcher recognized by the National Council of Science & Technology of Mexico (CONACYT) and is working with group research from Colombia, Spain and Dominican Republic. Actually, Dr. Garcia is author/coauthor in around 120 journals, international conferences and congress.

Giner Alor Hernández is a full-time researcher of the Division of Research and Postgraduate Studies in Orizaba's technological institute: Tecnológico de Orizaba. He received a MSc and a PhD in Computer Science from the Center for Research and Advanced Studies of the National Polytechnic Institute (CINVESTAV), Mexico. He has led 10 Mexican research projects granted by CONACYT, DGEST, and PROMEP. He is author/coauthor of around 130 journal and conference papers on computer science. Also, he has been a committee program member of around 30 international conferences sponsored by IEEE, ACM, and Springer. He also holds the position of editorial board member of eight indexed journals; he has been guest editor of JCR-indexed journals such as Journal of Universal Computer Science, Pervasive and Mobile Computing, Journal of Educational Technology & Society, Science of Computer Programming Journal, International Journal of Software Engineering and Knowledge Engineering, Computational and Mathematical Methods in Medicine, Journal of Medical Systems, Journal of Industrial and Management Optimization. He is the main author of the book entitled Frameworks, Methodologies, and Tools for Developing Rich Internet Applications, published by IGI Global Publishing. His research interests include Web services, e-commerce, Semantic Web, Web 2.0, service-oriented and event-driven architectures, and enterprise application integration. He is an IEEE and ACM Member. He is a National Researcher recognized by the National Council of Science & Technology of Mexico (CONACYT). ORCID: 0000-0003-3296-0981, Scopus Author ID: 17433252100.

Vesna Jankovic-Milic is an Associate Professor at the Faculty of Economics, University of Nis, Serbia. She holds an MBS from Faculty of Economics, Belgrade University, Serbia and PhD from Faculty of Economics, University of Nis. Her research interests include an application of quantitative, especially statistical, methods in economic research. She participates in various projects financed by the Ministry of Science, Republic of Serbia.

Lukáš Křen, graduate of Finance and investment management at Faculty of Business and Economics, Mendel University in Brno, Czech Republic.

Jose Roberto Mendoza Fong Industrial Engineering with specialty on Quality and Productivity. Entitled in the year 2009 on Institute Technology of Ciudad Juarez. Currently he is studying for a master's degree in industrial engineering with a specialization in logistics on Autonomous University of Ciudad Juarez.

Marija Radosavljevic is an Associate Professor at the Faculty of Economics, University of Nis, for scientific field Business Management. She was engaged as a researcher at the University of Economics and Business, Department for Production Management, Wien, Austria and at the Willamette University, Atkinson Graduate School Of Management, Oregon, USA. As user of Mevlana Academic Mobility she was guest professor at Akdeniz University, Faculty of Economics and Administrative Sciences, Antalya, Turkey. Her key interest areas are: quality management, process management, cost management. So far, she has published more than 130 papers and 4 monographs.

Athanasios Ragkos is an Agricultural Economist, currently a visiting Lecturer in Greek Universities. His main fields of expertise are non-market valuation techniques, optimization models, efficiency analysis and economics of rural development. He has published more than 60 papers in peer-reviewed journal and international Conferences.

Jorge Limon Romero is a professor of industrial engineering in the Faculty of Engineering, Architecture and Design at the Autonomous University of Baja California, Mexico. He has been President of the Industrial Engineering Academy at this faculty and he has also participated in several research projects. Dr. Limón is a member of the National System of Researchers of the National Council of Science and Technology in Mexico. His research interests include topics related to Six Sigma Methodology, Lean Manufacturing and applied statistics for process improvement.

Vagis Samathrakis since 1998 was Professor at the Department of Rural Development & Agribusiness Management at the Alexander Technological Educational Institute (ATEI) of Thessaloniki, and from October 2014 he is Professor at the Department of Accounting and Finance of the ATEI of Thessaloniki. He teaches Management, Entrepreneurship and Human Resource Management, Research Methodology, Portfolio Management and Business Economics. He is an external evaluator of European Community programs such as the Integrated Mediterranean Programs, the Regional Operational Programs, the LEADER etc. Since 1998 He has worked on topics such as the Competitiveness of Food and Beverage Companies, the E-business in SMEs in the Food and Beverage Sector, the Adoption of Information and Communication Technologies in Greek Agriculture and the Internet use by Businesses and Organizations in Rural Areas, the Adoption-Diffusion of Precision Agriculture in Greek Regions, the Farm Management and the Innovation and Entrepreneurship. His scientific work is published in scientific journals and presented at international conferences.

Laurence Saglietto is a Professor in Management at the Cote d'Azur University, France. She is specialized in Strategic Management and more precisely her research is focused on networks and Logistics. She is a permanent researcher at the GREDEG Laboratory.

Mirko Savic is a full professor at the Faculty of Economics in Subotica, University of Novi Sad. He is also a lecturer at the Centre for Applied Statistics at the University of Novi Sad.

Aleksandar Šević is the Lecturer in School of Business, Trinity College Dublin since September 2008 and Director of the MSc in Finance Programme since June 2010. Previously he held an academic position at the University of Newcastle, NSW, Australia and was a Research Officer at the Economics Institute in Belgrade, a leading Serbian economics research institution and consultancy house. He holds a BSc in Economics from the University of Belgrade, MA in International (Economic) Development from the Graduate School of International Relations, International University of Japan, and PhD in Finance from the Nanyang Business School, Nanyang Technological University in Singapore. He has published research papers both in Serbian and English. He is also a CFA Charterholder (since 2005) and CAIA Charterholder (since 2013).

Marta Simões is a Senior Lecturer at the University of Coimbra, Faculty of Economics and a researcher affiliated with GEMF and CeBER.

Martin Širůček works on the department of finance at Faculty of Business and Economics, Mendel University in Brno, Czech Republic. He focused on the topic connected with financial and capital markets, investment analysis and decisions. His article focused on the money supply and stock prices, on the stock bubbles, creation of portfolio and stock analysis. He is a member of exam board by European Financial Planner Association Czech Republic.

Alexandros M. Theodoridis is Lecturer in Animal Production Economics and Applied Statistics, at the Faculty of Veterinary Medicine, at the Aristotle University of Thessaloniki, Greece. He obtained a Diploma (BSc) in Agricultural Engineering (2001), from the Faculty of Agriculture, Aristotle University of Thessaloniki and an MSc in Economics, from the Faculty of Economics & Applied Economics, Katholieke Universiteit Leuven, Belgium (2002). He holds a PhD in Agricultural Economics obtained from the Aristotle University of Thessaloniki, Greece (2008). The PhD studies were funded by the Greek State Scholarship Foundation. His main research interests include agricultural economics, agricultural policy, animal production economics, statistical analyses and evaluation of experimental data and design of farm management surveys. Dr. Theodoridis has participated in several scientific projects funded by Greek governmental bodies, European Union and private companies and organizations. He has participated in 28 peer-reviewed journal articles, 3 book chapters, 14 conference papers and 8 conference announcements in various fields of Agricultural Economics and Applied Statistics. Dr. Theodoridis has been a member of the advisory committee for a PhD student and an external reviewer for 9 international scientific journals.

Franka Vrkić received her BSc degree in Communication in 2012 from the Faculty of Economics University of Split, Faculty of Economics. As a student she showed a great interest in Communication and Management topics, and during her study showed an impressive willingness to explore those fields deeper. During the course of her study she developed special devotions for the failed of Crisis Management what resulted with her decision to choose her master thesis in the field of Management, precisely Crisis Management. She obtained her MA degree in Management also from Faculty of Economics University of Split, Faculty of Economics in 2015. She currently works as accountant in private company in Split, Croatia.

Jovan Zubovic was born on June 26, 1970 in Belgrade where he completed primary and secondary school with excellent grades. Bachelor studies he completed in 1994 at Intercollege Cyprus, Limassol, with major is Business Administration, with an average of 3.386 (max 4). Postgraduate studies on major Marketing he completed at MSM - Maastricht School of Management outreach in Nicosia, Cyprus. Master thesis "Foreign Investments in Russia" he defended in 1996. (under Dean's Prof. Dr Andreas Polemitis supervision). Jovan Zubović has defended a docotoral thesis entiteled "Investments in Human Resources as a Factor for Attracting Foreign Direct Investments Focusing on Serbian Financial Industry" in 2009 on Belgrade banking Academy, Faculty for Banking, Insurance and Finance. Zubović was employed on the Institute of Economic Sciences in the period 2003-2012 as a research associate. In february 2012 he has moved to Economics Institute in Belgrade, where he has been seleced as deputy president of Scientific Council, and presided it as of 2013. Since Fabruary 2015 he is employed as a director of the Institute of Economic Sciences. Zubović is a memeber of the European Association of Labour Economists (EALE) as of 2011 and European Association of Agricultural Economists (EAAE) as of 2009. Since 1996 he has continuously participated in editing of scientific journals: - Since 2013 editor of journal Industrija - Since 2013 – member of the editorial board of International Journal of Young Researchers in Business Economics published by Mind Reader Publications New Delhi, India - Since 2012 - member of the editorial board of Journal of Sustainable Economies Management published by IGI Global, USA. - In the period 2009-2012 - member of the editorial board of the journal Economic Analysis. - In the period 2006-2008 – editor-in-chief of the journal Economic Analysis. - У периоду 1996-2006 – busines editor of the journal Маркетинг. Zubović has led several local and international projects that Economics Institute and Institute of Economic Sciences have realized individually or jointly with other institutions.

Index

H

I

J

L

M

O

P

R

S

T

V

W

www.ingramcontent.com/pod-product-compliance
Lightning Source LLC
LaVergne TN
LVHW060425300926
849162LV00006B/1531